WITH WINDOWS NT

MARK JOSEPH EDWARDS

A Division of
DUKE COMMUNICATIONS INTERNATIONAL
221 E. 29th Street • Loveland, CO 80538
(800) 621-1544 • (970) 663-4700 • www.dukepress.com

Library of Congress Cataloging-in-Publication Data

Edwards, Mark, 1961-

   Internet security with Windows NT / by Mark Edwards. — 1st ed.
     p. cm.
   Includes bibliographical references and index.
   ISBN 1-882419-62-6
   1. Computer networks—Security measures. 2. Internet (Computer
   network)—Security measures. 3. Microsoft Windows NT.   I. Title.
   TK5105.59.E38 1997
   005.8—dc21   97-33865
                                         CIP

Published by DUKE PRESS
DUKE COMMUNICATIONS INTERNATIONAL
Loveland, Colorado

Copyright © 1998 by Mark Edwards

It is the reader's responsibility to ensure procedures and techniques used from this book are accurate and appropriate for the user's installation. No warranty is implied or expressed.

This book was printed and bound in Canada.

ISBN 1-882419-62-6

1 2 3 4 5 6 WL 9 8 7

To my loving family and to my gracious friends,
I couldn't have done it without you.

ACKNOWLEDGMENTS

The following people were key to the development of this book. They are listed in alphabetical order, along with their contributions.

Andy Baron was born in Dushanbe, USSR, and is a graduate of Moscow State University (MSU). Andy received his Masters degree in Physics and Applied Mathematics in 1988 from the Moscow Institute of Physics and Technology, Moscow, Russia, and received his Ph.D. in 1993 from the same university. Before joining Midwestern Commerce as a director of technology in 1995, Dr. Baron worked at Microelectronics Center, a division of MSU, as a chief software engineer. Andy provided a portion of the material that formed the basis for Chapter 9, "Attacking Your Own NT Networks."

Philip Carden is an industry-recognized expert in network security. Philip is the Managing Consultant for The Registry's Network Systems Consulting Practice in New York and advises both corporate clients and vendor organizations on network security, network infrastructure, and intranet architecture. Philip frequently writes security-related literature and has been featured in *Windows NT Magazine*. His e-mail address is pcarden@tri.com. Philip wrote Chapter 10, "Firewall Basics," as well as part of Chapter 11, "How to Choose an Internet Firewall."

Rob Davis is a network consultant with a degree in Electrical Engineering from Texas A&M and a Masters degree in business from the University of Texas at Austin. Rob served as an officer on the USS *Jacksonville* nuclear submarine and previously worked for Deloitte and Touche in Austin. Rob currently works as a network consultant in Dallas, Texas, and can be reached at greenband@ poboxes.com. Rob compiled most of the information in Appendix A, "Out-of-the-Box NT Security Checklist."

Dr. Bill Hancock is a well-known computer consultant and engineer with more than 22 years of experience in the fields of computer science, network technologies, and electrical engineering. Dr. Hancock has been responsible for the design and implementation of more than 4000 systems and more than 3800 networks during his career. He has a formidable background in computer design and in network architecture from participating on operating system and network design teams at both DEC and IBM and from his current participation with the American National Standards Committee X3S3 (Data Communications), the International Organization for Standardization (ISO), and as leadership relations and membership relations director for the U.S. Chapter of the Digital Equipment Computer User's Society (DECUS), a large user organization devoted to sharing technical information. Dr. Bill Hancock wrote Chapter 5, "Multiprotocol Environments."

Alex Jules is currently a senior I/T consultant in Texas, working with a nationwide Network and Systems Integrator. He is a former IBM employee with several years of experience in LAN/WAN design and network management and has worked with several New York-based companies in tackling issues such as security in existing or new environments. He holds certifications in UNIX, Netware, and NT. Alex wrote Chapter 8, "Network Client and Workstation Concerns," and part of the material for Chapter 6, "Security Threats."

Mary Madden has been active in the networking arena for 10 years and can be reached at mtm@io.com. Mary has co-authored several books on networking and NT, including *Windows NT Networking for Dummies* and *Building Windows NT Web Servers* from IDG Books Worldwide. She has written numerous magazine articles and has been a technical editor for many books on networking. Mary wrote much of the material that formed the basis for Chapter 6, "Security Threats," and wrote Chapter 7, "Developing Effective Security Policies."

Marcus J. Ranum is CEO of Network Flight Recorder, Inc. and chief scientist of V-One Corporation. He is the principal author of several major Internet firewall products, including the DEC SEAL, the TIS Gauntlet, and the TIS Internet Firewall Toolkit. Marcus has been managing Unix systems and network security for more than 13 years, including configuring and managing whitehouse.gov. Marcus is a frequent lecturer and conference speaker on computer security topics. His Web site is at http://www.clark.net/pub/mjr. Marcus wrote part of Chapter 11, "How to Choose an Internet Firewall," as well as Appendix D, "Frequently Asked Questions About Firewalls."

Ned Rynearson is a Houston-based systems engineering consultant for Compucom as well as a Microsoft Certified Systems Engineer (MCSE), Microsoft Certified Solution Developer (MCSD), and Microsoft Certified Trainer (MCT). Ned spent over 14 years in the U.S. Air Force working in computer technologies. Since leaving the Air Force, Ned has been working privately in the Microsoft Backoffice arena. Ned wrote much of the material in Chapter 16, "Planning MPS Client Rollout and Support" and Chapter 17, "MPS Troubleshooting, Monitoring, and Maintenance."

I'd like to acknowledge all of the folks who use the Internet in a constructive manner by openly sharing their security-related follies, advice, and wisdom with everyone willing to listen. I've learned a wealth of information interacting with you all, and part of this book is an indirect result of the knowledge we've shared with each other. A special thanks goes out to the operators of the Bug-Traq mailing list, the NTSecurity mailing list, and the NTBugTraq mailing list — without your generous contributions to the Internet community, many people would still be in the dark about NT security. Thank you all.

And last, but *certainly* not least, thanks to all the great people at Duke Press and *Windows NT Magazine* who helped and encouraged me along the way. A special note of thanks goes out to **Janet Robbins**, **Mick Gusinde-Duffy**, **Marion Agnew**, **Martha Nichols**, **Dawn Cyr**, **Trish McConnell**, **John Morris-Reihl**, **Karen Forster**, **Dina Ralston**, **John Enck**, and **Eric Shanfelt** — thanks to all of you for your assistance, encouragement, and patience!

TABLE OF CONTENTS AT A GLANCE

TABLE OF CONTENTS

Part Two Foundations of Microsoft Security

Part Three Network Security — Principles and Practice

Part Five Microsoft Proxy Server

Part Six Security Resources

INTRODUCTION

Internet intruders come from all walks of life, and they all have their own reasons for breaching someone's network security — and they certainly aren't going away anytime soon. This book is designed to help thwart those intruders. After reading this book, you'll be better positioned to secure your NT networks from the would-be intruder. Rest assured that both the seasoned intruder and the rookie are also reading this book, and they *will* employ the contents against your networks. To protect yourself, you simply must apply the knowledge contained herein yourself. *As this book raises your awareness of ways to protect your NT networks, it simultaneously helps arm an entire new generation of NT attackers.*

Before you start reading this book, let me quickly point out that there is no such thing as a 100 percent secure operating system or network. The *only* way to completely secure your systems and network is to disconnect them from everything, including their power source. But don't let these facts get you down. Most operating systems, NT included, offer some type of out-of-the-box security. Further configuration, as well as adding third-party security tools, can go a long way toward creating a more secure network. This book offers useful insight into various means of strengthening your security. After you read it and put some its suggestions into practice, you'll find that you can achieve a comfortable level of security.

WHAT'S IN THIS BOOK

Although the information in this book is geared for people with little or no NT security knowledge, a seasoned security administrator may also learn new tips. This book covers a lot of ground, incorporating information that you would otherwise have to gather from several separate sources, including publications about TCP/IP protocols, Windows NT, and firewall technologies. This book serves as a single consolidated resource. I take a ground-up approach, starting with the TCP/IP network itself, moving to the NT operating system and network clients, followed by review and analysis of various security software packages that you can add to NT. In closing the book, I leave you with a set of reference appendices that point you to additional information.

This book has six parts. I begin in Chapter 1 by laying down the foundation of TCP/IP knowledge you need before you can adequately understand what you're doing when attempting to secure your networks. *Don't let Part One intimidate you, though.* Although it is technical and can be complex for the beginner, I present it clearly and concisely. If you're not interested in knowing what happens at the lowest levels of a TCP/IP network, simply skim Chapter 1 to become familiar with the terms. In this case, pay more attention to Chapter 2, where I discuss basic TCP/IP security in a broader scope. Chapter 2 covers overall TCP/IP security from a 10,000-foot view.

Part Two of this book discusses out-of-the-box NT security. Chapter 3 introduces the basics of NT's security capabilities. Chapter 4 explains the nuts and bolts of day-to-day NT security administration in a fair amount of detail. You learn the tools you have at your disposal, the concepts behind the use of those tools, and how to apply those concepts in your day-to-day administrative practices.

In Part Three, I explain the principles and practice of network security. In Chapter 5, I discuss the implications of today's multiprotocol network environment and how to assess the risks associated with the environment. In Chapter 6, you learn how to identify potential security threats. Chapter 7 covers the all-important security policies — what they are, why they're necessary, and how to go about developing a robust set of policies of your own. Chapter 8 addresses network client workstation concerns head-on. You learn about the common clients found on NT networks, some of the inherent risks of those clients, and how to alleviate those risks. Chapter 9 introduces you to the idea of breaking in to your own networks. I discuss in detail how your NT networks are attacked, teaching you the points of attack an intruder is likely to pursue, as well as offering you first-hand knowledge of how to replicate such attacks on your own. Chapter 9 puts you on a more even playing field against the would-be intruder. After you've completed this part of the book, you should know exactly how to think and act like an intruder — a key aspect of stopping them cold.

In Part Four, I give you a background in basic firewall theory and practice. Chapter 10, Firewall Basics, looks at what a firewall is and isn't and in the process explains the range of security options at your disposal. Tips for choosing an Internet firewall are in Chapter 11.

Part Five focuses on Microsoft Proxy Server (MPS). Because MPS offers an economical way to strengthen your overall network security, I think it's necessary to take a close look at it. Chapter 12 discusses Microsoft's Internet Information Server (IIS) in detail, because MPS is essentially a component that runs on top of IIS — to use MPS, you must know how to use IIS. In Chapter 13, you learn exactly what MPS can and cannot do for you. Chapter 14 helps you design your implementation. Careful planning leads to a smooth roll out. Chapter 15 is a hands-on, step-by-step tutorial about installing and configuring MPS. Chapter 16 helps you think about rolling out your MPS client software and discusses what you need to know to support MPS. Finally, Chapter 17 teaches you important aspects of monitoring, maintaining, and troubleshooting MPS in your environment.

The last part of the book is a set of appendices. Appendix A is an NT security checklist. Appendix B lists security resources accessible using the Internet. You'll find security-related Web sites, mailing lists, and Usenet newsgroups. Appendix C is a list of security vendors offering hardware- and software-based security solutions and a list of security consultants to assist you with your security needs. Appendix D answers frequently asked questions about firewalls.

This book also includes a CD-ROM, where you'll find several security-related utilities, tools, and software packages; instructions for the CD are in Appendix E. Some of the items included are various firewalls, port scanners, network-monitoring software, and virus detection and prevention utilities. Examine the contents and feel free to try them out. If you like a particular item, be sure to check the vendor's Web site for the most current version — development of security software is moving very quickly; undoubtedly a more recent version is available for your use.

CONVENTIONS

In this book, I introduce several terms and use some interchangeably. Intruders are known by many names. You've probably heard the terms *hacker* and *cracker*; by common definition, hackers are the nonmalicious group of computer break-in artists, while crackers are malicious. Of the two, crackers have ill intent, while hackers are merely on a mission of harmless learning. However, because many people don't realize the difference in these two sets of adventuresome folks, I use those two terms interchangeably in this book.

Also, you'll notice that even though this book is entitled *Internet Security with Windows NT*, I talk a lot about physical security. Physical security is just as important as network security, and neither is very useful without the other. I learned this fact first-hand during my experiences founding and operating a large Internet service provider in Houston, Texas. During my adventures at that firm, we connected hundreds of businesses to the Internet. Of all the companies we connected, few bothered to consider security as a necessity, and those that did take network security seriously didn't see the entire picture, paying little, if any, attention to the security on their premises.

To clarify the importance of physical security, let me offer you a simple analogy: Locking the front door to your house while leaving the back door wide open makes no sense. By the same token, an intruder who cannot enter your network using the "front door" network connection is likely to attempt some sort of physical access to penetrate your network.

HOW TO CONTACT ME

It's no big secret that I spend most of my waking hours interactively using the Internet. Therefore, the best way to reach me personally is by sending electronic mail. *Please* don't send messages asking me to troubleshoot your network security. Everyone's network is unique and must be handled differently. The time necessary for me to gain a thorough understanding of your environment makes it prohibitive for me to assist you directly except in a consulting capacity.

On the other hand, I don't mind talking about specifics at all. Just try to avoid generalized questions, such as "My network is acting strange, I think someone is breaking in. Can you help?" A more appropriate question is "Someone changed my home page; how can I stop this from happening again?"

Also, I'd love to hear any suggestions you have for further content, clarifications, corrections, or modifications that I might incorporate in future editions of this book. If you're a security vendor or consultant, send me your contact information. And if you produce security-related software, I'd love to include samples of your products on our CD-ROM as well.

Please don't be offended if I don't respond to your message immediately. I do answer all my e-mail, so please be patient with me. Send your correspondence to either *mark@ntshop.net* or *mark@ntsecurity.net*. And by all means, feel free to visit my Web site (http://www.ntsecurity.net), where I maintain a wealth of up-to-date NT security information and post my free monthly *NT Security Digest (NTSD)* newsletter.

CHAPTER 1

UNDERSTANDING TCP/IP

Many people don't know that TCP/IP (Transmission Control Protocol/ Internet Protocol) is an entire family of protocols or that TCP and IP are the parents of that family. This chapter describes TCP/IP in enough detail to give you a firm understanding of TCP/IP and its value. We also walk through the basic installation and configuration of TCP/IP on Windows NT 4.0 so you know what you're working with on your networks.

THE TCP/IP FAMILY TREE

The Transmission Control Protocol (TCP) and the Internet Protocol (IP) together form the basis for TCP/IP, a low-level driver that lets computers talk to each other using a network of almost any size. The Internet is connected using TCP/IP as its foundation.

TCP/IP was proposed in 1973. Nine years later, in 1983, a standardized version of the protocol was developed and adopted for wide-area use. In 1983, it also became mandatory that all connections to ARPAnet, the Department of Defense's predecessor to today's Internet, be made with TCP/IP.

TCP/IP was developed to solve several problems in moving data from point A to point B. The most important requirement was to guarantee delivery of data on a network that might be under attack from a foreign power. Because the Department of Defense (DoD) developed the Internet, this requirement was paramount and fairly predictable. If an enemy were to attack the military's computer systems and networks, data must continue to flow, secure and unhampered. The other established requirements were that data be moved efficiently and that its arrival be verified — yet the sending machine might not have any of the same operating characteristics as the receiving machine. TCP and IP both perform unique and vital functions that solve all the problems in moving data between machines over networks.

TRANSMISSION CONTROL PROTOCOL

TCP is the transmission layer of the protocol. Its primary function is to ensure reliable and verifiable data exchange between different hosts across a network. TCP performs its tasks by breaking data into manageable pieces and then wrapping the pieces with information called a *header* that routes the data to its final destination. TCP on the receiving machine then puts all the pieces back together, just as they were before the data was sent. The wrapped and bundled pieces are called *datagrams*.

The primary pieces of information in the TCP header are the source and destination port numbers, a sequence number for the datagram, and a checksum. Port numbers allow the data to be sent back and forth to the correct process running on each computer. (We cover ports in more detail later in this chapter.) The sequence number lets TCP reassemble the datagrams in the correct order. The checksum lets the protocol determine whether the data received is the data that was sent. The checksum calculates a number by adding all the octets of a datagram; this number is then inserted into the datagram's header. The receiving computer performs the same calculation, and if the two calculations do not match, an error occurred somewhere along the line, and the datagram is resent.

After the TCP header is inserted into the datagram, TCP passes the datagram to the IP protocol to be routed to its final destination. Figure 1.1 shows the layout of a datagram with its TCP header structure.

SOURCE PORT			DESTINATION PORT	
SEQUENCE NUMBER				
ACKNOWLEDGMENT NUMBER				
DATA OFFSET	RESERVED	FLAGS	WINDOW	
CHECKSUM			URGENT POINTER	
OPTIONS			PADDING	
BEGINNING OF DATA				

Figure 1.1
A Datagram with its TCP Header

INTERNET PROTOCOL

IP is the network layer portion of TCP/IP. IP actually moves data from point A to point B across a network. This movement of data is called *routing,* and that's really all IP does. (We cover routing in a bit more detail later in this chapter.) IP is typically considered unreliable, meaning that nothing guarantees that the data it routes will even arrive at its destination, much less in the order it was sent. IP relies on TCP to determine whether the data arrived successfully at its destination and to retransmit the data if it hasn't.

To route data, IP inserts its own header into the datagram after it receives it from TCP. The contents of the IP header are the source and destination addresses, another checksum, and the protocol number. The header informs routers (or gateways) along the way of the datagram's final destination. See Figure 1.2 for a layout of a datagram complete with its TCP and IP headers. The IP header portion has a gray background.

VERSION	INET HEADER LEN	TYPE OF SERVICE	TOTAL LENGTH	
IDENTIFICATION		FLAGS	FRAGMENTATION OFFSET	
TIME TO LIVE		PROTOCOL	HEADER CHECKSUM	
SOURCE PORT		DESTINATION PORT		
SOURCE ADDRESS				
DESTINATION ADDRESS				
ACKNOWLEDGMENT NUMBER				
DATA OFFSET	FLAGS	RESERVED	WINDOW	
CHECKSUM		URGENT POINTER		
OPTIONS		PADDING		
BEGINNING OF DATA				

Figure 1.2
Datagram with TCP and IP Headers

OTHER TCP/IP PROTOCOLS

The TCP/IP family consists of several other protocols typically referred to as *application protocols,* which are specialized protocols that use TCP/IP as their foundation. With the ever-growing popularity of the Internet, new application protocols are being developed at a blistering pace. Let's look at a few:

- Address Resolution Protocol (ARP) helps link a physical media access control address (an Ethernet address) with a node's associated IP address.

- Internet Control Message Protocol (ICMP) works at the IP network layer level and helps with network layer management and control, ensuring that errors are noted and corrected.

- Universal Datagram Protocol (UDP) is a connectionless protocol that is generally considered an unreliable way to send data across a network because it does not guarantee that the data sent will ever arrive at its destination. UDP is, however, a very efficient and fast way to send data because it does not have to connect and disconnect to send it, thus reducing network overhead.

- Simple Network Management Protocol (SNMP) makes it possible to collect information from network devices and lets network administrators manipulate configuration settings.

- Simple Mail Transfer Protocol (SMTP) allows for basic e-mail service across a network.

- Network News Transfer Protocol (NNTP) enables the propagation of public discussion forums.

- Telnet is a terminal emulation program that lets a user log on to a computer from a remote location.

- Internet Relay Chat (IRC) lets numerous users connect to a server, where they can all "chat" using real-time text-based messages.

- The World Wide Web, or the Web, as it's commonly called, is a hypertext transfer protocol that makes it possible to display documents containing clickable links to other documents.

- File Transfer Protocol (FTP) lets users transfer files across a network.

- Finger lets one user look up contact information about another user by asking a specific system for that information.

- Whois lets a user query the global Whois databases for contact and location information about a user or domain name.

- Gopher lets a user search for documents and files containing specific keywords and phrases.

- Archie searches for files by file name or parts of file names.

- RealAudio allows for the transmission and receipt of prerecorded and live audio across a network.

- VDOLive enables the transmission and receipt of prerecorded and live video across a network.

PORTS AND SOCKETS

Data sent from one computer to another on a TCP/IP network is sent to a *port* on the receiving computer. A port is like a person at a particular address. You can certainly send postal mail to any address you desire; however, you usually address the mail to a particular person or department so that it gets into the right hands. Ports let the correct process receive the data directly.

All ports are assigned unique numbers ranging from 0 to 32768. Today, many ports are numerically standardized and preassigned. For example, SMTP mail servers normally run on port 25, and Web servers normally run on port 80. TCP/IP uses a modifiable lookup table, usually stored in a file called Services, to determine the correct port for the correct data type. Ports may be queried by name or number. Ports can sometimes be defined on the fly by a program that facilitates other actions.

TCP uses the IP address of the receiving computer, along with the correct port number, to build the *socket address*. We discuss sockets later in this section; for now, just understand that sockets are low-level tools used to read and write data from, not to be confused with ports.

TCP creates a connection to the receiving computer using the socket address. Although TCP sometimes stays connected while data is being sent, staying connected while transferring data is not necessary and in fact is not the norm. After the data is sent, TCP simply disconnects from the socket. Furthermore, datagrams can arrive at the destination at different times and out of sequence. As I mentioned earlier, TCP/IP receives the datagrams and puts them together in the right order, complete with an acknowledgment to the sender.

Sockets are low-level interfaces to the TCP/IP family that were initially developed for Unix operating systems (the BSD Unix operating system was the first). Sockets are like files on your hard drive; you can read from them and write to them, which is exactly how they are used in a TCP/IP networking environment. A socket is created either to await a connection and any subsequent data exchange or to create a connection and initiate a data exchange. When a server uses a socket to wait for an incoming connection, it is a *passive socket*; when a client uses a socket to initiate a connection, it is an *active socket*. The only difference between active and passive sockets is the way different software packages use them.

THE FUTURE OF TCP/IP — IP NEXT GENERATION

As you may have gathered, TCP/IP is an ever-evolving family of protocols. With the explosion of the Internet, we are seeing some of the limitations of this protocol suite. One problem in particular is that we will soon run out of usable IP addresses under the current specification, with so many new connections to the Internet being built and installed every day. Another major issue is security. Both of these serious problems are being addressed by various consortia that are quickly finding the answers. Let's look at one of the foremost proposed solutions because it is likely to become a integral part of the protocol suite in the very near future.

The current version of the IP protocol is version 4, or IPv4, and the next generation, IPv6 or IPng (IP next generation), is set to become formally adopted. IPng was recommended by the IPng Area Directors of the Internet Engineering Task Force (IETF) at the Toronto IETF meeting held on July 25, 1994, as documented in RFC 1752, "The Recommendation for the IP Next Generation Protocol." (Request for Comments (RFCs) are a standard way to propose and debate the merits of any significant change or modification to a standard involving TCP/IP and the Internet in an open forum.) IPng was approved by the Internet Engineering Steering Group and made a Proposed Standard on November 17, 1994. The core set of IPng protocols was made an official IETF Proposed Standard on September 18, 1995.

IPng can be installed as a normal software upgrade to Internet devices and is interoperable with the current version of IPv4 found in today's TCP/IP protocol. IPng is designed to run well on high performance networks, such as Asynchronous Transfer Mode (ATM), and at the same time is still efficient for low-bandwidth networks, such as wireless networks. In addition, IPng provides a platform for new Internet functions that will be required in the near future.

IPng was designed to be an evolutionary step up from IPv4 but not to be a radical step away from it. Functions that work in IPv4 were kept in the IPng specification, and likewise, the functions that didn't work were removed. The changes from IPv4 to IPng fall primarily into the following categories:

- Expanded routing and addressing capabilities.
  - IPng increases the IP address size from 32 bits to 128 bits, which obviously supports more levels of addressing and a much greater number of addressable nodes. IPng also facilitates a simpler means of automatically configuring IP addresses.
  - A new type of address, the *anycast* address, is defined in IPng. An anycast address identifies nodes; a packet sent to an anycast address is delivered to one of the nodes. Using anycast addresses in the IPng

source route lets nodes control the path along which their traffic flows. IPng address types are discussed further later in this section.

- Header format simplification — Some IPv4 header fields have been dropped or made optional to reduce the common processing cost of packet handling and to keep the bandwidth cost of the IPng header as low as possible despite the increased size of the addresses. Even though the IPng addresses are four times longer than the IPv4 addresses, the IPng header is only twice the size of the IPv4 header.

- Improved support for options — Changes in the way IP header options are encoded allow for more efficient forwarding, less stringent limits on the length of options, and greater flexibility for introducing new options.

- Quality-of-service capabilities — A new capability enables the labeling of packets belonging to particular traffic flows for which the sender requests special handling, such as nondefault quality of service or real-time service.

- Authentication and privacy capabilities — IPng defines extensions that provide support for authentication, data integrity, and confidentiality. These definitions are included as a basic element of IPng and will be included in all implementations.

There are three basic types of IPng addresses: unicast, anycast, and multicast. *Unicast* addresses identify a single interface. *Anycast* addresses identify a set of interfaces so that a packet sent to an anycast address is delivered to one member of the set. *Multicast* addresses identify groups of interfaces, so that a packet sent to a multicast address is delivered to all the interfaces in the group. Multicast addresses in IPng supersede broadcast addresses.

IPng supports 128-bit addresses, or four times the number of bits as the IPv4 32-bit addresses. This 128-bit addressing scheme is several times the size of the current IPv4 32-bit address space — 4 billion squared times the current space, or 340,282,366,920,938,463,463,374,607,431,768,211,456 bits.

The Internet has a number of major security problems and lacks effective privacy and authentication mechanisms below the application layer. IPng corrects these shortcomings with two integrated options that provide security services. These two options may be used separately or together to provide different levels of security to different users. This feature is very important because different user communities have different security requirements.

The first security mechanism, the IPng Authentication Header, is an extension header that gives IPng datagrams authentication and integrity without confidentiality. Although the extension is algorithm independent and will support many different authentication techniques, the use of an MD5 security system has been proposed to help ensure this feature's interoperability within the Internet.

The IPng Authentication Header can eliminate a significant class of network attacks, including host-masquerading attacks. Using the IPng Authentication Header is particularly important when source routing is used with IPng because of the known risks in IP source routing. Its placement at the Internet layer can help provide host origin authentication to those upper-layer protocols and services that currently lack meaningful protection schemes.

The second security extension header provided with IPng is the IPng Encapsulating Security Header. This particular mechanism provides integrity and confidentiality to IPng datagrams. It's simpler than similar security protocols, such as the Network Layer Security Protocol (ISO NLSP), but it remains flexible and algorithm independent. To ensure this header's interoperability over the Internet, the Data Encryption Standard (DES) algorithm in the Cipher Block Chaining (CBC) mode (DES CBC) is being used as the standard algorithm. The DES CBC encryption process employs a 64-bit cryptographic key system.

Overall, IPng appears to be a very promising way of minimizing, if not eliminating, a few of the major problems in TCP/IP networking, especially Internet and security problems. You can expect every major vendor on the planet to adopt and implement this new protocol version in its hardware and software.

IP ADDRESSING EXPLAINED

So far, we have learned how TCP and IP work together to move data across a network. In this section, we cover what IP addresses are and what is needed in conjunction with an IP address to move data. This section helps you understand why IP addresses are so necessary and how they are used on TCP/IP networks.

ETHERNET ADDRESSES

Each Ethernet interface or Ethernet network card installed on a network has its own unique hardware address, known as an Ethernet address or media access control (MAC) address.

A MAC address is a 48-bit number that is preprogrammed by the manufacturer of the hardware device. MAC addresses consist of a unique six-part number annotated in hexadecimal; the value of each part ranges from 00 to FF. The first three parts of the MAC address are called the *organizationally unique identifier* (OUI) and are assigned by the Institute for Electrical and Electronics Engineers (IEEE). OUIs are purchased by Ethernet device manufacturers, who then assign the last three parts of the MAC address, thereby making each address assignment unique. For example, 01:b7:a3:0b:e1:19 is a MAC address, where 01:b7:a3 is the OUI and 0b:e1:19 is the unique number assigned by the manufacturer.

IP ADDRESSES AND CLASSIFICATIONS

TCP/IP requires each host on a TCP/IP network to have its own unique IP address. An IP address is a 32-bit number, represented by a four-part decimal number (*n.n.n.n*), with each of the four parts — called *octets* — representing an 8-bit portion of the whole address number. Each octet can have a value ranging from 1 to 254. IP addresses used on the Internet are assigned and regulated by the Internet Assigned Numbers Authority, who in turn delegates the assignment process to the InterNIC. You should ask your Internet Service Provider for IP addresses when connecting your network to the Internet.

Another term to know is *address pools*. Address pools are blocks of IP addresses that are commonly referred to as *networks*. There are five types of address pools: Class A, Class B, Class C, Class D, and Class E. The first octet of the IP address represents the Class A network number; the second octet represents the Class B network number; and the third octet represents the Class C network number. The fourth octet of an IP address represents the actual host number. When you put all the octets together (e.g., 207.91.166.2), you have an IP address. Class D and Class E networks are special networks. They're defined below, along with A, B, and C networks.

- Class A networks number large networks. The high-order bit of the first octet is always zero, which leaves seven bits in the first octet to define up to 127 networks. The remaining 24 bits of the 32-bit IP address are used to define the hosts, creating the possibility of 16,777,216 unique host addresses.

- Class B networks number medium-sized networks. The first two high-order bits of the first octet are always 10. Class B networks define up to 16,384 networks that can contain as many as 65,535 unique host addresses.

- Class C networks are typically used most often for numbering small networks. The first three bits are always 110, leaving room to define up to 2,097,152 networks, with each network having as many as 254 unique host addresses.

- Class D networks are made up of special multicast addresses that cannot be used for addressing devices on a network. The first four high-order bits are always set to 1110.

- Class E networks are reserved for experiments, with the first four high-order bits set to 1111.

IP SUBNETS

An IP *subnet* is a way of breaking a set of addresses, commonly referred to as an IP network, into smaller, more controllable pieces. When IP networks are subnetted, they can be routed independently to different gateways, which uses address space and bandwidth much more efficiently. An IP subnet operates by defining a *subnet mask*. The subnet mask is very similar in structure to an IP address in that it also has four parts, or octets. However, the allowable values of those octets are not quite the same as those in an IP address.

Subnet masks modify a 32-bit IP address by performing a mathematical calculation of the IP address and subnet mask at the bit level. Subnetting actually modifies the IP address by using the host address bits as additional network address bits.

The most common type of subnetting is performed on an even-byte boundary, although you may subnet a network using a bit boundary as well. An example of a subnet mask for a Class C network using an even-byte boundary is 255.255.255.0. If you use a Class C network address pool of 207.91.166.0, with usable host addresses ranging from 207.91.166.1 through 207.91.166.254, in combination with a subnet mask of 255.255.255.0, then all the addresses in that pool can be routed to the same gateway, and all are considered a part of the same logical IP network.

Subnetting can reduce the size of routing tables, minimize network traffic, isolate networks, maximize performance, and enhance your ability to secure a network. How you implement subnetting depends on many factors related to the use and design of your network.

MULTIHOMING

A host may have more than one IP address; these hosts are known as multi-homed hosts. Normally, hosts have just a single IP address; however, multihoming is necessary for several purposes, including establishing virtual Web servers. Multihoming can be useful for routing on a host computer containing more than one network card. Each card has its own unique IP address, and in practice, each of those cards could be connected to different physical network segments. With this type of configuration, more than one route to any given host can exist, which increases the probability of reaching it. This setup is useful when a network link goes down or becomes saturated with traffic.

ASPECTS OF TCP/IP

TCP/IP relies on certain functions and configuration settings to operate correctly. In this section, we look at some of the most crucial aspects of the protocol suite and other functions on which it depends. Pay special attention to these items because without an understanding of them, you're probably going to find yourself either suffering from a big headache or pulling your hair out from frustration.

GATEWAYS AND ROUTING

Routing is the process of getting your data across a network. Routing a datagram is very similar to traveling in your car. Before you drive off to your destination, you must determine which roads you are going to take to get there, and sometimes you have to change your mind along the way, altering your route for any number of possible reasons — a road may be closed, or traffic may be too heavy on a certain highway. TCP/IP routing follows this same concept.

The IP portion of the TCP/IP protocol takes care of identifying the starting point and the destination for your data. If IP doesn't know the address of the destination for the datagram and can't find out, it sends the datagram to its *gateway.* Typically, each host on a TCP/IP network has a gateway — an off-ramp for datagrams that are not destined for the local network. If a datagram is sent to the gateway, the gateway then takes on the job of forwarding the datagram to the remote destination.

Each gateway has a defined set of routing tables that tells it the path to certain destinations. Gateways don't know where every IP address is, so gateways in turn have their own gateways. When a gateway doesn't know the way to a particular destination, it forwards the datagram to its own gateway. This cycle of *routing* is continued until the datagram finally arrives at its destination. The entire path traveled from the origin to the destination is called *the route.*

Datagrams may travel to a particular destination one way one time and another way another time. The route is determined by many variables that occur along the route. For instance, overloaded gateways processing too much traffic may not respond in a timely manner or may simply refuse to route your traffic, causing a timeout. That timeout causes the sending gateway to seek an alternative route for the datagram. A timeout could also be caused by network links or network devices being down or many other factors.

In most cases, routes can be predefined and made to remain static if need be. Alternative routes can also be predefined, providing a maximum probability that your datagrams will arrive at their final destination. The way routing is handled on your network is purely a matter of preference. You should note that improper routing can lead to poor network performance; network routers may become overburdened with traffic or may inadvertently assign longer routes than necessary.

HOSTS, HOST NAMES, AND DOMAIN NAMES

The word *host* describes various devices on the network. Technically, any device on a network that has some sort of address and is capable of sending and/or receiving data or information can be called a host. A printer can be a host, a network fax machine can be a host, and a computer system can certainly be a host. However, hosts are usually thought of as computer systems on a network. On most networks, hosts have names. On TCP/IP networks, hosts have names that are a subset of domain names.

Internet host names are an easy way to remember a long decimal IP address. A host name is typically the name of a device that has a specific IP address. A host name and a domain name make up a *fully qualified domain name*. For example, www.ntshop.net is a fully qualified domain name, where www is the host name and ntshop.net is the domain name. Hosts on a network use names the same way people use names. We all have a Social Security number, and we can certainly remember that number if need be, but imagine if all of your friends and associates had to be called by their Social Security numbers instead of regular names! We use words as names instead because they are easier to remember. Likewise, it's easier to remember www.ntshop.net than it is to remember 207.91.166.2.

DOMAIN NAME SERVICE

Domain Name Service, or DNS, cross-references specific information to translate host names and domain names to IP addresses and vice versa using a lookup table that the network administrator defines and configures. For example, when you type www.ntshop.net in your Web browser, the DNS server returns 206.91.166.2 as an answer, allowing the Web browser to locate the server and load the home page.

Although you can run a TCP/IP network without it, DNS is considered an essential part of any TCP/IP network because it makes the task of remembering addresses much easier. Although humans think best in words, computers work best with numbers. DNS lets the human remember the name while DNS remembers the corresponding numbers, much like a phone book.

DNS tables compile records that are defined in a particular structure. Depending on the record type, the structure can be composed of four or five parts, but for the purposes of this book, we'll focus on the three important parts: the host name, the record type, and the host address pointer.

DNS tables can store several different types of records. The most common record types are address records, mail exchange records, and alias records. Let's look at address records, commonly referred to as A records. A records correlate host names to IP addresses. An address record entry for a host named "mail" in the "ntshop.net" domain is shown below.

        mail.ntshop.net.   IN   A   207.91.166.2

The next record type we'll look at is the mail exchange record. Mail exchange records point to the mail servers for a given domain name and describe where mail for that domain should be sent. It is possible to specify several mail servers in order of preference for a given domain, thereby increasing the probability that mail will arrive at its destination if one of the servers is down or not responding.

When one mail server tries to send mail to another mail server, it first queries the DNS server for the list of mail servers for that domain. Once that list is obtained, the servers are tried in the order of preference listed — if the first mail server listed does not respond, the second one is tried, and so on. If by chance none of the mail servers responds, the mail is returned to the sender. In the typical set of mail server records below, the MX portion of the entry specifies that the record is a mail exchange record, and the numbers 10, 20, and 30 indicate the order of preference.

yourhost.ntshop.net.	IN	MX	10	mail.ntshop.net.
yourhost.ntshop.net.	IN	MX	20	mail2.ntshop.net.
yourhost.ntshop.net.	IN	MX	30	mail3.ntshop.net.

CNAME records, or canonical name records, are also called alias records. CNAME records allow hosts to have more than one name. For example, you may want your Web server, named www, to run your FTP server as well. You could simply create a CNAME record that creates an alias of "www" for "ftp." CNAME records depend on previously defined address records, so you need to establish an address record for "www" before "ftp" would be usable. Sample CNAME records and their associated address records are shown below.

www.ntshop.net	IN	A	207.91.166.2
ftp.ntshop.net.	IN	CNAME	www.ntshop.net.

When you put all these record types together in a file, you have a DNS table:

mail.domain.com	IN	A		207.91.166.2
mail2.domain.com	IN	A		207.91.166.198
www.domain.com	IN	A		207.91.166.4
ftp.domain.com	IN	CNAME		www.domain.com.
host1.domain.com	IN	MX	10	mail.domain.com.
host1.domain.com	IN	MX	20	mail2.domain.com.

You can use other types of DNS records; however, we won't cover them all in this book. DNS can be a complex subject. You should seek out one of the many books devoted to the subject if you want a complete understanding of its intricacies.

MICROSOFT'S WINS SERVER

Windows Internet Naming Service (WINS) is an essential part of the Microsoft networking topology. WINS works with TCP/IP to map NetBIOS names to IP addresses. (NetBIOS is a session-layer protocol that manages data exchange and network access on Windows operating systems.) Because TCP/IP cannot operate with NetBIOS directly, it relies on WINS to get the job done.

WINS operates much as DNS does in that it maintains a table of NetBIOS names mapped to their associated IP addresses. The main difference between WINS and DNS is that the WINS server automatically builds and updates its own tables without user intervention, whereas DNS tables must be built and updated manually. Remember, DNS maps TCP/IP host names to IP addresses, and WINS maps NetBIOS host names to IP addresses.

Each time you need to access a network resource on a Windows NT network using TCP/IP, your system needs to know the host name or IP address. WINS lets you continue using the NetBIOS names that you have already become accustomed to.

The WINS server's IP address is defined when you configure TCP/IP after installing Windows NT, as you will see later in this chapter. When a Windows NT machine running TCP/IP is booted and attached to the network, it uses the WINS address settings in the TCP/IP configuration to communicate with the WINS server. The Windows NT machine then gives the WINS server various bits of information about itself so that the WINS server may include that information in its dynamic tables. WINS periodically refreshes this information so that its table remains current and accurate.

With the release of Windows NT 4.0, Microsoft included its own DNS server, which is designed to interoperate with the WINS server. Microsoft's DNS server includes a new DNS record type, the WINS record. This record, when defined, tells a DNS server to query the WINS server for host IP address information. In effect, this feature lets the DNS server look up the IP address of a host name that may not be in the DNS tables.

One real advantage to this setup becomes apparent when you use Dynamic Host Configuration Protocol (DHCP) to dynamically assign IP addresses to machines on your network. You may recall that DNS requires static IP addresses to be defined for each host and that DNS has no way of knowing when that address changes. With WINS at its side, a Microsoft DNS server can automatically keep up with the ever-changing IP addresses by simply relying on WINS to track them automatically. Then, when DNS needs to know an IP address, it can ask the WINS server.

You can certainly use WINS and DNS on your network, or you could use one without the other. Your choice should be based on whether your network is connected to the Internet and whether you use DHCP. If you use DHCP and are connected to the Internet, you're probably going to find that things work best with both WINS and DNS installed.

INSTALLING TCP/IP ON WINDOWS NT

Now that we have a basic understanding of TCP/IP and how it works on a network, let's walk through installing and configuring TCP/IP on Windows NT Server 4.0. In this section, we work with these basic assumptions:

- you are using an Internet domain name of "company.com"
- your server's TCP/IP host name is "www"
- your server's IP address is 204.176.47.2
- your server has a subnet mask of 255.255.255.0
- this particular server has only one network card installed
- you have a WINS server installed and running with an IP address of 204.176.47.1

Follow these steps to install TCP/IP.

1. Open the Control Panel by clicking Start, choosing Settings, and clicking Control Panel. A window containing all the installed Control Panel applets will appear.
2. Once the Control Panel is active, scroll down until you locate the Network icon (Figure 1.3) and double-click on it to bring up the Network Configuration dialog box (Figure 1.4). Select the Protocols tab and click Add.

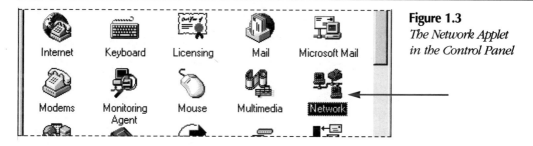

Figure 1.3
The Network Applet in the Control Panel

3. The Select Network Protocol dialog box will appear (Figure 1.5). Scroll down the list of available protocols until you see TCP/IP Protocol. Double-click TCP/IP Protocol or click the protocol and click OK to add it to your network configuration.

Figure 1.4

The Protocols Tab of the Network Dialog Box

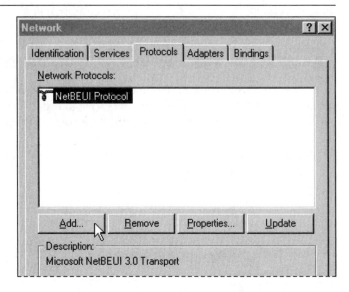

Figure 1.5

Adding TCP/IP to the Network

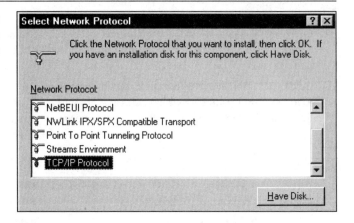

4. You may be shown a dialog box like that in Figure 1.6, asking whether you have a DHCP Server on your network and if you want to use it for dynamic IP address assignment. In most cases, you'll want your server to have a static IP address, so click No even if you have a DHCP server on your network.

5. Next, the Network Protocol dialog box asks where it can find the Windows NT installation files it needs to complete the TCP/IP setup. They should be in the same place you installed your Windows NT from, usually your CD-ROM drive. Insert your CD-ROM, enter the drive letter in the

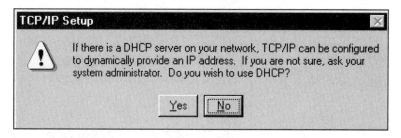

Figure 1.6
*Answering the
DHCP dialog*

dialog box as shown in Figure 1.7, and click Continue. TCP/IP Setup copies the necessary files to your hard drive and closes the dialog box to continue the setup procedure.

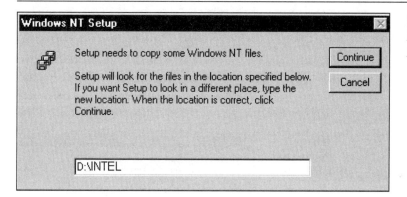

Figure 1.7
*Locating the
Installation Files*

6. Now that all the necessary files have been copied, you need to set the properties of the TCP/IP drivers. Windows NT TCP/IP setup will continue by rebuilding the registry entries and bindings for the network. It will detect that TCP/IP has not been configured and bring up the TCP/IP Properties dialog box (Figure 1.8).

   The first tab is the IP Address tab. Make sure your network card is displayed in the Adapter list. Next, select Specify IP Address and fill in the IP Address, Subnet Mask, and Default Gateway fields. The Advanced button presents a dialog box that lets you add more IP addresses and gateways and manage some aspects of TCP/IP security. Because we assume that this host has only one gateway and one IP address, we won't go into the Advanced dialog box at this time, but we cover the TCP/IP security settings later in this book.

7. Click the DNS tab to display the DNS properties (Figure 1.9). First, type **www**, which is the host name. Now fill in the Domain field with your domain name or your ISP's domain name; remember, we're using "company.com" for this example. Now click Add under the DNS Service Search Order list box. You will see a dialog

Figure 1.8

Configuring the Address, Subnet, and Gateway

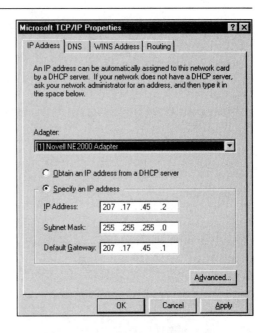

Figure 1.9

Configuring DNS Properties

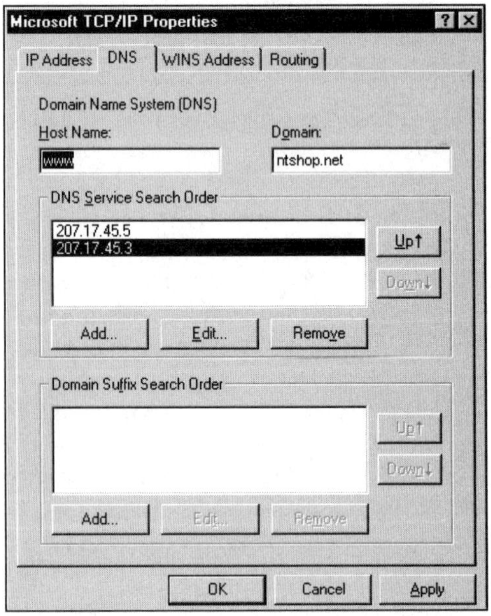

box where you enter an IP address of your first DNS server. After you have entered the first DNS server's IP address, click OK, then click Add again to add your second DNS server's IP address, if you have one. Windows NT lets you specify up to three DNS server addresses.

The Domain Suffix Search Order provides a list of domain names to search when you specify only a host name. Suppose you want to ping a host named mail.ntshop.net (ping sends a test packet to a host and waits for a response indicating that the packet arrived successfully). Open a DOS console window, type the command **ping mail**, and the TCP/IP protocol automatically appends your default domain name to the end, making it mail.ntshop.net, where mail is called the *prefix*, and ntshop.net is the *suffix*. Adding domain names to this list allows other domains to be searched automatically for a host with this same name. This feature can be very useful on some networks; however, for this installation example, we'll leave this list blank.

8. Click the WINS Address tab to display the WINS Address properties, as shown in Figure 1.10.

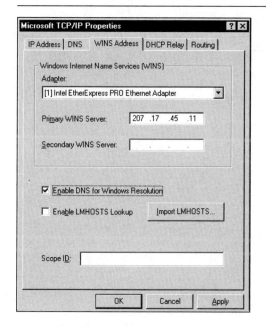

Figure 1.10
Configuring WINS Address Properties

Type the IP address of your WINS server in the Primary WINS server box. If your network has more than one WINS server, type the IP address of your secondary WINS server in the Secondary WINS server box. We want

Windows NT to use DNS to look up TCP/IP host names and addresses, so select the checkbox beside Enable DNS for Windows Resolution. By default, the Enable LMHOSTS Lookup checkbox is selected. In this example installation, we want to rely only on DNS for lookups, so clear this box. LMHOSTS Lookup is a method of name resolution that uses a text file similar to DNS tables. However, it differs from DNS in that it maps IP addresses to NetBIOS computer names, similar to the WINS server, except that the table must be updated manually.

All computers on a TCP/IP network must use the same scope ID. Ask your network administrator whether a scope is defined for your network and type the scope ID in this field. If you don't have a scope on your network, simply leave this field blank. Most Windows NT networks don't use a Scope ID.

9. Next, click the DHCP Relay tab (Figure 1.11). DHCP lets workstations and servers be assigned IP addresses automatically. The primary reason for using DHCP is that it can provide a centralized method of managing IP addresses. We won't delve into all the details of DHCP in this book, and for example purposes, we'll assume that you are not using a DHCP server on your network, so no changes are necessary.

Figure 1.11

*Specifying
DHCP Settings*

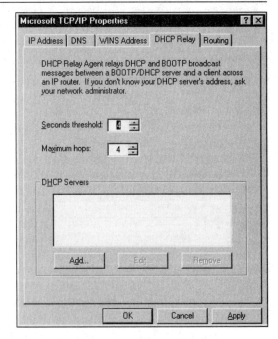

10. Now click the Routing tab to display the routing properties (Figure 1.12). The Routing dialog box has a single checkbox labeled Enable IP Forwarding. IP forwarding allows datagrams to be forwarded on a multihomed host. A multihomed host has more than one network card installed or more than one IP address assigned to a network card. With multihomed hosts, sometimes datagrams need to be routed between the network cards to other parts or segments of the network. This setting is a key factor in establishing a secure network segment and is covered later in this book. For now, do not select the check box.

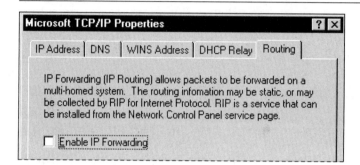

Figure 1.12
Routing Option

11. Now that you've completed configuring the TCP/IP properties, click OK to finish the setup process. The Binding Review is completed, and a dialog box asking whether you want to reboot now appears (Figure 1.13). It is always best to reboot whenever Windows NT asks you, so click Yes. Windows NT will write your settings to the registry and reboot. The registry can be viewed and modified with Regedt32.exe, which we cover later in this book.

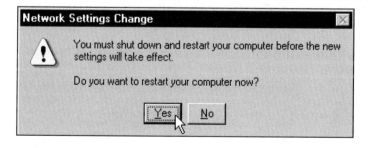

Figure 1.13
Reboot Dialog Box

12. After the server has rebooted, you can log on and test the configuration using the Ping utility. Open a DOS console window by clicking Start, selecting Programs, and choosing MS-DOS. When the DOS window

opens, type the following command: **ping 127.0.0.1**. You should see a response similar to the one shown in Figure 1.14.

Figure 1.14

Testing the Local Host with Ping

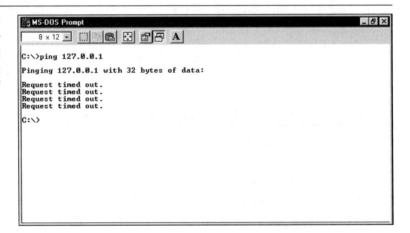

Ping sends a diagnostic packet to the address specified and waits for a response for a predetermined amount of time. We use the address 127.0.0.1 in this instance because it is a special loopback address designed for testing. If Ping does not receive a response in the predetermined amount of time, a time-out error is reported, as shown in Figure 1.15.

Figure 1.15

Timeout Error from the Ping Command

```
MS-DOS Prompt
8 x 12
C:\>ping 127.0.0.1
Pinging 127.0.0.1 with 32 bytes of data:
Request timed out.
Request timed out.
Request timed out.
Request timed out.
C:\>
```

13. After you have pinged the localhost address, you should try to ping another host on your network to make sure everything is working correctly. For example, if you have another host on your network with the IP

address 207.91.166.199, you can ping that address, as shown in Figure 1.16. You may also want to test your DNS or WINS setup at this time as well. You can do so by pinging a host by name that has a DNS entry or WINS server configured.

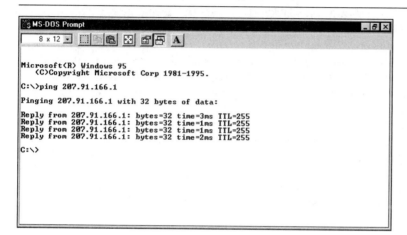

Figure 1.16

Pinging Another Host on the Network

Also, if your network is already attached to the Internet, you can test your gateway by pinging a host that you know is somewhere on the Internet. For example, you could try pinging the Windows NT Magazine Web server by typing **ping www.winntmag.com**. You should always get a response similar to the one shown in Figure 1.14, except that the response times might be a bit longer, because your packets have to travel across the Internet and back.

Now that you have installed TCP/IP on your Windows NT machine, I'll remind you that you have made an excellent choice for a networking protocol. TCP/IP is absolutely the most performance-oriented protocol you can use, and when it comes to connecting to the Internet, there is simply no other choice.

SUMMARY

Now that we have a basic understanding of TCP/IP and how it works, it should be clear that TCP/IP has many advantages. When you use TCP/IP on an intranet with Windows NT, you gain one distinct advantage over using TCP/IP with other types of network operating systems: ease of configuration and use. You should also understand that literally hundreds of vendors are creating software for the Windows NT operating system, which obviously increases the likelihood of finding software that does what you need.

Another major advantage of using TCP/IP and Windows NT on your intranet is the cross-platform connectivity. TCP/IP is available for almost every operating system in production today. Because TCP/IP is a standard family of protocols, connecting dissimilar operating systems is a breeze. You can connect new systems to older legacy systems in a snap. For example, if your network is composed of Apple Macintosh systems, minicomputers, mainframes, Unix systems, IBM PCs running Novell, and IBM PC-compatible systems running some version of Windows, the components *normally* would not be able to communicate with each other at all. But with TCP/IP installed on each of them, they are all capable of communicating and transferring data back and forth with ease. This flexibility is not possible with any other networking protocol today.

TCP/IP is the revolution that the computer industry has needed for a long time; however, it has taken the vast popularity of the Internet to institute its widespread implementation. Here are some of the major benefits of using TCP/IP:

- TCP/IP is a routable protocol with the ability to send datagrams using a very specific route, which in turn reduces traffic on other parts of a network.
- TCP/IP has a lower overhead than other protocols, which allows much larger networks to be constructed.
- TCP/IP is reliable and has efficient data delivery mechanisms.
- TCP/IP is standardized for cross-platform implementation, making TCP/IP able to send data between computer systems running completely different operating systems, from PCs to mainframes and almost everything in between.
- TCP/IP provides a common addressing scheme across all operating system platforms.
- TCP/IP can run over a variety of network types including Ethernet, Token Ring, X.25, Frame Relay, and even dialup lines.

CHAPTER 2

NETWORK SECURITY OVERVIEW

Now that you have an understanding of TCP/IP and some of its counter-parts, let's get a bit more familiar with TCP/IP security in general. After a brief look at the cost of poor network security, this chapter examines the history of TCP/IP security, the most popular methods of securing a network, and some of the potential dangers. You then get some insight into the mind of a potential intruder, which will make you more effective in preventing unauthorized access to your networks. The last section lists common places a network is vulnerable.

THE COST OF POOR SECURITY

Companies with poorly designed or no security systems are suffering enormous costs. The cost of a security system is far less than the cost of intrusion. A quick look at some of the figures can be a wake-up call for network administrators and business owners alike.

According to one study conducted by the U.S. Senate's Permanent Investigations Subcommittee, intruders cost businesses more than $800 million in 1995 alone, with U.S. companies losing more than half of the total. The study reported that in most cases, the breaches were not reported to law enforcement agencies for fear of bad publicity.

In 1995, the Department of Defense (DoD) computer networks experienced more than 250,000 attacks, and that rate of attack is expected to at least double every year for the foreseeable future. It is believed that these attacks were successful about 65 percent of the time. Even though some attacks to DoD systems are only a nuisance, some are a threat to national security. In the spring of 1994 at an Air Force laboratory in Rome, New York, a pair of intruders successfully broke into the lab's computer systems more than 150 times. During their dances around the lab's systems, they collected the passwords of users and used those passwords to break into more than 100 other computer systems attached to the Internet. One of the perpetrators, a 16-year-old boy from London, England, was apprehended. The other intruder remains unknown and uncaught.

These facts should alert you to the potential dangers of intrusion. What will a break-in cost you? Perhaps your entire business. Again, don't take your network security lightly, and never assume you are *completely safe* from intrusion.

THE HISTORY OF TCP/IP SECURITY

As soon as someone discovered how to connect computers to form a network, someone else immediately tried to infiltrate that system. Network security has come a long way. Let's take a walk through time and see where we have been, where we are, and where we are going.

YESTERDAY

In the very early days, all we had to work with were simple password schemes. Users picked a password and used it to access a computer system and its resources. The idea of creating networks of computers to share information and resources opened up a whole new can of worms. It became possible to reach out to systems besides your own without leaving the comfort of your own machine.

TCP/IP was vulnerable from the very beginning. In TCP/IP's very early days, circa 1983, not many people were seriously concerned about security. The excitement at connecting dissimilar systems overshadowed any concern for securing the connection. TCP/IP was designed to be a networking protocol without protection, not to offer any built-in security mechanisms — it travels across a network, which leaves the protocol open to interception along the way. The evolution of TCP/IP security was really the evolution of network security. Any resource accessible over the network presented a potential security risk to be exploited in some manner. To understand the nature and evolution of network security, we must consider that people used computers primarily to communicate. Sending electronic messages and transferring files were the most popular uses of networks.

TCP/IP was almost immediately adopted in the Unix community and first appeared in the BSD Unix operating system. When that great marriage took place, Unix became vulnerable. Every connection between a Unix system and a network like ARPAnet was open for exploitation. (As you recall, ARPAnet was the forerunner of today's Internet.) The Internet quickly became dominated by Unix operating systems (and remains so today). Unix includes known security flaws, especially in services such as e-mail. As Unix Sendmail and FTP were ported to other operating systems, so were the bugs and flaws. Fortunately, many of the systems using these services had different underlying structures that helped provide a natural protection against their flaws.

For example, intruders used Sendmail to instruct a system to mail them its password file. In the hands of an experienced intruder, the password files could be deciphered easily. However, systems such as Windows NT did not become vulnerable to this type of flaw because Windows NT does not store its passwords in an easily accessible file that it can simply e-mail or transfer out of the system.

As I mentioned, in the early days, security was based on passwords, which remain the last line of defense. However, as time went by, engineers focused on eliminating security flaws introduced by poorly engineered software. They came up with newer and more powerful encryption mechanisms to protect password files that were obtained by an intruder. They created ways to hide password files altogether, making them difficult to locate. Eventually, they began to look at the network and TCP/IP themselves as ways to prevent an intruder from ever reaching a computer on the network. If you can prevent unauthorized traffic, even a poorly protected software package running on a networked computer is instantly far less vulnerable to attack.

The engineers' work was made more difficult by the way the Internet evolved. Most of the early computer systems on the Internet belonged to universities and government agencies, which believed that the Internet should provide free access to all information. If a few people abused that free access, then that was the price. Even today, many universities on the Internet follow this philosophy, imposing very few restrictions. Unfortunately, when one person creates a liberty, another person will exploit that liberty.

TODAY'S NETWORK SECURITY

In today's world, security is of paramount concern. Networks have proven themselves invaluable in the world of commerce. If the old saying "money makes the world go around" is true, in the very near future that saying will become "networks make the world go around" as more businesses adopt wide-area networks as their vehicle for commerce.

Today, network security takes many forms, and a wide range of protection mechanisms are at your disposal. Innovations in password protection include heavier encryption schemes and password-choosing programs that attempt to crack a password before it's allowed to be used. The engineers who investigated minimizing network traffic have created a broad range of solutions that are available for today's networks. Because TCP/IP transmits data in packets, it makes sense for networks to identify and control those packets as they enter a network environment. Engineers have invented wonderful instruments of protection, such as packet filters, application gateways (proxy servers), and circuit-level gateways, each of which we discuss in more detail later in this chapter. Engineers have even come up with such high-tech devices as magnetic card keys, optical retina scanners, and fingerprint readers that are all available today. They've also introduced some simpler protection mechanisms, such as timers that limit the times of day a user can access a system.

Today's security world is much more high-tech than that of the past. However, security has not reached perfection by any means. New ways of protecting computers, networks, and their resources are still evolving in many different ways.

Each time we develop a new way of disseminating information across a network, we open up a whole new world of security issues and concerns. Yesterday it was Sendmail software, and today it's the World Wide Web. Fortunately, the Web is so popular that almost every major software development firm has adopted its technology and is improving it. Now some of the greatest and most powerful minds will undoubtedly take on security issues and find solutions very rapidly. For example, Microsoft and Visa are working with other firms to develop secure means of transmitting electronic payment information across the Internet.

The Orange Book

The DoD views security seriously, and rightly so. The best-known of the DoD's publications on security is the Orange Book, which is short for DoD standard number 5200.28, *Trusted Computer System Evaluation Criteria*. The Orange Book provides technical criteria for hardware, firmware, and software security, along with associated technical evaluation methodologies that support data security. We discuss the Orange Book and other DoD security publications in more detail in Chapter 3.

The Orange book categorizes security in four divisions, some of which have subdivisions:

- Division D: Minimal Protection — Systems such as DOS fall into this division because they have almost no protection schemes.

- Division C: Discretionary Protection — Most widely used operating systems profess to comply with Division C, Class 2 security (C2). However, there is a difference between being C2-certified by the National Computer Security Center (NCSC) and complying with Division C2 security.
    - Class 1 (C1): Discretionary Security Protection
    - Class 2 (C2): Controlled Access Protection

- Division B: Mandatory Protection — A system must provide mathematical documentation of its security and be able to maintain its system security even while the system is down.
    - Class 1 (B1): Labeled Security Protection
    - Class 2 (B2): Structured Protection
    - Class 3 (B3): Security Domains

- Division A: Verified Protection — A system must prove that it matches the specifications to the letter.
    - Class 1 (A1): Verified Design
    - Beyond Class 1

Any computer system that allows open and unrestricted access falls into security Class D. Most commercial operating systems are in the C1 and C2 categories. The Class B divisions are less practical to implement in a typical business environment. Class B and Class A systems are most often found where the absolute highest levels of security must be maintained at all times; for example, in some government-run computer systems. For a look at the Orange Book, point your Web browser to http://tecnet1.jcte.jcs.mil:8000/htdocs/teinfo/directives/soft/stan.html. For further sources of information, see the Bibliography.

Windows NT is in the C2 security division. One criterion for meeting this guideline is that you must keep the server behind a constantly locked door. C2 security capabilities weren't in Windows NT in the first release. Microsoft implemented C2 so that it could bid on government contracts for operating systems that require certain levels of security.

Microsoft and Netscape are two key players setting standards for securing systems and data transmissions. Netscape proposed and deployed the Secure Socket Layer (SSL), which is a way for Web browsers to exchange data with a Web server using secure data encryption methods. Visa, MasterCard, and other companies are developing their own security standards for electronic commerce.

THE SECURITY OF TOMORROW

We can look into the future with relative ease and see quite clearly that security is still improving. In Chapter 1, we discussed IPng, which gives TCP/IP the ability to protect itself from tampering. You can expect this new protocol to be adopted and quickly put into use. In addition, all the software- and hardware-based security technologies that currently lend protection to TCP/IP will evolve to give greater protection to this next-generation protocol.

For a clearer view of the direction security technologies are headed, we need only look to the medical and science communities. Their technologies, such as fingerprint readers, body temperature patterns, DNA decoders, and other high-tech means of positive identification, will be adopted in the computer security world at a blistering pace. These types of technology will improve security at both the system level and network level, offering new ways to authenticate network traffic origins and destinations.

Whatever technologies are in vogue, the network security of yesterday, today, and tomorrow can be reduced to one word — *diligence.* Good security is, and always will be, a cycle of diligence in monitoring security, analyzing data, and implementing procedures.

SECURITY METHODS

You can secure a TCP/IP network in many different ways. We cover the most common methods briefly in this section and in more detail in Chapter 17. To choose your methods, you need only ask yourself one simple question: "What am I trying to protect, and who am I protecting it from?" Specifically, we will look at

- firewalls
- packet filters
- proxy servers and application gateways
- circuit-level gateways
- physical isolation

- protocol isolation
- monitoring and auditing

FIREWALLS

You'll hear the term *firewall* used often. In a sense, "firewall" is a generic term because a firewall is simply some type of mechanism — hardware, software, or both — for protecting your network from the outside world.

Unfortunately, some people think they're protected if they install a firewall. Those people could not be more misinformed. If you think firewalls are fool-proof, consider France's Maginot Line. The Maginot Line was a defensive wall 62 miles long, armed to the hilt with artillery and soldiers, that was designed to keep the Germans out of France after World War I. Some French thought it was the perfect defense, but the Germans had another idea — they simply walked around it. There's more than one way to get past a barrier, including a firewall, and you can bet some intruder will find it.

According to International Data Corp., the threat of intruders penetrating networks attached to the Internet has sent worldwide firewall sales skyrock-eting from about 10,000 units shipped in 1995 to a projected 1.5 million by 2000. Some industry sources predict that this market stimulation will drive prices for an average firewall from around $16,000 today to about $650 in 2000. Companies like Ascend Communications (http://www.ascend.com) already sell their packet-filtering firewalls for as little as $500, although they're alone in this price range at the moment.

Even with a firewall in place on your network, you could still be a sitting duck. The firewall itself is not always the root of the security problem. Many network professionals overlook even the simplest security practices. For example, a man named Rica works for a large corporation and provides computer security and firewall penetration tests. He breaks into Fortune 500 companies' firewall-protected systems to see how effective the firewalls really are. His results are not pretty. In his eight years of break-in attempts, he's been caught in the act only once! When any of his clients eventually discovered he had been dancing around their internal networks, it was usually after he'd been in for several weeks.

Why is he able to break in undetected so successfully? Most security violation logs in firewall systems detect and record 50 to 60 percent of all unautho-rized access attempts. Mr. Rica gets in because the network security professionals charged with handling those systems do not monitor the logs closely enough. In some cases, they don't monitor them at all. Real intruders could be slipping in right under their noses.

Never assume an intruder won't go around or through your firewall. It's always prudent to know all the possible entry points of your system. Even inexperienced intruders could enter your system through any piece of software that lets one computer communicate with another. Some of these entry points lie in your network hardware, such as bridges and routers, and others are in your software systems, like your mail FTP server. You should identify all TCP/IP-enabled devices on your network, both hardware and software, and route traffic away from them when possible. This one step greatly minimizes your overall security risk. Don't put all your eggs in the basket labeled "firewall." You must define and develop security policies that include heavy monitoring if you want your firewall to be an effective deterrent.

Figure 2.1 illustrates a generic firewall implementation. Here are four questions to ask when considering a firewall for your network:

- What functions do you want the firewall to perform?
- What level of control over the network and firewall do you need and want?
- How much money can you allocate toward getting it done right?
- How much will it cost to maintain the firewall?

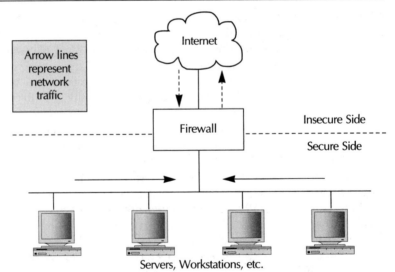

Figure 2.1
*Generic Firewall
Implementation*

PACKET FILTERS

Packet filters typically limit packet traffic to and from hosts on your network, based on an intricate set of rules that you define. Packet filters come in two varieties: hardware-based and software-based. A hardware packet filter is typi-cally a standalone router that filters packets as they enter and leave the router. A software filter runs on a network server that acts as a routing gateway.

As discussed in Chapter 1, each TCP/IP packet traveling through a net-work contains a header that holds certain information, including the source and destination addresses and the destination port number. A packet filter uses this information to decide how to handle the packet, based on the rules you establish that tell the router how you want to handle each packet type. As the packets flow through the router, the router compares each packet against the defined rule set and decides whether the packet can pass through.

You can define the source and destination addresses and the types of ports that packet filters recognize. The best packet filters by default deny all traffic unless it is expressly given permission to pass. Because you must pur-posely create a rule that allows certain traffic to pass, you are less likely to leave parts of your system exposed accidentally. Figure 2.2 shows a typical packet filter installation on a network.

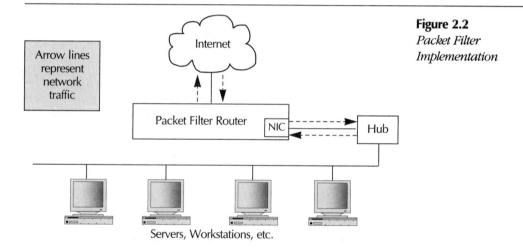

Figure 2.2
*Packet Filter
Implementation*

Servers, Workstations, etc.

Keep in mind that packet filters can have certain weaknesses stemming from their inner workings as traffic analysis agents. Because they simply look at packets and decide how to handle those packets based on port numbers and IP addresses, they can sometimes be spoofed (faked) into thinking a par-ticular packet stream is authorized traffic, when in fact it may not be.

We talk more about packet filtering systems and look a few of the best ones on the market later in this book.

PROXY SERVERS AND APPLICATION GATEWAYS

A *proxy server* is a server that is empowered to act on behalf of other computers on a network. A host computer running a proxy server is commonly referred to as an *application gateway*. Figure 2.3 shows a typical proxy server/application gateway configuration.

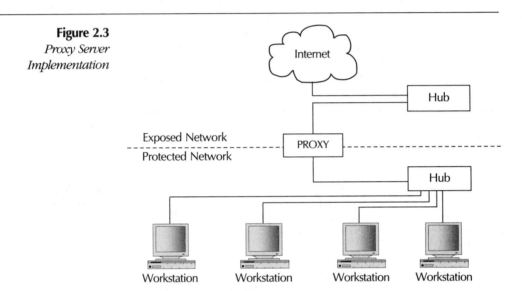

Figure 2.3
Proxy Server
Implementation

Proxy servers act as mediators between two systems attempting to communicate with each other across a network. The actual mediation process flows something like this:

1. A user connects to the application gateway via software that tells the proxy what system the user wants to connect to, and for what reason (such as a Web page request).

2. The gateway checks the user's source IP address and accepts or rejects it according to access criteria put in place by the administrator.

3. The proxy may authenticate the user by some means, such as a one-time password.

4. The proxy service creates a connection between the gateway and the host.

5. The proxy server passes data between the two connections.

6. The proxy server logs the connection information.

7. The proxy server repeats steps 5 and 6 until all the information is transferred. The disconnect process varies from vendor to vendor.

Because they protect the identity of the host, application gateways are a handy way to traverse a network anonymously. The source IP address of the host is never revealed to any system other than the proxy. They improve security because without knowing the true IP address of a host, it is next to impossible for an intruder to attack that machine. However, you should be aware that even the most minor mistakes in configuring the proxy and the network routing can leave you wide open to attack when you might consider yourself protected.

Proxy servers are an economical and reliable way to protect your computer systems from intrusion. Proxies strengthen the weaknesses associated with packet filters. Used together, they provide a higher level of security than if each is used independently.

Application gateways have a number of advantages over other types of security systems:

- Robust authentication and logging — the application traffic can be authenticated before it reaches internal hosts and can be logged in detail.

- Hidden information — the names of your internal systems are not revealed to external systems. Often, the application gateway is the only host name that must be revealed.

- Cost-effectiveness — third-party software or hardware for authentication and logging needs to be located only on the application gateway.

- Less complex filtering rules — the rules you establish for a combined packet filter/proxy server setup can be less complex than if the packet filter controls all aspects of application traffic by itself. When used with a proxy server, a packet filter simply allows application traffic destined for the application gateway and rejects all other traffic.

CIRCUIT-LEVEL GATEWAYS

Circuit-level gateways are similar to application gateways, except circuit-level gateways verify a TCP or UDP session but do not verify which application is being used. They simply allow a client to connect and send packets back and forth between the client and server.

The theory behind the circuit-level gateway approach to network security is avoiding any direct physical contact between the outside world and a machine on the internal network. In this scenario, a proxy address (or substitute address) is used as a contact to the outside source. Once information is transferred to that address, the proxy transfers information to the appropriate internal destination. This scenario helps deter hackers by limiting the amount of information individual machines share with the outside world, much like an application gateway. Unlike packet filtering systems, circuit-level gateways don't examine individual packets of information but accept multiple packets once they verify address information. Circuit-level gateways are rarely used alone; they are more commonly part of a larger security system package.

PHYSICAL ISOLATION

You should consider physically isolating systems on your network by placing them where they cannot be reached by TCP/IP traffic from anyone outside your network. This change alone can greatly minimize the possibilities of that system being attacked. If you set it up correctly, an intruder's only choice is to gain physical access to your facilities to get at the system. Facility access is a lot easier to control than network access. You should consider placing your systems behind a locked door with an alarm system in place, even during normal business hours. You may also consider using card key systems in which a user must have a card to log on to a system.

PROTOCOL ISOLATION

Protocol isolation techniques use network devices that do not require TCP/IP as the primary means of network communication. They use some other protocol, such as NetBEUI or IPX/SPX, to communicate on your local network. When these systems need to access the Internet, which requires TCP/IP, they go through some type of application gateway. Protocol isolation provides a great deal of protection because TCP/IP traffic cannot reach a system that does not run TCP/IP.

Microsoft's Internet Information Server (IIS) and Proxy Server (MPS), formerly code-named Catapult, both allow the use of IPX/SPX to gain access to the Internet with TCP/IP on client systems. Only the server runs TCP/IP, which leaves the client systems protected from attack. You can learn more about IIS and IAS at http://www.microsoft.com/infoserv.

MONITORING AND AUDITING

Monitoring your systems for availability is always a great idea. It can give you early warning signs of a possible intrusion attempt, and in lots of situations, you'll be able to stop an intruder before any real damage is done.

You can easily monitor your TCP/IP services with a number of programs that have been engineered specifically for that purpose. A typical program monitors your services at the port level, meaning that the program connects to the service and waits for a response. The program can page you, send you e-mail, and write an alarm message on the screen in the event of problems. The better monitoring software attempts to stop and restart services to get them to respond, and at least one of these programs even automatically reboots a nonresponsive Windows NT machine. One such software package is NTManage by LANWARE, Inc., which you can find on the Internet at http://www.lanware.net.

Windows NT comes with some fairly robust auditing capabilities. You should learn how the auditing system works and implement it on your servers. More important, and I cannot stress this enough, you must monitor the logs as part of a daily routine. It makes no sense to use an audit system if you do not review the logs regularly. Many networks use security systems, and intruders still find their way in. Why does it happen? In most cases, no one monitored the logs, and thus, no one detected the breach in time to stop it. *Monitor your logs diligently.*

THE INTRUDER'S PERSPECTIVE

To stop an intruder, you must *think like an intruder.* To do so, you need some basic information about the ways they behave. You need to understand their ethics and the tools they use to penetrate your systems.

HACKERS, CRACKERS, AND PHREAKS

The terms "hacker," "cracker," and "phreak" describe similar people with important differences. First, a *hacker* is an independent-minded law-abiding computer enthusiast. A hacker pursues the free-wheeling intellectual explo- ration of the potential of computer systems. Hackers are intensely interested in the system itself and enjoy relating to the machines. You can think of a hacker as a computerphile, a person totally engrossed in computer programming and computer technology. A hacker delights in possessing an intimate under- standing of the internal workings of a system — computers and computer net- works in particular. Hackers are usually the nonthreatening, nondamaging types of people, but many folks confuse the terms Hacker and Cracker, and use Hacker to indicate a malicious intruder. For this reason, we'll mainly use the term Hacker generically in this book to represent both good and bad com- puting explorers.

Crackers, on the other hand, are the ones to worry about. A cracker ille- gally accesses other people's computer systems for fun, profit, and personal gain. Crackers don't always harm a computer once they gain access. For some, the challenge of finding a way into a system and snooping around undetected is enough. The word is often used, confused with, and interchanged with hacker, although the meanings are not the same. Crackers definitely perpetrate some type of crime, whether they realize it or not.

Phreaks are another group altogether. *Phreaks* are mischievous individuals who delight in exploring and manipulating telephone systems and other audio-visual communication equipment. This interest first developed in the 1960s, before personal computers were widely available. In the early days, phreaks broke into telephone systems in an effort to make long distance calls without charge. Back then, everyone shared information on bulletin board systems (BBSs), which were accessible to most users only by long-distance phone calls. To gain access, phreaks used all sorts of ploys, mostly tone-producing devices because that's how most telephone switches were controlled. The switches recognize variations in audible tones and interpret them as commands. Phreaks know what these tones are, how to reproduce them, and how to use them to their advantage. Long-distance carriers such as Sprint and MCI suffered heavy losses at the hands of phreaks in the 1980s during the real heyday of phone phreaking.

Today, phone-switching equipment has become more sophisticated, making phreaking an extremely dangerous game to play — the likelihood of being caught is about 95 percent. Today's phreaks focus more on accessing telephone computers, much as crackers do, and also hijack voice mailboxes for personal use. Phreaks are still a threat because they will attack your company's PBX once they discover its existence.

HISTORY AND EVOLUTION OF HACKING

According to Bruce Sterling, author of *The Hacker Crackdown*, the roots of the modern hacker underground can be traced back most accurately to a now-obscure hippie anarchist movement known as *Yippies*. Because I agree with Bruce on this ancestry, this section is paraphrased from his book with permission.

The Yippies took their name from the largely fictional Youth International Party and carried out a lively policy of surrealistic subversion and outrageous political mischief. One of the most visible Yippies was Abbie Hoffman. Sought by federal authorities, Hoffman went into hiding for seven years in Mexico, France, and the U.S. While in hiding, Hoffman continued to write and publish work with help from sympathizers in the American underground. Hoffman survived mainly through false IDs and odd jobs and eventually underwent facial plastic surgery, adopting a new identity as Barry Freed. After surrendering to authorities in 1980, Hoffman was convicted on cocaine charges and spent a year in prison.

As the glory days of the 1960s faded, so did Hoffman's view of the world. He reportedly committed suicide in 1989, albeit under suspicious circumstances. Hoffman's FBI file was the single largest investigation file ever opened on an individual American citizen. Hoffman was a practiced publicist who regarded broadcast media as both a playground and a weapon. He manipulated network TV and other media with various lies, rumors, impersonation scams, and other distortions, all designed to upset law enforcement officials, presidential candidates, and federal judges. I think Hoffman knew the world was watching him, but what he probably didn't know was that he had inspired a new generation of activists who would use the popular new personal computer as an instrument against society. Thus, the hacker was born.

Hoffman's most famous work was *Steal This Book*, which publicized a number of methods by which young, penniless hippies might live off the fat of the American system. *Steal This Book*, whose title urged readers to damage the very means of distribution that had put it into their hands, might be described as a spiritual ancestor of the computer virus.

In effect, hacking got its start in the early 1960s, about the same time the first full-fledged time-sharing systems began to appear in universities around the globe. Computer wizards back then unofficially used storage areas of the systems for their own private experiments, ranging from programming adventures to computer games. In fact, if we can define technical hacking as the mischievous manipulation of technology, then we could say that hacking began even earlier, with antics such as rewiring elevators so they traveled to the wrong floor. However, most people consider hackers part of the computer world.

Toward the end of the sixties, the first experimental networks had arrived on the scene, including the now-legendary ARPAnet. At that time, computer hackers began venturing into what is now called cyberspace — that great expanse encompassed by the networks. The early hackers were, for the most part, privileged individuals who had access to a university's terminals and networks. But that profile changed as personal computers began to trickle into the market, along with low-speed and low-cost modems. BBSs began popping up everywhere, and users shared what they knew about breaking into computers.

In 1990, a nationwide crackdown on computer hackers was instituted, which resulted in arrests, criminal charges, at least one dramatic show-trial, several guilty pleas, and huge confiscations of data and equipment all over the U.S. The Hacker Crackdown of 1990 was larger, better organized, more deliberate, and more resolute than any previous efforts in the world of computer crime. The US Secret Service, private telephone security, and state and local law enforcement groups across the country joined forces in a determined effort to break the back of the electronic underground. It was a fascinating effort, with very mixed results.

The Hacker Crackdown of 1990 had another unprecedented effect — it spawned the creation of the Electronic Frontier Foundation (EFF), a new interest group dedicated to the establishment and preservation of electronic civil liberties. The Crackdown of 1990 created a continuing debate over electronic crime, punishment, freedom of the press, search and seizure, and ethics.

HACKER ETHICS — DO THEY EXIST?

Hacker ethics is a precarious subject. It seems contradictory that someone acting on the borderline of legality should have a set of ethics. Although most hackers insist that they do no harm and that the crackers are the lawbreakers, they do stray across the bounds of legality, often causing irreparable damage. However, hackers do have ethics, in a vague sense of the word.

The basic hacker ethic is that information should be free and that any information discovered by a hacker that may be valuable to others should be offered freely, no matter what source it comes from. This knowledge alone gives you a good idea of what you're up against. Here are few items that most hackers profess to include in their credo:

- Access to computers and any information that might teach you something about the way the world works should be totally unlimited.
- All information should be free.
- Don't trust authority, and do promote decentralization.
- Hackers should be judged by their abilities, not criteria such as degrees, age, race, or position.
- You can create art and beauty on a computer.
- Computers can change life for the better.

Some of these ideas make sense, and other parts obviously do not. We can never expect that all information in our society will become free to everyone; that much access would destroy our ability to compete. It seems that hackers lean toward a nonprivate life, in which people cannot keep anything about themselves or their activities private. This belief in itself makes them dangerous to your networks and your privileged information.

The hacker point of view has some merit, but it certainly doesn't justify their actions. One hacker has been quoted as saying, "Few people object to the sports of clay-pigeon shooting or archery, although rifles, pistols and crossbows have no real purpose other than to kill things — and hackers have their own code of responsibility too. Real hacking is not as it is shown in the movies and on TV. The sport of hacking may involve breaches of some aspects of the law, notably theft of electricity, theft of computer time, and unlicensed usage of copyright material; however, every hacker must decide individually the morality and legality of each instance as it arises."

I agree that killing animals for sport serves little, if any purpose, other than self-gratification. On the other hand, I also believe that hackers' unauthorized use of any type of facility also serves little purpose other than self-gratification and self-gain.

VIRTUAL GANGS

Just as the world has gangs that roam the streets, the world also has gangs that roam our electronic networks. These virtual gangs, if you will, are as serious a threat as a kid with a handgun in a street gang. Instead of a gun, they carry knowledge and vengeance. They want to free the world's information and prove to everyone that they cannot be stopped — a futile dream, but one that exists in the minds of virtual gang members. They are organized and thorough and have even formed worldwide associations, with regular meetings and conventions. Once such convention is the annual Ho-Ho-Con held each year near the end of the year. It may serve you well to attend one of these conferences occasionally, as federal law enforcement agencies do, just to keep up with trends and opinions.

You should understand the reality of these virtual gangs, if for no other reason than to understand that their power is in numbers. What one member may not know or have time to find out, another member will. This cooperation makes virtual gangs a more serious threat than the standalone intruder. Gangs attack and retaliate in force and in numbers, and when they do, it can quickly become a living hell on your network, with attacks coming from all different directions. On the bright side, protection against any intruder is also protection against virtual gangs.

INFAMOUS EXPLOITS

Various individuals and virtual gangs have perpetrated many publicized intrusions. You may recall the headlines from November 1989, when a gang crashed the computers at one of New York's public television stations, WNET, leaving the message, "Happy Thanksgiving you turkeys, from all of us...." Needless to say, that stunt caused quite an uproar and spawned numerous debates, leading the U.S. Congress to seek action to stop such shenanigans.

More recently, a young phone phreak and computer outlaw, Kevin M., made world headlines when he tapped the phones of the FBI agents assigned to catch him during a two-year manhunt. Kevin was finally caught in February 1995 after his foolish yet successful Internet attack on one of the foremost computer security experts, Tsutomu Shimomura. That attack provoked Tsutomu into a full-time search for Kevin. John Markoff, who had followed the story since profiling the hacker for the 1992 book *Cyberpunk*, reported the eight-week cyberhunt in *The New York Times*. Kevin, who grew up a shy loner in the Los Angeles suburb of Sepulveda, had gained notoriety earlier in his life by successfully breaking into MCI, the Manhattan phone system, and a NORAD defense computer system, foreshadowing the 1983 hacker film *War Games*.

Internet crackers recently infiltrated the Justice Department's home page, altering the official Web site to include swastikas, obscene pictures, and criticism of the Communications Decency Act. The official Web site, which was turned off by government officials when the intrusion was discovered, was changed to read "United States Department of Injustice," next to a red, black, and white flag bearing a swastika. The page included color pictures of George Washington, Adolf Hitler, and a topless photo of Jennifer Aniston. You can see a copy of the page as the crackers altered it at http://www.darkening.com/museum/museum/gallery/doj.

Law enforcement officials also recently charged a 21-year-old Argentinian with using the Internet to break into computer networks at DoD installations, NASA, Los Alamos National Laboratory, and several universities. The Justice Department is now seeking another man who is believed to have accessed confidential research files on aircraft design, radar technology, and satellite engineering.

Computer experts at Cambridge University are using the Internet to hunt for a hacker who breached their security systems to access some of the world's most sensitive research information. The authorities have no indication whether the hacker deleted or altered files, although it is possible. The intruder may have viewed or copied files belonging to world-renowned research scientists, giving the hacker an insight into commercially and academically sensitive material. The hacker used a sniffer, which sat silently within the computer system for four weeks, monitoring its activities. With the sniffer, the hacker could have compiled the passwords to give him unhindered access to every computer on the university's network.

Hundreds of cases similar to these go unreported or undetected. These few exploits are only the tip of the iceberg. The best of the best never get caught or detected at all.

INTRUDER HANGOUTS

Potential intruders have a number of well-known hangouts on the Internet. You should visit these sites periodically to keep up with the trends and movements. At the very least, you'll gain lots of insight into their methods and antics, which will give you a better understanding of the potential risks for your network.

A word of caution before you surf these sites: Be sure you check your security settings on your Web browser, making certain you've turned off all forms of Java and ActiveX. You need to ensure your visit to a hacker hangout doesn't turn out to be a reverse attack on your computer system during your visit, because sometimes these sites have malicious programs embedded in the Web pages that a user may never know about.

Web Sites

You should monitor these Web sites for new information:

- Phrack — http://www.fc.net/phrack. This site is an age-old publication for hacking, cracking, and phreaking information that dates from the early 1980s.
- National Hacker Association — http://junior.apk.net/~matto/index.html. This organization publishes monthly newsletters that offer information on the wide world of hacking. It's well worth the effort to join their mailing list and Web site.
- 2600 Magazine — http://www.2600.com. The 2600 club is named after the 2600 Mhz tone that, once upon a time, gave you control over a regional Bell company's trunk groups; at that point, you had complete control over that portion of the phone network. Monitoring this group will help you minimize fraudulent use of your phone systems.
- L0pht Heavy Industries — http://www.l0pht.com. This site offers hard-to-find files from the computer underground and beyond. It also contains security advisories.
- Hacker Hangouts Online — http://www.nando.net/newsroom/hack-sources. html. This site is a list of other sites where hackers, crackers, and phreaks hang out.
- Hack and Cracks — http://www.earthlink.net/~mumbv/index.html. This site contains loads of information and links to other hacker hangouts.
- Hackers Layer — http://www.cris.com/~lordsome/index.shtml. This Web site is an exhaustive resource of files, program cracks, hacking information, and links to other well-known Web sites hackers use.
- CERT — http://www.cert.org. The Computer Emergency Response Team runs this Web site. CERT typically watches for all new security threats as they become known and posts warnings and suggested solutions.

Usenet Newsgroups

Newsgroups are an open forum that should be monitored as well:

- alt.security — pertains to all security issues
- alt.hacking — focuses on hacking in general
- alt.2600 — pertains to the 2600 club
- alt.cyberpunk — discusses hacking and cracking openly
- comp.security.misc — provides a more serious discussion on security issues and concerns

Online Literature

- The Hacker Crackdown, by Bruce Sterling, is an electronically published book that chronicles government efforts to catch hackers, crackers, and phreaks. It is available free through many sites on the Internet, including http://www.cs.wesleyan.edu/HTML/The-Hacker-Crackdown.
- The Hacker Dictionary is a semi-humorous, semi-serious guide to hacker jargon. http://www.cnam.fr/Jargon/1.

INVITATIONS FOR INTRUSION

In this section, I cover some of the well-known problems with Internet services, showing you the major points of attack on your network. You should read this material carefully and scour your systems and network for signs of any of these vulnerabilities. In some cases, I may point out the obvious, but in others, I may not. In either case, all the information in this section is food for thought.

Remember this particular phrase whenever you are contemplating security issues in your environment: *Think like an intruder.*

FACILITY ACCESS

When people think of security, they often don't consider the floor space surrounding their systems and networking environment. An important aspect of securing your network is securing your facilities. Your security system could be as simple as housing your systems in a locked room or as complex as installing a high-tech intrusion detection system.

Never underestimate the lengths to which intruders go in their attempt to access your environment. Controlling access to your facility is just as important as any other part of securing your networking environment. Did you ever wonder who cleans your office at night while you're away? If not, you should. More people have access to your facilities and network than you probably realize, including your building management and their vendors, leasing agents with master keys to all suites, cleaning crews with master keys, and utility companies that provide services to your building.

A truly secure environment includes strict control over who has access to facilities and when. Remember, you can evaluate your present situation by thinking like an intruder. Here's a checklist (that by no means should be considered all-encompassing) to help you secure your environment.

Facility Access Checklist

- Who has keys to all the office doors?
- What's above those ceiling tiles — could someone crawl over the wall?
- Would a motion-detecting alarm be valuable?
- Who has access to your computers?
- Who has access to your administrator passwords, and how often are they changed?
- Is your cleaning crew bonded?
- Is your building management company bonded?
- Is your building's leasing company bonded?
- Do your network cables run through exposed and vulnerable areas of the building?
- Do you enforce policies about controlling visitors?
- Do your employees bring family members to work on weekends or after hours?
- Do you change locks and passwords when an employee leaves the firm?
- Do you let vendors and other employees know when someone departs the firm?
- Do you have a policy detailing what gets shredded before it is put in the trash?

These basic questions are a great starting point for evaluating your current situation. They can also help you arrive at better methods of controlling your physical environment. We'll talk more about policies and procedures in Chapter 7.

THE PASSWORD PLAYGROUND

Passwords are required nearly everywhere. You need a password to access almost any protected resource in a computing environment. As I mentioned earlier, carefully chosen passwords can go a long way to strengthen your overall security implementation. Intruders go to great lengths in their efforts to obtain your passwords.

The risks of not adopting a strong password-choosing scheme are numerous. Poorly chosen passwords are easily guessed by robotic software designed just for that purpose. To get an idea of just how easy it is to get a password-cracking software tool, point your Web browser to an Internet search engine such as AltaVista (http://www.altavista.digital.com) or Excite (http://www.excite.com), and type the keywords **"password cracker"**. You'll be amazed at how quickly you can find one and get it up and running. I put a password cracker to work on my own system's password file. Within eight hours, it had correctly found more than 190 passwords that it could use to gain access to my systems. I immediately changed all those passwords and instituted a very strict policy of password assignment that will help stop this situation from occurring again.

Most computer systems use a maximum password size of eight characters. However, Windows NT lets you choose even longer passwords. Choosing a good password is the real trick in preventing it from being cracked. The other side of the fence is that if your network transmits passwords in clear text, a sniffer can easily intercept them anyway. Although Windows NT networks don't transmit passwords in clear text over the internal network, some of the computers attached to your Windows NT network might. Examine each type of operating system you use in your environment so you understand what your goals must be.

Choosing good passwords is only part of the equation. You must also adopt policies and procedures that determine how those passwords are used and disseminated. Here are a few tips for choosing and using great passwords:

- Never use words that are in a dictionary. Intentionally misspell words, or simply make up a new word instead.

- Never use your name in any way, shape, or form. Also, never use any other information about you that could be easily discovered.

- Never use your family names, pet names, or other names or words that can be associated with you. If you're boating enthusiast, "sailing" would be a bad choice for a password, as would the words "captain" or "skipper."

- Never let anyone borrow your user ID and password, no matter who it is. It could cost you your job or your network's security. If you find yourself in a situation where you must let someone use your user ID or password, don't leave that person alone at a computer logged on with it. Change the password immediately after the person is done, and log the incident to protect yourself just in case.

- Never write down your passwords and leave them in your desk, purse, wallet, briefcase, or anywhere else. The rule of thumb here is if you can't lock it up, don't write it down.

- Never reuse old passwords.

- Never use the same password for multiple systems that you may have to access, unless you have a strong authentication system that governs such singular use of passwords.

- Never use the "save this password" feature found in many software packages. If you do, you may as well tell everyone what your password is up front.

- Do use at least six characters in your password at all times. If possible, use the maximum allowable password length. Remember, a password is meant to be difficult to discover, not easy to remember.

- Do use a combination of letters and other allowable nonalphabetic symbols. Replace letters with numbers once in a while, but not always. For example, you can use "1" instead of the letter "L" or a "4" instead of the letter "A."

- Do make passwords logically easy to remember, but only if absolutely necessary, and in those cases make them physically difficult to guess. For instance, "extreme" may at first seem like a good password, but "extr3m3" is a far better choice.

- Do change your password frequently, even if your security policies don't require it.

Normal Windows NT user accounts disable themselves automatically after a certain number of bad password attempts. A word of caution regarding the Windows NT Administrator user account: this account *does not* lock itself out for password failures unless you modify the NT registry. The Administrator account is thus incredibly vulnerable to attack because a would-be intruder could repeatedly attempt to guess a password until the password is discovered. The best way to guard against this vulnerability is to change the name used for this account. Don't leave it defined as "Administrator," and don't change it to something obvious like "Admin." Change it to something difficult to guess, yet something you won't forget.

SPOOFING

Spoofing occurs when IP packets from an intruder masquerade as packets from a trusted system. Spoofing lets an intruder on a TCP/IP network such as the Internet impersonate a local system's IP address. If other local systems on your network perform session authentication based on the IP address of a connection, they believe incoming connections from the intruder originate from a local trusted host and do not require a password.

This technique is especially damaging when connections are permitted without a password. It is possible for forged packets to penetrate a packet-filtering firewall if the router is not configured to block incoming packets that have source addresses in the local domain. This attack is possible even if no session packets can be routed back to the attacker. Note also that this attack is not based on the source routing option of the IP protocol.

Network configurations that are potentially vulnerable to IP spoofing attacks typically

- Have routers to external networks that support multiple internal interfaces
- Have routers with two interfaces that support subnetting on the internal network
- Have proxy firewalls where the proxy applications use the source IP address for authentication

IP spoofing attacks are very difficult to detect. The best defense against IP spoofing is to filter packets as they enter your router from the Internet, blocking any packet that claims to have originated inside your local network. Commonly called an input filter, this feature is currently supported by several major router manufacturers, such as Bay Networks/Wellfleet version 5 and later, Cabletron with LAN Secure, Cisco with RIS software version 9.21 and later, Livingston, and NSC. If your current router hardware does not support packet filtering on inbound traffic, you can always install a second router between the existing router and the Internet connection. The second router can then filter spoofed IP packets with an output filter instead. In any case, do not underestimate the dangers of becoming a victim of IP spoofing.

TELNET, RLOGIN, REXEC, AND RSH

Telnet, rlogin, rexec, and rsh are four programs that allow remote access to your network systems. Fortunately, none of these services come as part of Windows NT. You should never run these services on a Windows NT server unless you absolutely have to. You can enable remote connectivity in other ways that are far more safe than these services. Let's look at each of program and its intended purpose.

Telnet lets a user log on to your system over a network; the user eventually arrives at a DOS command shell. Once logged on, the remote user has the same abilities and commands as a local user sitting in front of the machine's keyboard. This scenario can be dangerous — only think about the damage a simple Delete command can do. There is no real need to run telnet on a Windows NT server. Keep in mind that a telnet service is the server aspect of telnet, and that a telnet client is completely different because it connects to the telnet service running on a given machine.

The rlogin service is similar to telnet in that rlogin lets users log on to a remote host and work as if they were sitting directly in front of the remote computer.

The rexec and rsh commands let you send commands to a specified remote host for execution. The difference between rexec and rsh is in security checking. With rexec, the remote host bases authentication on a user name and password. With the rsh command, the remote host bases authentication on user name and information found in either the hosts.equiv or .rhosts file. You should not run these services on your Windows NT machines because you can use other means (such as secure telnet) to get work done.

FILE TRANSFER PROTOCOL (FTP) SERVER

FTP lets a user upload and download files over a TCP/IP network. FTP servers are incredibly useful when configured correctly and offer a great way of moving files.

The FTP server found in Windows NT, like all others, lets a user log on from a remote location to transfer files. The user can log on either by using a valid Windows NT user name and a password or anonymously, if the FTP server is configured to allow anonymous logons. After logging on, users may navigate the parts of directory tree that they can access and upload and download files. You should take special care when you configure the file security settings for FTP users because you don't want to allow access to system files or other sensitive files inadvertently.

An FTP server running on a Windows NT machine presents most of the same inherent dangers as FTP servers running on Unix machines. Incorrect configuration can leave openings for intruders to exploit your data. You need to understand how file permissions are handled under Windows NT, and with that knowledge you can adequately protect your system when running an FTP server.

One basic rule: never allow the FTP server access to a non-NTFS partition. Only NTFS lets you set permissions correctly; DOS partitions offer no form of security. We discuss NTFS security settings in more detail in Chapter 3. Pay special attention to that chapter if you intend to run an FTP server on your network.

MAIL SERVERS

In the Unix world, Internet mail servers can be a real threat to security for a variety of reasons. In the Windows NT world, the threat is just as real if the server isn't configured correctly. The most popular Internet mail servers consist of two basic parts: the Simple Mail Transfer Protocol (SMTP) server and the Post Office Protocol (POP3) server. SMTP is a standard means of moving mail from server to server on a TCP/IP network. POP3 is a standard way for mail clients to receive mail from a mail server.

The security concerns in establishing and running your own Internet mail server revolve around its configuration. Some mail servers allow users a certain amount of control over aspects of their mail account, such as passwords, mail aliases, descriptions, vacation messages, and forwarding options. At first glance, these options don't sound like much of a security threat, but because they can be used to falsify identities or intercept mail, the potential for damage is great.

Intruders often spoof e-mail addresses, posing as another person by inserting that person's return e-mail address in their mail client and using that person's mail server to send mail. Perhaps they're trying to get sensitive information from one of your vendors, like your account number and the amount of open credit. Or perhaps they want to do some social harm by sending negative e-mail to others on the network. Whatever the reason, you can protect against it by using a mail server that can authenticate a connection before it's allowed to send mail. The SMTP/POP3 server found in Microsoft's Commercial Internet System platform (formerly code-named Normandy) is one such server. You can learn more about the Commercial Internet System platform at http://backoffice.microsoft.com.

Intruders also use mail servers to gain access to sensitive company information. If they crack the password to one of your mail accounts, they may be able to forward mail destined for that mailbox to themselves instead, or they may even simply log on and read it from the server. The two best ways you can protect yourself against any type of mailbox hijacking are to encrypt all your e-mail and to practice good password selection and rotation policies. Pretty Good Privacy (PGP), a popular encryption software, is compatible with many popular POP3 e-mail clients. PGP was created by Phil Zimmermann and uses the RSA and IDEA algorithms, which make it one of the best ways to encrypt information. You can get a copy of PGP from http://world.std.com/~franl/pgp/where-to-get-pgp.html.

Another way to protect your POP3 server, if your POP3 server doesn't have this ability built in, is to install a packet filter or some other type of firewall and limit access to the POP3 server to only those within your own networks.

You should be aware that intruders sometimes retaliate against others by bombarding their mail server with high volumes of mail or by sending mail with giant file attachments. High volumes of mail overload a mail server, rendering it incapable of doing its real job and creating useless messages that you must clean up. Likewise, sending giant files to a mail server can wreak equal havoc. The files eventually eat all your precious disk space, causing the server either to crash or to stop accepting new mail.

Unfortunately, neither of these scenarios can be prevented if you expect to keep an open channel for e-mail in and out of the Internet. The best practice is to monitor your logs and keep a close watch on your disk space utilization. If users frequently complain about missing mail or slow performance from your mail server, look closely at the server before space becomes a problem.

WEB SERVERS

A Web page may seem harmless, but it's what's in the Web page that counts. For the most part, Web servers are very secure software systems with only one job: to deliver Web pages to Web browsers. The jeopardy in a Web server comes from the way the Web pages are created and the content they hold.

In a Web page, a Common Gateway Interface (CGI) script, which is a mini-program, poses a potential problem. CGI lets programs output information to a Web server. CGI scripts run on your Web server when a Web page that has one is requested by a client. They can contain code designed to loosen security in any number of ways. Scripts can copy files, delete files, or even add or modify user accounts. Anything a programmer can think of is possible as long as the operating system allows it.

Protecting yourself against malicious CGI scripts under Windows NT relies on your Web server's ability to limit program execution to certain directories and your ability to correctly configure your NTFS file security permissions. A good Web server always lets you limit the directories from which a CGI script can run. You should consider letting your scripts reside in and execute from only one directory. Configure that directory's permissions for access only by the Web server and the administrator. This measure gives you greater control over scripts being placed on your Web server because users must ask the administrator to put them in the directory. You should also preview these scripts to see how they operate before you allow them to be used on your production Web server.

Microsoft's ActiveX and Sun Microsystems's Java are newer programming tools that you can use to create Web page content in the same way you use a CGI script. They both pose the same inherent dangers as CGI and thus should be treated with equal caution. The main difference between CGI and ActiveX or Java is that both ActiveX and Java can be made to run on the client's Web browser instead of the Web server. This setup presents a whole new set of dangers to guard against. An intruder can write some type of malicious code that causes plenty of irreparable damage when run on an unsuspecting Web-browsing computer.

ActiveX and Java have been available only for a short time, and intruders are already using these new programming tools. For example, I happened upon a Web site with an opinion poll. The poll asked whether viewers liked the Web site. Those who clicked "yes" were quickly sent to another pleasing Web page from that site. Those who clicked "no" were in for quite a surprise. The "no" button launched an ActiveX control that my Web browser ran, which spawned dozens of new Web browser clients on my desktop until my system ran out of resources and locked up. It certainly opened my eyes to the potential dangers of freely surfing Web sites. That ActiveX control could have done much worse things to my system than simply making it crash.

Microsoft's Web server, IIS, is covered in detail in Chapter 11. If you plan to run your own Web server under Windows NT, IIS is an excellent choice. Because it is seamlessly integrated into Windows NT, it adopts all the underlying security mechanisms provided by the operating system.

DENIAL OF SERVICE

One practice of torment intruders use is called *denial of service*, in which intruders bombard a system with unnecessary traffic on a certain port or group of ports so that the services using those ports cannot respond to genuine requests. A denial-of-service attack is one of the easiest and most common ways an intruder torments a network. I give an example of a real denial-of-service attack later in the book.

A denial-of-service attack can be launched on any TCP/IP-based service you provide access to from the Internet. Protecting yourself against denial of service is tricky in some cases. Without a packet filtering router or proxy server, you may not be able to stop such attacks. However, TCP/IP-based software that can close off traffic and limit access only to certain networks and users can help.

Detecting a denial-of-service attack is usually not difficult. If your mail or Web server is not responding, it could be under attack. A significant drop-off in performance is another prime indicator. Finding out who the culprit is can be another story. If your system software isn't logging connection attempts, you need a sniffing tool that lets you capture packets and look at the origin addresses. NetXRay is one software-based tool that can be invaluable when you experience various types of weirdness on your servers. You can get a copy of NetXRay at http://www.cinco.com.

KEYSTROKE GRABBERS

Keystroke grabbers are another way intruders gain access to your systems. Keystroke grabbers record every keystroke on a given computer's keyboard. A typical keystroke grabber records keystrokes on the machine the program is running on, so for it to work, an intruder must install the keystroke grabber on a particular machine. Intruders can install grabbers in one of two ways: by gaining access to your facility or by penetrating the system over your network.

One of the best ways to protect against keystroke grabbers and any other kind of unauthorized software installation is to use Microsoft's System Management Server (SMS) on your network. SMS performs many useful functions, including monitoring every piece of software that is installed on a system. SMS routinely inventories the systems, looks for changes, and alerts the administrator the instant something is installed or removed. This type of monitoring can easily tip you off to a keystroke grabber. If you want to see what a keystroke grabber can do, type **keycopy** or **playback** into an Internet search engine such as AltaVista (http://www.altavista.digital.com).

PACKET SNIFFERS

Packet sniffers monitor and capture every packet coming in and out of a network interface. With a packet sniffer, an intruder does not need a keystroke grabber.

Hardware-based sniffers usually must be physically connected to a network cable on your network, but software-based sniffers can be run from a workstation or even a dial-up link. Anything unencrypted is potentially useful to a would-be intruder. For instance, if your network transmits passwords over the network in clear text, a packet sniffer will capture them eventually. Your best protections against a packet sniffer are to encrypt all your sensitive data before it is transmitted over your network and to routinely change your passwords.

It is smart to get a software-based packet sniffer and see what your network reveals. Many good software-based sniffers for Windows NT systems are out there, including NetXRay, mentioned above. If you're using SMS in your shop, you may find the accompanying Network Monitor useful as well.

BACK DOORS

Once intruders successfully gain access to your systems, one of the first things they do is install some sort of back door that lets them come back in whenever they want. With Windows NT 4.0 and Service Pack 2, it is possible for anyone to add to an NT system a .dll (an executable program) that intercepts and records any password changes on the system. This .dll could store the password information in a place the intruder could access, such as the computer's Web server or in an e-mail message sent to the intruder. This fact is well known in the hacking community, and example source code is readily available for creating such a .dll.

Detecting back doors can be very difficult. As I mentioned earlier, running Microsoft's SMS server can go a long way toward detecting software installations, but the best practice is to monitor your system security and audit logs carefully. If you suspect someone may have installed a back door, you should immediately reinstall a *new copy* of your operating system. Do not perform an upgrade or even overwrite the old installation — completely reinstall a new copy in a new directory. This measure ensures that all files and data are reinstalled as shipped from the manufacturer, wiping out anything out of the ordinary.

VIRUSES AND TROJAN HORSES

Two of the most common and best-known threats to computer systems today are the virus and the Trojan horse. Viruses are rampant in the computing industry, with source code for numerous virus strains readily available all over the Internet. Thousands of strains of computer viruses already exist, and new ones emerge almost daily. They cover quite a range, from harmless viruses that simply put a message on the screen to downright nasty viruses that can destroy all the data they can reach on the local machine and the network. In most cases, viruses easily replicate themselves on every computer system and disk storage system they touch. Virus eradication can be a painful experience.

Trojan horses are a different breed of intrusion mechanism, named after the Trojan warriors who hid themselves inside a hollow statue of a horse. Once inside the fortress gates, the soldiers emerged to begin their killing rampage. Computer-based Trojan horses act in the same way. They get into your network systems through seemingly harmless software, and once in place, they create back doors, release viruses, sniff packets, or do almost anything else you can imagine an intruder doing. They are quite a dangerous threat indeed.

Your network can become infected with a virus or Trojan horse in a number of different ways, especially when connected to the Internet. For example, a customer can unwittingly give you an infected diskette or program file; someone can send you a seemingly harmless Microsoft Word document containing a Word macro with some destructive purpose; a user can download a software package that contains a virus; or friend borrowing your machine for a few minutes could unknowingly insert an infected floppy disk. The list goes on.

The best way to prevent virus and Trojan horse infections is to implement policies that mandate using a virus scanner at all times on all your computer systems. Here is a list of some of the more popular virus and Trojan horse protection packages available on the Internet:

- McAfee Scan — Virushield and AntiVirus NT, http://www.mcafee.com
- Cheyenne — NetShield, http://www.cheyenne.com
- Norton — AntiVirus, http://www.symantec.com/avcenter
- CT Software — SafetyNet Pro, http://members.aol.com/ron2222/snpro.htm
- TCT-ThunderBYTE — ThunderBYTE Anti-Virus, http://www.thunderbyte.com
- Trend Micro Incorporated — Interscan VirusWall, http://www.trendmicro.com

Many antivirus software packages are available, and they are simple to find on the Internet with a search engine. They are well worth the time and effort they take to locate and install.

SUMMARY

This chapter has given you some insight into the world of network security and the intruders who plague us all. By now, you should understand how security is evolving, where the ranks of intruders came from, what problems exist in Internet-enabled software systems, and where to start protecting those systems. Minimally, you should now understand that having great monitoring software and equipment can be invaluable in your security efforts. The rest of this book builds on this foundation, giving you a more detailed look at how to secure your Windows NT network environment.

CHAPTER 3

UNDERSTANDING BASIC WINDOWS NT SECURITY

Security is a crucial part of the Windows NT design. This chapter helps you understand how Microsoft has built the security model used in Windows NT. You learn the components the operating system uses to handle security and which tools you have at your disposal, as well as the roles they play.

The information in this chapter is very useful when you install Windows NT or any other part of Microsoft's BackOffice suite, such as Internet Information Server. Read the chapter carefully and take all the steps necessary to secure your systems. Remember, without a properly implemented security system, your server could become a playground for malicious intruders.

OVERVIEW

The security features in Windows NT are evolving quite nicely. Microsoft has had the distinct advantage of learning from decades of trial and error by other operating-system manufacturers. As a result, Windows NT offers one of the most secure and robust operating systems on the market.

In the early days of personal computers, the only operating system option was MS-DOS, which had absolutely no security. Neither did the first versions of Microsoft Windows. The first security features for Windows were provided by third-party vendors who wanted to add value to their networking solutions. With the release of Windows for Workgroups (WfW), we first saw the faintest hint of security. Its security was based on Microsoft's NetBEUI networking protocol, and it was rather weak, using a simple name-and-password combination that could be circumvented easily.

The real improvements in Microsoft security came with Windows 95 and Windows NT. Windows 95 provides much more control over access to computer and network resources, and even though the security in Windows 95 is not incredibly robust, it is a far cry from WfW: Some say that comparing WfW security to Windows 95 security is like comparing the strength of tissue paper to the strength of leather.

WfW uses a resource-level security implementation, in which access permissions are associated with each shared resource on the network. Administering resource-level security can be a royal pain on large installations because a user must be added to each shared resource individually before being granted access to that resource. Windows NT security, on the other hand, is based on a user-level security model, which means that each user account has a list of parameters that control which aspects of the system the user can access and how the user may access them.

Under Windows NT, permissions define the types of access allowed for each user and group of users. Windows NT maintains these permissions independently for each user. Managing Windows NT security, in effect, means managing users and groups, so you need to become very familiar with the User Manager and Windows NT Explorer. You also need to know the Event Log and other system monitors to determine and analyze activity on your network. I cover these tools briefly in this chapter and in much more detail in Chapter 4.

Windows NT security is very robust, protecting each shared resource in the system and on the network. When a user logs on to a Windows NT machine or a Windows NT domain, the operating system creates a unique access token for that user. This token identifies the user and all the user's associated groups. Each time the user requests access to a shared resource or the user's account runs a program, Windows NT checks the token against permission settings and returns a verdict that determines whether the access is allowed.

At the network level, Windows NT groups computers based on a structure called an *NT domain*. An NT domain creates a secure barrier between Windows NT networks, where users in one domain are not allowed access to other domains unless a trust has been established between those two domains. The NT domain model is a logical distinction; the computers participating in an NT domain are not necessarily connected to the same physical network. Windows NT can be configured to use either the NT domain models or the older workgroup model.

WINDOWS NT SECURITY ARCHITECTURE

The Windows NT security model is an integral subsystem — security affects the entire operating system. The security subsystem controls access to *objects* (such as a file or printer), which are sets of information made available for use on the network. After an object is made available on the network, it is called a *resource*. When an object is shared on the network, it becomes a *shared resource*.

SECURITY MODEL COMPONENTS

Windows NT security provides event auditing and detail logging and lets you monitor the access and use of various resources on your network. Windows NT security is, in many respects, much more secure than other popular operating systems in use today.

The Windows NT security model consists of several key components, each of which plays a vital role in the overall security model.

- Logon Processes (LP) — accepts logon requests from local users who log on locally (using the NT logon dialog box) and from remote users through remote logon processes.

- Local Security Authority (LSA) — ensures that users have permission to access a particular resource.

- Security Account Manager (SAM) — maintains the actual user account database in the registry and interacts with the LSA by validating users. The SAM database contains all the user and group permissions for a Windows NT domain (a copy of the SAM is located in %SYSTEMROOT\repair once you create an Emergency Repair Disk for system recovery).

- Security Reference Monitor (SRM) — ensures that a user or process has permission to access an object by checking the user's security profile. The SRM enforces access validation and any audit policies that have been defined by the LSA.

The individual roles played by these components in the overall security subsystem are shown in Figure 3.1.

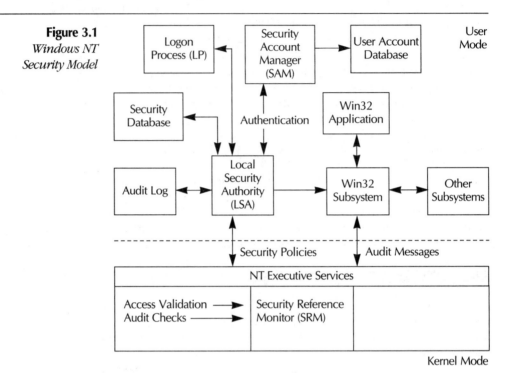

Figure 3.1
Windows NT Security Model

WINDOWS NT AND C2 SECURITY

The Windows NT security model was designed for C2-level compliance. C2 security is defined by the Department of Defense (DoD) as a baseline measurement of a secure operating system. The requirements for a C2-secure system are outlined by the DoD's National Computer Security Center (NCSC) in the publication *Trusted Computer System Evaluation Criteria*, also known as "the Orange Book" (for more information about the Orange Book, see Chapter 2). Microsoft worked closely with the NCSC throughout the development of Windows NT to ensure that both Windows NT Workstation and Windows NT Server comply with their requirements for a C2-secure system.

The NCSC has published different interpretations of the Orange Book that clarify its requirements for specific system components. One example is the NCSC's *Trusted Network Interpretation of the Trusted Computer System Evaluation Criteria*, commonly referred to as "the Red Book," which interprets

Orange Book security requirements as applied to the networking component of a secure operating system. The Red Book indicates how a network system should operate to meet Orange Book requirements for a C2 secure system. The NCSC has also published interpretations of Orange Book guidelines to help vendors ensure that their systems comply with Orange Book requirements. For example, the Blue Book interprets the Orange Book for subsystem components.

Today, network operating systems share key information and resources among many users throughout organizations of various sizes. Frequently, the information stored on network servers needs to be secure and is intended for use only by authorized individuals. These networks' ability to prevent unauthorized access to information is of paramount concern to the security and competitiveness of an organization.

Some of the most important requirements of C2-level security are listed below.

- The owner of a resource (such as a file) must be able to control access to the resource.
- The operating system must protect objects against reuse by other processes.
- Users must identify themselves through a unique logon ID and password, which must track the user's activities.
- Administrators must be able to audit security-related events, and the event logs must be protected from unauthorized access.
- The operating system must be able to protect itself against tampering.

Let's review some of these requirements in more detail. As I mentioned, under the C2 guidelines, the operating system must protect data stored in memory for one process so that it is not randomly reused by other processes. Windows NT Server protects memory so that its contents cannot be read after the memory is freed by a process. In addition, when a file is deleted on an NTFS partition, it's gone for good. Unlike DOS partitions, NTFS partitions do not include a way to undelete a file. Users cannot access a file's data, even when the disk space used by that file is allocated for use by another file.

On a Windows NT system, users must identify themselves by typing a unique logon name and password before being allowed access to the system. The system uses this identification to track the activities of the user. Authorized system administrators can audit security-related events and the actions of individual users, which are written to the Event Log where they may be easily reviewed.

Windows NT Server provides some excellent tools for managing and using these comprehensive security features.

EVOLUTION OF C2 SECURITY IN WINDOWS NT

Microsoft first signed a Letter of Agreement with the NCSC to evaluate Windows NT for C2 compliance in early 1992. Since then, Microsoft has worked closely with NCSC to ensure that Windows NT stays in compliance with the C2 guidelines. Because NCSC has found Windows NT's core components to be C2 compliant, users of Windows NT can build C2-certifiable systems. Windows NT Server 4.0 is also being evaluated as the networking component of a secure system, in accordance with the Red Book interpretations.

The Windows NT Server implementation of C2 security is based entirely on software. Windows NT users do not have to install additional hardware on their servers or clients to meet C2 security requirements. Some other operating system vendors use hardware components to provide some or all of the C2 security characteristics. Typically, the hardware components are client based and contain a CPU, memory, expansion BIOS, DES encryption hardware, network interface, and a hard disk controller. These hardware components intercept all file and server requests and route them through a specialized I/O card, which effectively displaces the operating system for certain kernel functions. Hardware-based C2 systems have their finer points, but I think basing a C2 security system in software components gives the operating system vendor, like Microsoft, a greater degree of control over development and evolution of the overall operating system product.

According to Microsoft, each Windows NT process and feature was designed with C2-level security in mind. Microsoft further states that two Windows NT features — its ability to separate users from their functions and its processes, such as identification and authentication — actually meet the Orange Book B2 security requirements.

REAL-WORLD SECURITY ISSUES

The C2 guidelines do not directly address a number of real-world security issues. The primary objective of the C2 guidelines is to give users a secure, usable system, and Microsoft has gone significantly beyond the implementation of C2 requirements in the development of Windows NT Server security.

Windows NT provides a set of comprehensive management tools that help administrators maintain security in their environments. For example, an administrator can control which specific users have access rights to which network resources, including files, directories, servers, printers, and applications. Access rights are defined on a per-resource basis, and all the resources can be managed from a central location.

User accounts can also be managed centrally. An administrator can specify group memberships, logon hours, account expiration dates, and other user account parameters, such as Remote Access privileges. The administrator can also establish an audit trail of all security-related events, such as user access to files, directories, printers, logon attempts, and other resources. The system can lock out a user after a prescribed number of failed logon attempts.

Administrators can force passwords to expire regularly, and they may also set password complexity rules so that users are forced to choose passwords that are difficult to guess. A simple logon procedure gives users access to the appropriate network resources as defined in their user profiles, which are established by the administrator. To prevent intruders from using packet sniffers to capture passwords transmitted over a network, user passwords are encrypted, users doesn't see or have access to the system-level encryption used on their passwords, and passwords are never passed over the network communications circuits.

When a user creates a resource, that user is considered the owner of that resource. Under Windows NT, users are able to define access rights and permissions for any resource they own. For example, if a user needs to share a specific document with other users, the owner may specify exactly who has read and write access to that document simply through the familiar Windows NT Explorer. Only authorized network administrators manage access to organizational resources.

Windows NT's security goes on to protect data, even while that data is in a machine's physical memory. Only authorized programs can access data stored in memory, which makes it impossible for rogue applications to hijack another application's data while the data is in the physical memory space of a Windows NT machine.

Building a secure network operating system environment requires careful planning and administration. Security features must be used throughout the entire system and network. Windows NT's security features are built into every facet of the operating system, which makes it a great choice for connecting your intranet to the Internet.

WINDOWS NT FILE SYSTEMS

Two basic types of file systems are available for use with Windows NT: File Allocation Table (FAT) and the NT File System (NTFS). Let's take a look at past and present features of these two systems.

THE FAT SYSTEM

In the early days of personal computers, circa 1981, IBM introduced the DOS operating system, which was developed by a young upstart company called Microsoft. DOS's file system was called the FAT system, named after the system's

File Allocation Table. The FAT system served its purpose until hard-drive technology had advanced enough to produce giant disk volumes that could store
gigabytes of information. As the disk drives grew, the search and retrieval
mechanism of the FAT system took longer and longer to produce results. In
addition, the FAT system allowed for a maximum of only 32 MB of file table
allocation. This limitation meant that as hard drives grew past the 32 MB
boundary, users had to partition the drives so that the FAT system could use
them. When MS-DOS 4.0 was released, its expanded FAT system used 16 bits
instead of only 12 bits to store file information, allowing for partitions larger
than 32 MB.

Under the FAT system, the root directory has a fixed size and location on
the hard disk. Directories are a special file type, with 32-byte entries for the
files they contain. Each 32-byte entry consists of the following file information:

- File name (an 8-character name with a 3-character extension)
- Attribute byte
- Modification time
- Modification date
- Starting allocation unit
- File size

Windows NT version 3.5 and later used the attribute bits to support file
names of up to 256 characters. Windows NT provides this same feature
without interfering with DOS access to the partition information. First, Windows NT stores the extra information in a conventional directory entry for the
file. Next, it creates one or more secondary directory entries that store the file
name information in 13-character increments and marks these entries as part of
a long file name by setting attribute bits. When DOS or a DOS-compatible
operating system accesses a file with all four attribute bits set, it simply ignores
the extra entries, acting as though they are invisible.

These tricks by Windows NT to lengthen DOS file names beyond the
older 8 plus 3 standard have some great merits. On the other hand, they have
caused problems for people who have used older disk repair utilities because
these utilities have no way of understanding the Windows NT enhancements.
Many a hard drive has been corrupted by these older utilities. To get yourself
on the safer side of the tracks, you should use only those FAT disk utilities
that are certified to be compatible with Windows NT. Better yet, you shouldn't
use the FAT system under Windows NT unless you have to because you'll be
giving up a wealth of security features found in NTFS. Remember: *The FAT file
system offers little or no security.*

NTFS

NTFS was designed specifically for Windows NT and includes most of the features found in other file systems. NTFS is incredibly important in securing a Windows NT machine. This section covers the NTFS basics.

Overview

NTFS includes many features not found in the FAT system and was designed to be reliable and efficient even when used on large disk volumes. NTFS provides a great balance of performance, reliability, and compatibility. Its design lets it quickly perform file operations like read, write, and search. NTFS allows long file names and maintains an 8 plus 3 file name for a given file so DOS programs can use it. It also supports case-sensitive file access for Unix-style programs and case-insensitive file access for DOS, OS/2, and Windows operating systems.

NTFS supports a variety of multiuser security models. Native NTFS security controlled with Windows NT Explorer is based on user accounts and user groups. NTFS obeys the POSIX (portable operating system interface for computing environments), which will please the Unix community. NTFS can also support the Macintosh security model by emulating an Apple-style file server, which simple FAT partitions cannot do.

Windows NT considers everything on an NTFS volume to be a file or part of a file. Every allocated sector on a disk volume belongs to a file, and even the file descriptors are part of a file. Each file has a record in a special file called the Master File Table (MFT), which is similar to the FAT table found in DOS.

Let's take a quick peek at part of the MFT. The first 16 records of the MFT are reserved for special use. The first record describes the MFT itself. The second record contains a pointer to the MFT mirror file, which is a copy of the MFT that is kept for fault tolerance and safety. If the first MFT record becomes corrupt, NTFS reads the second record. NTFS records the locations of the data segments of both the primary MFT and the MFT mirror file in the boot sector of the hard disk. A copy of the boot sector itself is recorded at the logical center of the disk. The third record of the MFT is the log, which is used for file recovery operations. NTFS writes updates to a log for each volume. After a system crash, this log can be used to straighten out problems almost instantly, producing a much faster recovery than with FAT.

Fault Tolerance

NTFS creates fault-tolerant disk subsystems in several ways. You should consider using some type of fault tolerance if your budget allows it. The built-in fault tolerance system can greatly enhance your ability to secure your data at the hardware level.

First, NTFS supports two types of disk sets that can be very useful: the volume set and the stripe set. A volume set is a way of grouping free space to appear as a single volume using a single drive letter. If an NTFS volume set fills up, it can be expanded by adding free disk space in another partition from the same disk or from another hard disk, up to a maximum of 32 areas of free space. The space on a volume set is used one disk at a time — the first one is filled before the next one is used. Volume sets do not offer any performance advantages, but they do offer a great way of growing a logical disk volume.

Stripe sets are a way of spanning information over multiple disks in a pattern. The data is "striped" across the disks so that a piece of the file exists on each drive. This sort of data storage increases disk I/O performance because each disk can process reads and writes simultaneously. Stripe sets consist of 2 to 32 disks, with some restrictions. The smallest disk in a stripe set is used as the baseline for all other disks. If you have two 4 GB drives and one 2 GB drive in a stripe set, each disk only offers 2 GB of storage to the overall set, for a total of 6 GB. On the bright side, the remaining free space can be used in other ways, like creating volume sets. Be aware that plain stripe sets offer no parity checking capabilities, so any data lost cannot be recovered automatically — recovery must be done manually using backups to restore the data.

Another method of fault tolerance, called *stripe set with parity*, is an altogether different method of spanning volumes. This type of subsystem requires at least three disks and no more than 32. As in the normal stripe set, this technique stripes data across the disks. The difference is the additional parity stripe that is written interleaved with the data stripes. The parity stripe is a byte parity of the data stripes at a given stripe level or row. This parity stripe is used to reconstruct missing or bad stripes during a read or write operation.

Stripe sets with parity are less vulnerable to failure because the parity stripes are not all stored on the same disk volume. When a data stripe is determined to be bad or missing, all the remaining good data stripes for that particular file are read, along with the parity stripe information. The data stripes are then subtracted from the parity stripe using the eXclusive-OR (XOR) mathematical function, and the result gives the missing data stripes.

Disk mirroring, a third form of fault tolerance, can be performed on either NTFS or FAT partitions. Disk mirroring requires two partitions on different disks, both using a single hard disk controller. Disk mirroring copies every file and directory on the first hard disk to a second hard disk. When one of the disks fails, the other is an instant replacement. You may also use partitions of different sizes, but remember that you may be wasting space on your drives if the sizes aren't the same.

Disk duplexing is essentially the same as disk mirroring, except that you use two controllers instead of just one. Each drive is placed on its own separate controller for complete hardware redundancy. The side effect of this configuration is that it can improve performance over standard disk mirroring. The Windows NT operating system sees no real difference between duplexing and mirroring; choosing between them is purely a hardware and performance consideration.

THE COMMON INTERNET FILE SYSTEM (CIFS)

CIFS is new to Windows NT. Introduced as a direct result of the increasing popularity of the Internet, CIFS is a protocol that interoperates with a file system to give access to shared objects across networks in a more seamless way. CIFS lets users work together over the Internet, an intranet, or some combination. CIFS is an open, cross-platform technology based on the native file-sharing protocols built in to Microsoft Windows and other popular PC operating systems and supported on dozens of other platforms, including Unix.

CIFS runs over TCP/IP and uses the Domain Name Service (DNS) for scalability. It is specifically optimized to support slow dial-up connections common on the Internet. With CIFS, existing applications and applications for the World Wide Web can easily share data over the Internet or an intranet, regardless of computer or operating system platform. CIFS is an enhanced version of Microsoft's open, cross-platform Server Message Block (SMB) protocol, the native file-sharing protocol in the Microsoft Windows 95, Windows NT, and OS/2 operating systems.

CIFS eliminates the need to use LMHOST files or WINS servers to locate remote computers for connectivity. The advantage of this newfound feature is most apparent when using a simple Web browser to make network connections to shared objects. A user can click a simple URL, such as http://207.91.166.199/docs/proposal.doc and immediately open "proposal.doc" on a remote system with an IP address of 207.91.166.199. The Web browser will attempt the connection and negotiate an authentication routine; both processes will be completely transparent to the user.

Microsoft has always been good at introducing useful functions, which has both positive and negative features. The positive side is that many products quickly become easier to use; the negative side is that end-user control is sometimes diminished or eliminated entirely. When a user loses control, problems can arise.

CIFS presents some inherent dangers when connecting Windows NT systems to the Internet. The dangers manifest themselves in the ease-of-use features. These dangers were clearly demonstrated in March 1997, when several university students discovered gaping problems in the protocol that let them initiate seamless connection negotiations without the user's knowledge by using a simple HTML-based Web page.

Microsoft is addressing these newfound problems and claims they are left over from the early days of CIFS development some ten years ago. On March 25, 1997, they released a document outlining proposed changes to the CIFS protocol that will help curb some of the security vulnerabilities, and these changes should appear in Service Pack 3 or 4 for Windows NT 4.0.

WINDOWS NT DOMAINS AND WORKGROUPS

Windows NT uses two basic models for structuring a shared resource environment suitable for use as a networking platform: *domains* and *workgroups*. A Windows NT domain is a group of servers that share a common security policy and user database. A workgroup is an organizational unit that groups computers that don't belong to a Windows NT domain. We'll discuss both structured environments in this section so you know exactly how to use either of them on your network.

Special Note

Experts agree that the best strategy for designing a Windows NT domain is to keep it as simple as possible and not use more domains than absolutely necessary. This approach keeps interdomain security risks and concerns to a minimum.

WINDOWS NT DOMAINS

A Windows NT domain represents a group of domain controllers, servers, workstations, user accounts, policies, and objects that can be used within the NT domain. The users belong to various user groups, where each user or group of users has varying access permissions to objects and network operations.

Domains are controlled by Windows NT Servers that have been installed and configured as either primary or secondary domain controllers. You designate Windows NT Domain Controllers when you install Windows NT. You are presented with three options that determine how the server software will operate on the network: as the primary domain controller, as a secondary domain controller, or as the server. Windows NT servers do not participate in domain-controlling tasks and thus have less operational overhead, which translates to better performance. If you install Windows NT as a network server and not a domain controller, you must reinstall the software later if you decide you want the machine to participate as a domain controller.

Domain controllers manage security access rights to the objects that are accessible on your network, including objects controlled by other Windows NT domains. Domain controllers that are part of the same domain share security policies and user account information through a process called *synchronization*, which lets the domain controllers replicate account information so that each controller has all the information and the information is current. Windows NT domain controllers can also share this information with other Windows NT domains through a trust relationship that can be established by the network administrators.

Windows NT domains should not be confused with TCP/IP domains. They are completely different and serve entirely different purposes. Also, the Windows NT host name, or machine name, is not the same as its TCP/IP counterpart.

DOMAIN TRUST RELATIONSHIPS

Windows NT domains can establish trust relationships. A trust relationship is a link between Windows NT domains that lets one domain recognize all users and global groups of another domain. When a domain trust is established correctly, a user needs only one ID to access resources of another domain.

Two types of trusts can be established between domains: one-way and two-way. In a one-way trust, one domain trusts the second domain, but the second domain does not trust the first domain. In a two-way trust, one domain trusts the second domain, and the second domain reciprocates by trusting the first domain.

Domain trusts reduce duplicate account information and the problems caused by unsynchronized account information. When trust relationships are established, user accounts and global groups can be granted rights and privileges in domains other than the one in which they were created. Trusts make administration much easier because you have to create a user account only once on your entire network. After it's created, the account can access any resource on the network, even another domain.

You can establish a model for an NT domain in a variety of ways. The right model for your purposes should be based on your network requirements and how you plan to control access to the objects on that network. The Windows NT Re-source Kit contains a very helpful tool to guide you in establishing your domain design. Here are four basic NT domain models that you might consider:

- Single domain — This model is used primarily for small networks with a limited number of users who don't need to be logically divided for management purposes. No trust relationships are required for this model.

- Master domain — User accounts are created in the master domain, whose main purpose is to manage the user accounts of all domains. All other domains trust the master domain.

- Multiple master domain — This model is used for larger network configurations that contain several master domains. All user accounts are created in one of the participating master domains. Each master domain has a two-way trust relationship with all the other master domains. The other domains trust all the master domains, but regular domains do not necessarily trust other regular domains.

- Complete trust — All domains on the network establish a two-way trust with all other domains on the network. Each domain contains its own user accounts and global groups that can be used on any of the other domains on the network.

When establishing domain trusts, it is always more secure to use the lowest possible trust level. In other words, don't create a two-way trust if you don't genuinely need it. Instead, use a one-way trust until the need for a two-way trust arises.

WORKGROUPS

The workgroup was introduced in Windows 3.x and later enhanced in WfW 3.11. Workgroups are not nearly as secure as Windows NT domains, but they do offer some nice features for small network environments.

In a workgroup, each computer is charged with taking care of its own user accounts and group information. Workgroup computers do not share this information with other computers on the network. Windows NT machines may participate in workgroups, and when they do, they maintain their own security policy and account information.

All users participating in a workgroup are called *global users*. (We cover global users later in this chapter.) When a user logs on to a computer over the network, the connection is authenticated on the remote computer by user ID and password. Workgroups are perfect for situations in which administration is not a big undertaking or concern. They are also good for networks that contain a mixture of Windows operating systems, particularly ones that don't use Windows NT.

USER ACCOUNTS

Windows NT user accounts are at the core of Windows NT security. Everything that happens in a Windows NT network can be traced to a specific user account authorized for the activity; even unauthorized activity is tracked. This section provides some insight into aspects of user accounts.

OVERVIEW

Because Windows NT is a user-level security model as opposed to a share-level security model, an administrator must create a user account for each user who wants access to resources controlled by Windows NT. When a user logs on using the account, the SAM checks the user logon information against the user database. When the logon is authenticated, the LSA generates a unique security token for the user that helps track the user's access rights and permissions.

Depending on your network's domain model, any particular user can have one or several accounts that allow various levels of access to workgroups and domains. This user account information could reside on the user's own computer, in the case of a workgroup account, or on a Windows NT domain controller or server. Where it resides isn't as important as how it is used.

The user accounts control access to resources. An administrator establishes privileges that give specific users the right to access a resource. If the user has the correct privileges, that user is allowed to access the resource. Windows NT also uses the accounts to create an audit trail. You can track most aspects of resource use, and the Event Log can show which user's action generated the logged event. There's nothing quite like a little positive identification to track and stop a would-be intruder!

ACCOUNT TYPES

Windows NT has two basic types of user accounts: global accounts and local accounts.

Global accounts are normal user accounts that are authenticated by the primary or secondary domain controllers or through trust relationships with other domains. Global accounts reside in the user's home domain and can be used to access resources in other Windows NT domains.

Local accounts are assigned in a domain to users whose global account is not in a trusted domain. Local account information is authenticated using information available only on the machine processing the logon. Local user accounts may be used only within the domain in which they are created and may not be used to access resources in other trusted domains. Local user accounts are typically used for WfW and LAN Manager users.

AUTHENTICATION

Windows NT systems that don't participate in a domain use the Netlogon system service to process logon requests for the local machine and to pass logon information to a domain server when necessary.

Netlogon replicates any changes in the security database to all domain controllers in the domain, including the SAM and LSA databases. A Windows NT Server's Netlogon service also synchronizes its user database in two situations:

- when a domain controller is first installed and
- when an offline domain controller's change log is full when it comes back online.

Netlogon also accepts logon requests and provides authentication information from the SAM database.

When a user logs on to a Windows NT machine that is not a domain controller, the system performs the *discovery process*, in which it locates the controller for the domain. If the computer is not part of a domain, the Netlogon service stops processing the logon request.

System-level communication between two Windows NT machines on a network is always performed on a secure channel. Windows NT creates this secure channel using a challenge-and-response combination issued by each Windows NT machine's Netlogon service. The secure channel is used by Windows NT to transmit API calls between the systems and to pass through user names and encrypted passwords. Once the secure channel has been established, Netlogon uses the following three special internal user accounts to maintain security on the channel:

- *Workstation trust accounts* let a domain workstation handle pass-through authentication for a Windows NT server in a domain. We'll talk more about pass-through in a moment.
- *Server trust accounts* let a Windows NT server obtain a copy of the master domain database from a domain controller.
- *Interdomain trust accounts* let a Windows NT server handle pass-through authentication from another Windows NT domain.

Pass-through authentication occurs when the local computer cannot authenticate an account. The user name and password are forwarded to a Windows NT server to attempt the authentication. For pass-through authentication to work properly, each Windows NT machine participating in a domain must be running the Netlogon service and its dependent Workstation service. The local Netlogon service sends the request to the remote machine's Netlogon service and waits for a response.

USER ACCOUNT MANAGEMENT

You manage user accounts in Windows NT using either User Manager or User Manager for Domains. These administrative applications provide a graphical interface to control all aspects of a user's account parameters. In the User Manager, you enable overall auditing and add, change, and delete user accounts and groups. The User Manager is discussed in detail in Chapter 4, "Nuts and Bolts of Windows NT Security."

USER RIGHTS AND PERMISSIONS

Setting up user rights and permissions is discussed in detail in Chapter 4. For now, you should understand one major difference between user rights and user permissions: User rights apply to system tasks, while permissions apply to objects.

USER RIGHTS

Two types of user rights, regular rights and advanced rights, authorize a given user to perform certain system tasks, such as modifying a printer share or backing up and restoring data. When establishing user rights and policies with the User Manager or User Manager for Domains, you will inevitably come across a list of rights that don't make sense to you at first. The tables in this section define each right so you know exactly what it is and how you might use it. Table 3.1 defines regular user rights and Table 3.2 defines advanced user rights.

TABLE 3.1 REGULAR USER RIGHTS

This User Right	Lets a User
Access this computer from network	Connect to a computer over the network
Back up files and directories	Perform backup operations
Change the system time	Set the system time on the machine's internal clock
Force shutdown from a remote system	NOT IMPLEMENTED
Log on locally	Log on at the local keyboard of a server
Manage auditing and security log	Set auditing preferences and view and delete the Security Log

continued

TABLE 3.1 CONTINUED

This User Right	Lets a User
Restore files and directories	Perform restoration operations
Shut down the system	Shut down a Windows NT machine
Take ownership of files or other objects	Take over ownership of an object that may belong to another user

TABLE 3.2 ADVANCED USER RIGHTS

This User Right	Lets a User
Act as part of the operating system	Have an account that acts as trusted part of the operating system itself, required by some subsystems under Windows NT
Bypass traverse check	Traverse a directory tree even when the user has no right to access the directory
Create a page file	Create a system page file (swap file)
Create a token object	Lets the LSA create access tokens. This right is for System-level access and is not assigned to normal users
Create permanent shared objects	Create permanent objects used by Windows NT
Debug programs	Debug programs running on Windows NT
Generate security audits	Generate audit-log events
Increase quotas	Increase each object's quota
Increase scheduling priorities	Increase the scheduling priority of a process
Load and unload device drivers	Load and unload device drivers
Lock pages in memory	Freeze pages in memory, which prevents them from being paged out of the system to the page file (swap file)
Log on as a batch job	Log on to the system and appear as a batch queue facility
Log on as a service	Perform security services

continued

TABLE 3.2 CONTINUED

This User Right	Lets a User
Modify firmware environment values	Modify the system environment variables (not to be confused with user environment variables)
Profile single process	Profile and observe a single process
Profile system performance	Profile and observe the system itself
Receive unsolicited device input	Read unsolicited data from an input device
Replace a process level token	Replace a process's access token

USER PERMISSIONS

User permissions apply to specific objects, such as files, directories, and printers. A typical permission grants access to a certain directory or a certain printer. Permissions are set and controlled by the owner or creator of an object. Only the system administrator can override permission settings, and only then after taking ownership of the object, at which point the ownership transaction is logged for security purposes.

Normally, user rights take precedence over object permissions. Let me offer an example using user groups, which I'll explain later; for now, just understand that user groups are basically a collection of user accounts with common rights. Now, let's say a user member of the Backup Operators group is performing a system backup. If a user had created a directory and denied the Backup Operators access, any member of that group could still access and back up the directory based on the right to back up files and directories assigned to the Backup Operators group, thereby overriding the creator/owner's permissions.

USER GROUPS

Windows NT user groups make it possible to assign sets of rights and permissions to several users at one time. When a user group is granted a permission or an access right, those permissions or rights are granted to all users who belong to the group. User groups are established and managed with the User Manager or User Manager for Domains. Windows NT includes three types of groups: global groups, local groups, and special groups.

GLOBAL GROUPS

A global group contains user accounts only from the domain in which it is created, and a global group may not contain any other groups. Global groups may be assigned rights and permissions for the domains in which they reside and the domains their home domain trusts. Global groups are an excellent way to export collections of users as a single unit to another Windows NT domain.

Windows NT creates three default global groups during installation: domain admins, domain users, and domain guests. The domain admins group is granted permission to modify and control certain aspects of the NT domain. The domain users group is granted lesser permissions that restrict their ability to manipulate the NT domain. The domain guests group is granted fewer permissions than other built-in groups because users in this group are temporary visitors on your network. You can, of course, create other global groups for your purposes. Table 3.3 defines the three built-in global groups that are created during a Windows NT installation.

TABLE 3.3 BUILT-IN GLOBAL GROUPS

Group Name	Description
Domain Admins	Users in this group can manage the workstations in the home domain and any other trusted domains that include domain admins as a member of their Administrators group.
Domain Users	Members of this group have access and abilities to workstations in the domain and even the domain itself. By default, all users are members of this group.
Domain Guests	A special group for users considered to be visiting (temporary) guests.

LOCAL GROUPS

Local groups contain user accounts and global groups from other domains. A local group can be assigned permission only for its own domain, and it can reside only on the Windows NT machine on which it was created. Windows NT creates several local groups when you install it as a server and a few more groups when you install it as a domain controller. Table 3.4 shows the standard local groups installed and their defined uses. Recommendations about using these groups appear in the "Recommendations" section at the end of this chapter.

TABLE 3.4 STANDARD LOCAL GROUPS

Group Name	Description
Administrators	This group is the most powerful because it allows the administration of every aspect of the NT domain and servers. Assign users to this group carefully. This group is the only one you are required to use.
Users	These users have minimal rights on a Windows NT server. They may create and manage local groups if they have logon permission and access to the User Manager utility.
Guests	This groups is for occasional or one-time users. Users in this group typically have very limited rights.
Backup Operators	These users have the authority to back up files and directories and restore files and directories. Backup operators may also shut down a Windows NT server if necessary.
Replicator	The operating system uses this special group to log the Replicator service on to the system. This group contains only a single domain user account, and there should be no regular user accounts in this group.
Everyone	This group is not a true group and doesn't even appear in the User Manager. However, it appears when you assign rights to resources, and it represents every user and account that exists on your domain. It's provided to make establishing unrestricted shares more convenient and easier.
Power Users	Users in this group can create and connect to network devices, actually defeating security measures that you have put in place. Be selective when assigning users to this group!

When you configure Windows NT as a domain controller, additional groups are automatically installed. Table 3.5 summarizes these groups.

TABLE 3.5 ADDITIONAL LOCAL GROUPS

Group Name	Description
Account Operators	Users in this group may use the User Manager for Domains utility with only a few restrictions. They may create, modify, and delete local and global accounts and groups any way they wish, except for the following groups: Administrators, Domain Admins, Account Operators, Backup Operators, Print Operators, and Server Operators. Account Operators cannot manipulate the Administrators group in any way, nor can they change security policies; however, they can use the Server Manager to add machines to the domain, log on at a server console, and shut down a server.
Print Operators	Members of this group can create, modify, and delete printer shares. They may also log on to Windows NT servers and shut down Windows NT servers.
Server Operators	This group has all the rights necessary to manage the domain's servers. Members may manage printers, manage network shares, perform backups and restores, format drives, lock a server, change the system date and time, log on to Windows NT servers, and shut down Windows NT servers.

SPECIAL GROUPS

Table 3.6 defines several special groups that you may come across now and then in lists when assigning permissions and rights.

TABLE 3.6 SPECIAL GROUPS

Group Name	Description
Interactive	All users using the computer locally
Network	All users connected to a computer across the network
System	The operating system itself
Creator/Owner	The creator/owner of an object (such as files, directories, or print jobs)

You aren't required to use any of these local and global groups other than the Administrators group, which is necessary for performing system-level administration. They are all provided for your convenience, and you should use them based on the authoritative rights they confer to users. When assigning users to groups, never take a shot in the dark when deciding which group to put them in. Refer to this list or establish a new group and restrict the permission for that group accordingly. Mistakes in assigning users to groups or assigning rights and permissions to groups can greatly compromise your security.

SHARED RESOURCES

A shared resource, sometimes called a *share*, is any object that has been made available on the network. The most common types of shared resources are files, directories, and printers, although a few other specialized shares are established by the Windows NT operating system. The person or process that establishes a shared resource becomes the creator or owner of that share.

The process for sharing files, directories, and privileges is detailed in Chapter 4. Briefly, when establishing an object as a share, the user must first choose a unique name for the share and then assign access permissions to users and groups that are allowed to access it. After this information has been established, it is used to create the *security descriptor*, a set of security attributes that secures it against unauthorized access. Each security descriptor consists of four parts:

- Owner security ID — indicates the owner of the object, which is either a user or a group
- Group security ID — an ID used only by the POSIX subsystem, usually ignored by the rest of Windows NT
- Discretionary access control list — controlled by the owner of the object, it reflects the users and groups that are granted or denied access to the object
- System access control list — controlled by security administrators, it defines which audit messages will be generated by the operating system

MONITORING TOOLS

Windows NT comes with several great monitoring tools that you will find useful in gathering and analyzing information about your systems. Each has its own function and purpose, and you should understand when each one is most helpful. This section reviews the tools built into Windows NT, giving you an overview of their functions and features.

EVENT VIEWER

The Event Viewer, detailed in Chapter 4 and shown in Figure 3.2, is one of the most important tools at your disposal. The Event Viewer lets you analyze and review the three basic logs: the system log, the security log, and the application log. Each of these logs tracks specific information and event types.

- System log — events related to system-level activities, such as drivers loading and unloading and services starting and stopping
- Security log — events related to security activities, such as invalid attempts to log on and failed access attempts
- Application log — events related to specific applications, such as a UPS service performing self-tests and messages that software backups are complete

Figure 3.2

The Event Viewer

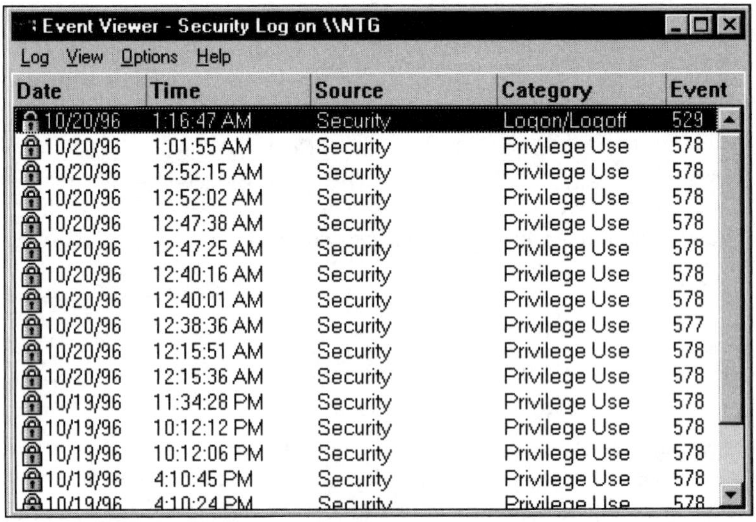

Date	Time	Source	Category	Event
10/20/96	1:16:47 AM	Security	Logon/Logoff	529
10/20/96	1:01:55 AM	Security	Privilege Use	578
10/20/96	12:52:15 AM	Security	Privilege Use	578
10/20/96	12:52:02 AM	Security	Privilege Use	578
10/20/96	12:47:38 AM	Security	Privilege Use	578
10/20/96	12:47:25 AM	Security	Privilege Use	578
10/20/96	12:40:16 AM	Security	Privilege Use	578
10/20/96	12:40:01 AM	Security	Privilege Use	578
10/20/96	12:38:36 AM	Security	Privilege Use	577
10/20/96	12:15:51 AM	Security	Privilege Use	578
10/20/96	12:15:36 AM	Security	Privilege Use	578
10/19/96	11:34:28 PM	Security	Privilege Use	578
10/19/96	10:12:12 PM	Security	Privilege Use	578
10/19/96	10:12:06 PM	Security	Privilege Use	578
10/19/96	4:10:45 PM	Security	Privilege Use	578
10/19/96	4:10:24 PM	Security	Privilege Use	578

You open the Event Viewer by clicking Start, selecting Programs, choosing Administrative Tools, and then clicking Event Viewer.

I can't overstate the importance of the Event Viewer in the overall scheme of security. *You must monitor these logs regularly* if you expect to have any success in securing your system. Most network break-ins occur on secured systems that were not properly or routinely monitored. Don't become the next casualty on the information superhighway — monitor your logs!

SERVER MANAGER

The Server Manager is a neat little tool that gives you a bird's-eye view of several aspects of your Windows NT server at any moment. The Server Manager has two basic views: one showing the computers that are members of the domain (Figure 3.3) and one showing details about any given computer in the domain (Figure 3.4).

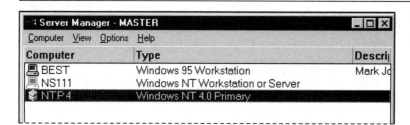

Figure 3.3
Server Manager Window

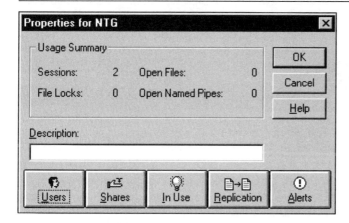

Figure 3.4
Properties for Computer NTG

As shown in Figure 3.3, the server view lists each computer in the domain, along with that computer's operating system type. You can scroll through the list and double-click an individual computer to present its properties and characteristics (Figure 3.4).

The Properties dialog box contains several buttons along the bottom. The buttons, labeled Users, Shares, In Use, Replication, and Alerts, give you access to information about that particular computer. Let's look at each type of information.

- Users — Clicking this button brings up the dialog box shown in
  Figure 3.5. It displays which users are connected to the server, which
  machine they are connected from, how many resources they have open,
  how long a user has been idle, what time a user connected to the server,
  whether a user is a guest, and which resources that user is currently using.
  You may disconnect a user from a given resource or from all resources
  using the buttons at the bottom.

Figure 3.5

*User Sessions
Dialog Box*

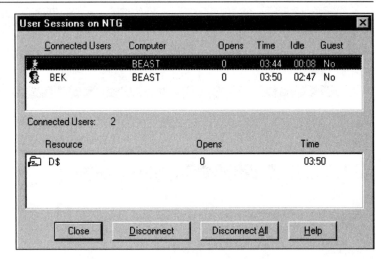

- Shares — Clicking this button on the Properties dialog box (Figure 3.4)
  brings up the dialog box in Figure 3.6. It displays the objects that have
  been defined as shared objects on the network. The window shows the
  share name, the number of connections to the share, the actual resource
  location, connected users and their time connected, and whether the share
  is currently in use by the user.

- In Use — Clicking this button on the Properties dialog box brings up the
  dialog box shown in Figure 3.7. It displays the resources that are currently
  open for use on the system. It shows the total number of open resources,
  the total number of file locks currently in place, who opened a resource,
  who the resource was opened for, number of locks for the resource, and
  the true path to the resource.

- Replication — Clicking this button on the Properties dialog box brings up
  the dialog box shown in Figure 3.8. It displays the directories that have
  been established to use to export and import data to and from other systems. You manage aspects of the settings using this dialog box.

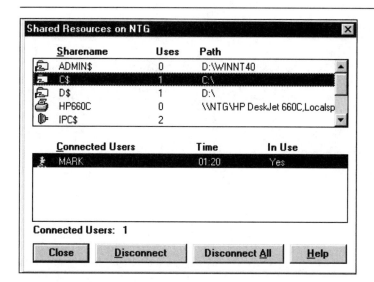

Figure 3.6
*Shared Resources
Dialog Box*

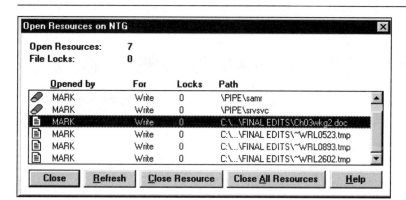

Figure 3.7
*Open Resources
Dialog Box*

- Alerts — Clicking this button on the Properties dialog box brings up the dialog box shown in Figure 3.9. It lists who receives administrative alerts sent from this machine and lets you add and remove users and computers to receive alerts.

The Server Manager consolidates several Windows NT dialog boxes, making server management easier. In addition to actions in the above dialog boxes, other useful tasks can be performed with the Server Manager. You can

- list all shares for a given server
- establish new shares

Figure 3.8

Directory Replication Dialog Box

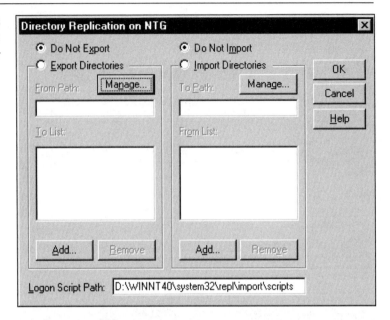

Figure 3.9

Alerts Dialog Box

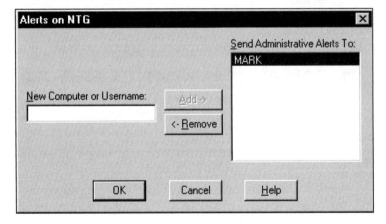

- adjust access permissions of a share
- list services running on a remote Windows NT machine
- stop and start individual services on a Windows NT machine
- adjust the startup properties of services on a Windows NT machine
- send a message to all users of a Windows NT machine

- synchronize all domain controllers in the entire domain
- add and remove member machines from the domain
- list only workstations in the domain
- list only servers in the domain
- list all machines in the domain

NETWORK MONITOR

The Network Monitor is a sometimes-overlooked arrow in the quiver of Windows NT weapons. The Network Monitor, shown in Figure 3.10, collects packet information from the network that you then display and analyze. The software and an administrative interface come as an installable service with Windows NT 4.0. The software lets you capture traffic only on the machine where it is running. For Network Monitor to capture packets from other machines, you must use the version of Network Monitor included with Microsoft's Systems Management Server.

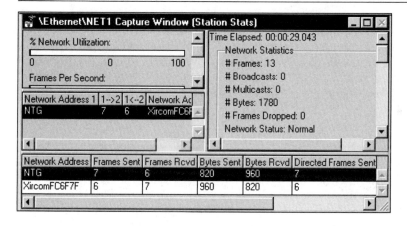

Figure 3.10
Network Monitor
Dialog Box

Network Monitor lets you define filters that can capture specific types of packets, limiting the data that is captured. Once packets have been captured, you can examine them individually to learn information such as the source MAC address, destination MAC address, source IP address, destination IP address, protocol type, and packet data description. Other information that depends on the packet type and protocol type is also available. Figure 3.11 shows several captured packets. The first captured packet is from a host named NTG, which is querying a DNS server at IP address 128.9.0.107 for the IP address of a host NS2.Netropolis.net.

Figure 3.11

Sample Captured Packets

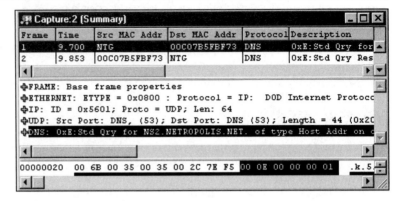

Captured packets can be an invaluable tool in your efforts to diagnose network trouble. I can cite a perfect example from my own experience. A Windows NT server runs the DNS service for my Internet domain Ntshop.net. One night while I was working on this book, I noticed a significant drop-off in the performance of my server. At first, I thought someone might be sending me a giant e-mail, because this machine also runs my Internet mail server. However, after a moment or two, the performance was not back up to speed, so I checked the Task Manager statistics on CPU usage (the Task Manager is covered later in this chapter). The statistics showed that the DNS process was using as much as 85 percent of the processor, with no signs of slacking off. Naturally I was curious about the cause because I run a relatively low-traffic network with almost no DNS queries to speak of.

I decided to capture some traffic on this server to see what was going on. I configured my packet sniffer to grab only DNS queries and ran the sniffer until it captured a few dozen packets. Because it was being bombarded with DNS traffic, it didn't take long. One look at the packets showed me the IP address of a DNS server on the Internet that was looking up information for an Internet domain for which my DNS answers queries. The captured information showed me where the packet came from and what the packet data was to be used for — a DNS lookup query. The problem was that I did not have the domain in my DNS tables yet because the domain was not in use at the time. When the remote DNS server queried my system for nonexistent domain records, it caused my DNS server to begin an endless loop, which was eating all my server's horsepower. I stopped the DNS service, added the missing domain information, and restarted the service. My server's performance went back to normal.

From this example, you can learn two lessons: first, the unintentional denial-of-service attack on my DNS server affected the performance of my

entire system; and second, network monitors can be invaluable resources for
tracking down trouble, especially would-be intruders.

PERFORMANCE MONITOR

Performance Monitor, which is built into Windows NT, is a fabulous analytical
tool. As its name implies, this tool offers insight into the performance characteristics of a given system service or process, using the standard interface
shown in Figure 3.12. Performance Monitor lets you monitor both the computer it's running on and other computers on your network.

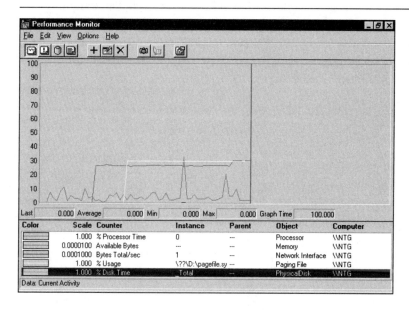

Figure 3.12

*Performance
Monitor Window*

Performance Monitor watches the behavior patterns of system objects,
such as the processors, memory, cache, threads, processes, and network traffic.
Each object that can be monitored has a set of counters that can provide information such as queue lengths, device use, delays, throughput, and internal
congestion. The software provides charting, alerting, and reporting capabilities
that reflect both current activity and ongoing activity. You can open, browse,
and chart log files, just as if they reflected activity being tracked at that
moment. In addition, this tool lets you

- view data collected from any number of computers simultaneously
- view and change charts to reflect current activity

- view counter values that are updated at a frequency you define
- export data from charts, logs, alert logs, and reports to spreadsheet or database programs for further manipulation, review, and printing
- add system alerts that log events in the Alert Log and notify you by reverting to Alert view, logging the event in Event Viewer's Application log, or issuing a network alert
- run a predefined program either every time or only the first time a counter value goes over or under a value you define
- create log files containing data about objects on different computers
- append selected sections of existing log files to a single file, forming a long-term archive
- view current activity reports or create reports from existing log files
- save individual chart, alert, log, and report settings, or save the entire workspace setup to reuse later

When you monitor a system using this tool, you are really monitoring the behavior of its objects. Remember, an object is simply a standard mechanism for identifying and using a system resource. Objects represent individual processes, sections of shared memory, and physical devices. With this knowledge, you can use Performance Monitor to detect subtle problems on your systems that may in fact in be early warnings signs of intrusion. For example, if you notice that your Remote Procedure Call (RPC) processes (Rpcss.exe) use 90 percent or more of your CPU time consistently, you can suspect a denial-of-service attack is underway. In a nutshell, this tool gives you a baseline for gauging normal system performance, which in turn you use to detect abnormal system performance.

Performance Monitor groups object counters by object type. For each object, a unique set of counters produces statistical information. Certain types of objects and their associated counters are present on all systems. However, other counters, such as application-specific counters, appear only if the computer is running the associated software. Not all software packages produce counters for use with Performance Monitor, but most of the better ones do.

Each object type can have several instances. For example, machines with multiple processors have multiple instances for those objects. The physical disks on your systems are object types with an instance for each disk on the system. Some object types, such as memory, do not have instances, because they are viewed as single units. If an object type has multiple instances, each instance may use the same set of counters to track data.

What is the significance of all these objects and the ability to monitor them? Performance Monitor can often identify an area of the system that is dragging performance to a screeching halt, allowing you to determine who or what is causing the problem there.

Microsoft's IIS Web server and all other parts of the IIS suite provide performance counters that can be a big help in gauging traffic loads and general use. Learn to use Performance Monitor, and you'll find that you'll not only be able to tune your Windows NT server for optimum performance, but you'll also be able to sense and locate causes of performance degradation as they are happening.

TASK MANAGER

The Task Manager is easily launched by simply pressing the Ctrl-Alt-Delete key combination and selecting Task Manager from the menu. The Task Manager presents a wealth of useful information, some of which is similar to that found using Performance Monitor. Task Manager provides a quick and simple way to view running processes, their memory usage, CPU time, and other vital information. Let's look at each tab in the Task Manager.

The first tab, Applications, is shown in Figure 3.13. It shows each open application in the Task column, along with its status. You may also launch a new task using this dialog box.

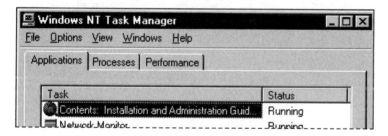

Figure 3.13
*Task Manager,
Applications Tab*

The second tab, Processes (Figure 3.14), shows every process running on the machine in the Image Name column, along with other vital information such as process ID, CPU time, CPU usage percentage, and memory usage.

The third tab, Figure 3.15, shows CPU and memory use, histograms for that data, total handles, threads and processes, commit charge usage, physical memory usage, and kernel memory usage.

The Task Manager gives you data on some of the same resources you can monitor more accurately with Performance Monitor. However, the Processes tab is especially useful, because you can quickly see which processes are using the most memory and CPU time.

Figure 3.14

Task Manager,
Processes Tab

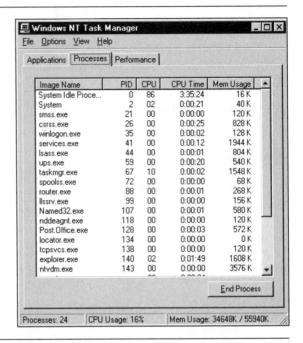

Figure 3.15

Task Manager,
Performance Tab

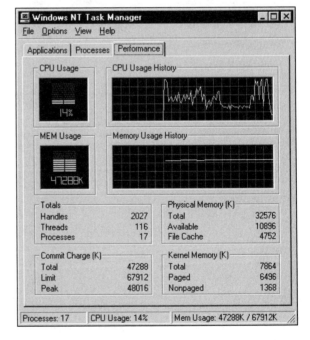

RECOMMENDATIONS

This section offers a few recommendations that should help you establish security for your network environment. You should re-examine these concepts in the context of your own environment before you use them.

- Windows NT Server cannot protect critical business data if the operating system is not running. You need to secure your server hardware physically. Put your servers behind a locked door in a well-ventilated area.

- Use power-on passwords that prevent intruders from starting an operating system other than Windows NT. Power-on passwords are a function of the computer hardware, not the operating system. The procedure for setting up the power-on password depends on the type of computer you are using, but it is normally established by adjusting some features of the ROM BIOS.

- Keep all your files on Windows NT file servers.

- Do not let anyone but select administrators have access to the shutdown features of the operating system.

- Using the system ROM BIOS, disable all floppy drive use on the server.

- Use servers that come in cabinets with a locking mechanism that does not allow the cabinet to be opened without the key. Most clone computers can be opened quickly with a simple screwdriver — a nice feature at times, but bad for security.

- Shred your paperwork before tossing it into the trash — you never know who may be digging around in there after hours.

- Routinely change passwords. Enforce the use of long, difficult passwords.

- Use the feature (introduced in Windows NT 4.0 with Service Pack 2) that lets you add DLLs to Windows NT for strong password checking. Service Pack 2 includes a sample DLL called Passfilt.dll. A few third-party DLLs offer the same function.

- Never write down passwords unless you can lock them up afterward.

- Never lend your user ID and password to someone else.

- Don't assume someone standing by you isn't looking over your shoulder.

- Routinely monitor your system performance and system event logs for oddities.

- Disable the Guest account and Guest group.

- Minimize the rights of the Administrator account so that it is essentially crippled, and then create another account to be used with administrative rights instead. This tactic keeps hackers guessing and makes the account you really use for administrative tasks harder to crack.

- Minimize membership in the Administrators group.
- Eliminate the Everyone group and replace it with another group and another name of your choosing.
- Disable unnecessary network drivers and unbind them from network cards that don't need them.
- Don't run software that you don't need.
- Use the NTFS file system instead of FAT whenever possible.

SUMMARY

This chapter has covered some of the basic security features of the Windows NT operating system. We've looked at the file systems, user accounts, user groups, domains and trust relationships, administrative tools, user rights and permissions, network resources, and the overall security architecture of Windows NT. This information should be a great foundation for understanding what you have and how it all works together as you establish and manage your network security. The next chapter gets into the nuts and bolts of this same information, taking a more hands-on approach.

CHAPTER 4

NUTS AND BOLTS OF NT SECURITY

To adequately secure your systems, you need to understand the
mechanics of Windows NT's underlying security system because most
software written for Windows NT relies on Windows NT's internal
architecture to control access to network resources. In this chapter, you
learn security considerations of users, groups, file systems, and printers.
I also describe how to use logging and auditing features in NT to help
secure your resources. Finally, we look at security considerations for
several aspects of your network:

- RAS Security
- TCP/IP security
- domain trust relationships
- Windows NT installation
- IIS installation
- FTP and gopher
- Windows NT Services

Remember, you should maintain the point of view that anyone is a
potential intruder.

USER SECURITY

Before you establish a Windows NT network, you need to thoroughly understand several aspects of user security. Pay close attention to the details of the accounts we cover in this section — the Administrator account, the Guest account, and user accounts. Much of the security in Windows NT depends on the permissions you grant and deny each user. Mistakes in granting permissions can lead to devastating consequences down the road, leaving your network vulnerable to intrusion.

ADMINISTRATOR ACCOUNT

The Administrator account, which is added automatically during Windows NT installation, has a far-reaching impact on security. You define a password for this account during installation, and you should guard this password carefully. After setting up a Windows NT server and establishing the Administrator account, your next step is adding a user that you assign to the Administrator account. This user has the permission to administer the Windows NT domain, including users, groups, and resources. You should also add that user to the Administrators group, which gives it permission to manage all aspects of the NT domain. I explain user groups in more detail later in this chapter.

In theory, the Administrator account can be shared by more than one user, each of whom has the account's password. Although this setup might be convenient, is it a very bad security mistake that should be avoided at all costs. Instead, you should establish an individual account for each user who is granted permission to administer the domain so that you can create an audit trail to show exactly who did what and when. When administrators share the Administrator account, you have no way to know exactly who was using the account.

Be very careful to whom you give administrator privileges, because these users can change any part of the operating system they want. Users with administrator privileges should be monitored closely to ensure that the Administrator account is not misused.

One of the best ways to secure against unauthorized use of the Administrator account is simply to establish a new account, give it administrative privileges, and change the privileges on the old Administrator account to provide no access whatsoever. This approach keeps hackers busy trying to hack into an account that gains them nothing.

GUEST ACCOUNT

Another special account is the Guest account. When Windows NT 4.0 is installed, it automatically adds and disables the Guest account. Because the account is disabled, no one can use it to log on to the network. In my experience, leaving this account disabled has always been effective, unless you are absolutely sure that you need to use it.

For the most part, the Guest account is an easy way to give occasional or temporary users very limited access to the Windows NT domain resources. Some Windows NT services also use the Guest account to log on. However, using the Guest account gives you no sure way to know who did what on the network. For all intents and purposes, it can be viewed as a way to log on to the network anonymously. Some networking professionals even recommend that you leave the Guest account set with no password in place. In my opinion, this is a big mistake.

A better way to handle services that rely on the permissions of the Guest account is to establish individual user accounts with limited permissions that can be used by any Windows NT service that needs to log on to the network. This way, you'll have a better audit trail showing which services or users performed each particular action. All Windows NT services let you configure the account they will use to interoperate with the operating system. If you take the time to manage these services properly, you'll be doing yourself a big favor.

USER ACCOUNTS

User accounts are managed by a network administrator, who creates an account for each user in the domain who needs to use network resources. Windows NT generates a unique security ID for each user account, and that unique ID is stored with the user's permissions and rights as part of that user's profile. When a user attempts to log on, Security Account Manager checks the logon information against the user information in the user accounts database and tries to authenticate the logon. If it is successful, the Local Security Authority creates an access token for the user, and the user is then logged on.

In the Windows NT security model, the two types of user accounts are called *global user accounts* and *local user accounts*. Global user accounts are users accounts established in those users' home domain. Global users are authenticated by the primary or secondary domain controllers or through trust relationships established with other Windows NT domains.

Local user accounts participate in a domain through some type of remote logon. In this case, a remote logon isn't necessarily a remote communications link such as a dial-up connection; instead, a remote logon means simply that the user is "remote" from the domain (s)he is logging on to. The workstation and user do not belong to any domain other than the domain the user account has been added to, so a user who is a local user and not a global user must be authenticated only by the Windows NT server that the account is being created on. That user cannot be authenticated through a trust relationship with another domain. Sound confusing? It's really not. For example, you may have a network composed of Windows NT domains and Apple Macintosh systems. Users that belong to the Macintosh community are local users and are subject to the limitations of that user type.

Creating User Accounts

Let's walk through the steps that add a user to the Windows NT domain. You manage user accounts with either the User Manager or the User Manager for Domains. The only difference between the options is that the User Manager for Domains lets you access user account information on other trusted NT domains.

1. To open the User Manager, click Start and choose Programs, Administrative Tools, and User Manager. Figure 4.1 shows the User Manager dialog box.

Figure 4.1

User Manager

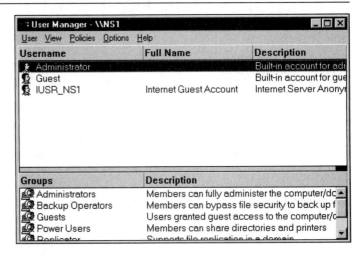

2. To add a user, select New User from the User menu. You are presented with the User Properties dialog box in Figure 4.2. Type a Username, Full Name, Description of the user account, and the password. You may need to adjust the check boxes in this dialog box; the meanings are defined in Table 4.1.

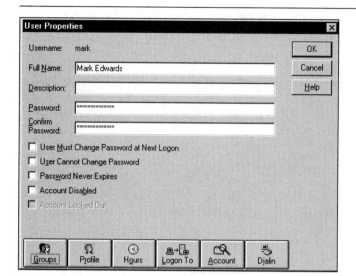

Figure 4.2
User Properties Dialog Box

TABLE 4.1 USER MANAGER CHECKBOX DEFINITIONS

User Must Change Password at Next Logon	Establishes the password as temporary until the next time the user logs on, at which point the user must change it.
User Cannot Change Password	Prevents the user from changing the account password.
Password Never Expires	This password never expires and is not required to be changed at regular intervals. Selecting this checkbox *is not recommended!*
Account Disabled	This account is disabled and cannot be used to log on to the network.

I recommend that you not use the User Cannot Change Password setting, because this setting circumvents effective password policies. You should routinely change your account passwords. Although this setting could be useful in instances where a Windows NT service must log on to the system with a user account to function properly, you could easily change passwords for your system services.

3. After you have completed the main dialog box, you need to review the other settings, so click Groups. You'll see a dialog box like the one shown in Figure 4.3.

Figure 4.3

Group Memberships Dialog Box

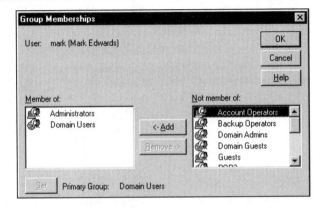

Notice that the two groups have different icons. The globe behind two users represents a global user group. A terminal behind two users represents a local user group. We discuss global and local user groups in the next section. In this example, we assume you're adding a user to the Administrators Group, so highlight the Administrators group and click Add. Then click OK to establish the group.

4. To review the user profile, click Profile in Figure 4.2. The dialog box shown in Figure 4.4 will appear.

Figure 4.4

User Environment Profile Dialog Box

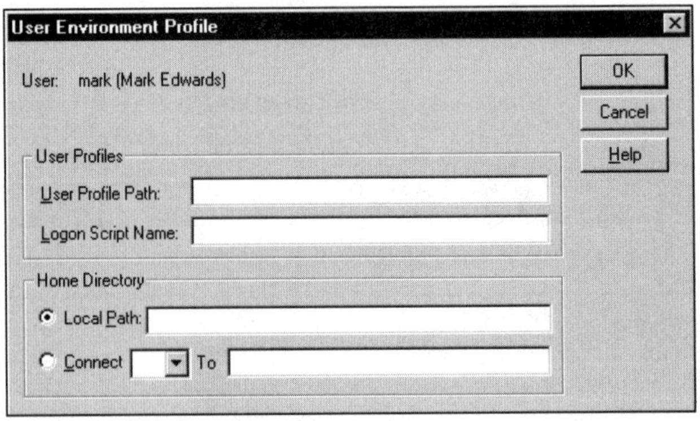

The settings in the User Environment Profile dialog box can be very useful in managing users. You can set the Profile Path, Logon Script Name, Local

Path, and connection information. We won't set any of these options for our example, but here are their definitions:

- Profile Path lets you define local, mandatory, or roaming profiles for the user. Profiles store various aspects of the user's account, including desktop settings and program settings. Local profiles are created the first time a user logs on and are available every time the user logs on. Roaming profiles are downloaded from the path specified whenever the user logs on at any machine on the network and are updated when the user logs off. Mandatory profiles are created by an administrator, can't be modified by the user, and are updated when the user logs off.

- Logon Script Name is the name of a command file or batch file to be run on the client machine when the user logs on.

- Local Path lets you define a modified path for the user where you can locate the user's files and programs. This path is the default for File Open and Save As dialog boxes.

- Connect To assigns a network drive and path to be used as the local path. It overrides the Local Path setting.

    Click OK to return to the dialog box in Figure 4.2.

5. Next, let's look at the Hours dialog box. Click Hours in Figure 4.2, and you should see the Logon Hours dialog box (Figure 4.5).

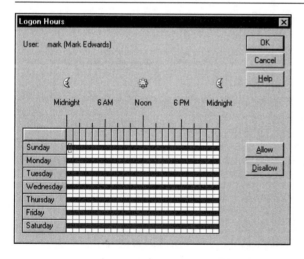

Figure 4.5

Logon Hours Dialog Box

Here, you can define the hours a user can log on to the network. By default, all users are allowed to log on at any time of day, any day of the week. However, you may want to restrict your users unless you are sure they need to access the network during non-standard business hours. Simply click the hours and the correct day, then click Allow or Disallow. The allowed times are indicated in blue. Click OK to return to the User Properties dialog box.

6. Now let's set workstation options. In Figure 4.2, click Logon To, which presents the dialog box in Figure 4.6.

Figure 4.6
Logon Workstations Dialog Box

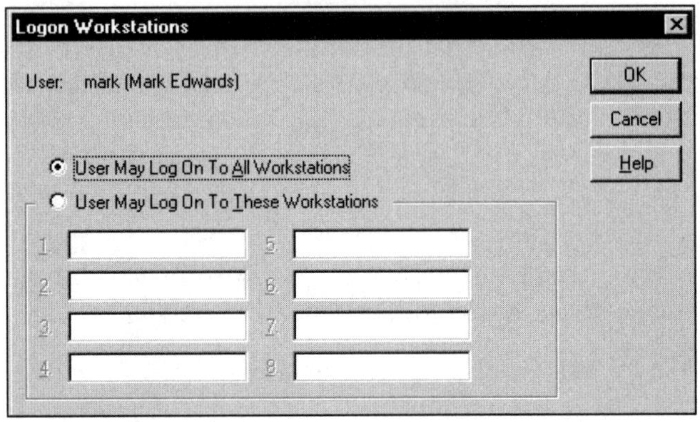

The Logon Workstations dialog box has two basic settings: User May Log On To All Workstations, and User May Log On To These Workstations. These settings let you restrict the workstations that a user can log on to the network from. By default, the user can log on to the network from any workstation. To restrict the user, click User May Log On To These Workstations and type workstation names in the fields below. Click OK to return to the User Properties dialog box.

7. Now let's look at account information. In Figure 4.2, click Account, and the Account Information dialog box (Figure 4.7) will appear. The first parameter you can set determines when the account expires. After an account expires, the user cannot log on until the account is reset. By default, accounts are set to never expire. However, pay attention to this account setting and be sure to set a short-term or temporary account to expire so that you avoid leaving a back door open to an ex-employee or a former temporary employee.

At this dialog box, you can also set the type of account, but because account types are covered later in this chapter, we won't go into them here. For our example of adding a user to the Administrators group, select Global Account. After your settings are complete, click OK.

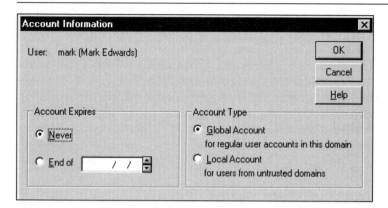

Figure 4.7
*Account
Information
Dialog Box*

8. The last item to review here is the Dialin Information dialog box, which you open by clicking Dialin in Figure 4.2. Windows NT uses domain-based security for Remote Access users. Figure 4.8 shows the dialog box where you define whether and how a user dials in to the network.

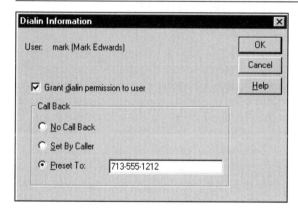

Figure 4.8
*Dialin Information
Dialog Box*

To give the user access to the network via a dial-in connection, simply select the Grant Dialin Permission to User checkbox. Next, review the call-back settings, which define how the user connects when (s)he calls in. Your options are

- No Call Back — the user is connected immediately without a call back. This setting offers the lowest level of security because no verification is performed.

- Set By Caller — the user provides a number that the dial-in server calls before it lets the user log on to the network. This setting offers a medium level of security that works well when users travel.

- Preset To — the user is called at a predefined phone number set by the administrator and then is logged on to the network. This setting offers the highest level of security because the user must call from a predetermined location and phone number and only the administrator can change it.

The call back features add a layer of security — you can ensure that the user trying to log on remotely is doing so from an authorized phone number. If you implement Remote Access Server (RAS) on your network, I highly recommend that you use the highest level of call back security that is feasible for your users. Intruders love unattended dial-up systems! When you've set the Dialin permission for the user, click OK to return to the dialog box in Figure 4.2.

Now we've gone through the steps for adding users to the Windows NT Server and Windows NT domain. We discuss the complexities of user security policies and permissions later in this book.

GROUP SECURITY

The Windows NT method of grouping users is a powerful way to manage many users. The features and controls help ease administrative duties and help control access and permissions. This section covers the ins and outs of establishing a secure user community.

OVERVIEW

User groups are collections of users who have the same set of rights and privileges. Windows NT has several helpful predefined groups. The most important predefined group is the Administrators Group. Users who belong to this group have complete control over domain security and certain hosts on the network, so be careful which users you assign to this group. Users in this group can make detrimental changes to your security settings.

In Windows NT, you may also define your own groups. Once a group is defined, you can establish customized rights and privileges for the group. For example, if your system includes contact management software, you may want that software accessible to certain users and inaccessible to others. You could establish a group called "Contacts," give that group permission to access the shared directory where the contact management software resides, and add your selected users to the new group. You can easily give groups of users access to resources without giving each user those permissions one by one.

As I mentioned earlier, Windows NT has two types of groups, *global groups* and *local groups*. Global groups contain only individual user accounts for the domain in which the global group is created; global groups cannot contain other groups. Global groups are useful in granting permissions and rights to access local resources or resources in trusted Windows NT domains. Windows NT includes three predefined global groups: Domain Admins, Domain Users, and Domain Guests.

Local groups can contain both users and global groups that have access rights and permissions to object resources on the network. Local groups allow the export of users and groups from other domains into the local domain. A local group has permissions and rights only inside the domain in which it was created. Windows NT Server includes six predefined local groups: Administrators, Users, Guests, Backup Operators, Replicator, and Power Users. If you install Windows NT Server as a primary or secondary domain controller, three additional local groups are established: Account Operators, Print Operators, and Server Operators. These groups are discussed in detail in Chapter 3.

ADDING USERS TO GROUPS

Managing groups and adding users to groups is a simple process. To begin, you must be logged on with administrator privileges, and the users must already be in the user database. Then simply open the User Manager and double-click the group you want to administer. In the example that follows, we add a user to the Administrators group.

1. Click Start and select Programs, Administrative Tools, User Manager or User Manager for Domains. The User Manager dialog box (Figure 4.9) appears.

2. Double-click the Administrators group in the lower window to bring up its local Group Properties dialog box (Figure 4.10). It includes all the information related to the group and buttons that let you add and remove members.

3. Click Add; another dialog box will appear, shown in Figure 4.11, that displays all the users and groups. Select the user you want to add from the list of names and click Add. The user is added to the group, and the name is shown in the Add Names box in the bottom window. Click OK to return to the local Group Properties dialog box.

Figure 4.9

User Manager

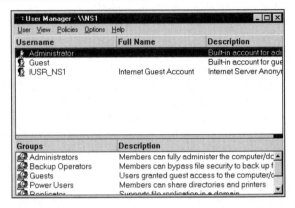

Figure 4.10

Local Group Properties Dialog Box

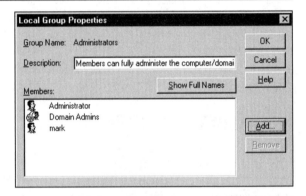

Figure 4.11

Add Users and Groups Dialog Box

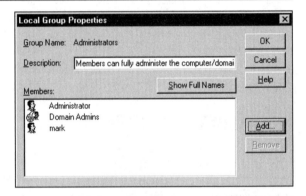

4. When you click OK in step 3, the user becomes part of the Administrator group. The user is listed in the Members list box (Figure 4.12). Click OK to close the dialog box.

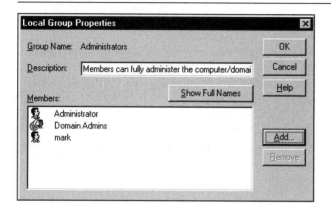

Figure 4.12
Local Group Properties with User Added

Manipulating groups of users is a powerful feature of Windows NT that gives you lots of control over security and other aspects of your NT domain. Be sure you make groups work to your advantage, because they can minimize a lot of the tedium you'd face if you managed users as individuals. In Chapter 6, I outline some changes you should make to some of the pre-existing local groups.

FILE SYSTEM SECURITY

File systems are at the heart of any computing system and network. Most operating systems offer the same basic sets of file system security features, and none should be overlooked or taken for granted. Proper understanding of the underlying file system in Windows NT gives you invaluable insight into the security of Windows NT servers and workstations. This section walks you through establishing security controls in this environment.

OVERVIEW

Windows NT Server 4.0 supports two basic types of file systems: FAT and NTFS. Although Windows NT 3.51 also supported the High Performance File System (HPFS), which was developed for IBM's OS/2, as of Windows NT 4.0, that file system is no longer supported by Microsoft. Chapter 3 contains an in-depth discussion of both FAT and NTFS so I only summarize their features here.

The FAT file system has no security features to speak of. You can set the attributes of a file to "system" or "read only," which makes it more difficult to accidentally delete a file. The only real advantage of the FAT system is that MS-DOS supports it. If you're connected to the Internet, FAT is a bad choice. *Don't use it.* The only exception is if you're using a non-Intel-based computer system, such as the DEC Alpha. RISC-based processors such as the Alpha require a small DOS partition for Windows NT to be installed and run correctly. In these cases, create only a small partition — about 5 MB — to meet Windows NT's needs. Be sure to install the operating system on the NTFS partition, and do not use the smaller DOS partition for anything other than the few files Windows NT places there during installation. Be sure you don't accidentally give your FTP server access to that partition!

In contrast, NTFS offers robust features to control access to the hard drives and their contents. It also offers significant performance advantages over FAT file systems. NTFS features include

- Support for setting permissions on files and directories
- Faster access to larger sequential access files and random access files
- Long file names and directory names, which can be up to 254 characters long
- Automatic conversion of long file names to the DOS 8+3 standard when the files are accessed by DOS workstations on the network
- Files and directories sharing with Macintosh systems
- Efficient use of drive space

After you convert your file system to NTFS, you can't access the NTFS partition through DOS. DOS doesn't understand NTFS and cannot read its data formats correctly. To get around this problem, you can obtain a utility from the Internet called NTFSDOS, which is a set of drivers loaded during a DOS boot sequence that lets DOS read an NTFS partition. Using NTFSDOS is a heavily debated topic, and I believe that NTFSDOS poses several risks to security. We discuss NTFSDOS in detail in Chapter 9 — be sure to understand the implications before deciding to use it in your environment.

If you are one of the many administrators converting a Novell Netware server to Windows NT Server, I offer you some words of caution: You cannot simply convert the file system to NTFS — this process destroys all the data on the Netware volume. To convert properly, first back up your Netware server and install Windows NT Server. After Windows NT is installed and your hard drives are formatted to NTFS, restore your data to the hard drive.

SHARING DIRECTORIES AND FILES

Now let's talk about Windows NT file system security. File system security has four basic parts: share permissions, directory permissions, auditing, and ownership. Servers on a network act as repositories for various types of data files and software programs that can be accessed and run across the network by users. However, before files and programs can be accessed by users across the network, they must be *shared*.

Sharing a directory lets users connect to the shared object (the *share*) and use it as if it were a local drive on the user's workstation. Once a directory has been shared, its contents are accessible to the users who have permission to access the share. The administrator may impose restrictions on the shared directory, providing a higher degree of control over that resource.

Sharing directories is easy. You begin by opening Windows NT Explorer, as shown in Figure 4.13. (The Explorer is Microsoft's replacement for the File Manager and first appeared in Windows 95.)

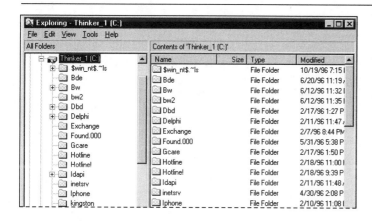

Figure 4.13
Windows NT Explorer

1. To share a directory, find the directory in the left window of the Explorer. Right-click the directory name and select Sharing from the menu (Figure 4.14).

2. The Sharing dialog box has three tabs: General, Sharing, and Security (Figure 4.15). The Sharing tab is selected by default, so let's begin there. At first, Not Shared is selected for the directory. To share the directory, select Shared As; the directory name will appear in the Share Name field automatically. The name in this field is the name users see. In some cases, it may be useful to use a descriptive share name like MSOffice, and in others disguising the function of the share by giving it a nondescript

Figure 4.14
Explorer's Directory Menu

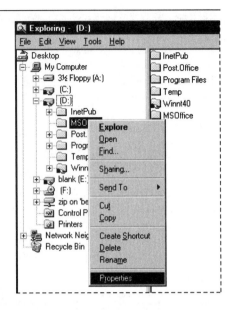

Figure 4.15
Directory Sharing Dialog Box

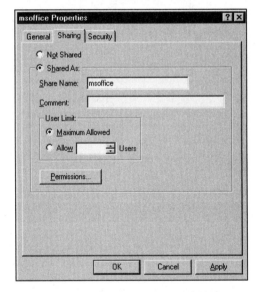

name is better. Because users can also see the Comment field, you can use this field to give more information to users. For instance, you may have an old version of MSOffice installed along with a new version of MSOffice; you could use the comment field to describe the versions, such as "MSOffice Version 6.0" or "MSOffice Version 7.0". The comment field is not required; however the Share Name field must be completed.

3. Next, let's look at the User Limit settings. These settings can be very useful for controlling server loads. You can select two basic settings: Maximum Allowed and Allow Users. Maximum Allowed means that Windows NT lets users connect to the share, up to the maximum number of users that the server can handle. The Allow Users option lets you limit the number of simultaneous connections to the share.

   This feature can be very beneficial in controlling various aspects of the shared directory, depending on your needs. For example, you might want to let only a few people connect to the share to ensure that the server doesn't get overloaded. Or you might have a set number of licenses for a software package in a shared directory and you don't want to exceed the software license.

4. The final task on this tab is setting permissions for the share. Clicking Permissions brings up the dialog box shown in Figure 4.16.

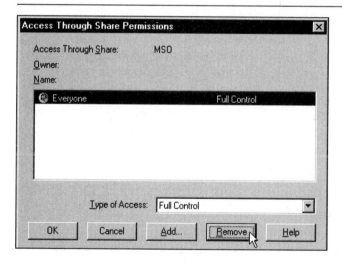

Figure 4.16

Access Through Share Permissions Dialog Box

By default, each share you define allows access to the Everyone group on Windows NT, which encompasses every user in the domain. In this instance, we don't want everyone to have access, so we remove this group by selecting Everyone and clicking Remove. Remember that you should establish a new group that includes all users and use it instead of the Everyone group. If you establish a share that actually will be used by everyone, assign your replacement group to the permission list instead.

5. We want to add permission for a group of users to access the share, and we have two choices: adding individual users one by one or adding a user group. Click Add from the Access Through Share Permissions dialog box. You'll see a dialog box like the one in Figure 4.17.

Figure 4.17

Add Users and Groups Dialog Box

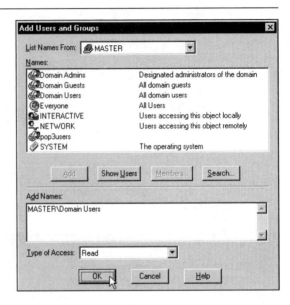

The Add Users and Groups dialog box shows all the defined groups in your domain, with the Add Names list box empty. To view the domain users in the list along with the groups, click Show Users. In this example, we want to give access permission to a user group called Administrators, so select the Administrators group in the list and click Add to put the Administrators group in the Add Names list.

Next, we define the type of shared access the group can have by clicking Type of Access. You have four types of access to choose from:

- No Access — The groups in the Add Names list do not have access to this share. You can use this option to complement the Everyone group. Give the Everyone group access to the share and exclude users and groups in the Add Names box from having access to the share.

- Read — The defined set of users and groups have read-only access, meaning that they cannot change, delete, or modify the contents of the share in any way; they can only read from it.

- Change — Users can read and write to the shared resource, but they cannot delete it.

- Full Control — Users and groups of users have the ability to do with the share what they may. They can read it, write to it, execute programs in it, add files and programs to it, and even delete it entirely. Be careful about giving this type of access to your shares. Assigning Full Control can defeat your attempt to secure your network server's resources.

Bear in mind that these options define access to the shared resource, not access to the directory that already existed before it was shared. Directory permissions must also be set to allow users access. We want the Administrators to have full control over the share, so select Full Control and click OK to establish the permissions and close the dialog box. Click OK again to close the Access Through Share Permissions dialog box. At this point, you are back at the Sharing tab (Figure 4.15).

6. Now that we have completed the addition of the permissions for the Administrators to access the share, click the Security tab. The dialog box shown in Figure 4.18 will appear. This dialog box is divided into three areas: Permissions, Auditing, and Ownership.

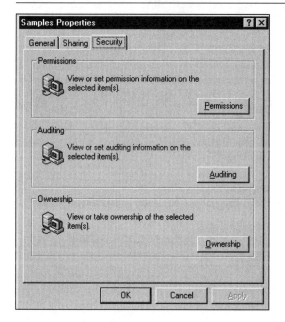

Figure 4.18
Security Tab

7. First, click Permissions. The dialog box shown in Figure 4.19 will appear.

Figure 4.19

*Directory Permissions
Dialog Box*

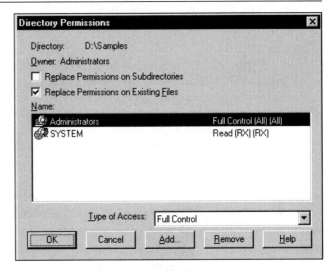

As you see, it is similar to the one you use to add users and groups to the share; however, here you assign directory permissions, not the share permissions.

Let's examine the types of access you can assign to the shared directory. The options are slightly different than those found on the Sharing permissions property page. You can assign nine types of access to a shared directory:

- No Access — No access of any type is allowed to the files in the directory. Specifying No Access for a user prevents any access even if the user belongs to a group that has access to the directory.

- List — Allows viewing of files and directories and navigating into the directory's subdirectories.

- Read — Allows the same permissions as the List permission plus the ability to run programs in the directory and its subdirectories.

- Add — Allows adding files to the directory and its subdirectories but does not allow access to the files contained in the directory unless access is allowed by other directory or file permission settings.

- Add & Read — Allows the permissions of the Add permission plus the permissions of the Read permission.

- Change — allows the same permissions as the Add & Read permissions plus deleting the directory, its subdirectories, and files.

- Full Control — allows users and groups of users complete control over the directory. Full Control gives the user Change permission plus the ability to change permissions on the directory and its files and take ownership of the directory and its files. As with the Share Permissions, Full Control can defeat your attempts to secure your network server's resources.

- Special Directory Access — presents a special dialog box, like the one shown in Figure 4.20, that lets you customize the permission settings for this directory and its files.

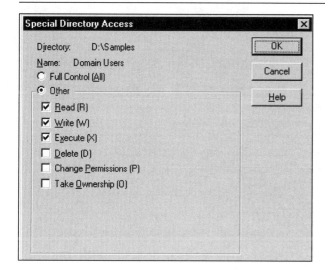

Figure 4.20
Special Directory Access

- Special File Access — allows the same permissions as the Special Directory Access settings with one addition, Access Not Specified, which prevents files from inheriting permissions from the directory. By default, all files in a directory inherit the permissions of the directory they reside in. The Access Not Specified prevents this inheritance, which lets you customize the permissions of each file. Figure 4.21 shows an example of this dialog box.

Figure 4.21

Special File Access

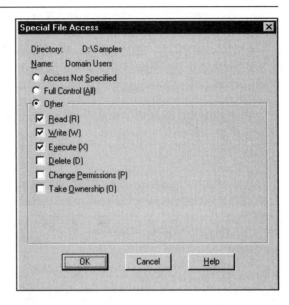

The settings of the Special Directory Access dialog box are itemized below:

- Read (R) — Allows viewing the names of files and subdirectories
- Write (W) — Allows adding files and subdirectories
- Execute (X) — Allows changing to subdirectories in the directory
- Delete (D) — Allows deleting the directory
- Change Permissions (P) — Allows changing the directory's permissions
- Take Ownership (O) — Allows taking ownership of the directory

8. Now that we've covered file and directory permissions, close the dialog box by clicking OK, which takes you back to the Directory Permissions dialog box (Figure 4.19). You need to understand the ramifications of the two check boxes on this page. The Replace Permissions on Subdirectories box propagates your permission settings all the way down the subdirectory tree. Check this box if you want your permissions to be the same on all files and subdirectories of this share. The default sets permissions on the directory and its files, not its subdirectories.

By default, permission settings apply to files in the directory as well as the directory itself. Clear the Replace Permissions on Existing Files check box to apply your permission settings to the directory only, but remember, if the Replace Permissions on Subdirectories box is checked, the subdirectories will have the permission settings, too. Click OK to close the Directory Permissions dialog box.

9. Next, let's look at the Auditing portion of the Security tab (Figure 4.18). Click Auditing to display the Directory Auditing dialog box (Figure 4.22).

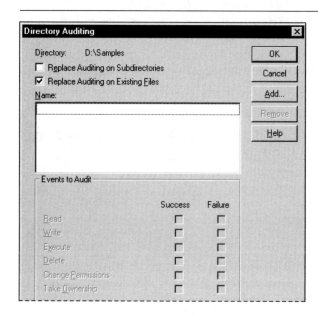

Figure 4.22
Directory Auditing Dialog Box

First, add users and groups to the audit list by clicking Add; the process is very similar to adding users and groups in previous steps. Any users or groups added to the list become part of an audit trail that is written to the Event Log for your review. For our example, select the Administrators group.

You can audit several events for a given share; the audit trails are written to the Windows NT event log. The events that may be audited are

- Read — Audits the display of file names, attributes, permissions, and owner

- Write — Audits the creation of subdirectories and files, changes to attributes, and display of permissions and owner

- Execute — Audits the display of attributes, permissions, and owner; and switching subdirectories

- Delete — Audits the deletion of the directory

- Change Permissions — Audits the changes to directory permissions

- Take Ownership — Audits the changes to directory ownership

Select the events you want to audit, then look at the two check boxes at the top of the dialog box. Although their names are slightly different, they present essentially the same options as those discussed in Step 8 and have the same effect on how the audit trail is established. Select the Replace Auditing on Subdirectories and Replace Auditing on Existing Files check boxes as necessary and click OK to set the audit trails and close the dialog box.

10. Next, let's review the Ownership portion of the Security tab (Figure 4.18) and its effect on security. Click Ownership to open the Owner dialog box (Figure 4.23).

Figure 4.23
Owner Dialog Box

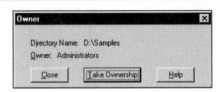

This dialog box has three simple buttons: Close, Take Ownership, and, of course, Help.

All files and directories on an NTFS partition under Windows NT have a single owner. When a file or directory is created, the person creating it is its initial owner. The owner of an object has the ability to grant permissions for that object, which controls how the file or directory is used. The owner and members of the Administrator group can grant permission to other users to own a file or directory.

Any administrator can own a directory or file; however, an administrator cannot actually *transfer* ownership to other users (but they can grant the *right* to own), preserving the security mechanism designed into Windows NT. For example, if an administrator takes ownership of an object and changes the permissions, then that administrator can access a file on which you have set the No Access permission. If you check the ownership of that object, you can see that the ownership had somehow changed, and by examining the Event Logs, you could find out who had violated the permission you previously set on the file object.

The best practice is to check object ownerships regularly. Equally important, you should establish a firm degree of auditing and always include in your security routines a check of the event log for security-related events. I cover auditing and the event log in detail later in this chapter.

11. Finally, let's look at the General tab (Figure 4.24). The General tab displays information and lets you set the attributes of a file or directory. First you see the file or directory name, along with its associated icon. Next, you see Type, Location, Size, and Contains information for the file or

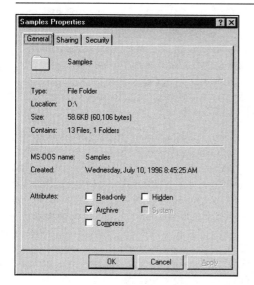

Figure 4.24
General Tab

directory. In Figure 4.24, the Type is a File Folder, also known as a directory, that is located on D:\ and is 58.6K. The Contains data is the number of subdirectories and files in the folder. Then we see the DOS file name and the day, date, and time the directory was created. The DOS file name is the 8+3 form of the file name that DOS-based operating systems use.

At the bottom of this page, we see the file attributes. File attributes give you some control over the directory. The five attributes of any file or directory under Windows NT are defined as follows:

- Read-only — Selecting this box prevents the file from being rewritten or deleted accidentally.

- Archive — Selecting this box means that the file should be archived. Some backup software programs use this setting to determine whether a file needs to be backed up.

- Compress — Selecting this box means that this directory will be compressed. Windows NT can compress files and directories on the fly, which can save precious disk space.

- Hidden — Selecting this box hides the file from the DOS DIR command and Explorer. Hidden directories and files cannot be used unless you know their name and location. Hiding files can be useful in some cases, using the basic principle that "what others can't see, they can't mess with." However, beware: there are several ways of finding all hidden files on a given hard-disk partition, so don't assume hidden files and directories are safe.

• System — System files typically are part of the operating system and are required for it to run properly. By default, system files do not show up in the Windows NT Explorer. Never delete files with this attribute unless you are absolutely certain that you know exactly what the file is and that you can do without it.

You can see that two sets of parameters establish file system security: file system parameters and shared resource parameters. File system security parameters actually sit underneath the shared resource security parameters, and each complements the other. The combination provides a great deal of control over access to the resource.

To clarify: essentially, file system security and shared resource security are the same in that they offer control over access to a resource. However, they work in tandem, since each relies on the other. For example, if you shared a directory called Temp on your hard drive and gave the Domain Admins group permission to access the share, their attempts at access only work completely if the permissions on the Temp directory itself *also* allow access permission for the Domain Admins group.

Exercise caution when establishing shared resources, and take the time to control them correctly. Also, don't overlook the importance of establishing audit trails for your resource usage. Audit trails do generate work for the network to handle, but the cost is far less than a potential intrusion.

PRINTER SECURITY

Printer security is an important issue but can be overlooked when you establish the printer as a shared object on the network. You don't want someone to hijack your print queue and take copies of your documents, do you? Establishing printer security is not that different from establishing shared file and directory resources; however, it has its own set of parameters that should be configured carefully. Printer security comes into play when a user logs on to the printer server itself at the server's local console or connects to a shared printer resource across the network.

1. For example, let's assume that you have already installed an HP Deskjet 660C printer driver, and you want to establish the device as a shared object on your network. Begin by clicking Start and selecting Settings, then Printers to bring up the Printers folder, where you see the icon for your installed printer(s).

2. Right-click on the HP Deskjet 660C icon and select Properties. The dialog box shown in Figure 4.25 appears; you can see that it has several tabs.

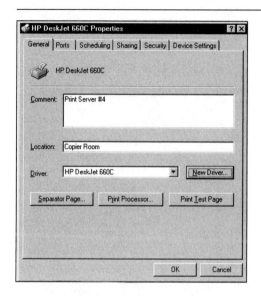

Figure 4.25
Printer Properties

Because we are focusing on printer security in this section, I only cover the options that pertain to security. At the General tab, which is the default, type information in the Comment and Location fields as necessary and make sure the correct printer driver for your printer is selected in the driver field.

3. Click the Scheduling tab to display a dialog box like that shown in Figure 4.26. On this tab, we consider the Available and Priority settings. The Available setting lets you define the times of day the printer is available to produce output. Select From to enable the From and To time settings. This setting is useful for limiting printer access to only certain times of day. Any attempt to use the printer outside this time window will fail, and the user will be unable to print.

   The Priority setting lets you adjust the priority of the printing order of your documents. Higher-priority documents print before lower-priority documents. In this example, we leave the priority set to the default setting of low, or priority one, which means low-priority documents have the same priority as higher-priority documents.

4. Next, click the Sharing tab to display the dialog box shown in Figure 4.27. Here we establish the printer share and assign permissions for users and groups. First, select Shared and type a name in the Share Name field. The

Figure 4.26
Scheduling Tab

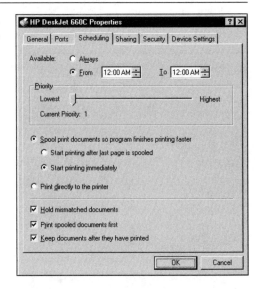

Figure 4.27
Sharing Tab

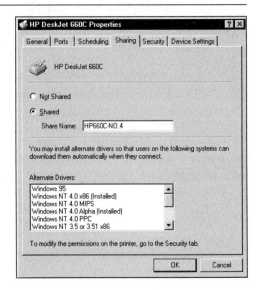

Alternate Drivers list box lets you install alternate drivers for other operating systems that may need to use the printer share. This particular setting has no impact on security, but select any additional drivers you may need. Bear in mind that you need the diskettes for each print driver that you select to install, so have them handy.

5. Click the Security tab. The dialog box, shown in Figure 4.28, should look familiar if you read about file security.

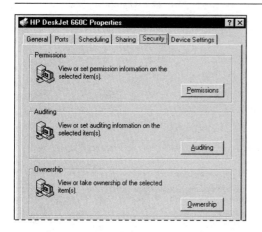

Figure 4.28
Security Tab

First, click Permissions to display a dialog box like that shown in Figure 4.29.

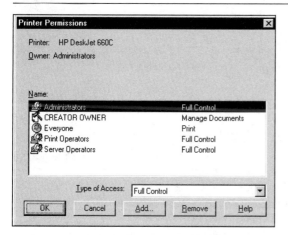

Figure 4.29
Printer Permissions

Click Add to add users and groups to the Name box. To adjust the type of access for any user or group assigned to this share, select that name from the list and click Type of Access. The four types of printer access are

* No Access — Any user or group has absolutely no access to this shared printer. This setting is useful in conjunction with the Everyone

group, simply excluding the users and groups that you do not want to have access.

- Print — Users and groups can send documents to this shared printer.
- Manage Documents — Users and groups can manipulate the documents in the print queue. They can re-prioritize them, place them on hold for printing at a later time, or delete them.
- Full Control — Users and groups have the same rights as in the Manage Documents permission and can delete the share or change the owner of the printer share as well.

Click OK to return to the Properties dialog box.

6. Click Auditing on the Security tab to display the dialog box in Figure 4.30.

Figure 4.30

Printer Auditing

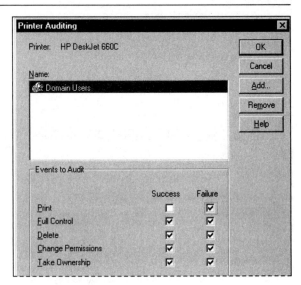

In this example, we establish auditing for everyone, so click Add, select the Everyone group (or your new group that gives access to all users), and click OK. You can audit the success and failure of several actions: Print, Full Control, Delete, Change Permissions, and Ownership. For this example, we assume that we want to audit the success or failure of Change Permissions and Delete, which deletes the share, so select both the Success and Failure boxes for those two audit types. Click OK to complete the audit settings.

To establish any type of auditing, you must use User Manager to turn on auditing for the entire system. Doing so implements individual auditing for some aspects of Windows NT but certainly not all aspects, and in these cases, the audit switches simply act like an On/Off switch.

7. Now let's click Ownership on the Security tab. A dialog box letting you take ownership of the share appears. Here, the owner can adjust the permissions of the share in the same way as the owners of files and directories can. Click OK to close the ownership dialog.

You can now click OK to close the Print Sharing dialog box. You have successfully established this printer as a resource that users and groups on your network share.

LOGGING AND AUDITING

Windows NT logs three types of events: System, Security, and Application. Each type keeps its own records, and each log can be viewed in the Event log in the Administrative Tools folder. Each log tracks a basic set of parameters for its events: the date and time, the source of the event, the event subcategory, the event ID, user-related event entries, and the machine name of the system where a particular event occurred.

The Event log, like most utilities in Windows NT, uses standard icons to represent the urgency of a log entry. The information icon is a blue circle with the letter "i" in the center, the warning icon is a yellow circle with the letter "i" in the center, and the error icon is a red octagon with the word "stop" in the center. Information entries simply give you information and usually do not indicate a serious problem. Warning entries are items that Windows NT warns you about because they may require some action. Error log entries are serious; you should always handle them immediately.

By default, Windows NT establishes some level of logging. You can enhance the logging levels of a Windows NT server by turning on the audit trails in the User Manager. Open the User Manager and select Audit from the Policies menu. Windows NT displays the Audit Policy dialog box (Figure 4.31).

Here, you can enable the success or failure of several actions for auditing:

- Logon and Logoff — Tracks each attempt to log on to or off of the server directly or through a domain controller; also tracks network connections.

- File and Object Access — Tracks the use of those resources in the domain for which you set auditing; also tracks print spooling.

- Use of User Rights — Tracks how user rights are used. When a user exercises a right, it's logged for tracking (except for logons and logoffs, which are tracked by the Logon and Logoff setting).

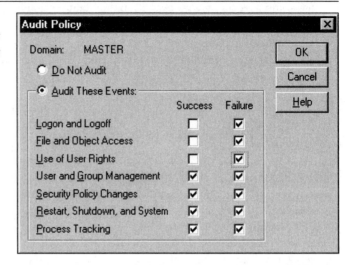

Figure 4.31
User Manager Audit Policy Dialog Box

- User and Group Management — Tracks the creation, change, or deletion of a user account or group; when a user account was renamed, enabled, or disabled; and password changes.

- Security Policy Changes — Tracks changes in the User rights, Audit policies, or trust relationships of the domain.

- Restart, Shutdown, and System — Tracks when a user either starts up or shuts down the server and when an event occurs that affects the entire security system or event log.

- Process Tracking — Tracks program activation, indirect object access, and process exits.

To be security aware, you should always use some sort of auditing configuration and review the logs routinely. Don't be too concerned about the disk space the logs use, because you can adjust the size of your logs with the Log Settings option on the Event log's Log menu.

SYSTEM LOG

Now let's look at some log entries you may encounter. First, let's look at a System event. Assuming you already have the Event log open (Start button, Programs, Administrative Tools, Event log), select System from the Log menu. In the window, you'll see a list of events that have been logged. You can quickly view details about any event by simply double-clicking an entry in the list (Figure 4.32).

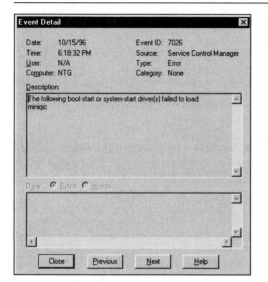

Figure 4.32
System Event Detail

The System Log tracks all successful and failed events, including events that take place during system startup. Typical system events include services starting, drivers loading, disk capacity checks, and other network administration concerns. The particular event shown in Figure 4.32 was logged because a MINIQIC tape backup driver failed to load properly.

SECURITY LOG

The Security log, selected from the Log menu and shown in Figure 4.33, tracks all security-related events.

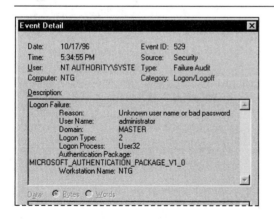

Figure 4.33
Security Event Detail

Typical entries are generated by the system using built-in security policies and policies you define while establishing audit trails. The security log shows items such as logon attempts and object access. In the example in Figure 4.33, a failed logon attempt shows someone attempted to log on with the Administrator account at 5:34 PM on October 17, 1996. The entry also says that the system used in the failed attempt was called MACHINE. The reason for the entry was an unknown user name or bad password. Some words of wisdom: *Watch your security log religiously.* As I mentioned earlier, most security breaches go undetected for some time after they occur.

APPLICATION LOG

Application logs contain information generated by application programs on the network. An *application* in this case is any type of software other than the Windows NT operating system. In Figure 4.34, the log entry shows that the DNS server ran its routine maintenance as scheduled.

Figure 4.34
Application Event Detail

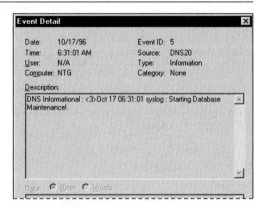

Once again, never underestimate the value of auditing and monitoring. Audit trails and the Event log are invaluable security tools that you should overuse. Logs can lead you directly to information valuable to your security efforts. They can detect intrusion attempts while they are occurring, and they can help you track down a perpetrator quickly. Be certain that your security procedures mandate the regular use of these tools.

RAS SECURITY CONSIDERATIONS

In this section, I don't give instructions about installing the Remote Access Service (RAS). Instead, let's establish RAS dial-up security. Establishing user accounts for RAS is similar to establishing user accounts for local network access, with a few additions.

First, grant your RAS users the ability to dial in to the network by adjusting the user parameters with the User Manager, as described in the User Security section of this chapter. Next, you should examine the call-back setting for the user; remember, the call-back setting lets you force a user to dial in to the network from a specific phone number. For a more detailed explanation of the callback setting, see the User Security section of this chapter. For security's sake, you should consider always using RAS's callback feature.

After users connect to the network through RAS, they have the same rights and privileges they have when they log on to a workstation that is physically wired to the network. In fact, RAS treats a modem as an Ethernet device and extension of the network.

Another important aspect of RAS security is your ability to define the protocols that can be used over a dial-up connection. If parts of your network use a protocol like IPX/SPX and you don't want dial-up users accessing those parts, simply disable that protocol under RAS when you install and configure it. This method of isolation is commonly known as a protocol barrier.

All user access via RAS is logged to the Event log, and you can review it with the Event Viewer. Also, you can use the RAS Administrator program to monitor in real time all RAS connections to the network.

MICROSOFT TCP/IP SECURITY

Windows NT 4.0 includes TCP/IP network configuration options that let you filter packets from certain types of protocols destined for the TCP/IP network. You can limit three types of network traffic: TCP, UDP, and IP. Traffic is limited based on the port address that is the traffic's destination. It stands to reason that if traffic cannot reach a particular TCP/IP port on your server, it cannot present much of a security risk.

For a list of service types and their associated ports, look at the Services file in the \%SYSTEM_ROOT%\SYSTEM32\DRIVERS\ETC directory, where %SYSTEM_ROOT% is the directory where you installed Windows NT (such as WINNT40). This file lists most but not all of the common protocols.

Let's look at the TCP/IP security settings available under Windows NT 4.0.

1. First, open the Network dialog box from the Control Panel, and select the Protocols tab. Double-click TCP/IP Protocol, click Advanced, select the Enable Security check box, and finally, click Configure. The TCP/IP Security dialog box (Figure 4.35) will appear. This box lets you set three groups of settings: TCP, UDP, and IP. For each, you can choose to Permit All or Permit Only. For example, let's assume we want to allow access only to the Web server port, which is normally port 80 and uses TCP.

Figure 4.35

TCP/IP Security Settings

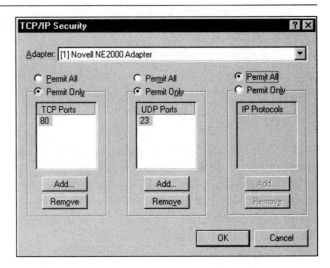

2. To restrict access to all TCP ports except port 80 for the Web server, first click Permit Only in the TCP group of settings.
3. Next, click Add, type **80** for the port number, and click OK.

You just successfully eliminated all TCP traffic to your server except Web traffic destined for TCP port 80. You can use this dialog box to permit access to any ports — you need only know which protocol type it is and the port number for the protocol.

Packet filtering is a powerful way to control access to your server. After you turn it on at the Enable Security check box, the packet filtering mechanism denies all access to all ports. This feature is the sign of a good filtering subsystem because you must make a conscious decision to allow access to each port individually. Although making these decisions on individual ports can be a tedious task, the benefits of taking the time greatly outweigh the cost. In many cases, using this feature can also save you the expense of an external packet filter. Don't be afraid to implement this part of Microsoft's TCP/IP security.

In addition, Microsoft introduced support for the Point-to-Point Tunneling Protocol (PPTP) in Windows NT 4.0. PPTP is a new networking transmission technology that supports multiprotocol virtual private networks, which enable secure access between systems using the Internet. We talk about PPTP in detail in Chapter 8, but for now, you can see in Figure 4.36 that enabling PPTP is straightforward; simply select the Enable PPTP Filtering check box.

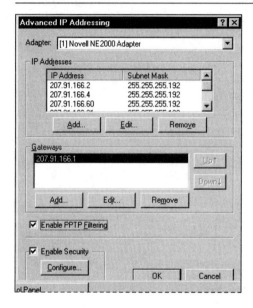

Figure 4.36
Advanced IP Addressing Dialog Box

DOMAIN TRUST RELATIONSHIPS

As I mentioned earlier, the Windows NT domain is entirely different from the TCP/IP Internet domain. The Windows NT domain serves as a barrier between network communities. Windows NT domains cannot even acknowledge each other unless they are properly introduced through what is known as a trust relationship.

So what's a trust relationship under Windows NT? Quite simply, it's a link between Windows NT domains that allows one domain to recognize all users and global groups of another domain. When a domain trust is established correctly, a user needs only one ID to access resources of another domain. Trust relationships are explained in more detail in Chapter 3.

Establishing trust relationships is a simple process that consists of two basic steps:

1. The first domain permits a second domain to trust it.
2. The second domain trusts the first domain.

To establish a two-way trust, simply perform both of these steps on both domains. You establish trust relationships with the User Manager for Domains; to get there, click Start, select Programs, Administrative Tools, and User Manager for Domains. After the User Manager for Domains is open, select Trust Relationships from the Policies menu. For our example, we assume we're establishing a one-way trust (Domain2 trusts Domain1) and that you're already logged on with administrative privileges.

1. Click Add next to the Permitted to Trust this Domain box, and type **Domain2**.
2. Type a password in both the Initial Password and the Confirmation Password boxes.
3. Click OK and then Close.

Now you've permitted Domain2 to trust Domain1. The trust is not complete until Domain2 enters the parameter to trust Domain1, as shown in the following steps:

1. Click Add next to the Trusted Domains box.
2. In the Domain box, type **Domain1**; in the password box, type the password established in the previous steps.
3. Click OK and then Close.

Domain2 now trusts Domain1. Terminating a trust relationship is just as easy as establishing it. One domain must stop trusting another domain, and the other domain must remove the permission for the first domain to trust it.

Now that the trust it set up, you should be aware of a few changes to your network:

• The trusted domain now appears as an optional domain in the logon box on Windows NT machines. Users from the trusted domain can log on to workstations that trust it.
• The trusted domain's users and groups now appear in browse lists.

- You can make network connections to shared resources on the trusting domain's servers.

Domain trusts are useful in most Windows NT network environments. Security is always a concern when giving access to users in foreign domains. You should follow these precautions to ensure that someone on the Internet running Windows NT can't hijack the trust: never use a blank password and always make sure that the trust relationship kicks off within 15 minutes after you create it. It is easy to guess a blank password, so even though the password you assign is only temporary, always assign one. After the trust is actually established, Windows NT immediately generates a new internal password that is never revealed to any user and secures the trust with this new password.

NT INSTALLATION CONSIDERATIONS

When you install Windows NT Server or Windows NT Workstation, be sure that all your other Windows NT domain controllers and backup domain controllers are live on the network before you begin. Before a Windows NT machine can join a domain, it must be authorized by a domain controller, which must be available on the network during the installation. Having all the domain controllers live on the network lets you avoid accidentally installing two primary domain controllers in the same domain and ensures that that particular machine is authorized to join a given domain.

In any network build-out, you should think carefully about how to structure your domains and networks. Consider who will administer them and how users will be allowed to access their resources.

Be careful to record the Administrator password and keep it in a safe place behind lock and key. As soon as you have the server up and running, immediately add at least one user account to the Administrators group, as a safety net. With this user account, you won't be forced to reinstall Windows NT from the ground up if you lose your Administrator password. You cannot easily recover a lost password under Windows NT, just as you cannot only recover a deleted file on a Windows NT system that uses NTFS.

IIS INSTALLATION CONSIDERATIONS

The Internet Information Server, Microsoft's Web server software, relies almost entirely on Windows NT for most of its security functions. The underlying Windows NT security subsystems give IIS the features for user and file system security. Step-by-step instructions for installing and configuring IIS are in Chapter 11; here, we look at security issues to consider.

IIS sets most of the security parameters for you during default installation. However, you should still pay attention to the home directory for your Web site files and the user name IIS uses for anonymous logons.

Consider locating your Web pages on a separate Windows NT server if possible. Although it may degrade performance, this setup makes it harder for an intruder to penetrate your Web site because the intruder must attack an additional system. In almost all cases, I recommend that you never use your Web server for other types of work — for example, as a file server — because Web servers are notoriously vulnerable to attacks.

Anonymous logons are necessary if you want your Web site available to the general public over the Internet because they don't require a username and password. Most public Web sites use only anonymous logons. However, you should set up your anonymous logon carefully. When you install IIS, the installation routine creates a generic account name that the IIS services use to facilitate anonymous logons. The account's name is IUSER_MACHINENAME, where MACHINENAME is the NetBIOS name of your computer. Immediately after you install IIS, open the User Manager and change the user name of the IIS user account. Intruders prey on this account, hoping that someone has mishandled the security settings. Giving this account an obscure name can help prevent future security mistakes and limit intrusion attempts. Be sure to triple-check all the security settings, and don't forget to include to set up policies and procedures for managing and using this account.

Don't set up a Web server just for the heck of it. You should know the purpose of any piece of software before you place it on your system. Although your purpose and intent may change over time, you should have at least an initial purpose for setting up a Web server. If your purpose includes delivering Web pages that contain sensitive information, you need to establish some security for the directories that contain the sensitive information and policies and procedures reflecting how it is managed.

You can establish user names and passwords to control access to parts of your Web site. IIS provides three ways to authenticate users: anonymous, clear text, and Windows NT challenge/response. Use them to your advantage.

Do not overlook the possibility of a denial-of-service attack, which burdens your system with traffic and requests, rendering it unable to respond. IIS lets you control the total bandwidth that your Microsoft Internet services use. You can use this feature to limit the output from the FTP, gopher, and Web servers to certain predetermined levels of traffic. You set this limit with the Internet Service Manager.

Another neat feature of IIS is that you can restrict or grant access by IP address. This feature is handy if you want only local users or a select group of users to access the server. You configure this feature at the Properties dialog box for the Web server in the Internet Service Manager. As Microsoft's CIS platform, formerly codenamed Normandy, is likely to be used more often, you need an understanding of how access can be controlled. CIS is a higher-end Internet publishing platform encompassing IIS (among other software) and comes complete with membership systems that rely heavily on correct permission settings.

You also need to consider the programs you may run from your Web site, including CGI Scripts, .dlls, .exe files, .com files, ActiveX scripts, and JAVA scripts. From a security perspective, these programs can be very dangerous. For a detailed explanation of their drawbacks, review Chapter 2 carefully and read Chapter 13. One major problem is using ISAPI .dlls on IIS. ISAPI programs run in the security context of IIS itself, which usually runs under the all-powerful System account; connecting users and ISAPI scripts fall under the security context of the IUSR_MACHINENAME account. Although this setup implies that ISAPI scripts are highly regulated, a malicious programmer could code an ISAPI script to revert its security context to the all-powerful System account. It takes only a simple line of code containing the following function call:

```
RevertToSelf();
```

When this code is executed, the ISAPI script reverts to the original security context, which is the System account. Because the System account can perform any possible action on a Windows NT system, the ISAPI script immediately becomes a major security threat. With additional coding, an ISAPI script can introduce a virus, trojan horse, back door, or other security threat. The only way I know of to protect yourself is to examine any ISAPI program carefully before running it on your system.

FTP AND GOPHER SECURITY CONSIDERATIONS

FTP lets users upload and download files from your system. Gopher lets you make documents and information available for access across the network. Users can search gopher documents through keywords contained in the files.

FTP and gopher are potentially dangerous services to run on a network. Some people recommend never using these tools; however, I think you can use them safely if you are careful in securing and monitoring them. Because FTP and gopher let a remote user access the server and download information, security is important. Establishing security for either service is essentially the same, so I cover them in this section together.

One way to control access to FTP and gopher is by limiting access to certain IP addresses. Follow these steps:

1. Double-click the gopher icon in the IIS Manager.
2. Choose the Advanced tab.
3. Choose Granted Access or Denied Access.
4. Add exceptions using the Add button. When you add exceptions, you specify which computer or group of computers, by IP address, is granted or denied access. After clicking Add, either choose Single Computer and type the IP address or choose Group of Computers and type the IP address and subnet mask.

If you choose to grant access to all computers by default, you can specify which computers are denied access; if you choose to deny access to all users by default, you can specify which computers are allowed access. Either way works well; your choice depends on the number of addresses you have to restrict or grant access to.

You can enable anonymous logons for FTP by selecting Allow Anonymous in FTP's Service dialog box under the IIS Manager. The System Event log records "anonymous," the logon ID, and the password for anonymous logons. Allowing anonymous access can add lots of users, and you should set it up carefully if you plan to use it.

You need to understand one aspect of FTP: FTP is controlled by file permissions. A user must have access permission to the FTP service's home directory. Without this permission, even users with valid IDs and passwords will be denied access. Anonymous logons for all Microsoft services run under the IUSR_MACHINENAME account, so triple-check the permissions of that user account. When establishing an FTP server in Windows NT, people are most likely to overlook this setting. If you are troubleshooting a user who cannot FTP successfully, double-check the file permissions for the FTP service's home directory. Minimally, they should allow read and execute access for the directory and read access for the files.

I do not recommend allowing anonymous FTP access to your system — one mistake on your part and the intruder is in.

Anonymous logon is the only way to access gopher. You establish access to the gopher service through an anonymous account the same way you establish it for FTP, except that with FTP you can require a valid user ID and password, and with gopher you don't have the option.

WINDOWS NT SERVICE CONSIDERATIONS

Lots of software for Windows NT runs as a system service. In many cases, these services require a user account to log on to the system to perform their duties. Automated backup software is a prime example of this type of software.

The real danger in these system services isn't in the services themselves, but in the user accounts they require. Many installation programs try to take burdens off the system administrator by automatically creating generic accounts for their software packages to use. The problem is that potential intruders know what these user account names are, just as you do. A potential intruder can use one of these accounts to access your system if the accounts are not limited correctly.

System services accounts as a rule do not require the "Access this computer from network" permissions; they normally use the "Log on locally" permission. Each software system is different and has varying permission requirements. You should analyze each to learn which user accounts they require. Once you have determined the most basic level of permissions they need, eliminate all other rights before installing the software.

SUMMARY

In this chapter, you learned how to add users and set their permissions and associated access rights, and how to create new user groups and add users to those groups. This chapter has also given you many tips for eliminating some of the potential dangers of users and groups under Windows NT and some suggestions to consider before installing Windows NT and IIS. You have also learned how to establish shared resources and audit trails and how to review audit trails using the Event Log. Security is a complex undertaking that only becomes more complicated as your networking environment grows. Use this information to your advantage and be decisive when establishing parameters for your underlying subsystems.

CHAPTER 5

MULTIPROTOCOL ENVIRONMENTS

Windows NT's base operating system includes TCP/IP, Novell's IPX (for accessing Novell NetWare servers), NetBEUI, and AppleTalk because most NT configurations use more than one protocol, and NT is a robust vehicle to deliver multiprotocol services. However, delivering these multiprotocol services is not without hazard. This chapter discusses the architecture of Windows NT's multiprotocol environment and ways to secure this environment from network attack with firewalls, encryption, and authentication.

You should understand up front that multiprotocol networks are significantly more difficult to secure than single protocol networks, and that they require layered security, just as single protocol networks do. This chapter, primarily written by Bill Hancock, demonstrates why layering security is important and should give you a clear view of the potential problems you face in these network environments.

THE PREVALENCE OF MULTIPROTOCOL NETWORKS

Networks based on Windows NT usually incorporate multiple protocols. To compound the problem, some applications, such as Microsoft's Source Safe, use only the NetBEUI protocol to operate between systems. When NT systems are used in a network in a factory or on a production line, customized protocols often control specific machinery. These protocols are typically nonroutable (like NetBEUI) and are definitely not part of the TCP/IP suite. Therefore, securing an NT network environment requires a lot more effort than securing just IP and its associated transports and applications.

Even if IP serves as the primary corporate protocol, IP is often revised extensively to support additional network types, addressing types, applications, and other technological changes. Therefore, you're likely to run the "old" version and the "new" version of IP at the same time on the same system as you convert to the new version. (Any network manager can tell you horror stories about converting to a new version of practically any protocol. Almost without exception, most companies run both versions during testing before going to the new version because of the problems that invariably occur with any new protocol.) Any security solution must work with many protocols, even simply different versions of the same protocol.

In practice, nearly all corporate networks are multiprotocol. Besides all the protocols included in Windows NT, you might have to protect the SNA-related protocols that dominate mainframe environments and DECnet, LAT, various hardware-specific protocols, and many non-IP protocols that are widely used with midrange computers. Many corporate networks operate between 6 and 18 protocols besides IP.

Preventing a network attack, especially when a large number of attacks are inside jobs, requires security for *all* protocols, not just IP. In a trusted network environment (as with most non-Unix servers), IPX and NetBEUI reign supreme, as do other non-IP protocols, and any of these may be used to gain access for an attack on a server.

The industry trend is to require faster and faster connections to the local and remote user. Before long, cable television systems and the many other technologies being developed to provide high-speed connections to homes will be the norm, especially for telecommuting and remote access. In addition, protocols that many industry observers had said would disappear have lingered for a long time and are expected to survive for many more years. SNA, DECnet, and IPX grow in corporate networks and show no signs of disappearing completely. In fact, many purchasing projections predict increased demand for some non-IP protocols based on the sales and growth of different server architectures. Even in pure IP networks, the evolution of IPv6 requires support for more than one version of the protocol suite as the network grows. For these reasons, supporting multiple protocols will continue to be the norm.

NT'S MULTIPROTOCOL ARCHITECTURE

Figure 5.1 illustrates the multiprotocol architecture of the NT operating environment. As you can see, NetBEUI has an alternate link to the Microsoft protocol bindery. This link presents a problem for system security, because some actions and programs take advantage of this built-in back door to gain access to the system.

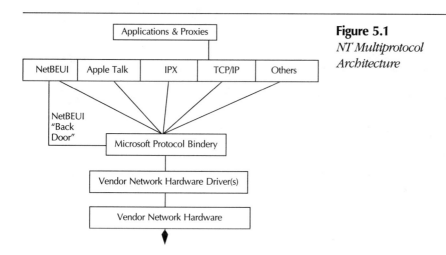

Figure 5.1
NT Multiprotocol Architecture

The back door is included to support applications that use NetBEUI, such as SMS and other third-party facilities that require remote bootstrap facilities. In effect, under specific conditions, NetBEUI facilities may compromise NT security measures. For example, proxy servers such as Microsoft Proxy Server 1.0 do not necessarily prevent access to NT through other protocols and applications, such as IPX with X.400.

Some firewall vendors have implemented their own user-mode solutions for NT for TCP/IP only. (For more in-depth consideration of specific firewall products, see Chapter 11.) These solutions are implemented as standalone firewalls that require dedicating the entire NT system to firewall operations, as shown in Figure 5.2 (you'll also see the NetBEUI backdoor that I talked about previously).

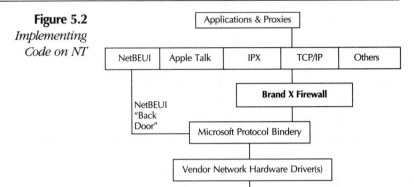

Figure 5.2
Implementing Code on NT

This setup presents the following obvious problems:

- It does not protect other applications that require other protocols to execute.
- The NetBEUI protocol back door is still active and may compromise the firewall.
- User-mode code causes serious performance degradation of the system.
- No other applications may run on the system while it is used for firewall software.
- No additional protocols in the network may be used or secured in a manner similar to IP.
- It is valid for only the current version of IP and doesn't take into consideration dual-stack TCP/IP systems, which will be common as users upgrade to IPv6.
- Because of other ways to implement protocols in MS-DOS or other emulation modes, the IP filtering illustrated does not necessarily provide any protection for any IP session that does not go through the firewall.
- Any NT security holes are still accessible unless you filter every protocol that you can implement on the system.

To compound the problem, you can bypass NT's native protection by implementing a protocol stack in the MS-DOS "virtual machine" environment and connecting to external systems. This method bypasses any security facility looking at TCP/IP native-mode stack access to the network and provides access to the system. Other holes have come and gone in different versions of NT and probably will again as NT matures and expands its capabilities.

NT'S MODES OF OPERATION

The NT system architecture (in Figure 5.3) has two modes of operation: *user* and *kernel.*

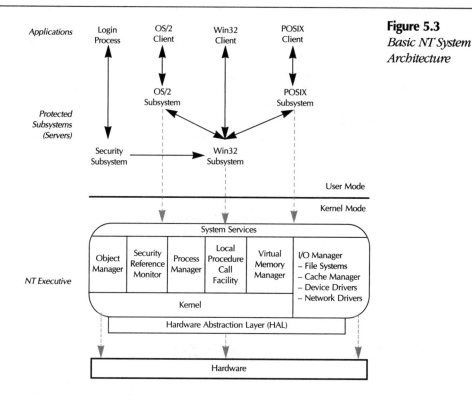

Figure 5.3
Basic NT System Architecture

Any network security software that is not implemented as a kernel-level service dramatically degrades the NT operating environment because of context-switching. A *context switch* is a technical function that is required to move between user mode and kernel mode; it is triggered every time user-mode security software needs access to system services or networks.

Most protocol stack facilities run in kernel mode and are usually implemented as driver facilities; only a few applications on the protocol stacks run in user mode, and they are controlled through context-switching. It is important to provide proper security for the kernel protocols to make them impervious to attack. Implementing security services in kernel mode minimizes context-switching and increases performance dramatically.

A LAYERED APPROACH TO NT NETWORK SECURITY

Network security in any environment is best when approached in layers or tiers, particularly in multiprotocol environments. Think of layers as separate security controls, each isolated from the others, each with its own specific tasks, yet all designed to work together — one layer assists another if a particular layer is breached. One advantage gained in a layered approach is that adding security to the network from source to destination adds more control points and more places where you can inspect network traffic.

In a layered environment, a given layer implements specific security measures that are duplicated on subordinate layers. If an intruder breaches a layer, another layer discovers the breach and informs the security staff that an upper-layer breach has occurred. When an alarm goes off, you know that a breach of the outer layer has occurred. A security measure in another layer traps and identifies the breach, and you know that the attack is contained and documented. With this method, no further intrusion is allowed without staff intervention.

Trying to breach layered security is like pole-vaulting over a moat of alligators (layer 1) into an electric fence, which has an alarm (layer 2). Getting over layer 1 (the alligators) may not set off any alarm because the breach is so clever, but when the pole vaulter hits the electric fence, sparks fly and the vaulter's presence is obvious. What happens from there is up to the network or security manager.

IMPLEMENTING LAYERED NETWORK SECURITY

A layered security system minimizes the chances that a network attack gets to a sensitive system or user data and maximizes the chances of detecting security threats before they reach a significant asset. To implement layered security, we need to consider some significant points about firewalls and routers, because these tools can be important components in a layered security setup. Firewalls are also covered in more detail in Chapters 10 and 11.

Firewalls and routers are substantially different, yet both are necessary. Routers move traffic between networks, a function essential to any network configuration using routed protocols like TCP/IP (NetBEUI cannot be natively routed). Because you can configure routers to provide specific frame- and packet-filtering, they are frequently sold and configured as firewalls (typically called *screening routers* when used in this capacity). One firewall product in particular, FireWall/Plus, supports an internal Cisco router hardware card but does not implement routing facilities in the firewall software itself. Allowing a firewall to also perform routing presents some very serious security and performance deficits, which are easiest to show in contrast to firewalls' capabilities.

True firewalls provide packet processing and filtering in an environment that is similar to a router's, but much more secure. While routers only translate and move packets, firewalls:

- Securely report activity to and from the firewall system. Most routers do not locally generate and store event logs and reports; routers with logging ability usually generate and store them on a remote system, thus compromising the security of the reporting mechanism.

- Give you a graphical interface to manage filters. In contrast, most routers have a command-only interface that is a basic method of configuring and using the router. To take advantage of a router's filtering and "firewall" abilities, you must possess in-depth expertise.

- Provide advanced filtering designed for security operations. Routers filter packets but are not designed with the rule bases required to implement security policies. Using advanced filtering and predefined security rules, a firewall can rapidly implement security policies.

- Can off-load filters from the router systems. When you implement filters in a router, the router's computational engine must search the filter structures each time a packet comes in. This search degrades the router's speed and keeps the router from doing what it was designed to do: route packets. A firewall provides robust, high-performance filtering, thereby implementing security policies without degrading the router's performance.

In fact, you can use routers to breach network security. A router implements a protocol's routing layer. If the router is breached by an attack or a software flaw in the routing code, you can use the router to compromise the internal corporate network. A true firewall does not implement the routing protocol, so even if the firewall is breached, an intruder doesn't automatically have access to the routing protocol and therefore can't get to the internal network. Many Unix-based firewall systems implement a full IP routing layer.

With that said, let's look at the one-layer network security implementation shown in Figure 5.4. The padlock symbol in the figure indicates a layer of security. A network is more vulnerable when only a firewall (a single layer of security) is used on an Internet connection. In this configuration, an attacker who gets around the firewall system can attack the NT server from the network if the right protocols are in place and left unprotected.

Figure 5.4
NT's Vulnerability to Attack

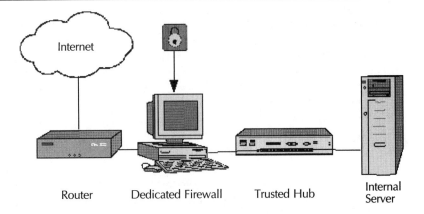

Router   Dedicated Firewall   Trusted Hub   Internal Server

Screening incoming packets with a filter on your router adds another layer to the network security architecture, as shown in Figure 5.5.

Figure 5.5
Placing a Screening Router

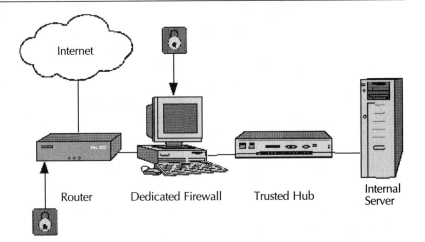

Router   Dedicated Firewall   Trusted Hub   Internal Server

In this configuration, it is both wise and necessary to duplicate some security rules in both the firewall security rule base and the router filter rule base. Particularly important are those rules that allow or deny types of access, such as Web, FTP, and e-mail. In fact, not replicating certain rules may cripple that particular function altogether; for example, if you allow Web access through the firewall but the router blocks port 80, Web access is effectively broken.

Once in place, the layers effectively detect breaches. For example, if a Telnet filter in the router denies all Telnet access, no Telnet functions should arrive at the firewall system. If the firewall also denies a Telnet connection from the untrusted Internet side, an arriving Telnet connection lets the security manager know immediately that something happened in the router because the Telnet attempt actually reached the firewall. It's then important to check the router.

Filters in your router should

- Pre-screen security threats and dismiss them from the connection path
- Offload security-checking from the firewall except when the router doesn't screen the attempted function properly
- Offload packet-filtering functions from the firewall
- Let the firewall detect problems in the router

You can add yet another layer of security by using a switching bridge in the hub to control traffic directions and provide additional layers of packet filtering (Figure 5.6).

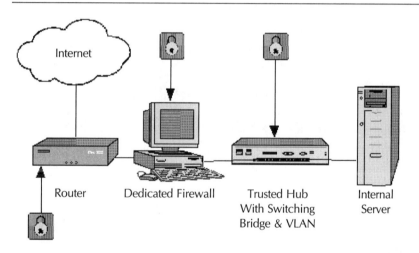

Figure 5.6

Implementing a Switching Bridge

Router   Dedicated Firewall   Trusted Hub With Switching Bridge & VLAN   Internal Server

Using hub-based virtual local area network (VLAN) software in the switching bridge, a feature available from some but not all switching-bridge vendors, further protects the network path from attack.

Sometimes using a firewall on an active client or server system acts as another security layer, as shown in Figure 5.7. This method, although functionally similar to the system firewall discussed above, is different in both its security rule base and its performance. The security threat is reduced because a real firewall is in the network path *before* the firewall on the internal server or client; this "real" firewall pre-screens connections coming toward the client or server. Server-based firewalls give you a final layer of network security before any intruder can reach the server operating environment.

Figure 5.7
Adding a Server-Based Firewall

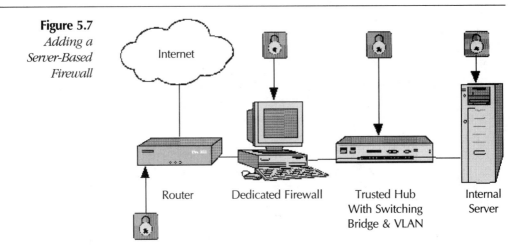

Router   Dedicated Firewall   Trusted Hub   Internal
                                        With Switching   Server
                                        Bridge & VLAN

If you implement layered security throughout your corporation, you can set different levels of security for different aspects of the network, depending on the criticality of a component to the company. In the above VLAN configuration, at least four layers of network security would have to be breached before the server's operating assets are vulnerable. Of course, using four layers of security may be overkill for your needs — some networks need this level of security, and some don't. It's a decision you'll have to make based on your company's data.

You can add more layers of network security with authentication facilities, encryption, digital signatures, and other security methods that can be used in many different layers of network protocols, including applications. If you implement them properly, you can add different security features so that they are transparent to your users' activities as long as the user attempts to access authorized systems and facilities.

PROTECTING AGAINST ATTACKS FROM INSIDE

Network firewalls and other layered security measures are a bottleneck at strategic points that prevent wholesale attacks on a network from the outside. It's fairly common to put a firewall facility between your internal system and known troublesome (and hostile) networks, such as the Internet. However, most companies do not implement firewalls between different company divisions, sister-company networks, customer networks, and other third-party or vendor-supplied network connections — but perhaps they should.

In a typical "trusted" attack on an NT server, a program initiates a file transfer *from the server* to an untrusted entity during off-hours. Many companies might not suspect this activity as a form of intrusion because few companies think about their systems voluntarily moving data from the trusted side, unassisted by a connection initiated from the untrusted side of a network connection, and they don't monitor for it. Ironically, the bulk of network attacks — in some cases as many as 80 percent — actually come from internal entities that are part of the corporate resource list. On average, internal and external attacks are more balanced, but the actual ratio of inside to outside attacks depends on your network. Because firewalls and filters work not only with incoming requests but also with outgoing requests, layered network security can help keep sensitive assets *in* as well as keeping attackers *out* of asset collections.

CLIENT ATTACKS — A NEW THREAT

Recently, network security defenses have concentrated on keeping attackers at bay from servers. The problem, especially in the past three years, has shifted toward attacks on client-side connections, whether those clients are on the local network or telecommuting from a remote location.

In Apple Computer's Mac OS V7.1 and later versions, AppleTalk is able not only to access servers, but also to let the client publish itself as a disk service in a network and let other clients access the disk services — typically referred to as *peer-to-peer* networking, similar to that seen in Windows for Workgroups. Peer-to-peer access requires no intermediary system for connections to be made and maintained. Using this type of configuration, in effect, gives a workstation the capability to act as a server, and as such, that workstation should be protected with its own layers of security.

Let's not discount new types of connectivity not quite yet in the mainstream, because in the very near future, high-speed residential connections will become more popular and used as a means of home Web surfing and quite possibly telecommuting. Bill Hancock uses use a 7 Mbps cable TV connection from his home to the Internet. This connection acts like a standard Ethernet connection (it even provides a standard RJ45 UTP connection on the set-top box connection to the cable broadband network), and it works like a standard Ethernet connection with the client software. This Ethernet-like convenience means that it is trivial to load a protocol analysis tool on the workstation client and view activity on the cable television network — activity that consists of traffic created by other people in the neighborhood, including their user passwords, file transfers, and network locations. When all traffic can be seen in the clear by placing a protocol analyzer or packet sniffer on a network client, *nothing* is secure.

TELECOMMUTERS — ANOTHER CLIENT SECURITY PROBLEM

Some studies project that workers in more than 60 percent of information-related jobs will telecommute more than 40 percent of the week by the year 2000. Telecommuters represent special security problems: they require support for high-speed network connections, and they keep sensitive corporate information at their homes. Sensitive information outside the physical perimeter of the company and the handful of established remote access facilities is more vulnerable.

Because telecommuting is becoming more common, high-speed network connections via cable television networks, Asymmetric High Speed Links (AHSL), and other technologies may become the normal mode of connection. Client computers hooked to networks such as cable television become "information appliances" (and much easier targets for the kinds of attacks described in the previous section) because they are continually connected to the network. Telecommuters will be subject to systematic network attacks no differently than corporate networks connected to any untrusted network. Figure 5.8 shows a typical dial-in or ISDN connection path, and Figure 5.9 shows a typical cable TV connection protocol.

Figure 5.8
Telecommuter Connection Path

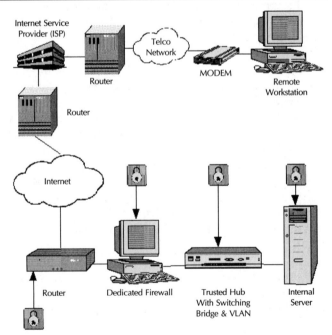

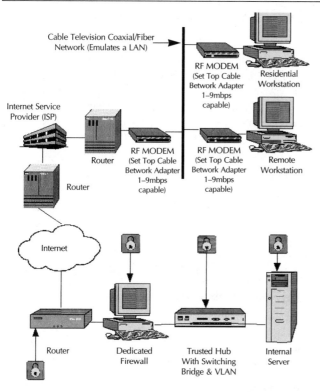

Cable Television Coaxial/Fiber
Network (Emulates a LAN)

RF MODEM
(Set Top Cable
Betwork Adapter
1–9mbps
capable)

Residential
Workstation

Internet Service
Provider (ISP)

Router

RF MODEM
(Set Top Cable
Betwork Adapter
1–9mbps
capable)

RF MODEM
(Set Top Cable
Betwork Adapter
1–9mbps
capable)

Remote
Workstation

Router

Internet

Router

Dedicated
Firewall

Trusted Hub
With Switching
Bridge & VLAN

Internal
Server

Figure 5.9
*Typical Cable TV
Internet Connection*

    Because most client computers can't provide a firewall in the remote or
residential computer, the chances of being attacked when connected to public
high-speed networks is extremely high and has a high potential for success. A
1996 U.S. General Accounting Office report showed more than 240,000 attacks
on the U.S. Department of Defense (DoD) unclassified networks; the report
suggests that more than 64 percent of the attacks were successful — and DoD
takes security very seriously. What will happen to the millions of telecommuters who connect to their office facilities with no network security and who
leave their home-based systems turned on all day while at the office and also
while connected to the high-speed network provided by the cable television
vendor? Free-lance attacks will be the norm, and these attacks will be successful, unless some preventive measures are taken. For example, a home PC
user could load a PC based firewall, like McAfee's PC Firewall; if a telecommuter needs to connect to your corporate network, you should consider virtual
private networking (VPN) tools, which authenticate remote users and encrypt
network traffic, protecting it from prying eyes.

VIEWING INTERNAL NETWORK TRAFFIC

Collecting data on in-path transactions on the Internet via a dial-up connection requires some specific levels of expertise. In contrast, very inexpensive or free software that can analyze Ethernet-like cable TV connections is available for NT and other systems; data passing over the connection is easily visible in standard ASCII format. For example, the packet breakout in Figure 5.10 shows the user's password for an anonymous FTP session between a remote NT network connection and an FTP server at IP address 129.170.16.79.

Figure 5.10

Packet Breakdown for an FTP Session

```
Flags:          0x00
  Status:         0x00
  Packet Length:85
  Timestamp:      15:35:27.247
  Filter:         IP
Ethernet Header
  Destination:  00:00:0c:19:99:49
  Source:       00:05:a8:00:84:3b
  Protocol Type:0x0800  IP
IP Header - Internet Protocol Datagram
  Version:              4
  Header Length:        5
  Precedence:           0
  Type of Service:      %000
  Unused:               %00
  Total Length:         67
  Identifier:           19528
  Fragmentation Flags:  %010  Do Not Fragment
  Fragment Offset:      0
  Time To Live:         255
  IP Type:              0x06  TCP
  Header Checksum:      0xdde2
  Source IP Address:    192.246.254.153
  Dest. IP Address:     129.170.16.79
  No Internet Datagram Options
TCP - Transport Control Protocol
  Source Port:      2050
  Destination Port: 21  FTP - File Transfer Protocol
  Sequence Number:  1241405969
  Ack Number:       1629760546
  Offset:           5
  Reserved:         %000000
  Code:             %011000
            Ack is valid
            Push Request
  Window:               17688
```

continued

```
Checksum:            0xf86c                                      Figure 5.10
Urgent Pointer:      0                                           Continued
No TCP Options
FTP Control — File Transfer Protocol
  FTP Command:       0x50415353  (PASS)  Password
  Password:
  rmasey@network-1   72 6d 61 73 65 79 40 6e 65 74 77 6f 72
6b 2d 31
  .com               2e 63 6f 6d
  Newline Sequence: 0x0d0a
Frame Check Sequence:  0x06c1fd4a
```

The packet breakout above was captured with an off-the-shelf tool and was performed with the current versions of FTP, TCP, and IP (version 4). It is trivial to capture information on shared networks, and the current implementations of cable TV and shared high-speed LAN environments (such as Ethernet/802.3, Token Ring/802.5, and FDDI networks) do not protect against it. Network protocols, as shipped from vendors, do not encrypt data streams, and information carried in a protocol is visible to anyone who knows how to read the information in a packet.

On intranets, most protocols don't employ encryption; those that do employ it use encryption only to establish sessions or for password security. The problem is that some devices, such as Netware-aware printers, don't support encryption for passwords, so the encryption feature is commonly disabled to allow users access to printers. Just because a security feature exists doesn't mean it's used properly, or even at all.

On corporate networks, users often maintain a common format for IDs and passwords to save confusion when accessing many different systems and servers. Therefore, securing one protocol is not enough. If users access a network using the same ID and password in an unencrypted session that they use for encrypted sessions and the password is compromised for an unencrypted session, then the password is also compromised for the encrypted session. To properly protect network connectivity, all protocols must be encrypted for all transactions and all packets must be controlled (firewalled) when they arrive at the destination to keep users from accessing sensitive information and to protect the user's client system integrity.

SECURITY SOLUTIONS — ENCRYPTION IS NOT ENOUGH

Although encryption can be valuable, encryption modems and encryption software for a specific protocol do not solve the end-to-end network security problem. Encryption is very good at authenticating a specific remote entity and at hiding any transaction over the network from observers of the traffic being transferred. However, encryption has its limitations.

Encryption is much like giving someone you trust the keys to your house so that no one can see your friend accessing your house and no one can see what your friend is doing between his/her house and your house. This privacy is good. What is not so good is that encryption does not stop a trusted user from attacking the destination system's services. For example, encryption may ensure that only corporate users access a system, but encryption does not restrict what a trusted user may be allowed to access and extract from the server. It's like letting someone you trust come in the front door but not restricting where that person can go inside the house and what that person can deliver to or remove from the house.

When used with encryption, firewalls at the destination or source of a network session add the filtering and security controls required for network security on a client or a server. Encryption ensures that the connection is allowed and protected from observation. Firewall facilities on the client or server restrict where incoming or outgoing connections can access data on entities on the client or server. By setting up specific firewall rules on the client and server in addition to encryption software, the security manager can properly protect system resources from systematic network attacks.

AUTHENTICATION — MORE THAN JUST PASSWORDS

On many systems, authentication is left to passwords, which can be broken, spoofed, overridden, or stolen. Token authentication, such as security cards, improves the security authentication offers, but cards can be stolen, lost, and cumbersome to manage. Certificates, which are becoming increasingly popular, act as a digital driver's license of sorts because the issuing certificate authority acts as a credible third party, vouching for you. However, the certificate management process, the certificate authority itself, and other management areas could be compromised and cause security problems. Hardware-embedded authentication is better than software, security-wise, but it is still difficult to manage.

Increasingly, users are using a single logon for all protocols because they don't understand or care that the system they wish to reach from their NT workstation is an IBM mainframe running SNA. Users want to identify themselves to the network entity once and travel throughout the network, regardless of protocol, without logging on again. To most folks, security is an annoyance, and anything that can be done to alleviate the burden makes them happy.

SUMMARY

In the Windows-NT environment, multiple protocols are the norm and will be for a long time, in part because companies have invested in mainframes and midrange computers that do not have, need, or want TCP/IP connectivity. Using Windows NT in the internal network environment means implementing multiple protocols. In some application environments, even on pure NT networks, protocols such as NetBEUI (a connectionless protocol originally used in LAN Manager) are necessary to satisfy corporate access requirements; therefore, securing many protocols is a necessary aspect of network security, and layering security measures is the safest way to go about it.

CHAPTER 6

SECURITY THREATS

In this chapter, we walk through areas that might pose security threats to your organization, internal and external, obvious and less obvious. Instead of separating internal and external threats, I divide the threats into physical and network threats. I also consider relationships with service providers that might cause problems and suggest a starting point for considering your own network security. But first, let's make sure we all understand exactly what we mean by security threat.

WHAT EXACTLY IS A SECURITY THREAT?

You may ask yourself, "Why should I worry about security?" When facing the issue of security, it's important to understand exactly what you are trying to protect. Information is at the heart of your organization — it's what holds your organization together and provides the means of productivity.

View your organization's information the way you view its furniture: If someone walked into your office, picked up all your furniture, and walked out with it, you'd be mad, plus you'd have to spend money on new furniture. If you still had the receipts from your furniture, you might be able to place a dollar value on the theft. But what if someone walks in (or travels through cyberspace) and steals your data? Would you able to put a dollar amount on its value? What if the intruder only read all your organization's trade secrets without actually taking anything?

Your organization's information is one of its assets. Your systems probably carry all your personnel records, contracts, sales information, private arrangements, schedules, research, and more — all of which can be deadly to a business if placed in the wrong hands. When contemplating information security, consider what people can access. Someone may be lurking at your office door in a manner that's not so obvious to you. He or she may steal your data in such a way that it's months before you realize what happened. And, unfortunately, the thief could be one of your own employees.

Theft and burglary are not the only security threats to your organization's data. Anything that poses a danger to your network, such as a fire or hard disk failure, is a security threat. For example, if your building is flooded by heavy rain, that's a security threat. If your computer room happens to be in the basement of that building, you probably have a major crisis on your hands that is just as dangerous to the welfare of your business as a cyberspace intruder.

A REAL STORY

Let's look at a real situation (names and places have been changed to protect the guilty). The head of the Human Resources department (Bobby Pin) sends e-mail to the President (Anna Cin) about the impending IS outsourcing deal. Bobby writes in his e-mail to Anna that certain employees in the IS department probably won't be picked up by the future outsourcing company. Bobby then attends a meeting, leaving his computer logged on — it's wide open for anyone to walk in and view everything on it, including the sensitive e-mail. Someone in the IS department (Pete Moss) walks in, sits down at the computer (remember, his job is to fix computers, so it's normal to see him sitting at anyone's computer), and reads the e-mail, thereby finding out that his department will be outsourced soon and that he won't be hired by the new company.

You don't think it can happen? It *did* happen at a large, well known international firm. Pete could access Bobby's sensitive e-mail because he set up the e-mail system for the organization and installed the client e-mail software on everyone's PC in the organization. During installation, Pete used the password of "PASSWORD" for everyone's computer and took the chance that Bobby never changed his password. Pete was right and could view, forward, and print all Bobby's e-mail. Bobby would never have tossed a paper copy of the memo in the trash can; instead, he would have shredded it. However, since he started working on a computer, he had become lax about handling sensitive data.

If you think this situation won't happen in your organization, think again. This story is just one example of a person accessing data s/he shouldn't. Those charged with protecting your network may in fact be poking into areas where they don't belong. You've heard the question, "Who's minding the store?" Well, it's up to each organization to be aware of every type of security threat on its systems. Failure to take this responsibility is simply absurd.

WHAT DO WE DO TODAY?

Do you remember when credit card vouchers had carbon paper in them? Then the news hit the streets that people, sometimes restaurant staff and sometimes criminals rummaging through garbage cans, were stealing the carbon paper and manufacturing fake credit cards. Credit card companies stopped making vouchers with carbon paper, but by then, many innocent shoppers were victimized.

Although that particular situation has changed, some of us give our credit card number over a cellular phone, not realizing that criminals can capture our information over the airwaves. Drug dealers using their cordless phones to conduct illicit business have discovered later that some baby monitors operate on the same frequency as cordless phones. Much to the criminal's amazement, the entire drug deal has been overheard (and even recorded) by their neighbors and police officers. You need to be aware of your organization's transmissions and the tools that can intercept and capture the data.

Have you heard of Tempest-compliant electronic devices? Did you know that someone outside your house or office building can capture your screen image with them? Equipment such as monitors and CPUs emit electromagnetic rays that can be captured and monitored by anyone with some electronics knowhow. Imagine the implications if someone monitored stock market computers and gained advance knowledge. Although it might seem like an extreme example, the story of one person's test to prove it could be done is at the following URL: http://www.thecodex.com/c_tempest.html.

STATISTICAL INFORMATION

This book wouldn't be complete without some statistics on security. Chapter 2 includes some statistics about the cost of security breaches. If you're still not convinced that the security of your information assets is important, here are some shocking facts. *Information Week*/Ernst & Young's fourth annual Information Security Survey of more than 1,300 IS executives in the U.S. and Canada revealed the following statistics about organizations and their attitude (or latitude) toward securing information assets:

- More than 50 percent of those surveyed indicated they had suffered financial losses from security breaches and disaster recovery
- 70 percent weren't able to calculate the amount of loss
- More than 25 percent calculated losses of up to $250,000, with some in the $1 million range
- 63 percent indicated the cause to be virus attacks
- 33 percent discovered attacks by insiders
- 17 percent discovered attacks by outsiders

The figures above indicate that one out of two organizations was hit by some type of security problem that caused them to suffer a loss. The other figures show that the losses were by no means insignificant. For more information about this survey, check http://techweb.cmp.com/iw/602/security.htm.

A LOOK AT PHYSICAL THREATS

When we talk about physical security threats, we mean more than just your network media and servers; we are also talking about your clients and client environment. It does no good to save a confidential file on the secure server if the user has a copy of the file on a loose floppy or laptop. If you want to protect information, you must deal with the physical security concerns of your environment, which is not always easy. If you lease floor space from a management company, you are dependent on that company. You may find that your management company doesn't care about your information security concerns, especially if you have already entered into a written contract and are trying to secure your assets after the fact.

Your network and its information are no safer than the premises in which they are housed. I once had a job at a billion-dollar world-renowned data processing company. I worked in a facility that was very well protected. It was so protected that I joked that it reminded me of the old *Get Smart* television show where Maxwell Smart walked through door after door after door, each of which locked behind him as he passed through. At my particular job site, I went through a barrage of security checks in a similar manner on the way to my workplace.

First, I had to get past armed guards and a locked door, surrounded by at least a dozen security cameras, with my ID badge and card key. From there, I rode an elevator to my particular floor, where I was immediately faced with another locked door to our suite that could be opened only with a specific card key at certain hours of the day. From that point, I'd travel down a hallway to yet another set of locked doors called the "man trap," which only one person could enter at a time. The man trap's dual-door combination was accompanied by a pressure-sensitive flooring that could detect the presence of more than one human body standing on it, at which point the door's locks would cease to open until all but one body left the flooring. Past this door, there was yet another locked door, also opened only with specific card keys at specific times of day. After I made it this far, I was in my work area but still had no access to a computer or terminal without an ID, a one-time password, and direct supervisory control.

This setup sounds pretty secure, doesn't it? It was intended to be — but it wasn't. I found two basic problems quite easily. First, for convenience, we had freight elevator access built into the secure room. Anyone who knew the location of the ground floor elevator doors could bypass more than half-a-dozen security systems, including all the cameras and ID checkpoints. I routinely rode this elevator when I was running late for work, and no one ever said a single word or even paid much attention. I could have been anybody stepping out of that elevator.

The second problem was that the pressure-sensitive flooring could be spoofed, and I proved it. One evening, after an office party, a couple of coworkers and I discovered that it was possible to give someone a ride right into the data center. The pressure-sensing systems of the floor looked for patterns of weight distribution on the floor in the form of two footprints; the systems didn't actually analyze the weight of the footprints themselves at all. In other words, if the security system sensed more than two feet on the floor, it triggered, so a simple piggy-back ride could evade the security system. The manufacturer's short-sightedness in not including weight analysis, combined with the buyer's complete faith, make up a definite "gotcha" in the security world.

Never ever assume you're completely safe, no matter what security you think you've got in place, no matter how much you spend — almost invariably, there's a way around it. You simply must protect the premises — not through expenditure alone, but also by continued analysis and testing.

Let me ask a question: Why put in a door with locks if you place the hinges on the outside, where an intruder can knock out the pins? Physical threats to your organization's data are sometimes the most obvious; however, in some cases, they're not. You need to examine every inch of your network facilities with a magnifying glass to find any oversights, including door hinges on the wrong side! Certainly you wouldn't leave your house without locking it. You wouldn't leave packages in your car without locking it, either. Leaving your car or home unlocked is an obvious threat. However, what about the "not-so-obvious" threats that lurk out there? Let's look at both obvious and less-obvious threats.

THE OFFICE ENVIRONMENT

Your office environment is your domain, and you should take complete control of it. However, remember that a casual office environment can be secure at the same time. You must determine a comfortable level of security. You can become so secure that working in the security environment is counterproductive — security becomes a form of overkill that makes work tedious beyond necessity. Don't overdo it, but by all means, don't underdo it either. You need to balance comfort and security by identifying your security needs and defining and enforcing policies that reflect them accurately.

Premises Access

Controlling visitors to your site can be a chore. Some people feel that too much "noticeable" security can alienate visitors or guests — but in reality, many visitors respect and admire the secured establishment. In either case, it's your site, so secure it as you see fit.

Two types of people visit any given site: those who belong to your firm and those who do not. You should handle visiting employees from other sites in the same way you handle employees from your own site. One firm I worked with was accustomed to handling employees visiting from their other sites. The travel department of the remote site called the IS department of the visited site to ensure that the visitor had controlled access to the network resources, with a limited-access ID and password set to expire according to the timeline of the employee's visit. They also made sure that a card access key gave access only to the appropriate rooms.

Site tours conducted for people who aren't employees should also be scheduled in conjunction with some security control. Don't let visitors roam freely. Make sure the staff knows people are coming in for a tour. You don't want sensitive data left on computer screens or desktops in plain view. *Shoulder surfers* — people literally looking over your shoulder — are a big risk to most businesses. Denying nonemployees access to the premises is one of the best ways to reduce this risk significantly, but monitoring their visits is a reasonable compromise.

You should also be leery of contractors and building maintenance people. Don't ever be afraid to ask for someone's credentials, and certainly don't be afraid to verify them with their home office. I know of several instances in which someone used a masquerade to gain access to a site. As a rule, all visitors should present ID. You can simply photocopy it for later reference if you need it. People who object to this exposure probably have something to hide, and you don't want them running loose in your facilities.

Often, employees need to come to the office after hours and on weekends and holidays. Workers with after-hours access should respect this privilege. You should stress the importance of maintaining control over access to the office. Employees may be tempted to bring someone into the facilities with them, particularly if they're not planning to stay long. Allowing your personnel to decide who comes and goes in and out of your site is a bad practice. They should not bring other people with them, no matter how inconvenient it may be to make other arrangements.

A woman brought her son into the office while she did some quick work on a weekend. Little did she know that her son was an amateur hacker and was shoulder-surfing while she worked to learn logon names and passwords. Armed with that information, he hacked into the corporate network once he got home. He was quickly detected and caught, and his mother was fired. This situation could have been prevented with a simple company policy about visitors.

Equipment Access

Access to equipment should be granted based on need. If only one person in your firm needs access to certain equipment, that equipment shouldn't be left in the open. Sooner or later someone will be tempted to do something s/he shouldn't. Equipment access can be especially hard to control in 24 × 7 shops, those that run 24 hours a day, 7 days a week. In one large international 24 × 7 concern, the office environment is fairly safe from intrusion during the day. However, after hours, workers can roam the facilities, gaining access to almost anything they please.

To secure your equipment, you can do many simple things that lots of shops overlook. For instance, you need to lock the doors to the rooms that house your servers and other vital equipment. Many server closets are dual-purpose rooms — some are used for storage or are shared cable closets. If room-sharing creates a lot of traffic in a room, it's a bad security practice. In most instances, room-sharing has evolved over time and may be difficult to change, but the security advantages gained by segregating the two can be significant. People who need access to your cables may not be the same people you want to have access to your servers.

If your organization uses electronic access cards, you should make sure access is restricted to your server closets. Don't just make assumptions; check with the people who assign the access cards and find out who currently has access to the sensitive areas of your premises. In one organization, an IS manager assumed that the IS staff were the only ones with access to storage rooms. They found out too late that they weren't. One particular room was listed as a general-purpose closet and many people had been granted access to it. As a result, another group of employees had been storing their paper supplies in this same room. Eventually, a small electrical fire that could have been avoided got out of hand because of the paper's high combustion rate. The damage was considerable. A similar situation occurred in a small hospital, where employees stored oxygen tanks in the same room as computer equipment. These types of scenarios are easy to avoid with simple and regular auditing routines.

Look at the current design and locations of your rooms. Don't rule out electronic eavesdropping as a tool against you. All types of electronic equipment, especially video monitors, emit noise. These emissions find their way into your building's wiring systems and radiate around the building following the wiring. In effect, this wiring is like a giant antenna, and sophisticated equipment can pick up these emissions and recreate computer displays very easily. Shielding your room and your equipment from electromagnetic interference (EMI) is always a good safety measure. Any wiring leading from a computer to any building wiring should be shielded, and if feasible, you should shield entire rooms. Devices to accomplish this are available today in most electronic stores.

Auditing your premises regularly is necessary for good site security. Be sure to check for loose, exposed, or insecure cabling. Check for inactive or open network cable drops, and disconnect them at your hubs until needed. Find out what's in your server rooms and network equipment rooms, and eliminate nonessential items from those rooms.

DESIGNING THE PERFECT COMPUTER ROOM

One of your first tasks should be to secure your organization's data with no public access. Usually you choose a room specifically designated for only computer equipment, with the following special considerations:

- Badge access — You should secure the door so that only people with permission can enter the room; ID badges are the best method of security. Don't bother getting a badge reader that doesn't record the time and identity of each person who enters the room. If this equipment is cost prohibitive, put a lock on the door and limit the number of keys you pass out. If possible, make people sign out for the key every time they need access to the room. This procedure sounds tedious, but it will be helpful when you do your first troubleshooting and need to know who the last person in the room was.

- Ceiling tiles — Now that you've secured the door to the computer room, stand in front of it and look up. If the building is designed with ceiling tiles, anyone can bypass your security door by popping up the tiles and climbing a ladder into your room. Ask your building maintenance company to secure those tiles or build the wall through the ceiling, all the way up to the bottom of the floor above.

- Motion sensors — If you establish badge access for entering hallways and rooms but use motion sensors for leaving rooms and hallways, pay attention. If you walk up to a closed door and hear a click, or if you can push the door to get out of a room, you've got this type of system. If you look up, you will see a sensor on the ceiling or on the wall. It detects motion by the door and unlocks it so you can get out. One company was robbed when intruders used a poster from the building's lobby to bypass this security system. When they encountered badge access doors, they slipped the poster under the door and wiggled it around until it set off the motion detectors and unlocked the door. The burglars then had free access to the entire floor.

- Video cameras — There's nothing quite like a photograph to prove guilt! You can buy inexpensive equipment that doesn't look like video cameras — the clock on the wall could actually be a camera. Some companies install cameras as small as the head of a pin in ceiling tiles and use tapes from these cameras after an industrial accident to determine whether the employee was following the rules.

- Window/Basement control — Don't put your computer room (or equipment) in the basement of any building because it might flood. Likewise, high winds can wreak havoc if you have windows near computer equipment; besides, intruders can break into windows on or near the first floor.

- Air conditioning — Because you shouldn't have windows in a computer room, you should plan for adequate ventilation and cooling. A four-day weekend in a stifling room (buildingwide air conditioning is often turned off beginning Friday night) can cause mechanical parts, such as disk drives containing data, to break down.

- Temperature sensors — Air conditioners break down from time to time, especially when you're not around. Invest in a room temperature sensor that pages you when the temperature rises or falls a certain amount. Some uninterruptable power supply (UPS) systems, which serve as battery backups when the power goes out, have this feature.

- UPS systems and a electric backup generator — It's best to tie your entire room into a big UPS system like those from Liebert. At the very least, connecting a standalone unit to the host computers alleviates some trouble in a power failure. When you tie a UPS into your system, set it up so that you are paged when the UPS is triggered. And although this suggestion may push the limit, tying your computer room's UPS system into the building generator buys you more time to get to the computer room before the computers run out of electricity.

- Access tracking — Do you make employees sign for keys and badge access? If you don't keep a centralized log on employees and the kinds of access they have to your premises and systems, you have no way to guarantee that employees who leave the organization lose their access. Do all your keys and card key badges say "duplication prohibited" on them?

- Housekeeping — You don't need to let the housekeeping staff enter the computer room; you don't generate enough trash to justify the security risk. Instead, keep a broom and dustpan in the computer room — and yes, use it yourself to sweep the room. When the trash can gets full, set it outside the computer room door. You don't know what the housekeeping staff is doing while you're not there to monitor their activities.

- Trash can — In fact, before you put the trash can outside the computer room, check what's in it. You should shred printouts of sensitive information before throwing them away. Trash reveals a lot about a person. Paparazzi sift through the garbage cans of famous people to find out what the stars are up to.

If your workstations are in a public place where a variety of people have easy access to your computers, and if the physical protection described in this section is cost-prohibitive, I recommend at least the following precautions:

- Protect domain controllers. Domain controllers keep user account databases, sensitive profiles, and most sensitive data. You should secure domain controllers (primary and backups) in a relatively safe place where at least a door and a lock will prevent an intruder from gaining physical access to the server.

- Do not store sensitive information on the workstations. Make the administrative password for every workstation different from the password on the domain controller.

- Remove floppy drives from these workstations or disable the floppy drive and set a CMOS password on every workstation. Of course, this precaution is not a complete fix, but it makes things more difficult for potential intruders.

WHAT'S OUTSIDE THE COMPUTER ROOM DOOR?

Now that you've secured your computer room, walk around the floors of your building and see what they tell you about the security of the rest of your system. Check again the location and contents of closets, as we mentioned earlier in this chapter. Anything that's connected to your system represents a potential point of entry. Isolated standalone machines seem to pose the smallest threat to your security, but even they can be targets, depending on the software and data you store there. Audit your building. Check for loose floppies or laptops, know where your key workstations are, and document the locked doors your servers are behind and who has access to them.

WHO'S IN CHARGE HERE?

What person do you think of first when you consider physical security? Start with your system administrator. Windows NT administrators are powerful. They can change any user password, change permissions, read any file on NTFS volumes, and erase all traces of the actions. The Somarsoft NT Security white paper (http://www.somarsoft.com/security.htm) recommends the following actions:

- Use only trustworthy people as administrators. Check the customer references of a potential candidate thoroughly, which will help determine an individual's trustworthiness. In many situations, you can dispense with an administrator; for example, if you own a small business, you can be your own administrator instead of relying on an outsider. Day-to-day Windows NT administration is simple enough that this option is realistic. When an outsider is required, the internal administrator can ensure that nothing suspicious is done.

- Have administrators work in teams and review each other's work.

- Establish and enforce a rule that no one, not even an administrator, is allowed in the computer room alone, especially after hours. If an administrator needs access to the computers after hours, the administrator should be accompanied by a security guard who is trained to ask what the administrator is doing, judge whether the answer or actions seem suspicious, and file a written report of the incident.

Anyone with access to your organization's facilities and information should be considered a security risk, no matter who they are. Employees are the heart of any organization. They are the producers and money makers, but that doesn't exclude them from being scrutinized. In today's corporate world, rival organizations can and will pay highly for valuable information, and sometimes the temptation is too hard to resist. Good background checks are always worth the money and effort, so don't overlook this aspect in your hiring process.

In addition, you need to understand what it takes to keep employees around. The last thing you need is your competitor hiring away the people that have a high level of exposure to your critical information. Your best bet is to take good care of those vital employees, making sure their needs are met. This simple practice goes a long way toward making sure those people stay with your firm.

MOBILE USERS AND LAPTOPS

Many users who have access to your system while on the road also have an office where they dock their laptops. An improperly docked laptop can be a security risk. An intruder can steal either the entire laptop or just a key component, like a hard drive.

Mobile users should also be careful of shoulder surfers while working on the road — perhaps their seatmate on a plane, train, or bus.

INTERNAL MEMOS

Internal memos are often a big security risk. Many companies send memos to large distribution lists and lose control of how the recipients pass along the information. Sensitive memos lying around or thrown in the trash without being shredded indicate a problem.

Control the distribution of your company memos the same way you control your computerized information. Your decisions should be based on the sensitivity of the information they contain. If the information could lead to any type of damage to your firm, control the dissemination carefully. Perhaps adding policies regarding sensitive information is in order.

CABLE AND CARDS

Don't cut corners on new or improved network infrastructure design. If you do, your organization may find itself ripping out and replacing cable just to catch up with the current technology. You should evaluate the growth of your organization by looking at the emerging higher-speed networking technologies.

Using Asynchronous Transfer Method (ATM) on your server backbone is a possibility, and Fiber Distributed Data Interface (FDDI) is a consideration if you can afford all that fiber optic cable, but for even more economical technology, also look into the newer high-speed Ethernet options and newer protocol standards like the Fast IP and VLAN standards.

Today, the prices for 100 MB Ethernet cards are close to the prices of older 10 MB Ethernet cards. Gigabit Ethernet is being pushed as a new industry standard, as is Tag Switching, the child of industry leader Cisco Systems. Tag Switching technology combines the performance and traffic management capabilities of the data link layer switching (layer 2) with the scalability and flexibility of the network layer routing (layer 3).

You have many options for enhancements when growing your network. The basic security premise of the physical network is to protect the cable plant. It doesn't help to secure your systems behind locked doors if an intruder can tap a cable in a hallway or storage room or plug into a network hub stored in a closet. Plan your wiring runs carefully; make them difficult to get at; and secure access to your bridges, routers, hubs, and other connectivity equipment by putting them behind locked doors and restricting access to the keys.

SERVERS

Your servers are probably the single most important devices on your network. Many IS departments have debated rack-mounting servers vs. leaving them in individual cases. Although the discussion can be interesting, the arguments for standalone servers aren't compelling enough for me to not rack-mount a production server when money permits the expense. The added security and ease-of-management benefits greatly outweigh the expenses.

Adding more standalone servers as your company grows takes up more floor space than rack-mounted systems because standalone servers are usually placed side by side instead of stacked, like rack mount systems are. Rackmount systems cost more money, but so does floor space, and you can take the rack mounts with you when you move. Furthermore, top-of-the-line rackmounting systems, like those from Compaq Computers, have locking doors and panels and can be bolted to the floor, which increases your security.

Don't overlook rack-mounted UPS units. Some UPS units can monitor temperature and humidity changes. By increasing the sensitivity of these types of settings, you can track environmental changes that occur when doors open and close. Your results may vary, but it's another step in monitoring all aspects of your servers. Sensitive UPSs can detect when doors have been left open mistakenly, an ability that could lead to early detection of a possible intrusion attempt.

NAÏVE EMPLOYEES

Don't let your employees be naïve about information. You should make sure they know what is and is not proper procedure for revealing or changing information stored by the company, such as phone numbers and passwords. If you don't teach your employees how to handle situations, they are left to make decisions for themselves, often poor ones.

Potential intruders use *social engineering* against employees such as help desk operators, receptionists, programmers, and analysts. Social engineering occurs when intruders manipulate employees or vendors to get crucial information. The bigger the organization, the more likely it is that intruders try this trickery. You may be surprised how easy it is to get someone on your help desk to reset a password. You should establish and enforce explicit policies regarding information dissemination.

You may also need to protect the employees from themselves and each other. I've heard too many horror stories about users accidentally deleting another user's files for one reason or another. You may also want to consider incremental backups of your data. Archiving data incrementally, with historical revisions in place, can help protect against similar accidents. It also lets users pick up close to where they left off in cases of loss.

TRASH CANS

When asked to evaluate the security of a given firm, I like digging in the trash cans (dumpster diving). You may be amazed at what you can learn from other people's trash or recycling boxes. You often find entire reports that were discarded because of a simple formatting error, passwords written on scraps of paper, "While you were out" messages with phone numbers, old file folders with documents still in them, or diskettes and tapes that weren't erased or destroyed, all of which could help a would-be intruder.

And who are those people on your cleaning crew? We've already decided the cleaning crew won't enter the computer room, but don't forget the other trash cans. If federal agencies deem it necessary to do background checks on people who have access to their waste baskets and shredders, you probably should as well.

On a visit to a local help desk, I noticed a detailed diagram of a network and its routers, including which ports were blocked — and even more horrifying, the ports that weren't! Although the network administrators were aware of the holes, which was gratifying, finding those holes detailed on paper discarded in a trash bin was truly horrifying.

The best practice is to cross-shred all your paper and physically destroy all magnetic media to make it useless to an intruder. In several instances, corporate spies gathered enough sensitive information from the trash of their competitors to drive them out of business. Information leaks definitely harm your business, so don't take that trash can for granted.

VOICE MAIL

Because intruders can access voice mail systems through a phone line, you should think of voice mail systems in the same way you think of your other physical systems. Voice mail systems store and forward messages, and some allow access to outside lines from within the voice messaging system. Intruders love to find this access, because it lets them make free long-distance calls. This kind of telephone fraud costs corporations millions of dollars a year. It's relatively easy to prevent if you configure your voice mail system properly and maintain control over the instructions for its use. Be sure to check your voice mail systems and understand their capabilities.

PREVIOUSLY OWNED CLIENT PCS

No matter which file system you use, you can usually reclaim lost information in a variety of ways — Norton's Unerase and Unformat utilities, the Windows 95 and Windows NT 4.0 recycle bins, or reclamation facilities that can repair your damaged hard disk bit by bit. Finding out who has access to those utilities is just as important as locking cabinet drawers in the HR department. Something perceived as harmless — like swapping machines for a user whose machine has died — can lead to big security holes because users can get information from an improperly wiped disk.

In one case, a used-computer dealer, in a routine examination of equipment purchased at a Department of Justice auction, discovered information intact on the hard drives — including lists of people in the Witness Protection Program! In another horror story, a medical charity gave a friend some computers that contained a list of local people who had been diagnosed with AIDS. I hope these stories make my point: Wipe your hard drives with specialized tools, or better yet, take the financial loss and physically destroy them.

POWER-ON PASSWORDS?

Power-on passwords, a BIOS feature that requires you to type a password before the system even boots, are incredibly useful in the business environment. Many applications can recover documents lost during power failures; for example, if you're working on a document in Microsoft Word and the machine loses power, the machine can retrieve a cached version of the document when the power comes back on and Word is reopened. If your loss of power occurs near the end of the day and you go home before power is restored, the document you were working on is immediately vulnerable — if you don't use a power-on password.

Another argument for power-on passwords relates to Windows NT servers. Windows NT is a secure operating system if it's configured correctly. But that security can be compromised easily with a DOS boot disk and NTFSDOS (see Chapter 8 for more about NTFSDOS), which can bypass security and mount Windows NT's NTFS disk partitions. Power-on passwords can prevent this breach by letting you remove the floppy boot sequence.

A LOOK AT NETWORK THREATS

Let's talk about your network. Your network is probably the most heavily used vehicle for disseminating your organization's information. Your network lets you share information, and if you're connected to the Internet, you've just opened your network's doors to the outside world. Networked systems, whether connected only internally or to the external community, pose the highest risks. You should always give special attention to security when planning your overall network design. If security is an afterthought, you must give special attention to redesigning that same network.

This section isn't an all-encompassing list of network threats; as soon as someone posts a definitive list, someone else will invent another way to penetrate your system. Instead, I start with the obvious and work my way down to the not-so-obvious. Although you may have encountered some of the situations in this list, I hope some items may open your eyes to risks you haven't even thought about.

ASKING FOR HELP

Lots of people use the Internet for help on certain issues, including security. When participating in a mailing list, Web site, Usenet newsgroup, or any other public information system, *never* give details that aren't necessary. Deliver information on a "need to know" basis only. Intruders routinely monitor most aspects of the Internet, looking for possible targets.

Here's a true case: Recently, someone posted a message to a security mailing list asking for help securing WebSite Web server software. Immediately, I informed the user that this software has several known and published exploits, and I told him how to fix it quickly. Within 15 minutes of his post, his site was down, crashed by an intruder. If he had excluded from his message the fact that he was running WebSite software, he probably wouldn't have been touched at all. Fortunately, his systems and data weren't harmed, but they could have been.

WHAT'S IN THE CACHE?

Caching is covered in detail in Chapter 8, so I include only a brief summary here. Most operating systems, including all versions of Windows, have some type of password caching, which can be compromised. For example, Novell client software loaded on a Windows 95 machine stores passwords in the system swap file, which a simple text editor can read. Survey your operating systems, and learn how to disable password caching of all types.

FILE SERVERS OR HOST SYSTEMS

If you have a network, chances are that you have a server system. Because you're reading this book, I assume that you have at least one Windows NT server. We've already talked about locking up these host systems physically. The next step is to secure your user accounts properly, especially the Administrator account and Administrators Group — the ones that allow access to almost anything!

VIRUSES

Most organizations wait until they get hit with a virus before they spend the money on virus protection — a bad strategy. Once a virus infiltrates the network, it takes very little time to infect an entire organization. If you connect your network to the Internet, the danger of viral infection is extremely high. Your virus protection plan should protect both workstations and hosts. You'll find some great examples of virus protection software on the CD-ROM included with this book.

SNIFFERS

Besides being aware of network packet sniffers (which can intercept data across your network), you also need to develop a policy on their use (see Chapter 7). Sniffers can capture and decode all packets entering and leaving the wire, including the company president's e-mail. If you capture packets with a sniffer and send them to a third-party company to analyze a particular problem, that company should sign a nondisclosure agreement with your organization. If it doesn't, how do you know its employees are handling your data with prudence? Also, your administrators may need to use a packet sniffer to troubleshoot problems, so be sure you have an acceptable use policy regarding this type of software and hardware.

ETHERNET PORTS

Do you have empty network ports in your walls that you're saving for later use? These ports are an easy way to penetrate your network. Intruders can bring in a laptop and plug in to your system through one of these ports — particularly if they're using a sniffer. You should disconnect any unused wiring from your hubs.

BACKUP TAPES

Unprotected backup tapes are a network security risk. Password-protect them for read access. Don't store your backup tapes at your data center; instead, store them off-site. If backups aren't off-site and a fire in the building causes the host to go up in flames, any chance of restoring the data does, too. I recommend that you take backups off-site to a location that's 20 or more miles away from the host system at least once a week.

WIRETAPPING

When you run cable, make sure it is protected by at least one security mechanism — for example, anyone who needs to get to the cable must access your suite with a card key first. Intruders will go to great lengths to gain access to your cable and wiring, where they can easily eavesdrop or break into systems.

HOT-SWAPPABLE AND SPARE COMPONENTS

Do you invest in hot-swappable components for your network's critical components? You should consider it if your data is mission critical. It's important to analyze the business cost of network downtime. For example, if you could lose $100,000 for every hour the system is down, you've just built a business case for spending $10,000 on hot-swappable components that can be changed without taking the system down.

If you still think your organization can't afford hot-swappable components, keep spare parts, such as hard disks, memory, NICs, and modems, on hand. Anything that provides a vital link in your system should have a spare part on site.

USER PASSWORDS

Windows NT passwords protect a large part of your Windows NT system. Maintaining strict password policies limits the possibility of a password attack. The easiest way for someone to gain unauthorized access to your system is with a stolen or easily guessed password. It is very important that all Windows NT users, especially those with administrative rights, have long, complicated passwords that are impossible to guess. You can set passwords with User Manager or at the system logon prompt. Password scanning tools, like ScanNT by MWC, Inc. (http://www.omna.com/Yes/MWC/PRS-index.htm), help you implement your password policy. The program checks Windows NT user account passwords for "strength" against any password dictionary.

With the User Manager, you can also specify how quickly account passwords expire, which forces users to change passwords often, and limit the number of failed attempts to log on, which locks out an account when this limit is reached. For example, if you set a maximum of three bad password attempts with a 30-minute lockout after the third attempt, you can minimize the number of password attempts per day.

You can set such a limit on the Administrator's account in Windows NT 4.0, but you must purposely edit a Registry setting to activate it. However, instead of doing this, I strongly recommend that you remove the Administrator account's right to log on from the network, allowing the Administrator account to be used only when logging on locally — if at all. This way, even if someone discovers your Administrator password, the password works only from your server. It's also wise to minimize the number of users that belong to the Administrators group. As mentioned in Chapter 4, the best tactic is to not use the Administrator account at all, opting instead to use a substitute account with complete administrator privileges.

Brute force password attacks, which I discuss further in Chapter 9, exploit a user's account on a system. One of the most common brute force tactics is to look for default accounts on systems. Some versions of Windows NT Workstation by default install a Guest account enabled with a blank password. As we mentioned in Chapter 4, always assign the Guest account minimal privileges; unless you really need it, disable it.

USER AND GROUP ADMINISTRATION

User and group administration is crucial to any network environment. Be careful when assigning privileges and be sure that your policies are followed.

Be particularly careful with unnecessary accounts. Sometimes when employees leave a company, no one bothers to disable or delete their accounts (network, Internet, and voice) — much less collect their card keys and door keys. This oversight leaves the back door wide open for the former employee to dial in from home if your network maintains a dialup system. You should establish a procedure for employee access that starts with initiating access and ends with removing access as soon as access is no longer necessary.

Here are a few basic techniques to help you achieve a better level of security:

- Disable the Guest account until it's needed; disable old, unused accounts, such as those used by temporary employees or vendors.
- Create a new Administrator account by creating a new user and adding it to the Administrators group. Then revoke the built-in Administrator account's "access from network" right. You may even want to disable the Administrator account completely once you've established other users as members of the Administrator group.
- Replace the Everyone Group with a new group and revoke the Everyone group's rights in the Policies/User Rights menu of the User Manager.

SHARE AND FILE PERMISSIONS

As you create new shares, Windows NT assigns the Everyone group to them by default. Check the Security tab when establishing shared resources and minimize the number of users who have access rights. You can use Somarsoft's DumpACL, included on the CD-ROM accompanying this book, to review permission settings on your shared resources. DumpACL analyzes your shares and creates a report.

NTFS partitions have faster read file access than DOS partitions, and DOS partitions have faster write access than NTFS partitions. Some people take advantage of this knowledge to improve their system's performance for disk-intensive applications, such as SQL Server or the Windows NT paging file. If you use a DOS partition, be sure that you

- Do not share DOS volumes — they use the FAT file system, which offers no security. For safety's sake, use the Scheduler Service to perform an unshare command on that DOS partition every time the system starts up.
- Secure the server physically by keeping it in a locked room with controlled access.

E-MAIL ADMINISTRATORS

You should think about who handles your corporate e-mail systems. People have been caught reading others' e-mail. Sometimes it's necessary to read someone else's mail, but it can be avoided 9 out of 10 times. You probably won't ever know whether it's happening on your network, but you can put a policy in place to govern such instances (see Chapter 7) and require all e-mail postal officials to sign the policy.

UNWANTED TCP/IP PORTS

As you learned in Chapter 1, TCP/IP relies on ports to perform its tasks, and therefore it's not difficult to find active services. Routinely scan the TCP/IP ports on all the machines on your network, looking for ports that should not be "listening." This important procedure can reveal rogue services. For example, you may find an unwanted FTP server or a hidden Web server using company bandwidth. Intruders are known for installing rogue services on inconspicuous chosen ports, and your scans may pick up such an abnormality.

You definitely should monitor ports 137, 138, and 139, which allow direct network connections to shared Windows NT resources. You should block all access to these ports at your Internet router, which will prevent a potential intruder from gaining direct network access to your Windows-based systems.

BUILT-IN TCP/IP FILTERING

Windows NT 4.0 now includes built-in TCP/IP filtering. This feature is quite primitive and does not support Access Control, logging, or other advanced features commonly found in most firewalls. Nevertheless, this kind of filter system adds a layer to your network security. If you use this filtering as a line of defense, you should check the configuration routinely to make sure nothing has been changed. The Windows NT 4.0 TCP/IP filtering functions are in the Control Panel, Network, Protocols tab, TCP/IP, Security button.

Built-in filtering is most effective when applied to the LAN interface on a Windows NT-based Internet router because filtering can control which TCP and UDP ports can be accessed. The configuration dialog boxes for filtering provide only the option to "disable all except the following ports," which means turning on necessary ports one by one. This method is the best way to control a system — the result is tedious configuration but high protection.

NETWORK BINDINGS

I can't give explicit advice about network bindings because the correct settings for your environment depend on your network's structure and the protocols you use. However, you should review your network bindings and make sure nothing is set unnecessarily. The Somarsoft Web page offers good tips for basic binding arrangements on networks running only TCP/IP. You may want to unbind the SMB protocol from the TCP/IP transport, which prevents users on the Internet from connecting to your Windows NT-based shares. Somarsoft is located at http://www.somarsoft.com.

THE REGISTRY

Most Windows NT settings are kept in the Windows NT registry. You can configure the registry both locally and remotely, which leaves it open to exploitation. Be sure you disable remote registry access on your systems (Windows NT and Windows 95). I recommend changing the following registry entries; be sure to test these changes on a noncritical server before implementing them, because results vary from system to system.

- Remove the Everyone group permissions from HKEY_LOCAL_MACHINE and be sure you don't propagate the changes through the entire subtree.
- Set the following permissions throughout the entire subtree:

    HKEY_LOCAL_MACHINE\HARDWARE
    | Administrator: | Full Control |
    | local system: | Full Control |
    | users: | Read only |

    HKEY_LOCAL_MACHINE\SOFTWARE
    | Administrator: | Full Control |
    | local system: | Full Control |
    | users: | Read only |

    HKEY_LOCAL_MACHINE\SYSTEM
    | Administrator: | Full Control |
    | local system: | Full Control |
    | users: | Read only |

- Enable auditing with the Security | Auditing menu in the Registry Editor. Use an ordinary user account to check that the system works properly because many software packages require write access to several subkeys to run. Log on as an administrator and check the Event log to find out which registry keys require write access, then grant users write access to only those keys.

- To restrict network access to the HKEY_LOCAL_MACHINE on Windows NT 3.51 with Service Pack 2 or higher, create the key

    HKEY_LOCAL_MACHINE\SYSTEM\CurrentControlSet\Control\
    SecurePipeServers\winreg

and set the following permission for this key:

Administrator: Full Control

These recommendations tighten your overall system security. As I said, be sure to try these on a noncritical system, because changing registry permissions can render some software packages useless until the registry settings are adjusted correctly.

Instead of making the changes above manually, you can use a tool created by David LeBlanc called Everyone2User. You'll find Everyone2User on the Web at http://207.176.151.4/david.htm.

PBX SYSTEMS

Although telephone systems are not part of the Internet, I want to mention them while I'm talking about possibilities because you might connect your PBX to a network to automate its operation. Historically, teenagers perpetrated most network intrusions, and these same teenagers enjoy hacking phone systems.

If you use a sophisticated phone system and you don't require voice mail passwords, intruders can get into your voice mail system the same way they do networks. Even if you do use passwords, software programs can hack these phone systems using the same principles used to hack computers.

You should handle phone system passwords in the same manner you'd handle network passwords. Set up a minimum number of password guesses before locking out the account. Require users to have a password of 6 or more characters. Don't allow outside callers to call in and obtain an outside line — hackers love this feature. This function is common in busy organizations, such as hospitals and large firms with a lot of activity. Because some outside callers masquerade as if they are calling from inside the organization, if possible, don't allow outside lines to ring directly on internal call lines either, but instead force all calls to go through a main number and have someone act as the operator for the firm.

EXTERNAL LAN LINKS

For a variety of different reasons, businesses connect their networks to their business partners' networks. If you do, be sure you understand your partner's idea of security and install some type of traffic-limiting firewall between you and your partner. If their network is hacked, yours might be next! In other words, in cases like this, your network is no safer than its weakest connection point.

EXTERNAL WAN LINKS

Untrusted networks, such as the Internet, pose considerable risks. The best approach is to minimize all open access to your network from the untrusted network, which means closing unused or unnecessary ports at the firewall, using proxy servers, and maybe even using other technologies, such as virtual private networks or stateful inspection devices.

IIS

Internet Information Server (IIS) is a highly integrated Web server for Windows NT. IIS uses the Windows NT security database to authenticate Internet users. If you use IIS in an insecure mode and allow clear text authentication, hackers can sniff Windows NT passwords and use them to access your Windows NT server. Even if you use Windows NT Challenge/Response authentication, you still risk a brute-force password attack. If an intruder tries a brute-force attack on the IUSR_SYSTEMNAME account, which IIS uses for anonymous user access, and your policies enforce account lockout after a set number of bad password attempts, you could experience a denial of service. The attack would lock out the account, preventing any anonymous access.

Intruders know several ways to attack an IIS server. Your main defense is to load new service packs when they become available. Because service packs can sometimes break applications running on your Windows NT system, some consider keeping current a bad practice. However, remember that Microsoft rarely announces to the world new security problems; instead, they simply slip the fixes into service packs. Therefore, not loading service packs renders your system more vulnerable than it needs to be — *so load the service packs religiously.*

Running old versions of any software, especially Internet services like IIS, can lead to trouble. Versions of IIS before version 3 have many known problems that can easily lead to unwanted access. I post most of the exploits on my Web site, http://www.ntshop.net/security.

Also, using untrusted ISAPI programs, which are Web server scripts developed especially for IIS, with any version of IIS can be problematic. These scripts run under the authority of the IUSR_SYSTEMNAME account, and therefore inherit the account permissions of this account. However, it is incredibly simple to change the ISAPI permissions to the all-powerful SYSTEM account with one line of code: RevertToSelf(). When a script with this line is executed, the script gains system privileges, at which point it can do anything an administrator can do. This exploit is posted on my Web site, along with a sample ISAPI script that you can try. The best ways to prevent this problem are to not use ISAPI programs from untrusted sources and to not use any ISAPI scripts if you don't absolutely need to.

SOFTWARE FEATURES

When many people get a new software package, they dive in headfirst without reading the manuals or learning about new features, particularly when they're upgrading existing software. However, this approach is often a bad practice, because new features can leave data unprotected or overly exposed — or they can improve your security.

Many software packages contain built-in security features; you should use those features to your advantage. For instance, Microsoft Word's password protection feature lets a user protect a document from prying eyes, which may be just what you need to enhance your overall security — especially if you're handling a customer's proprietary information. Many software packages offer this type of function, and using it can go a long way toward deterring intruders.

The best practice is to proceed with caution. Whenever you contemplate an upgrade or new installation, keep security in the front of your mind. If you do, you'll train yourself to look at your situation differently, and more often than not you'll be able to recognize potential holes and problems before you become a victim of them.

UNTRUSTED RESOURCES ON THE INTERNET

Online networks, especially the Internet, are a Mecca for new and exciting resources — primarily software. But don't take these resources for granted; sometimes their developers have ulterior motives, such as infiltrating your network. Don't be naïve and blindly accept items from the Internet. We've all heard the old saying, "Never look a gift horse in the mouth," but when it comes to security risks, you should consider doing just that.

Shareware and freeware are two of the most enticing and dangerous types of software you can acquire because you have very little motive to trust the developers. Usually a shareware developer is just one person sitting in a bedroom someplace writing software because that's what that person likes to do.

We all appreciate a person's effort to develop something and give it away, but the problem is that intruders often use these types of software as a way to infiltrate your network.

The software may contain a virus that destroys your data or maybe even a Trojan horse that e-mails a person your passwords every time they are changed. (For more information about avoiding these types of threats, see the next section.) Think it can't happen? Take the case of Windows NT 4.0. Sometime in mid-1996, Microsoft quietly added a feature that calls a DLL any time a password changes or a new user is added. With this new feature, an intruder could easily create a Trojan horse that e-mails the user name and password to someone on the Internet. For an example of this exploit, along with some sample source code, point your Web browser to http://www.ntsecurity.net/security/passworddll.htm. Also, be leery of software you get through e-mail. Even a seemingly harmless Word document can contain dangerous macros that can harm your network.

AVOIDING THE PLAGUE

The virus and the Trojan horse suggest the wisdom of avoiding random relationships. Code-signing is new concept whereby developers add a verifiable digital signature to a software package, but this type of technology doesn't guarantee anything — it simply lets a person know where a piece of software was supposed to have originated from, through examination of a digital signature.

The best advice I can give is simply to not use untrusted software. Testing software on an isolated computer works to a certain extent, but the possibility still exists that some hidden command, variable, or switch could trigger some malicious activity, something you don't find until it's too late.

Viruses

A virus, as defined by the Semantec Anti-virus Research Center, is "a parasitic program written intentionally to enter a computer without the user's permission or knowledge." The word "parasitic" indicates that the virus, by attaching itself to files or boot sectors, replicates using the resources of the host system, continuing to spread and harming the host — just like a living virus. Though some viruses do little other than replicate themselves, some viruses can cause serious damage, affecting program operation and system performance. You should never assume that a virus is harmless and leave it on a system. You should always eradicate it immediately upon detection.

Most DOS- and Windows 3.1-based file viruses function under Windows NT also, especially if your Windows NT systems use the FAT file system, but NTFS-based systems are also vulnerable. The relatively good news is that a native Windows NT virus has not *yet* been created, at least not to my knowledge. The bad news is that it is possible to create native Windows NT viruses, and thus some ill-mannered person is probably writing one even as you read this book.

The Trojan Horse

Just as the name implies, a Trojan horse harbors a hidden feature that can do anything imaginable. One example is a shell script that performs a task such as faking the logoff sequence when the user isn't really logging off, thus leaving the system open, or faking the logon script, capturing user names and passwords for later use.

Windows NT takes a novel approach to preventing this faking by requiring the magic Ctrl-Alt-Del sequence to initiate user logon. However, according to Somarsoft's Windows NT security site (http://www.somarsoft.com), even this sequence won't stop hackers who can physically access computers and write their own Windows NT logon sequence emulator. After the user name and the password are grabbed for later use, the Trojan horse imitates the infamous Blue Screen of Death (the screen you see when Windows NT crashes), leaving the user thinking that the system merely crashed.

Other versions of Windows, such as Windows 95, are also susceptible to Trojan horses. Consider the impact of a simple keystroke-grabbing Trojan horse if a user logs on to that workstation as a Windows NT administrator — it would grab the user's password, which an intruder could then use to gain administrative privileges on the Windows NT network. These types of Trojan horses already exist and are readily available on the Internet; for examples, see my Web site (http://www.ntshop.net/security).

Dangerous Macros

A macro is a series of commands. Microsoft Word uses macros; the macros execute when documents load. Programs that use macros, such as Word, are a force to be reckoned with. Macro commands can actually delete files or even send files through e-mail to someone they weren't intended for. Microsoft is aware of this vulnerability and has taken steps to prevent dangerous macros, but you can't rely on them alone. Be careful about accepting program files containing macros from unknown or untrusted sources — they could ruin your system.

Uncontrollable Web Controls

The huge popularity of the Web has spawned new development tools, some of which can be used to create reusable objects and scripting code, commonly referred to as controls. Some of these tools, including ActiveX, VBScript, Java, and JavaScript, can all damage your system if the tools have unforeseen bugs. In

February 1997, a German television station aired a segment showing a computer programmer who had successfully developed a simple ActiveX control that could be embedded in any Web page. When a user visited a Web page with that control embedded, the control opened a copy of Quicken, a popular accounting software, on the user's computer, and inserted a transaction. The point of the demonstration was to show the weakness in the security of these tools. For an online example showing how easy it is for an ActiveX control to launch a program from a Web page, point your browser to http://www.ntshop. net/security/ActiveX.htm. This page has a simple control that opens a copy of Notepad and inserts some text. This demonstration should raise your eyebrows a little.

Protecting yourself against attacks from malicious Web controls takes just basic common sense, with a little pain and suffering mixed in. If your Web browser supports any of the development controls I mentioned, disable them. When you are surfing a Web site that you know you can trust, turn them on only while surfing that site, and turn them back off when you're finished. I know this process is tedious, but it might save you a lot of grief down the road.

Here are some other good policies to implement that can help minimize potential damage from uncontrollable Web controls:

- Backup policy — Back up all your important data regularly and frequently. Backup policies are a necessary part of your security. In the worst-case scenario, you'll be able to restore your files from the backup.

- Software policy — You should have policies about downloading active content (scripts or other controls that execute on the end user's machine) from public Web pages.

- Anti-virus software — In any environment, you should use virus protection to prevent this type of infiltration.

- Encrypting information — Several packages offer encryption. Two of the more popular are pretty good privacy (PGP) and RSA SecurPC.

    - PGP, a public-key encryption system, is available for many platforms. PGP uses the strong Rivest-Shamir-Adleman (RSA) public-key encryption algorithm and can secure such items as your personal files and public messages. With PGP, you can communicate securely with other people, without having to meet to exchange secret keys. It also includes support for digital signatures, making it possible to sign public messages without the risk that someone will modify the message. PGP is used worldwide for secure e-mail communication.

        PGP lets users generate their own pair of private and public keys. You publish the public key to everyone; someone sending you a file uses it to encrypt a file or a public message. You keep the private key secret and use it to decrypt files or messages that were encrypted with the public key. The principles of public-key cryptography are documented in the PGP software distribution (freeware versions of the PGP also include source code). Information on current PGP versions can be obtained at http://www.ifi.uio.no/pgp/versions.shtml.

- RSA Data Security, Inc., incorporates strong RSA cryptography into the file systems of many operating systems. RSA SecurPC is a corporate security solution and a personal security tool that integrates with the operating system. For example, on a Windows-based PC, it becomes part of the Windows 95 Explorer or the File Manager in Windows 3.1 or Windows NT; on the Macintosh it integrates with the Finder. A user can define a set of files and directories or folders that are automatically encrypted and decrypted when they enter or exit Windows or shut down or start up their Macintosh.

MONITORING AND DETECTION

Logs are a snapshot of time on your network. These historical records are invaluable in tracking down network problems, especially security-related problems. Protect your system logs fiercely, because they may contain vital information such as network addresses, machine names, user names, and bad passwords. Treat your logs like any other piece of secret information.

It is well known in the security world that most network break-ins occur on networks that have some security but aren't monitored closely enough. Therefore, I cannot stress enough how important it is to monitor your network — watch its performance and read your logs, in detail, often. Failure to do so gives an intruder a big opportunity to penetrate your network.

With Windows NT, you should read the Event log details and use the Performance Monitor, as well as other tools. Monitoring can often alert you to suspicious activity before it results in damage. Watch the Event log for oddities such as event code 529 (invalid logon attempts) repeating many times, which could indicate that your system is under a password attack. Also, watch for event code 517, which indicates someone has cleared the log file. To cover their tracks, hackers routinely delete system logs after they enter a system.

Using the Performance Monitor, check the list of processes running on the server and look for processes that should not be running. You can also monitor many different aspects of the Windows NT system with this tool, such as Errors Access Permissions (EAP), Errors Granted Access (EGA), Errors Logon (EL), and Logon Total (LT) — each of which counts its respective transactions: EAP counts denied object access; EGA counts errors in attempting to grant access to an object; EL counts total errors logging on; and LT counts total logons. These types of statistics serve as a way to monitor security.

If your company runs Internet services, you should consider installing a package that can monitor these services and alert you to any unusual events. A copy of this type of software, NTManage, is on the CD-ROM accompanying this book.

DOCUMENTATION

We purposely listed this item last because it's the least-desired job of any network administrator. However, as you see in a moment, it's necessary and a helpful place to begin evaluating your security. Use the documentation guidelines in Chapter 7 as a basis for your network documentation. NetSuite (http://www.netsuite.com) provides a handy way for you to document your existing network, along with wiring and cabling specifications. Additionally, LANware's NTManage (included on the CD-ROM accompanying this book; also at http://www.lanware.net) also helps you document your system and builds a database of IP address assignments at the same time. Failure to document your network puts your organization at substantial risk, since eventually you'll lose mental track of all the modifications you've done to your network. When a security problem occurs, you may not be able to locate the source of the problem quickly to stop whatever is happening during your perceived security problem.

THE RISKS OF OUTSOURCING

If your organization outsources any or all of your IS functions, you need to place some checks and balances on that outsourcing company. Typically, these outsourcing companies back up and store your data, provide communications links, and maybe even run your help desk for you. The key is that these companies, in an effort to save money, sometimes combine your data with other company's data on one system or one database. You need to know who has access to your information. It's important for you to ask the outsourcing company how they separate data and how they put in safeguards between organizations and partners. You should ask them at least the following questions, and consider ending your relationship with them if they aren't answering positively:

- Is my organization's data stored on a separate hard disk or host?
- Who has access to my organization's data? List all names and the reasons they have access.
- Does your organization perform background checks on its employees?

- Are your employees bonded?
- Does your organization have a disaster recovery plan? If so, provide us with a copy.
- Does your organization subcontract work to other companies? If so, to whom and why?
- Does your organization share any communications links with other organizations? If so, what safeguards are in place to separate transmissions and data?
- Does your help desk require my employees to give a security code before changing passwords?

You risk a lot if you outsource your most critical assets without thoroughly investigating the company providing these services to you. Never assume that a "reputable" firm has its own security issues in order. Find out for yourself, and if you can't, select another partner.

DO YOU TRUST YOUR ISP?

I think it was Bruce Springsteen who said, "Blind faith in anything will get you killed." When it comes to selecting an ISP, don't trust it until you know it well, because this "blind faith" may get your network "killed." Trusting the company also means trusting its employees, whom you don't know. I say this from experience, having founded, operated, and sold one of Houston's largest ISPs. Don't get me wrong, I'm not saying my company was not trustworthy — we absolutely were. I'm saying that my customers almost never checked us. They simply called us and said "I need to connect my Windows NT network to the Internet" and we'd do it for them.

Today, I don't run my own Internet link through my old company because I don't own it anymore and I don't know what's going on over there. I know that they don't pay as much attention to security since I left. After selling my company, I chose a new ISP, whose owner I know personally. I learned about his employees — the people who would handle my link and therefore have the knowledge necessary to sniff packets coming from my network. The more I learned about them, the less I trusted them. Almost all his system administrators seemed to have some connection to or history with the hacker underground, which is sometimes good because these guys know most of the exploits and can prevent them. The owner hired them for their backgrounds, but apparently, the temptations were too great.

I began experiencing what I can only call "weirdness" on my personal workstation. I began looking into what was causing the oddities. To rule out a source-routed packet attack (which my router blocks — but you never know!),

I changed the IP address of my workstation to one I've never used before. Within a matter of minutes, I captured several log entries on one of my systems that showed that one of my ISP's servers was sending packets to this new address. How could they have known I was using this new address this quickly? Eventually, I decided that they must be monitoring a range of addresses on my network — without my knowledge or permission — and in that process found this new address moving packets out to the Internet.

I was incredibly aggravated, so I sent an e-mail to the owner telling him what I had discovered and told him very politely to "make it stop, and do it yesterday, not tomorrow." Now I must assume that my ISP was intercepting all my private mail and other correspondence. I moved my Internet link to a new ISP — but not before I personally visited that ISP and received background information on its network administrators and a controlled tour of its network shop.

The lesson here is that you shouldn't completely trust anyone at all — especially your ISP. Remember, all your outbound Internet traffic goes straight through its network and can be captured and examined at will. Perhaps operating with a sense of paranoia when it comes to selecting an ISP and using its services is in perfect order here — which is my newfound practice.

WHERE TO START?

Now that you are aware of all these security threats, how do you go about systematically protecting yourself against them? A good place to begin is answering the question, "What do I have at my disposal?" You don't know what you need if you don't know what you have. We consider thorough network documentation in the next chapter, but here's a place to start. Let's talk about your existing environment.

EXISTING ENVIRONMENT

Start with a good site survey to reveal what you have on hand and what you need to protect.

Equipment and Software

To begin with, inventory your equipment and software systems and determine what software is running on which platforms. Depending on the size of your network, you may want to do a full inventory, which is also great for insurance purposes. You may even want to hire an outside firm; Tally Systems has long been a leader in wall-to-wall inventory audits.

You may also want to consider software that keeps track of your inventory. Instituting a network management and inventory application suite like

Microsoft's Systems Management Server (SMS) or IBM's Tivoli Management Platform (TME10) is always beneficial. These types of software systems can determine hardware platforms, system configurations, and system software content surveys and can alert you when changes are made to systems. A full-scale inventory audit may take a lot of personnel time at first, but once you've got it done, it's much easier to keep up-to-date.

Identify and classify all your systems. Many different classifications can be applied to your hardware and software. The following list offers some example categories for classification:

- Strategic — Strategic systems conform to corporate computing direction and standards. New purchases should use the strategic platform as the preferred solution. The strategic direction is the most practical, multi-purpose, scalable, cost-effective solution.

- Tactical — Tactical systems are production systems that are no longer the strategic computing direction but still serve practical roles in the current computing environment. These systems must be maintained or replaced with strategic systems.

- Legacy — We all have the black sheep that we wish would disappear, but we can't make them. These older systems must still be used but are not in the strategic direction of your organization. Many e-mail systems and database applications fall into this category, and this technology must be supported.

- Unsupported — An unsupported system can't feasibly be supported by your organization or any other. Many legacy systems move into this category quickly in today's world. You should consider phasing out this equipment in favor of newer technologies that are easier to secure and support.

Network Documentation

Documentation is vital to any network installation. Make sure your network and its modifications are thoroughly documented as part of the installation process, not as an afterthought. Lack of documentation routinely costs firms money when they need to reconstruct their systems.

Detail your network protocols on your network maps to help you understand what's flowing through your network, any trends or patterns, and your traffic load. Good network maps are invaluable in troubleshooting and securing networks. I give you a documentation outline in the next chapter.

Keep your network maps under lock and key as you would any sensitive information; don't post them on a wall for everyone to see. Although you may be proud of your network design and your network map may be impressive, it's still proprietary information that you must protect.

ADDITIONAL REQUIREMENTS

Once you've evaluated and documented your entire network, you should have a clear view of what you currently have on hand. Now you need to determine any additional equipment you need once you've chosen your methods of protection.

Hardware

After the evaluation, most companies conclude that they're underpowered in some areas and overpowered in others. A 500 Mhz DEC Alpha running file and print services for 50 users is a bit of overkill. Look at the loads on your servers and balance those loads either by moving users off overworked servers to underused machines or by taking ad vantage of inter-operability and inter-changability features of those machines. You may be able to get away with swapping hard drives.

If you plan to install software-based security systems, you'll need hardware to run it on. Learn the requirements of any particular software and determine whether your current platforms are adequate. You may find that you need a few minor upgrades.

Software

After you identify all your available software platforms, you can start by using any deterrents those packages offer. For example, most network operating systems allow some type of auditing, so make sure it's enabled and monitored closely.

Almost every company will need at least one additional software package to deploy adequate security protection schemes, unless you're planning to use hardware-based tools. Appendix C lists most security software vendors for NT; use it as a guide in researching your additional software needs.

Network Connections

Connections are another overlooked area when planning network installations. One of the most tedious aspects of network planning and maintenance is keeping up with the ever-growing changes and demands. The best practice when considering new connections or changes to current connections is user need, not administrator convenience. In all cases, it's best to segregate network traffic both by load patterns and by access patterns.

What I mean is that you should try to develop your network the way you develop and segment your business — isolate your accounting people on a network segment and isolate your sales staff on a different network segment. This segregation makes it easier to control network traffic with intelligent hubs and routers. If no physical path to certain data systems and information exists, accessing that information is much more difficult for an intruder and any impact from a successful attempt is minimized.

THE FUTURE OF MICROSOFT SECURITY

Microsoft's security consciousness is rising rapidly. More people are becoming concerned about security, especially because the Internet has become so popular. Windows NT 5.0 will sport the Kerberos authentication protocol and other important enhancements, such as new switch settings that control clear text and challenge/response authentication. Microsoft also makes development kits that add security to custom-built applications, like the Microsoft Security Framework. Not only will Microsoft continue beefing up security potential, but so will third-party developers who create applications for Windows NT environments.

Code-signing techniques, which authenticate the origin of a given piece of software, are gaining popularity. Although this technology has problems and risks, it does offer a level of assurance when you obtain software in nonstandard ways, especially downloading it from the Internet.

Windows NT 4.0 includes the new Point-to-Point Tunneling Protocol (PPTP), which is a way to create an encrypted private network connection between systems. Using this technology, you can span your LAN to another LAN in some distant location safely by using the Internet as an inexpensive means of connectivity. Also, you can use PPTP with your telecommuters to better secure your systems. Telecommuters can use the ISPs of their choice, making a PPTP connection back to your network with less risk of packet sniffers and other snooping techniques obtaining sensitive information.

Microsoft has also released a new router technology, called Routing and Remote Access Server (RRAS, formerly code-named Steelhead), which you could combine with the MS Proxy Server to create a very robust front line of defense. Watch for RRAS to be developed even further, quite possibly into a full blown firewall/router product with MPS 2.0.

SUMMARY

This chapter covers some broad categories of your environment that can pose risks to your network. We considered security threats in general, specific physical threats and network threats, and questions to ask outside service providers. In the next chapter, I present ideas for policies that safeguard against some of these security threats.

CHAPTER 7

DEVELOPING EFFECTIVE SECURITY POLICIES

In this chapter, we look at some ways to create and enforce security policies for your network. Remember, securing your network from attack incorporates more considerations than just your Internet connection, so we look at all kinds of security issues. I give you a sample Security Manual, a starting point for a Disaster Recovery Plan, and an outline for a Network Documentation Plan. When your network is running fine, this kind of documentation seems unnecessary, but its value becomes apparent when you discover a network problem and it takes you two extra days to fix it because the network isn't documented. Finally, we look at what you should do if you experience some kind of threat to your network's security.

IN THE BEGINNING

If you want your employees to take security seriously, you need to develop sound policies within the organization, educate users on these policies, and enforce the policies rigorously. If you take security seriously, your attitude will permeate the entire organization and minimize the monkey business that comes from within.

To add a further complication to the already complex matter of security, many organizations outsource their IS functions, allowing an outside company to manage their data. You need to incorporate controls and measures into your policies to make sure the outside company handles your data, a vital company resource, with confidentiality, integrity, and safety.

You should visit the National Computer Security Association (NCSA) Web site (http://www.ncsa.com/hotlinks) to stay up-to-date on relevant issues. The site includes great links to other security-related sites, focusing on policies, software, and security firms.

To begin your quest for security policies and procedures, ask yourself the following questions to see whether your organization is on the right track:

- Does our organization have a security manual for our employees?
- Do we have guidelines to follow when ordering hardware and software?
- Do we require all purchasing to go through a centralized group or individual?
- Do we require cost/benefit analysis and risk analysis for all new systems, including software?
- Do we consistently update our network documentation and associated maps?
- Do we have a disaster recovery and business resumption plan?
- Do we know who is responsible and accountable for our systems at each level?
- Do we have policies for system integrity, confidentiality, and information privacy?
- Do we have formal audit plans at all levels?
- Do we communicate information on a timely basis to our users?
- Do we include our users in the development of our policies?
- Do we require our employees to study our policies?
- Do we require our employees to sign a document proclaiming they will adhere to policies?

- Do we require the same of our business partners that we're physically networked to?

- Do we learn details about our networking partners and their employees, such as our ISP?

Depending on the type of business you're in and the way you actually conduct business, you could ask yourself a lot more questions. Your best bet is to assemble a team of the people who run your departments and flush out concerns. These issues will help you form an extensive list of questions that examine every aspect of your business in relation to security.

DEVELOP SOUND POLICIES

As I have said, intruders can come from outside or they can be right in your own back yard. Before you do anything in relation to the Internet, your organization needs to develop and enforce security policies. All eligible employees should be required to sign your organization's policy forms, and the completed forms should be part of each employee's Human Resources file. Current employees should sign the forms as part of continued employment.

If you outsource your IS functions, those employees should sign custom-tailored security forms, too. You should have some legal review of your forms and policies to ensure that you have some type of legal recourse for violations after the forms are signed.

At least every six months, your legal counsel should review your policies in light of current workplace legislation. In today's high-tech world, laws and technologies are changing very rapidly, and the ones that don't change are being interpreted in new ways. The policies you put in place today may not be meaningful in six months. For example, have you ever seen a "noncompete agreement" that companies routinely require employees to sign? They often don't hold up in court, usually because their wording is too restrictive. Your company can't legally "unfairly" restrict someone from doing business, and "unfairly" is subject to different interpretations. For example, if you require employees to sign a nondisclosure agreement to protect your in-house information, the time period you specify in that document may be longer than the law allows, and thus, the entire document may be held up as invalid. So check your policies.

Before you try to implement security policies, get buy-in from your users and from high-level managers; if you have a chief information officer (CIO) or a chief technical officer (CTO), start there. Although enlisting management support may delay the development of your policies, upper management must support and enforce these policies if they're to carry any weight. Any policy that states "employees will be dismissed immediately for violating the policy" must be supported by upper management so no one becomes an exception to the policy — which leads to overall noncompliance and possible discrimination suits.

In addition to forms that the employees sign, create a security manual separate from the employee handbook so the employees clearly understand the policies. A sample outline to use as a starting point is in the next section.

Decide or discover ahead of time where money to handle security problems will come from. For example, will money be taken out of the employee merit increase pot, the profit sharing pot, or some other source? Do you have a little excess in your budget that could cover it? Security breaches and threats cost organizations real dollars. If you know where the money to pay for mistakes or carelessness comes from, you can share this information with the employees so they understand the implications.

Different employees may sign different forms. For example, although in theory your customer service representatives don't need to sign an e-mail confidentiality agreement, it wouldn't hurt to have them do it anyway. The next section discusses forms that you may include in your security form portfolio — again, seek the final advice of your company's attorney.

FORMS FOR ALL EMPLOYEES

Keep in mind two points: first, your forms should clearly state the consequences of deviating from policy and procedure (e.g., dismissal, demotion, or criminal charges); and second, you should always word the documents in a nonthreatening way — you don't want to discourage people from working at your company by making them feel that you run your own little police state.

Confidentiality Agreement

All employees should sign a form stating that they will keep all organizational data confidential while they are employed and for some period after they leave your firm. Besides a definition of the term "confidential material," the form should include specific actions that the employees agree to, such as:

- They move confidential data and material only to those places you specify (for example, can they take it home for work reasons?).
- They don't leave confidential material out in the open (e.g., on their desktop); instead, they keep it only in locked drawers.
- They stamp all confidential material "Confidential" in red ink.
- They keep *all* confidential material in specially marked containers and shred the paper or delete the electronic files when their usefulness has past.

Badge/Password Agreement

All employees should sign an agreement indicating that they will

- Not give their badge or passwords (voice mail, network, Internet, or other) to any other employee
- Not leave workstations logged on to the network unattended
- Install power-on passwords for laptops and screen-saver passwords for workstations

Hardware Security Agreement

This policy should require all employees to secure the equipment they are assigned. For example, laptops lying out on the desk are easily stolen; if possible, you should require employees to lock laptops into docking stations.

This form should be very specific and should be based on the type of equipment that you give to your employees. It should also state how employees should handle equipment they have control over, including your network servers, wiring, and phone systems. This policy should also restrict them from modifying their equipment in any way.

Software License Agreement

It's imperative that you have all employees sign a form indicating that they will not

- Copy software off the network for any reason without permission from a specific person or persons
- Download software from the Internet for any reason
- Install software on the network
- Install software on their own PCs
- Disable or tamper with the virus protection software on their PCs
- Remove software or manuals from the office premises without written permission from a specific person or persons

Some of these items may save you headaches and legal problems if the Software Publisher's Association (SPA) comes knocking at your door. This group chases down software piracy and software license violators.

FORMS SPECIFIC TO IS EMPLOYEES

The following forms are only suggestions; you should contact your lawyer before attempting to draw them up. These forms are the minimum suggested; your organization may require more.

Security Agreement

All your IS personnel should sign a form agreeing to at least the following actions:

- They will fill out an incident report for any incident or hazard (current or future) that could pose a threat to the organization's safety or security at any level.
- They will fill out a report on any individual that does not follow the organization's security policies and procedures.
- They will fill out these reports in a timely manner, if not immediately. You should define what you mean by "timely" based on your firm's needs for that information.

E-Mail Postmaster Agreement

People charged with maintaining or operating the e-mail system for the organization should sign a form stating

- They will handle this responsibility with integrity, confidentiality, and discretion at all times.
- They will not monitor or read e-mail unless the intervention is required to reroute an e-mail message in transit. In such a case, they will read only the header information necessary to send the e-mail to the destination or back to the sender. Of course, if your firm routinely monitors e-mail contents, then this agreement may not apply.

Network Administrator Agreement

Because network administrators typically have full access to the network and all its contents, they should sign a confidentiality/integrity/ethics agreement that covers all of the aforementioned policy content, insofar as it applies to your network environment — a sort of blanket agreement. In other words, if you don't use e-mail, then you don't need e-mail policies and agreements.

EDUCATE THE USERS

Your users will be more likely to comply with your organization's security policies if they know why the policies are in place. For example, they may be aggravated by the 60 extra seconds the virus protection software adds when they boot up or insert a floppy disk. If you explain how fast a virus can infect a PC or network and the damage that can ensue, they may understand that 60 seconds a day is nothing. In addition, you want to educate them of the potential danger of just one person failing to meet this obligation — the ripple effect.

If you simply hand them the policies or your security manual, you are leaving it up to them to interpret your policies. As you probably know, you can give the same paragraph to ten different people and each interprets the same words differently. So give policies to them in writing, explain what the policies mean, and help them understand why they are in place. Your policies or security manual should also contain a blanket statement that says they agree to ask for clarification in the unlikely event they do not completely understand the purpose of any policy.

I suggest you host a seminar, either for the entire company or by department, depending on the size of your firm. Keep this seminar succinct but meaningful. To help your presentation, bring in a company that specializes in security solutions, because those companies can give examples of real situations where organizations lose money because of lax security policies. Point out that when an organization loses money from security breaches, it leaves less money for raises. When you explain security in terms of its financial impact on employees, you might raise awareness.

Many organizations, particularly manufacturing plants, post the number of days it's been since an accident. You may find a similar security posting — it's been X number of days since a security violation — effective in your organization. The more awareness you create in the organization, the better off your life will be.

Speaking of awareness, I suggest you host a security awareness week once a year to keep the fire lit under the employees. Use this time to bring them up to speed on new knowledge and inform them of any serious problems that have occurred at other firms. You may even include a "security awareness" section in your company's monthly employee newsletter. Remember the old adage "out of sight — out of mind"? You simply can't afford this scenario in your business when it comes to security.

As vital as it is to educate employees, listening to them is critical, too. It could be beneficial to institute an open-door policy or "no questions are dumb" policy. Two or more heads are always better than one when it comes to security.

ENFORCE THE POLICIES

Policies are useless if you don't enforce them. Not only do your users need to understand the financial implications of security problems to your organization; your users also need to know what will happen to them if they don't follow the policies to the letter.

I suggest that you rate the seriousness of security threats to your organization and decide on action based on how much risk the threat imposes. Immediate dismissal is not unheard-of for actions that put the company in a vulnerable position, such as pirating software. Companies can be assessed $100,000 – $500,000 fines for this breach when caught (notice that I use the word "when" here, and not "if"). It's not fair to other employees if one employee puts the company at risk. It's also not uncommon to give employees one written notice before termination. However, one slip-up can cost your organization a lot of money, so your company should determine what's best.

One organization I know of teaches security by example. They walk around and look for workstations left unattended, logged onto the network, with no password restrictions. From those workstations, they send an e-mail resignation notice to the employee's boss similar to the one below.

> Dear Boss:
>
> I must give you my two-week notice of resignation, effective immediately, because I've been caught leaving my workstation unattended, which is a violation of our company's security policy.

This technique is *definitely* effective. Imagine leaving your workstation unsecured and finding out that you resigned from the company without even knowing it. Somehow, you have to explain to your boss that you didn't write the note.

Regardless of how you choose to enforce your policies, be consistent with every employee, don't play favorites, and take swift action to correct problems.

SAMPLE OVERALL SECURITY MANUAL

This section gives you an outline of a rather encompassing security manual to prepare for your employees. Giving them a manual clearly communicates what your organization expects of them, and they can keep it at their workstations and refer to it as needed. As you compile your security manual, you may want to talk with your Human Resources department to see if they have other safety or security information they'd like to include in the manual; at the very least, you may need their approval for your manual. If your organization follows specific Occupational Safety and Health Association (OSHA) regulations, your manual may be quite large; in that case, you may want a section in it specifically for Network Security, or place that information in separate notebook.

For an exhaustive (and I do mean exhaustive) security manual that includes bibliographic information, links, and software information, check the InterNIC site (http://ds.internic.net/fyi/fyi8.html). Although the outline below is not all-encompassing, I hope it gets your creative juices flowing.

INTRODUCTION

In this section, explain why security is important to the company. If you design a security seminar for the employees, you can take material from your seminar to use in the introduction.

EMERGENCY NUMBERS

In case of an emergency, who do you want your employees to call? If you have dedicated security personnel on site, which is unlikely unless you're a large corporation, who should an employee call first — internal security or the police? If it's an internal problem, who in the IS department should they contact? If you don't give specifics, you've left the employees open to make their own decisions, which we all know aren't always the same decisions we'd like them to make.

BADGE AND PASSWORD REGULATIONS

Even though you've designed a form for each employee to sign concerning badge and password access, you should reiterate their responsibilities here. You may also include a copy of the blank form here so they can see it and remember that they signed it.

If you require employees to wear badges, you should consider a policy requiring all visitors to wear special badges. Visitors may be required to sign a visitor book, obtain a badge, and be escorted while in the building. If visitors are required to wear badges and be escorted, you should include information on the procedure to follow if employees notice an unescorted visitor or someone without a badge following them into a controlled area.

A policy on lost and forgotten badges is also a good idea. Most large firms that are serious about security do not let employees into the facilities without their personal badge. If for some reason they forget their badge, they absolutely must go home and get it before being allowed any type of access — this sort of practice builds discipline and diligence, but may be too restrictive for your environment. You may instead want to adopt a policy of how often an employee can be issued a temporary badge before some type of disciplinary action is taken.

PROPERTY SAFETY AND CLASSIFICATION

If you follow the policy suggestions in the previous section, the employees also signed a form requiring them to secure all computing assets as if they were their own. In this section of the manual, you should itemize exactly what you expect the employee to protect and how — for example, locking laptops into docking stations or having signed property passes for equipment leaving the building.

Hopefully, you carefully track all equipment telecommuting employees use. If they must sign a property form, state so here. Also, make sure someone is responsible for getting the equipment back when employees leave. I know of one case where an employee left a firm and managed to keep two very expensive notebook computers worth more than $10,000 — the company never asked for them back. He embarrassed them all by returning the laptops months later in front of the firm's bosses.

COPYRIGHT AND LICENSING INFORMATION

Most employees know that it's a copyright violation to photocopy an entire book, magazine, or other published materials. However, you should remind them of that and state that your organization does not condone it. You also want to inform them that copying software is a big no-no, and tell them why. Include a copy of the policy form they signed. Tell them who the SPA is, and the consequences when the SPA knocks at the door.

Employees need to know that any work they create while on your time or using your resources belongs to your organization. It should be considered proprietary information.

Does your organization classify material as confidential? If so, you need to advise your employees of the specific handling requirements (e.g., red "Confidential" stamp, document shredding or special document storage requirements).

TELEPHONE SECURITY

You should require your employees to use passwords on their voice mailboxes. Here, you should state that policy and why you have it. You may also want to warn employees that they are *never* to transfer incoming calls to outside lines. Receptionists are particularly vulnerable to this request.

You should also consider regulating how employees handle requests for information about your organization. For example, if *LAN Times* calls someone in the IS department, do you want that employee granting an interview and representing your organization? Probably not. Tell your employees who should get these calls. You'd be amazed at what can be learned from a simple phone call to an unsuspecting employee.

PRIVACY

Some companies take the position that an employee on the premises is subject to monitoring, including videotaping, reading e-mail, or listening to voice mail. This section of the manual is a great place to announce whether surveillance cameras are used in your organization. Because of privacy laws, you may need to also post this information at the entrances to your building. You can also include information about how e-mail and voice mail are treated within your organization. Products are available that monitor e-mail for certain key phrases. Some organizations use this software only in outbound e-mail to make sure that employees in different companies aren't colluding on prices. Regardless of your organization's stance, you may want to make the information available to your employees here.

You should also warn your employees that they represent your organization on the Internet. If they surf the *Playboy* Web site, it's your organization's information that is being transferred to that Web site. They need to be aware of the marketers on the Internet that gather this information for profiling and reuse.

IMPORT/EXPORT REGULATIONS

Does your organization have international branches? If so, you need to be aware that sending software, e-mail, faxes, and other information to an international location may be considered "exporting." You need to advise your employees of your policy. You (or your company attorney) may need to consult the U.S. Department of Commerce about some issues.

TRAVEL

Employees need to know your policies on handling equipment and data when they travel. For example, do you want them to avoid working on a laptop on an airplane because of shoulder surfers or corporate spies? If so, tell them very plainly right here.

Can employees discuss your organization's business in public areas? They probably shouldn't, and you should put this in writing. You don't want anyone talking about serious business transactions at a restaurant where other people may be able to eavesdrop on them. Don't think for a minute that a corporate spy won't follow your people around looking for an opportunity to hear something.

DISASTER RECOVERY PLAN

If your organization doesn't have a disaster recovery/business resumption plan, you're risking the security of your network — one fire could put your company out of business. The goal of a disaster recovery plan is to get your organization back to some working state so it can resume business as soon as possible after a disaster occurs. Many consulting companies specialize in disaster recovery, including Rothstein Associates, Inc., in New York (info@rothstein. com or http:// www.rothstein.com). The measures I outline below will help you develop a disaster recovery plan.

FORM AN INCIDENT RESPONSE TEAM

When an incident occurs on your network, whether it's a natural disaster or a virus, you should not try to fix the problem alone. Before a problem occurs, you should form an incident response team (IRT) that consists of a well-rounded group of people from all aspects of your business, not just IS employees. As it develops your disaster recovery plan, this team can express business needs from perspectives other than just the IS department. When a problem occurs, this group should be notified first — in fact, the first person notified of any problem should be the person whose job it is to call the other IRT members — and each person charged with handling a certain aspect of business resumption. Be sure to design your plan so that the recovery tasks can be performed in parallel wherever possible to reduce your overall recovery time.

RATE THE DISASTER LEVELS

Most plans categorize different disaster scenarios and explain what to do in each case. You rate a disaster in much the same way as hurricanes and earthquakes are rated. For example, a Category 1 disaster might indicate all building facilities are useless for more than seven days. A Category 5 disaster might mean only one floor is useless for a day.

INTERVIEW YOUR ORGANIZATION

Ask yourself whether some job functions are more critical to the continued success of the organization than others. I don't mean you should decide that one employee is more important than another; instead, you should consider whether certain job functions and data should be restored before others. For example, most Customer Service departments are critical to an organization because they take orders that generate cash flow. If you can't take orders, you can't generate revenue. Therefore, your Customer Service Department's 800 number or other telephone lines must be restored immediately, along with the representatives that answer that line. You have to decide the order in which to restore your organization and make sure that the most important business functions are back "on-line" first, so to speak.

Your team should interview department heads and explain the business resumption plan. Department heads should help the team decide the order in which departments are restored to business functionality and exactly what those departments require. Some departments may not need a backup site; their employees may be able to continue their business from home.

You may want to run through your recovery plan, perhaps on a weekend or at night. Being prepared is one thing; having been through a simulation is entirely another thing — it makes your recovery smoother and less frightening.

STEP-BY-STEP PLANS FOR EACH RATING

Your plan should include step-by-step instructions about what to do for each category of disaster, how to do it, and what escalation procedures to follow. Escalation procedures generally dictate who gets notified of a problem, and at what time intervals those persons are notified. It would also dictate a series of corrective measures at specific intervals as well. For instance, if a server crashes, how long can it be down before you call a manager to inform them you're having trouble getting it back online? And likewise, how long would you attempt to revive a dead system before putting the backup system into service? It should also include the list of who to call (along with the phone numbers) — the first order of business is to call the member of the IRT that's responsible for calling other members of the IRT.

You should consider arranging with your business management company for a backup site to locate certain employees during restoration. At this backup site, you'll need computers and phones for those employees to work on and a server to which you can restore the network's data. How much will all this contingency planning, not to mention recovering from a disaster, cost? It depends on your backup site arrangements and whether you hire a consulting company to help you.

DOCUMENT THE PLAN

You can include your Disaster Recovery Plan in your Network Documentation notebook; however, I suggest creating a separate notebook for it. Why? Because you'll pass out two copies of this notebook to every member of the team — one for the office, and one to take home in case disaster strikes at night or during their off hours. This level of preparation may seem like overkill to you, but if disaster strikes and you're not prepared, you should consider yourself "unemployed" when your organization loses money for each day its doors are closed. Many firms simply go out of business after serious disasters, but you can avoid this drastic course of action by planning and preparation. In fact, some insurance companies now require disaster recovery plans to obtain certain coverage.

RECOVERY PLAN OUTLINE

- IRT members' names, office/home phone numbers, pager numbers
- The order in which people are to be notified in the event of a disaster
- Emergency numbers
    - Company president's home and office phone number
    - Fire department
    - City and county police departments
    - FBI
    - Secret Service
    - The Computer Emergency Response Team (CERT) phone number and address (CERT is explained later in this chapter)
    - Building maintenance number and off-hours phone and page numbers
    - Company lawyer's name, phone number, and address (include emergency number)

- Backup site for business resumption
- Order of business resumption — a list, by department, of which data to restore first
- Hardware necessary for business resumption — what phones and computers employees will need in the backup location
- Business resumption plan

NETWORK DOCUMENTATION

As I mentioned in Chapter 6, network documentation is extremely important. By network documentation, I don't mean writing the administrator's password down somewhere! I mean a comprehensive paper record of your network's ins and outs, preferably in a three-ring binder, organized with divider tabs. I like the paper method because you can glance through it in a hurry when the system is down, and if you only have a computerized version and that particular computer is down, you're out of luck. The binder doesn't preclude keeping it in electronic form on the network where it is backed up.

Several programs can assist you with network documentation, like Net-Suite's Advanced Professional Design and Audit programs (http://www.netsuite. com) and the LAN Support Group's BindView EMS (http://www.bindview.com). If you have Microsoft's SMS product, you can automate some of your inventory analysis. Additionally, products like NTManage from LANWARE (http://www.lanology. com/ntmanage) map a network completely and build an IP address assignment database at the same time. Appendix C contains a comprehensive list of vendors.

One of the most important aspects of network security is to maintain network logs. If you have snapshots of your network when it's healthy, you have a baseline to use as a comparison when something goes wrong. You need to also monitor the logs for suspicious activity. For example, if you see someone repeatedly trying but failing to log on, an alarm should go off in your head. Don't assume the user is having trouble remembering the password; you may in fact be experiencing an attempt at intrusion by an outsider. Check it immediately. Remember, most network break-ins occur on networks that were not monitored closely enough.

Below is a sample outline (along with the suggested tabbed dividers) that you can use to get started. Although it's not as comprehensive as you may need, it *is* a good start and you can add to it as appropriate.

SAMPLE NETWORK DOCUMENTATION NOTEBOOK

Introduction Sheet

- Vital contact information

  - Network administrator name, e-mail address, and phone and pager numbers

  - Backup network administrator name, e-mail address, and phone and pager numbers

- IS managers' names, e-mail addresses, and phone and pager numbers
- IRT roster with phone and pager numbers
- Help desk number (if applicable)
- Computer Emergency Response Team (CERT) **(412) 268-7090**

- Vacation schedules (someone in Jamaica probably won't come to work right away if your office is in Austin)
- Company name and address
- Documentation notebook owner and contact information
- Date of last network documentation revision
- Who to contact for corrections, additions, and updates

Asset Management

- Purchase orders for network equipment and software, arranged alphabetically
- Warranty information for all network equipment and software, arranged in alphabetical order by vendor
- Maintenance agreements for all network equipment and software, arranged by vendor

Server Configurations

List the following information for each host or server:

- Its name and purpose (e.g., AUS101 — file and print services for building 2)
- Its status (i.e., mission critical, non-mission critical)
- The manufacturer and serial number
- Make and model
- Vendor name, address, and phone number
- Date and purchase and location of purchase order (should be in the Asset Management tab, above)
- Warranty and maintenance information
- Amount of RAM
- Disk drive(s)

  - Make and model
  - Serial numbers
  - Hot-swappable?

- IDE/EIDE/SCSI

- NIC(s)
  - Make and model
  - Serial number(s)
  - IRQ/Base I/O
  - Driver version
- CD-ROM Drive(s)
  - Make and model
  - Serial number(s)
- Tape drive
  - Make and model
  - Serial number
  - Tape software name and version
- Desktop operating system or network operating system type and version (including items like Service Pack levels and patches and serial numbers)
- Applications (including utility, debugger, and tools software) and version information
- Application licensing and purchasing information (include how software metering is used)
- Fault tolerance
  - RAID level (if applicable)
  - Duplexing used?
  - Mirroring used?
  - Hot-swappable parts?
- Other

Workstation Configurations

Working from the above list for servers, compile applicable information for each workstation.

Printer Configurations

- Make and model
- Serial number(s)
- Amount of RAM

- Printer name(s) and location(s)
- IP address(es) if applicable
- Network attachment type (e.g., JetDirect card, print server, etc.)

Cabling Plan

- Cabling company name, phone number, address, and hours of operation
- Wiring specifications and categories
- Building distance measurements
- Topology (Ethernet, Token-Ring)
- Topology distance limitations
- Wiring closet locations
- Distribution frame information
- Color code used
- City, state, and building code regulations and compliance information (e.g., plenum rating)

Communications

- Local telephone company (telco)
    - Name, address, and emergency phone number
- Link information
    - Account number and circuit ID for each telco line (e.g., T1)
    - Communications line phone number (e.g., ISDN)
    - Cable number (telco usually has its own cable numbers)
    - Type of link and speed (e.g., analog, digital, ISDN, 56K, T1)
    - Monthly cost as purchased
    - Fault tolerance: are any lines used as backup links? If so, which ones?
- PBX equipment
    - Vendor name, address, and phone number
    - Make and model
    - Software version
    - Telephony employed?
    - Call-tracking employed?
    - Analog lines connected to PBX? If so, how many?
    - Special considerations

- Routers
  - Make and model number
  - Serial number
  - Software version level
  - Hard copy of current routing tables
  - Vendor name, phone number, and physical and Web addresses; tech support hours of operation
  - IP addresses

- Modems/multiplexers
  - Make and model
  - Serial number
  - Speed
  - Vendor name, phone number, and physical and Web addresses

- Hubs/MAUs
  - Make and model
  - Serial number
  - Number of slots and cards (if applicable)
  - Management software version
  - Vendor name, phone number, and physical and Web addresses

- Other — you should list other network components such as ATM equipment

Internetworking

- ISP information
  - Name, phone number, and physical and Web addresses
  - Monthly charge
  - Type of connection and total connection time allowed per month (if not a dedicated link)
  - Gateway IP addresses and subnet masks
  - DNS primary and secondary addresses
  - Address assignments and subnet masks
  - Special configurations for this particular ISP

- Server Information
  - FTP server

- Directories used for each purpose
- Allow anonymous logins?
- List of users with FTP access
- Web server
  - HTML version used for Web pages
  - Copyright notice on home page
  - Date of last revision on home page
  - CGI scripts used?
  - Java used?
  - Maintenance scripts used and the intervals they run
  - Permission settings
  - Virtual directories and virtual server information
- Gopher server
  - Directories used
  - Document types allowed
  - Permission settings
- E-mail server
  - Domain names served
  - Software version and serial numbers
  - Host name and IP addresses
  - MX Priority number for DNS
  - Aliases used
  - Distribution lists used, along with member user names
- DNS Servers
  - Domains and sub-domains served
  - Root servers used
  - Server configuration (caching only? primary or secondary?)
  - IP addresses
  - Machine names
  - Software versions, patches or modifications, and serial numbers
  - Hard copies of the DNS tables

- TCP/IP information
  - IP address pools, range, and Class (A, B or C)

- Subnet masks
- Company distribution of IP addresses per network segment

- Domain Names
  - Domain assignments, enterprise wide
  - Sub-domains established
  - Domain contacts

- Firewalls
  - Vendor name, phone number, physical and Web mail addresses
  - Software and hardware version numbers and patches
  - Serial numbers
  - All filtering rules applied
  - Placement on the physical network in regards to wiring

Diagrams

Network schematics of the following components:

- LAN (including topology, hubs, routers, servers, and floors)
- WAN (including line speeds, routers, and cities)
- Internet connections
- Floor plan blueprints or CAD drawing

Maintenance Log

- Daily routines
- Weekly routines
- Monthly routines
- Trend analysis
  - Network percentage uptime and downtime
  - Capacity planning
    - Disk utilization
  - CPU utilization
    - Web server utilization
  - Problem analysis
    - Suspicious activity
    - Relevant incident reports

System Error Logs

- Date of the error
- Reason for the error
- Fix for the error

Change Management

- Moves, additions, and changes
- Special rights (people given unusual network access)

HOW TO HANDLE A SECURITY BREACH

So you've accumulated all kinds of information and organized it so that it's easily accessible. What do you do when something threatens the security of your network? Let's walk through some actions that will help you determine what do to when you detect or encounter a real or potential problem.

GATHERING NECESSARY INFORMATION: A CHECKLIST

First, you need to decide whether the problem is currently taking place, whether you see only the potential for a problem, or whether the problem occurred earlier and you're just now detecting it. Once you've determined this, you'll know whether you have a few minutes to collect your thoughts or whether you need to be on the phone right away. The following suggestions can be applied to instances of a perceived network threat. They don't necessarily apply to some type of physical threat, such as someone breaking into the building or an unknown person in the facilities.

- Stay calm. This advice sounds really basic, but you'd never believe how many alarmists think of panic and doom in situations like this. A clear head helps you solve the problem methodically and helps you when contacting personnel about the problem.
- Grab a blank notebook, a pen, and your network documentation book. You want to record everything — every move you make and who you talk to and when. In these situations, we often find fixes by trial and error. Although some of us claim to have great memories, most of us forget details when we're under pressure. Therefore, as you make changes to the system and test them, record the changes and the results. As you make phone calls, log them. You want this information not only for tracking but also to help you write your follow-up report.

- Have your network backup tapes handy. Keep two copies, one on-site and one offsite, or keep your single copy offsite within quick retrieval distance from your offices in the event it's needed. You might not need them, but sometimes you must go back a few days or a month and look at your network's state then to help you determine how healthy or unhealthy it is now. Remember the movie *Disclosure*? The plot hung on the fact that someone destroyed e-mail messages but forgot that the messages still existed on backup tapes.

- Call your IRT. When you discover a problem, you need to contact the team and gather all the brains you can to approach the problem.

- Take a snapshot of your network. If you follow the advice earlier in this chapter, you already have a snapshot of your network when it was healthy. Now, you want to get a snapshot of it at the earliest time you discover a problem.

- Save all your system logs from every single system that creates them. You can use these logs to determine the extent of any potential damage and to reconstruct a break-in, step by step.

- Contain the problem. Disable routers or any other equipment to contain the problem to a minimal number of sites.

- Determine the problem and its extent — what happened? Did you discover a new account with administrative access that you didn't set up? Was confidential data accessed? Are strange things happening to the users' PCs?

- Try one thing at a time and then test. Have you ever made five changes that fix a problem, only to discover that you don't know which of the changes actually corrected the problem? If you have a security problem on your network, you need to know exactly what caused it and what fixed it. Be methodical, take things step-by-step, and document your steps.

- If you have found evidence of an intruder, contact your local law enforcement agency. The question is, which one — the local police, the FBI, or the Secret Service? The answer depends on the potential damage. The FBI has no interest in "tiny matters" such as an employee using another employee's card key to get into the office on a weekend, even if it *is* against your policies. On the other hand, if that employee stole a computer, the FBI might want to know but would probably point you to your local police, because it's a theft. However, if you think that employee was selling that computer to a competitor to give your competitor an edge, the FBI might be interested. If you find any unauthorized user entering your network from the Internet, you should call your local FBI office. They'll be interested, because they work around the clock tracking these hackers — who are probably breaking into more than just your network.

For an excellent viewpoint on handling security problems, check out the following Web site: http://www.ds.internic.net/fyi/fyi8.html#incident-handling.

USING CERT TO YOUR ADVANTAGE

Now that you're prepared and armed with some information, it's time to take action. Call the Computer Emergency Response Team (CERT) at (412) 268-7090. Keep this number handy! According to their Web page, "The CERT Coordination Center was formed in 1988 to serve as a focal point for the computer security concerns of Internet users." In a nutshell, CERT concerns itself with responding to computer security incidents and offers product vulnerability assistance. They are not interested in natural disasters or internal theft. CERT coordinates certain security activities, such as following through to make sure that the right people are working on the problem. They also coordinate legal activities if needed. CERT is also on the Web at http://www.cert.org.

An outside intruder could be someone from another state or country, where other laws apply. If you feel the need, contact your organization's lawyer. Chances are, though, that your attorney isn't experienced in handling these situations. Again, CERT is your best first phone call. They want you fill out a form on their Web site; I suggest copying the form locally before you encounter any problems. Keep the sheet in your network documentation notebook so that when you detect a problem, you can begin recording information that will help them help you.

If you determine that one of your employees inappropriately accessed some data, then you might prefer to involve your own Human Resources department instead of contacting CERT. A breach of this nature may involve firing an employee, depending on how your organization decides to handle such matters.

COST OF INCIDENT

If at all possible, determine and document the cost and potential impact of this incident to your organization. You should include information like cost of personnel involved to handle the incident, revenue lost because of system outages, legal costs, and any other associated costs. This information could be handy if you go to upper management to push for more equipment or software to prevent future incidents. You may also be able to recover damages from a convicted intruder.

FOLLOW UP

Meet with the IRT and determine whether this incident was caused by a policy or procedure that was outdated or ineffective. It's important at this stage to change or better enforce your policies and procedures to ensure that the problem does not recur. It's also important to analyze whether your security plan and IRT worked smoothly. If not, what information did you need that you didn't have? Could any software, tools, or documentation speed up incident recovery? Use your cost analysis above to justify any new software or equipment, and always use a security breach to learn how to defend against it in the future.

INCIDENT REPORT

Once you've fixed the problem, you need to write an incident report. This report should contain copies of the log you kept while working on the problem. It should also note any changes you made to policies to prevent this type of incident from occurring again. File these reports in an overall log book, or in a separate notebook designed for this purpose.

SUMMARY

In this chapter, we covered a broad range of topics that focus on developing sound security practices and policies. We looked at why you need to institute policies in your organization and some content you may need to include in your policies. We also saw the framework for a working network documentation notebook — one you can begin filling out immediately and revising to fit the needs of your organization. I also pointed you to some great Web sites that have done a lot of research in each area of security, all of which you should visit regularly, because information changes rapidly. Last, I gave you instructions to follow when you do experience some kind of security threat.

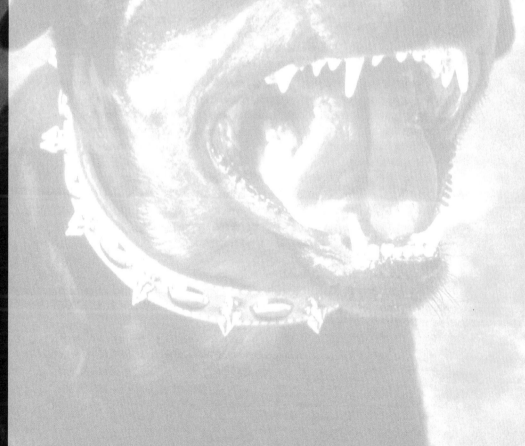

CHAPTER 8

NETWORK CLIENT AND WORKSTATION CONCERNS

In this chapter, we walk through some familiar and not-so-familiar steps
in securing network clients and workstations. The purpose of this
chapter is to help you understand some of the pitfalls in setting up the
more popular clients and to show you how their operating systems may
affect your organization's security. We also discuss securing some of the
file systems on particular network clients.

THE NETWORK CLIENT AND ITS HISTORY

Before you can secure a client, we should first discuss what a client is in its current state, its historical state, and its future state. Understanding client evolution can give us some insight into the emerging technologies in store for us in relation to security.

A *client* is any device that is directly or indirectly attached to a network or to another device on a network. Many people mistakenly assume that a client is only one particular flavor of workstation (a workstation running a particular kind of software, such as Windows 95, Windows for Workstations [WfW], or Windows NT Workstations). However, a client can be, for example, a workstation, a server, a printer, a fax machine, a hub, or a router. Servers can also be a type of network client. Therefore, for the purposes of this chapter, we approach the server from a different perspective, treating it as a client to address those concerns.

One of the earliest network clients, still in use in various forms, is the *dumb terminal*, or simply a terminal. Terminals exist in one form or another in both hardware and software implementations. One of the more popular software implementations is the VT-100 (Virtual Terminal, type 100).

Although this device is called a dumb terminal, it has many advantages. In particular, a dumb terminal is easy to manage and its security is easily localized to clusters of these devices. In the context of a network, particularly in a mainframe environment, a *cluster* is a group of I/O (input/output) devices, such as terminals, computers, or printers. A cluster shares a communications path, usually provided by a cluster controller, to a host machine. Clustering terminals was a tiered approach to isolating and troubleshooting problems. A network environment made up of several controllers was monitored and polled for status at a set interval, and if communications could not be established during the poll, the controller or the device that was causing the problems was fixed. This topology relied on quite a bit of manual intervention, which eventually led to large staffs on many help desks.

The problem with this dumb terminal model of network organization was that it worked on the assumption that the client could always communicate with the server, which we know is not always the case. When communications were interrupted, so was the work flow.

Over the years, the dumb terminal gained some intelligence and took some of the load off the centralized host it was connected to. This development was a move toward the *distributed computing model* or *client/server model*, in which the client (terminal) offers a front-end interface and simple processing capabilities and the centralized host system does the back-end processing work. A good example of this model in today's world is a client/server database such as SQL Server.

As the price of storage media dropped, operating systems could economically reside on the local workstations, replacing the model in which several workstations shared one operating system that resided on the centralized host. The hosts became a place where people could access limited or legacy applications and share their information through file services.

Eventually, entire applications resided on a client workstation. The client in this setup is called a *fat client*, where "fat" refers to a complete application residing on a client workstation — not to be confused with the old DOS file system. Fat clients are, naturally, the opposite of thin clients, which run applications that reside on a server instead of the local client system. The fat client has its pro and cons. Some of the advantages are reduced network traffic and speed improvements. Have you ever tried running a shared copy of MS Word over a 4 MB Token-Ring network? It's slow!

Some common problems of the FAT client still exist: inefficient management, difficulty in updating client software, problems in maintaining client hardware and software inventories, the possibility of viruses, and inefficient backups — storing vital company information across several machines makes backing up all your information very tedious.

Today, the industry seems to be shifting back toward the terminal model, now called the network PC, or *thin client*. The thin client offers a vast improvement over the old dumb terminals. Because of its excellent client/server architecture, the Web has been instrumental in pushing this technology along. A thin client now offers more power than a dumb terminal and has less management overhead; the management process has returned to the administrators, making for centralized control.

Because clients can be any resource connected to your network — a computer, gateway, printer, communication link, or software application that provides a point of entry to the network — the roles of client and server can be reversed or confused in *peer-to-peer network environments*. For instance, in a WfW environment, your machine can be both a workstation and a server — a *dual resource* — but it's still a network client. The many types of network clients are all resources that need to be secured properly because they all serve as potential entry points to the your network.

CLIENT DATA TRANSMISSIONS

We've already established that information traveling across your network is your organization's life blood. You're probably already aware of most of the information traveling your network, but I'm sure you've overlooked some items that are "your information." In fact, the *keys* to your information are routinely transmitted across your network, so let's examine just how secure these keys really are.

AUTHENTICATION SECURITY

When users log on to your network, they are probably (at least they should be) prompted for a user name and password. The user name/password combination is one of the primary building blocks of any secure network. What happens to the user name and password (both of which are part of your sensitive company information) once users hit Return to log on? Well, the information becomes vulnerable to interception and possible misuse.

One illustration shows a simple yet fatal flaw in native FTP services. In some organizations, FTP is not prohibited completely, and in others, it is heavily used. Although using FTP can be advantageous for your Unix clients that need to pull files from your server, the user name and password are transmitted over the wire in *plain text*. Anyone running a packet sniffer on your network can easily grab user names and passwords. We discuss this problem in more depth in the "Sniffing Your Wire" section later in this chapter. FTP is not the only culprit with poor authentication; other services such as Telnet are just as dangerous.

When clients access resources controlled by Windows NT, user names and passwords are never transmitted across the network in clear text — instead, they're encrypted, which provides a higher level of security. (For those of you familiar with Novell Netware, this protection is somewhat comparable to NDS.) During the logon process to an NT-controlled resource, your logon information is encrypted and sent over the network wiring to a domain controller for authentication. Although any encryption brings a higher level of security to the equation, Microsoft's method of encryption has been criticized as weak and breakable, mostly by people in the Unix community who hate Microsoft technology. Although cracking NT passwords is possible in certain instances using specific tools, the likelihood of it happening is greatly reduced by loading and implementing service packs. Keep in mind, now, that decrypting NT passwords is not necessary for them to be useful as a means to get into your network. On the other hand, the critics' point is well taken: No encryption is entirely safe indefinitely. As the horsepower of newer processors increases, so does the likelihood they can break encryption schemes.

Let's delve a bit further into the subject of encryption. Many network operating systems rely on this tactic to protect information traveling across the network.

AUTHENTICATION ENCRYPTION SCHEMES

The encryption/decryption methods for some of Microsoft's software systems have always come under fire. Their weaknesses have been chronicled on many Web sites that also give you utilities to decrypt data encrypted by some of Microsoft's methods. For example, it's relatively easy to obtain a program that cracks Microsoft Word document passwords. However, with the latest releases of its products, especially Windows NT 4.0, Microsoft has made many enhancements.

Another way to enhance media authentication security is to use third-party authentication systems such as Kerberos. Although Kerberos is not currently supported on Windows NT 4.0, Microsoft has claimed that Windows NT 5.0 will fully support Kerberos authentication.

Kerberos is used in many open network computing environments, most commonly in the Unix world. Kerberos uses the model of a trusted third-party authenticator, dividing the network computing environment into trusted and untrusted participants. It converts an untrusted network client into a trusted network client through authentication (positive identification), allowing a network application to securely identify its peers. The client is *trusted* in that each of its peers believes Kerberos's judgment as to the identity of the other. Kerberos's authentication model, which uses a trusted server to hold the initial encryption keys, is used for authenticating other network clients.

SNIFFING YOUR WIRE FOR CLIENT INFORMATION

In several places in this book, I've mentioned the security threat introduced with a network sniffer; we look at sniffers in more depth here. In essence, a network packet sniffer is no different from your typical radio frequency scanners, which simply sniff the airwaves for someone talking on some type of radio device and let the user listen in on the conversation. Cordless phones are another easy target. (Incidentally, I highly recommend that you get rid of any cordless phones, especially in the workplace — or restrict your conversations on them to non-sensitive topics.) Packet sniffers do the same thing, except a bit more thoroughly.

A network sniffer, or a sniffer program, captures packets from your workstation and any other clients operating on your network. Sniffers occasionally get packets that are somewhat cryptic, and it takes the intruder some time to decipher the information, but it's not too difficult — especially if the information is transmitted in clear, unencrypted text.

For example, a user placed a call to my help desk staff because he was having difficulty getting to one of my Unix hosts on the network. I asked the user to "ping" the host by name and by IP address, and he couldn't. After a slew of other scripted questions, I sent a technician to check out his network cable, which was faulty, so we replaced it. I then asked the user to FTP a file from one of our hosts. Meanwhile, I set up a capture session with a packet sniffer to ensure that the packets were leaving his workstation correctly, and I looked at a few of them to make sure they weren't fragmented. After a successful FTP session, his problem was solved. At that point, I mentioned to the user that he misspelled the day of the week he was using for his password! Boy, was he surprised. As you can see, it's a great idea to restrict the use of any network packet sniffers to only the essential (and trusted) staff members. If knowledgeable members of your IS staff are malicious or simply mischievous, they can capture packets and re-create security keys that were never meant to be disclosed.

Although you're not likely to leave a sniffer lying in the open, a user could bring in a software-based network sniffer and run it from the workstation. Low-end software sniffers may not have all the analyzing functions that a Network General brand hardware-based sniffer has, but even low-end sniffers are capable enough to be serious security threats. You shouldn't be surprised that many of these applications are available on the Internet. They are posted for general use on many sites, and some good-natured network monitor manufacturers, who really mean well, have evaluation copies available for downloading.

Those of you who use network analysis and systems management software may be familiar with such products as Microsoft's SMS and Novell's LANalyzer and ManageWise, which have their own network monitors. Each has packet capturing capabilities and can be run on low-power machines with many different network cards.

One of the best ways to stop software-based network sniffers is to use only network cards that don't allow promiscuous mode operation. Normally, a network card grabs only packets that are destined for that particular network card, but when you put a card in promiscuous mode, the card then captures *all* packets it sees, regardless of their destination. Without a promiscuous network card, software-based packet sniffers are useless. This feature is the reason many organizations demand that their procurement department regulate the purchase of network cards to only those cards without this capability. This policy doesn't stop users from inserting their own network cards, but products like Microsoft SMS Server can immediately detect such an addition and you'd know to reprimand the culprit.

REMOTE CLIENTS AND REMOTE ACCESS SERVICES

As we discussed earlier, telecommuting adds new security requirements to your organization. Many users are now doing their work from home or from a hotel room while they're on the road. With the advent of telecommuting, many types of new clients are emerging.

Whether the user dials in to the network with an Ethernet-based remote access server, such as a Shiva LANRover, or to a bank of modems attached to your NT server, security issues still exist. IS departments are handling the securities issues in various ways. Advanced call-back verification and data encryption are two features that larger companies can afford; however, you also have inexpensive alternatives to remote access security systems, like the Remote Access Service (RAS) in Windows NT Server.

RAS is the server end of the connection. Windows NT Workstation, Windows 3.11, and Windows 95 all have client versions that ship with these individual packages. DOS clients and clients for earlier versions of Windows are in the \CLIENTS\RAS directory of the NT Server installation CD.

Also included in RAS are two TCP/IP-compatible protocols that are fairly new to Windows NT: Point-to-Point Tunneling Protocol (PPTP) and Multilink Point-to-Point Protocol (MPP). PPTP lets users create a secure virtual connection between their private networks using the Internet as the WAN. PPTP was introduced by the Internet Engineering Task Force (IETF), and Microsoft leads the effort by packaging the protocol in Windows NT 4.0. The protocol uses the same encryption methods used in RAS and supports TCP/IP, IPX/SPX, and NetBEUI. The really nice thing about PPTP is that you no longer have to maintain large blocks of modems for dial-in access. Your users can connect directly to the Internet through the provider of their choice, at which point they can easily build a PPTP connection to their "home" network.

Multilink PPP allows the use of multiple phone lines to build higher-bandwidth links. A user dials in to a network one or more times, using one or more modems. Upon connecting, the MPP protocol "bonds" the connections, dynamically expanding the bandwidth according to the modem speeds. For example, if you make two MPP connections to the same server at 28.8 Kbps, you have approximately 56 Kbps of usable bandwidth.

I won't go into all the details of establishing RAS connections, because that topic is better left for books focusing on NT administration. However, I will stress that you should use the RAS's Call-back function to its greatest extent when you allow inbound callers, and whenever possible, use PPTP for all your connections. PPTP is an encryption protocol that runs on top of a PPP connection, and using such a protocol obscures your data from prying eyes as it travels across an untrusted network. You can find some great information in Microsoft's Knowledge Base, http://www.microsoft.com/kb. Search for document Q121877, which details routing IP over RAS connections, and Q161410, which details setting up a private network connection over the Internet using PPTP. Both documents will help you establish secure RAS connections.

Before you connect an NT system to the Internet using RAS or any other communications method, make certain that you've already secured the system with the modifications suggested throughout this book.

Special Note

CLIENT APPLICATIONS DEVELOPED IN-HOUSE

Many organizations work hard at developing their own in-house applications, particularly companies that require specialized transaction-tracking. Companies usually develop their own applications because commercial applications aren't robust enough or customizable enough to meet a company's direct needs.

The security problem with many in-house applications is that they seem to spring up almost overnight, out of nowhere, and soon proliferate on desktops with almost no in-depth thought given to security design. "After-the-fact" re-engineering for security can often take months to implement correctly. For example, an organization wrote a database application that actually opened multiple TCP and UDP ports for access, ports that were once off-limits and secured. These ports included TCP 137, 138, and 139, which are crucial for sharing resources and are a major security problem for NT networks. If the application-development group had consulted with the security group, the ports would have remained closed. Instead, the application-development group had to re-engineer the application, probably taking the project over the estimated developmental time and budget limits.

The best way to avoid this problem is to both have and enforce a good security policy. This policy should describe how applications interact with the network at all levels. In fact, it would be wise to have your security personnel interact directly with your developers to best ensure your objectives are met. Your policies should also provide for independent software audits, which can often find security oversights, leftover test hooks, and sometimes even back doors left by a malicious or disgruntled employee. Chapter 7 gives detailed information about establishing effective policies.

WINDOWS 95 CLIENTS

Any client operating system that doesn't force a user to log on is a security problem, and Windows 95 is no exception. We all know that Windows 95 asks a user to log on, and most of us also know that simply hitting the Escape key bypasses this requirement. With Escape, you bypass the 95 logon authentication; although you don't have access to NT controlled resources, you do have access to a workstation attached to the network, which could be the first step toward penetrating network security. Someone gaining access to a Windows 95 machine in this way can introduce some type of Trojan horse, which can do almost anything the developer wants, including activating itself when a user logs on the network correctly.

Windows 95 has other problems as well, including one found with most Intel-based workstations — the ability to boot from a floppy disk. This ability is one of the single biggest gaps in workstation security today. One of the best ways to prevent a machine from booting from floppy is to simply remove the floppy drive. This may not be feasible for you, so instead, you can adjust the BIOS settings. Most BIOS these days allow the user to specify the disk seek order when booting up. By default, you should set this to look for a C: drive first, and an A: drive second. This way, the BIOS always sees the hard disk before the floppy, and never boots from floppy. Of course, you also need to use the BIOS password protection to stop someone from going in and changing this setup back. Windows 95, like WfW, caches passwords to a file. These files, which are in the Windows installation directory, are named *username*.pwl, where *username* is the actual name used to log on or access a resource. Using software available through the Internet, these password files are easy to crack. The best way to eliminate this problem is to turn off password caching on all Windows 95 machines. Follow these steps:

1. Open Regedit by clicking Start and then Run. Type **Regedit** and click OK.
2. Find the following registry key:

   HKEY_LOCAL_MACHINE\SOFTWARE\Microsoft\Windows\ CurrentVersion\Policies\Network

3. Right-click the right windowpane and choose New, then DWORD Value.
4. Name this value DisablePasswordCaching.
5. Double-click this new parameter, and set the value to 1.

For more information about Windows-based workstation security problems, look at my Web site: http://www.ntsecurity.net/security.

Windows 95 also lets you use a Policy Editor (poledit.exe) that can, to some extent, control what a user can and cannot access on the Windows desktop. If you use Windows 95 on your network, you should use this tool. The Policy Editor lets you create a default user profile that you should restrict from using sensitive applications such as the Control Panel applets and the DOS Command Shell. A user's personal profile establishes access restrictions when the user logs on to the workstation. If a policy for the user does not exist, the user falls under the default user profile. This utility doesn't eliminate booting from a floppy disk to gain access to the workstation, but it does handle a large part of the problem caused when users bypass logon authentication by hitting Escape — even then, their sessions are governed by the default user profile.

You can easily enable Windows 95 to use user profiles:

1. In the Control Panel, open the Passwords applet.
2. Click the User Profiles tab.

3. Enable "Users can customize their preferences and desktop settings."

4. Reboot the system.

Given the amount of risk Windows 95 presents in a network environment, your best bet is to upgrade these operating systems to Windows NT Workstation. Meanwhile, you should download and install the latest patches and Service Packs for Windows 95 from Microsoft's Web site (http://www.microsoft.com). These patches eliminate lots of the known problems, but certainly not all.

WFW CLIENTS

WfW is no better than Windows 95 at securing a workstation — in fact, it's worse. WfW password files (*.pwl) can be cracked easily. In fact, several password-cracking programs are readily available on the Internet. If a user happens to use the same password at the workstation level as for the NT domain, it is incredibly easy to infiltrate the network — just copy the *.pwl file and crack it. Your best bet is to disable password-caching by setting the flag in your System.ini file as follows: In the [NETWORK] section of the System.ini file, add a line saying "passwordcaching=no" and restart Windows.

Another problem in both WfW and Windows 95 is the system that controls access to shares. The controller for shares requires only a password to use a shared resource such as a drive or directory, where user-level access control requires user authentication. Using share-level access control is the worst possible way to share resources, especially because so many people create the shares with no password in place! Even if passwords are defined, they're usually poorly chosen and easily guessed with a dictionary-based password cracker.

Simply put, you should upgrade all your WfW computers to Windows NT Workstation. The investment is well worthwhile and completely changes the level of security on your networks. For more information about Windows-based workstation security problems, look at http://www.ntsecurity.net/security.

DOS WORKSTATIONS

It is silly at some level to talk about DOS-based workstations because DOS is natively ignorant to the entire concept of networking. To be useful on a network, DOS requires some type of redirector, such as Microsoft networking or Novell Netware.

DOS workstations have all the same vulnerabilities as Windows 95 and WfW computers. One of the main issues for the DOS workstation, or any workstation that allows a DOS prompt, is a utility called NTFSDOS. This utility gives the DOS workstation direct access to an NTFS file system. NTFSDOS is discussed in detail in Chapter 9.

MACINTOSH CLIENTS

Integrating Macs on an NT network can pose additional security risks. NT does a good job of connecting Mac clients for resource-sharing, but you should be aware of some limitations before deploying these attractive machines on your network.

- NT Remote Access doesn't support AppleTalk, so Mac clients can't dial in to an NT server.
- Mac clients don't support logon scripts.
- Mac clients don't take advantage of user profiles.
- For Mac clients to participate in interdomain trust relationships or see resources from other NT Server domains, Services for Macintosh must be enabled in each of the domains residing on the same network.
- Mac clients, by default, send passwords in plain text over the network wire for authentication. Passwords are encrypted *only* when using Microsoft Authentication for Macintosh.

NOVELL NETWARE CLIENTS AND SERVERS

Microsoft has gone to great lengths to make NT integrate well with other network operating systems, particularly the ever-popular Novell Netware. Microsoft has developed a set of applications that specifically integrate Novell into Windows NT environments. The core set of these applications is listed below.

- Client Services for Netware (CSNW)
- Gateway Services for Netware (GSNW)
- File and Print Services for Netware (FPNW)
- Directory Service Manager for Netware (DSMN)

Let's look at these in detail so you understand the implications of using these services in your NT environment.

CSNW is an NT-based 32-bit redirector that lets your NT systems access the Netware environment as if the client were any normal type of Netware client. You can add CSNW to an NT server by choosing the Add Software option in the Control Panel. You don't need to configure the Netware servers except to add the necessary user account.

GSNW lets the users of an NT server access Netware resources as if they were normal Netware clients, without requiring the installation of any client software on the client machines. GSNW creates a user account called NTGATEWAY on the Netware 3.x or 4.x server running bindery emulation. All users accessing the Netware resource through this service have the same access restrictions and permissions as those established for the NTGATEWAY user account. The GSNW translates the native Microsoft Server Message Block (SMB, discussed later in this chapter) to the Netware Core Protocol (NCP).

FPNW allows the integration of NT servers into an existing Netware environment by providing utilities such as ATTACH, LOGIN, LOGOUT, SETPASS, MAP, SLIST, CAPTURE, and ENDCAP. One of the options given to an FPNW server is the ability to respond to the Get_Nearest_Server request generated by Netware clients. During installation, FPNW creates the SYSVOL directory (which becomes the root directory for Netware clients) and the LOGIN, MAIL, SYSTEM, and PUBLIC subdirectories. The SYSTEM directory is empty, and the LOGIN and PUBLIC directories don't contain much. The familiarity of the directory structure makes adapting to the new server simple once you understand it. Keep in mind that installing FPNW enables an NT server to provide both SMB and NCP, both of which can make an NT server vulnerable to attacks. Also remember that when a user logs on to NT Server running FPNW, that user is actually logging on to a bindery emulated by FPNW, not an actual Windows NT domain.

DSMN lets you synchronize your Netware bindery accounts with your NT user accounts. DSMN requires GSNW, which must be loaded before installing DSMN. With DSMN, users need only one account and password to access both Netware and NT servers, which can make life easy for the user. On the other hand, if the user's password is compromised on either system, it's compromised on both, so be careful to develop policies about passwords, their storage, and their use.

You'll probably find that it's easier to administer your heterogeneous environments if you use these applications, but you should note certain considerations. In particular, if your workstation is a Netware client (client meaning *any* Netware agent) accessing both an NT gateway to the Internet and another Netware system, your workstation also becomes a gateway from the Internet to your network. This means that it might be possible for an attacker to route traffic through your machine back to your Novell systems. To prevent this type of attack, you should probably use two or more network cards and adjust the bindings on the cards so that one card is used for Internet access (TCP/IP only) and the other card is used for Novell IPX traffic.

In the specific case of Microsoft's GSNW, concerns are more critical. One problem is that the user account used for gateway services can have only one set of permissions. Therefore, if an intruder gets through your firewall (if you have one), the intruder has whatever permissions the user account has.

Consider this problem as well: DSMN lets you synchronize your user accounts, but if you have a secure Netware environment and an insecure NT environment, you run the risk of compromising your secure Netware environment. The same arguments can be made for all your mixed environments that are integrated. To secure one end, you may have to loosen security on the other end. If you must loosen security at one end to achieve your integration goals, be careful in defining where your network ends and your Internet connection begins.

WINDOWS NT WORKSTATIONS

Although security issues still exist when either Windows NT Workstation or Server is used as a client, it is one of the most securable clients you can obtain today. I stress that administrators should administer their networks from a Windows NT system of some sort, *not* from other Windows clients such as WfW or Windows 95. Although performing some administrative duties at a user's workstation can be quick and convenient, in most cases you leave a cached copy of your password on their machine; this cached copy can be cracked easily.

One of the biggest security problems with NT Workstation is that users who administer the servers and domains tend to leave these workstations logged on with no screen saver or screen saver password. Many administrators leave User Manager for Domains running on their desktops indefinitely, not realizing that anyone gaining access to that machine can access the domain. If you administer your network from your NT workstation (which is a great idea), secure your workstation just as you'd secure an NT server, right down to the last nut and bolt — and don't forget to load the service packs!

SHARING WINDOWS NT WORKSTATIONS

If you happen to be in a situation where it seems practical to share your workstations among users (such as lab and clean-room environments), securing those machines becomes a key factor in your overall security efforts. If you must share workstations, use Windows NT 4.0 Workstation. Under NT Workstation, users may personalize their desktops in some ways, which is handy; to let users personalize their desktops, set up "roaming profiles" for the users and establish default permissions.

The correct way to set up default permissions on a workstation is to set the system's file and directory permissions as follows:

User/Group	Type of Access
System	Full control
Administrators	Full control
Users	Read only

Once the previous step has been performed, set the permissions on the %SYS-TEMROOT%\SYSTEM32\CONIFG directory as follows:

User/Group	Type of Access
System	Full control
Administrators	Full control
Creator Owner	Full control
Users	Add permission

This setup lets users of this particular machine create profiles but does not give them access to someone else's.

Now, on your Temp directory, set the following permissions:

User/Group	Type of Access
System	Full control
Administrators	Full control
Creator Owner	Full control
Users	Read/Write/Execute (under Directory Access)

Performing these steps takes you a long way toward securing your NT system. Keep in mind that some applications require write access to the application directory for storing data. Some older applications require write access to %SYSTEMROOT% to store their associated .ini files. You should dispose of the older applications that use .ini files in favor of newer versions that store information in the NT registry.

REMOTE REGISTRY ACCESS

One great aspect of any network operating system is that you can make your machine accessible to other network clients and servers. Unfortunately, at the same time, this accessibility leads to an insecure system. If you're familiar with NT, you definitely know about the registry. But did you realize that your registry is vulnerable to attack?

In Windows NT 3.51, a feature was built in to Windows NT that let any machine on the network (with the proper tool) access the registry. Almost no security was included to prevent this access. Fortunately, this problem was fixed in Windows NT 4.0 Server with the introduction of this registry key:

HKEY_LOCAL_MACHINE\SYSTEM\CurrentControlSet\Control\
SecurePipeServers\winreg

Note that *this registry key is not present on Windows NT 4.0 Workstation*, but it can be added easily. The presence of this key disables remote registry access for anyone other than users who belong to the Administrators group. Another way to disable access to the registry is to tighten permissions by removing the permission for the group Everyone at the root of the HKEY_LOCAL_MACHINE hive. *Do not* propagate this change to the lower keys in the hive. *Be careful:* Although this method correctly secures an NT 3.51 registry, it may actually cause some applications to run incorrectly. Testing this change on nonproduction servers is worth the time and effort it takes to figure it out. Also, keep in mind that this change can easily be undone if necessary.

You may want to take advantage of the DumpACL tool by Frank Ramos from SomarSoft (if you didn't notice, Somar is Ramos spelled backwards). This tool explores potential permission holes, which may have been set either by default or by an administrator inadvertently. Appendix B tells you how to contact SomarSoft.

UNIX CLIENTS

Unix clients inherently support some networking scheme. For a long time, the Internet was proliferated with Unix systems. Only recently (relatively speaking) are other TCP/IP-based operating systems being used as Internet gateways. Unfor-tunately, Microsoft hasn't designed a networking client for Unix; therefore, all access to and from a Unix box is in the form of platform-independent, protocol-specific services. This section focuses on some of the common problems that plague Unix systems and protocol-specific services.

Before I dive off the deep end talking about Unix in an NT environment, let me emphasize that you need to stay on top of all the CERT advisories for your particular Unix variety. You should also subscribe to the BugTraq mailing list, which routinely posts messages about security holes in Unix, along with fixes to the problems. You can subscribe to BugTraq by sending e-mail to listserv@ netspace.org with the words "subscribe bugtraq" in the body of the message. No subject for the message is needed.

I'm not going to tell you about all the problems with today's Unix implementations. Instead, I'll repeat something I said earlier in this chapter: In a mixed-platform environment, holes in the security of one operating system can lead to security breaches of other secured systems. If your NT servers have access to an unsecured Unix system, it makes absolutely no sense to secure them. If intruders can't get into your NT system directly, they'll probably look for another system on your network that they can get into; after that, any system that your compromised system "sees" is also vulnerable to attack.

Having said that, some of the glaring problem files that you should look out for in a Unix environment are .netrc, .rhosts, and other similar files. These files contain logon names, machine names, and password information in ASCII. For convenience, many users like to synchronize all their passwords, and if users have their user name and passwords listed in one of these files, your network is wide open. If you've got Unix machines in your network environment, you shouldn't use these files.

Another easy action you can take is to disable your root user accounts on all your Unix machines. Rename them, or at least restrict users from logging in as root. Users that require root access should use the "su" (switch user) command for gaining root account permissions. This method of gaining root access creates log entries that you can audit.

THE NETWORK FILE SYSTEM (NFS)

The Network File System (NFS) is a distributed file system developed by Sun Microsystems, Inc., that lets a computer on a network use files, peripherals, and other network resources as if they were local resources. NFS is, in a sense, platform independent and can be found running on mainframes, minicomputers, RISC-based workstations, and even personal computers.

NFS is a popular way of sharing file and directory resources in cross-platform environments. Unfortunately, NFS, like so many other software packages, was not designed with security in mind. In fact, many scripts that exploit its poor authentication algorithm already exist and are located on the Internet. Microsoft does not produce an NFS server native to Windows NT, but many third-party developers have created NT-based NFS solutions.

With NFS, resources are mounted and shared from a server, and NFS requires special client software to access an NFS-mounted resource. Because of the way NFS shares resources across a network, the shares are susceptible to attacks like resource-spoofing. Many organizations have opted for alternative file-sharing systems such as the Andrew File System (AFS), which is more secure than NFS, but also more expensive.

MICROSOFT'S SMB PROTOCOL

Microsoft's Server Message Block (SMB) protocol shares files, printers, serial ports, and communication abstractions, such as named pipes and mail slots, between computers on a network. SMB was originally defined in 1987 in a Microsoft/Intel document called Microsoft Networks/OpenNET-File Sharing Protocol; it was subsequently developed further by Microsoft and others. In this section, I briefly explain the SMB protocol so you understand its nature and the implications of using it. You can find the SMB documentation on Microsoft's FTP server (ftp://ftp.microsoft.com).

SMB is a client/server request/response-based protocol, in which the client generates requests and the server sends back a response. The only exception to the request-response model occurs when the client requests an opportunistic lock (called an *oplock*) and the server subsequently must break the previously granted oplock because another client has requested a file open with a mode that is incompatible with the granted oplock. In this case, the server sends an unsolicited message to the client signaling the oplock break.

Clients connect to servers with one of many protocols: TCP/IP, NetBIOS over TCP/IP, NetBEUI, or IPX/SPX. Once connected, clients can then send commands (SMBs) to the server that let them perform tasks such as access shares, open files, and read and write files.

SMB provides two types of security: share level and user level.

- Share level — protection is applied at the share level on a server. Each share can have a password, and a client needs only that single password to access all files under that share. This security model was the first one SMB used, and it's still the only security model available in the Core and CorePlus protocols. WfW's Vserver.exe implements share-level security by default; so does Windows 95.

- User Level — protection is applied to individual files in each share and is based on user access rights. Each client (or user) must log in to and be authenticated by the server. Upon authentication, the client is given a UID, which it must present on all subsequent accesses to the server. This model has been available since LAN Manager 1.0.

Quite a few SMB clients are available commercially; the main clients come from Microsoft, including WfW 3.x, Windows 95, and Windows NT. SMB clients are most evident when you use the File Manager or the Windows 95 Explorer, because these tools let you connect to servers across the network. They are also used when you open files with a UNC (universal naming convention) such as NET USE X:\\SERVER\SHARE. Other SMB clients available are the SMBCLIENT from Samba and SMBFS for the Linux version of Unix.

Several SMB server implementations are also on the market, including Samba, WfW 3.x, Windows 95, Windows NT, the PATHWORKS family of servers from Digital, LAN Manager for OS/2 and SCO, VisionFS from SCO, TotalNET Advanced Server from Syntax, Advanced Server for Unix from AT&T, and LAN Server for OS/2 from IBM.

If you run any of the software packages listed, you probably wonder which TCP and UDP ports are used by SMB for file- and print-sharing — the answer is ports 137, 138, and 139. Port 137 is used by NetBIOS name services, port

138 is used for NetBIOS datagrams, and port 139 is used for NetBIOS sessions. Unless you find them absolutely necessary, you should disable these ports for both ingoing and outgoing traffic. Intruders *easily* use these ports to gain access to your network. The next section discusses the vulnerabilities of the SMB protocol and explains one of the popular ways that intruders use it to their advantage.

SAMBA

Samba is one of the more popular communications suites that uses the Microsoft SMB protocol, and one of the more dangerous as well (more on the dangers in a moment). Samba is a freely available SMB server that works with most of the popular Unix platforms, such as OpenVMS, Linux, Solaris, SunOS, HP-UX, ULTRIX, DEC OSF/1, Digital Unix, Dynix (Sequent), IRIX (SGI), SCO Open Server, DG-UX, UNIXWARE, AIX, BSDI, NetBSD, NEXTSTEP, and A/UX. You can find Samba at http://samba.anu.edu.au/samba.

Samba implements the NT LanManager v0.12 protocol dialect, but Samba servers cannot directly participate in an NT domain. They can, however, participate in browsing and can even become a browse master on an NT network. (Don't confuse Microsoft network browsing with Web browsing here. They are entirely different. Microsoft network browsing is viewing the network systems and resources, as seen in Server Manager, using NT Explorer, File Manager, or with the Net View command.) Samba can process logon requests for Windows 95 systems and implement user-level security. With Samba, shares can be made public, where access is mapped to the owner of the particular share, who can control other users' access to the share.

The big danger with Samba was discovered by accident, as a byproduct of the actual development process. That is, the makers of Samba did not intentionally create the danger for exploiting Microsoft network shares, but Samba can in fact exploit network shares quite easily. When a WfW or Windows 95 machine shares any folder (making it a network resource), bugs in Microsoft's SMB implementation (over all network protocols) allow users access to the entire drive with whatever permissions they got with the share. These resources are advertised on a browse list that is available by default to anyone on the local network and to anyone on the Internet who knows the machine's IP address. Any user sharing a folder on a TCP/IP network without a password opens the whole disk to the entire Internet — all an intruder needs to do is locate the machine. Users with a password should remember that Windows has no protection against brute force password-guessing other than setting account lockout priorities. Now might be a good time to remind you yet again of the importance of choosing incredibly difficult passwords!

Microsoft quietly released a patch for WfW in October 1996 and publicly announced a patch for Windows 95 on October 20, 1996. These patches have not been tested rigorously, but they appear to fix the problem. The release version of Windows 95 prevented Samba clients from issuing a "cd.." command below the shared folder "root" but did not limit the use of the "cd../" command. The patches and Microsoft's press releases about this problem are available on Microsoft's Windows 95 Updates Page. Keep in mind that the patch works only on the US/English version of Windows 95 at the time of this writing; all non-English versions of Windows 95 are still vulnerable to this exploit!

A FEW WORDS ABOUT NT FILE SYSTEMS

Although file system security is emphatically stressed on Windows NT servers, it is often overlooked on the workstations. NTFS should be the only file system used on NT machines attaching to your network. Allowing or creating a dual-booting NT system is also highly discouraged for security purposes. In other words, don't install non-NT operating systems on the same machine you install NT on, and always use NTFS instead of FAT.

Someone who can boot your machine with either DOS or Linux can access information on an NTFS partition with tools that can read raw sectors and information. NTFS security permissions work only when NT is in control. FAT is highly susceptible to virus infection. Attacks on the Master Boot Record (MBR) can leave a FAT disk partition inaccessible, affecting productivity at the very least. Symantec has a white paper (http://www.symantec.com) about how viruses work in the Windows NT environment.

THE NEXT STEP: COMMON INTERNET FILE SYSTEM (CIFS)

Now that you see the dangers inherent in Microsoft's SMB, we're ready to move to the next step of file system evolution. The next incarnation of SMB, and the next evolution of implementations like Samba, is the Common Internet File System Protocol (CIFS).

The Internet is rapidly opening up new and innovative ways of communicating, for individuals and organizations alike. Past Internet use has been limited to simple one-way file transfers or read-only browsing; however, today's Internet users demand greater interactivity and functionality. CIFS supports richer, more distributed applications over the Internet. It defines a standard protocol for accessing remote file systems over the Internet, letting groups of users share documents across the Internet or within corporate intranets.

CIFS takes advantage of the SMB protocol that lets users natively share file and print services (i.e., Microsoft Windows 95, NT, and other PC-based operating systems) and extends those abilities and attributes to the Internet. CIFS is also supported on non-PC-based operating systems like OS/2 Unix and VMS. It incorporates the same type of high-performance, multi-user read and write operations that make up today's infrastructure. It uses TCP/IP and the Internet's Domain Name Services (DNS) for scalability, and it's optimized to support slower-speed dial-up connections.

CIFS is not intended to replace HTTP; instead, it will complement HTTP while providing more sophisticated file sharing and file transfer than older protocols such as FTP. CIFS enables all applications, not just Web browsers, to open and share files securely across the Internet.

CIFS lets multiple clients access and update the same file while preventing file-sharing conflicts; it also supports aggressive caching mechanisms, including read-ahead/write-behind without loss of cache coherency. This new file system also offers increased fault tolerance, increased support for slow modem dial-up lines, anonymous and secured file transfers, and ease of administration for security policies. Additionally, users will be able to interact with a file without downloading it to the local drive first.

AT&T, Data General, Digital Equipment, Intel, Intergraph, Network Appliance, and SCO are all working actively with Microsoft to support CIFS. CIFS is already widely supported in commercial software products such as AT&T Advanced Server for Unix, Digital's PATHWORKS, HP Advanced Server 9000, IBM Warp Connect, IBM LAN Server, and Novell Enterprise Toolkit, among many others, and is also part of the Samba file- and print-sharing software discussed earlier in this chapter. CIFS is definitely something to look forward to, and perhaps we'll see this new file system creep out of Redmond in Windows NT 5.0 and in service packs for NT 4.0.

SUMMARY

From this chapter, we can see that workstations and other network clients can be a real challenge to manage. They can, however, be secured with constant monitoring, good policies and procedures, user education, and constant evaluation. We cover Windows clients, Unix clients, Netware clients, and even some hardware that you wouldn't automatically think of as network clients.

All the information in this chapter has shown you that you should not leave a single stone unturned when it comes to securing devices attached to your network. You now know that any device attached to your network can become an instant security risk for one reason or another.

CHAPTER 9

ATTACKING YOUR OWN NT NETWORKS

As I've said before, to beat the intruder, you have to think and act like the intruder. This chapter shows you some ways to test your own networks against attacks, using some of the same tactics intruders use. We look at critical areas, explaining why these areas are vulnerable, the tools to use to test the vulnerability, what to expect during your testing, and possible ways to eradicate the problems.

Keep in mind that any tool that manages, implements, or controls network security can be used against your network. This chapter doesn't cover every single attack that could ever happen to your Windows NT network, but using its suggested tests can improve the security of your networking environment. After you read this chapter and follow my advice, you'll have a better understanding of the potential dangers and know how to test your NT systems for them.

ATTACKING THE SYSTEM

I assume that you have already connected, or are going to connect, your NT network to the Internet. In this light, you need to tighten security on your NT systems as best you can. A good perimeter defense network eliminates most security problems on your systems. On the other hand, one slip on the firewall administrator's part or one small bug in the firewall code could leave your network exposed to the entire Internet community. Therefore, it is always prudent to secure your systems in as many ways as you can. Don't simply rely on the firewall to do its job — some day it may not be working exactly as you expected.

UNDERSTANDING UNC

The Universal Naming Convention (UNC) is a standard way to name applications that enables users to

- browse documents on the network directly and
- open an application's files on remote machines without requiring the user to specify the location of the file on the network or connect to that network.

Universal names are location independent (that is, they don't necessarily reside on the same machine each time they're used) and let users attach to network shares (files and printers) and transfer files to other computers. To see your network in one of the ways potential intruders do, you need to understand the UNC.

Overview

Under DOS and MS Windows systems, the location of static files is usually specified by the standard drive and directory naming convention; for example, C:\Dirname\Filename.txt describes the location of a file named Filename.txt located on the C: drive in a directory called Dirname. In contrast, the UNC achieves network integration and interoperability by defining a command line that can be used from any DOS prompt to manipulate shared resources like printers and files.

Once a resource is established as shared, it is automatically available using a standard UNC. The UNC uses the syntax \\Server\Share, where Server is the server name and Share is the shared resource name. Let's look at an example. Suppose you have a Docs directory located on an NT server called Corp somewhere on your network and that this directory's share name is Docs1. The correct UNC for this shared directory is \\Corp\Docs1, where Corp is the name of the server where the file is located, and Docs1 is the name of the share. To mount this share so it can be accessed at a local machine, a user could open a DOS command window and type this command:

NET USE X:\\Corp\Docs1

After the user types this Net command (more on Net commands later in this chapter), Windows NT begins security checks on the share's permissions to see whether this user has access to the resource.

Known Issues of the UNC

Because the Windows NT and Windows 95 APIs both support UNC, most software tools for these platforms support the UNC. As you can see in the examples below, the UNC can make life much easier in cases such as copying one file to 100 separate NT workstations or analyzing 100 different files on 100 different workstations. You can do these tasks easily with a batch file and the UNC; otherwise you'd have to map 100 network drives from your administrative computer to get the job done. Your batch file program to copy these files might look like this:

```
xcopy \\system1\share1$report1.doc
      \\server1\reports\report1.doc
xcopy \\system1\share1$report1.doc
      \\server1\reports\report2.doc
xcopy \\system1\share1$report1.doc
      \\server1\reports\report3.doc
xcopy \\system1\share1$report1.doc
      \\server1\reports\report4.doc
xcopy \\system1\share1$report1.doc
      \\server1\reports\report5.doc
etc.
```

UNC does have one funny little bug. If you issue the command

```
copy existing_file \\SERVER_NAME\C$\nul
```

you create a file called nul in the directory represented by C$, which is normally the root directory of the C: drive on the server named SERVER_NAME. This "nul" file cannot be removed using standard NT tools like File Manager or Windows Explorer, and this file is a frustrating puzzle for the system administrators once they find it. The file can be deleted only with the following command:

```
del \\server_name\c$\nul
```

Interesting, don't you think? Using this particular hole, a malicious intruder may copy a large file, causing NT to unnecessarily use disk space to store that file.

Another twofold problem with the UNC is that installing Windows NT establishes some default shares, which are referred to as *administrative shares*. By default, these shares are named C$, D$, E$, etc.; one is created for each physical disk partition on the system. If your system has three disk partitions, three shares are created. These shares point to the root directory of each partition, which means that the permissions are set so that only a member of the Administrators group can use them. On the surface, these shares seem like a great thing, because you don't have to share them yourself before you can use them, and, in fact, they do come in handy at times. However, they can also be used to attack your system.

Intruders worth their salt know about these shares and their default names. They also know that most NT administrators don't rename their Administrator account, and therein lies the problem. These shares can be used to hack away at the Administrator account, which is never locked out because of bad password attempts, something else intruders already know. Potential intruders can sit at their machines on the other side of the planet, running a simple dictionary-based password-cracking program that tries to mount the share over and over, using a new password each time, until the true password is discovered.

To eradicate this problem, you should

- Rename the Administrator account to something obscure.
- Rename administrative shares to something obscure.
- Block TCP and UDP ports 137, 138, and 139 to your systems, thereby blocking NetBIOS access to the system. These ports are used for communication when exercising actions against a command containing a UNC.

You should also know that intruders can access several hidden system-level shares. For example, the IPC$ share is used by the system, but an intruder could easily attach to this share with the following command from an NT system:

```
NET USE \\SERVER\IPC$ "" /USER: ""
```

This command connects to the IPC$ share anonymously — without a user name or password. The intruder can then fire up the Registry Editor, User Manager, Event Viewer, or any other tool. Microsoft is fixing this little-known anonymous access and the fix should appear in the new CIFS protocol once it's released in Service Pack 3 for NT 4.0.

You can practice a little "security through obscurity" by hiding shared resources so they don't appear in the File Manager or Explorer or from the Net Use command by simply appending a $ (dollar sign) to the end of the share name — for example, name the share Docs1$ instead of Docs1. This way, a user needs to know the share name beforehand to easily gain access to it. While you're at it, it's also a great idea to rename (delete and re-create) your C$, D$, etc., shares. Because they're created by default, everyone knows they exist.

On the other hand, you can completely disable these default shares by editing registry keys. To disable the shares completely, edit the following registry keys:

- For servers: HKEY_LOCAL_MACHINE\SYSTEM\CCS\Services\ LanManServer\Parameters\AutoShareServer

- For NT Workstations: HKEY_LOCAL_MACHINE\SYSTEM\CCS\Services\ LanManServer\Parameters\AutoShareWks

Change the key setting to 3D0 and reboot. You'll see that the default administrative shares have been disabled.

SOFTWARE ASSISTANTS

Each software package described in this section is used theoretically as an administrator's tool. These tools are extremely useful for administering NT domains, servers, and workstations. On the other hand, this software is also an essential part of a hacker's toolkit. A skilled intruder does the same things an administrator does; intruders are simply in a more difficult position because they do not have legitimate access to the system and its resources. I strongly recommend that you *remove all these programs and any other administrative tools from your production servers, especially those servers that are visible and accessible from the Internet.*

Addusers.exe

An important part of any system-level security policy is the user account policy. If you happen to handle only 5 to 20 accounts, you will probably be happy with the User Manager, because it provides an easy-to-use graphical interface. Unfortunately, it's not particularly useful if you have lots of users to manage — a command-line utility is a far better way to administer lots of user accounts.

Addusers.exe is on the Windows NT Resource Kit CD-ROM. This utility creates, lists, or deletes user accounts and groups on a specified computer. When listing accounts, Addusers.exe creates a comma-delimited text file, which you can easily import to programs such as Microsoft Access. The Adduseres.exe utility helps you maintain your user database integrity. You can maintain the database directly or distribute your user database to other systems; in either case, you can make sure that no unwanted accounts are added to the database.

Administrator permission is required to add new accounts, but only user-level permission is required to dump accounts. You can find out the syntax for the Addusers command by typing **ADDUSERS /?** at any command line.

For example, to list the entire user database for a particular machine, simply put Addusers on that machine or use Addusers from a machine that has access to the one you want to list, and type the following command:

```
addusers \\COMPUTER_NAME /d accounts.lst
```

This command produces the accounts.lst file in the current directory. The file is comma delimited and has the record structure shown below:

```
User Name, Full Name, Password, Comment, Home Drive,
    Home Path, Profile, Script
```

At first glance, you might think that this tool dumps out user passwords, but don't get excited, because it doesn't. The password field is for *adding* users only. To get an idea of what this file's contents may look like, review the following sample, in which every line past *user9* refers to groups and members.

```
Administrator,,,Built-in account for administering the
    computer/domain,,,,
Guest,,,Built-in account for guest access to the com-
    puter/domain,,,,
user0,New User,,Comment for user0,,,,
user1,New User,,Comment for user1,,,,
user2,New User,,Comment for user2,,,,
user3,New User,,Comment for user3,,,,
user4,New User,,Comment for user4,,,,
user5,New User,,Comment for user5,,,,
user6,New User,,Comment for user6,,,,
user7,New User,,Comment for user7,,,,
user8,New User,,Comment for user8,,,,
user9,New User,,Comment for user9,,,,
Global Group Name, Comment, Users
None,Ordinary users,Administrator,Guest,user0,user1,
    user2,user3,user4,user5,user6,user7,user8,user9,
Local Group Name, Comment, Users
Administrators,Members can fully administer the
    computer/domain,Administrator,Domain Admins,
Backup Operators,Members can bypass file security to
    back up files,
```

```
Guests,Users granted guest access to the
   computer/domain,Guest,
Power Users,Members can share directories and inters,
   user0, user1, user2, user3, user4, user5, user6,
   user7, user8, user9
Replicator,Supports file replication in a domain, Users,
   Ordinary users, Domain Users, user0, user1, user2,
   user3, user4, user5, user6, user7, user8, user9
```

Adding users with this tool is fairly simple. The following batch file helps you automate the creation of new user accounts. This batch file, Add.cmd, requires these command line parameters: a user name, a full name, and a password, in that order.

```
REM ----------- NewUser.cmd: batch file to create new
   user account on the local NT system
REM ----------- first we create temporary file:
   "$$$.tmp" to use it as an input for addusers.exe
echo User Name,Full Name,Password,Comment,Home Drive,
   Home Path,Profile,Script>$$$.tmp
REM ----------- Append command line parms in to the file
   in proper format
echo %1, %2, %3, Comment for %1,,,, >> $$$.tmp
echo Global Group Name, Comment, Users >> $$$.tmp
echo ,,,>>$$$.tmp
echo Local Group Name, Comment, Users, >> $$$.tmp
echo Users,Ordinary users,%1 >> $$$.tmp
echo Power Users, Members can share directories and
   printers,%1 >> $$$.tmp
REM ---------- Add the New User
ADDUSERS /c $$$.tmp
REM ---------- Clean up now
del $$$.tmp
REM ---------- End Of Batch File
```

Using this batch file with the command line **ADD newuser realname test** creates the user account **newuser** for the person **realname** with the password of **test**. This batch file also places the user in the Users and Power Users Groups. Keep in mind that this batch file can be further modified to add other parameters you need.

Deleting user accounts with this utility is also simple. The following batch file, named Deluser.cmd, demonstrates deleting users.

```
REM -- DelUser.cmd: batch file to delete a user account
REM -- first we need to create temporary file: $$$.tmp
   to use it as an input for AddUsers.exe
```

```
echo User Name,Full Name,Password,Comment,Home
    Drive,Home Path,Profile,Script>$$$.tmp
echo %1,New User,%1,Comment for %1,,,,>>$$$.tmp
echo Global Group Name, Comment, Users>>$$$.tmp
echo ,,,>>$$$.tmp
echo Local Group Name, Comment, Users,>>$$$.tmp
echo ,,,>>$$$.tmp
rem Delete the User
AddUsers /e $$$.tmp
REM -- Clean up
del $$$.tmp
REM -- End Of File
```

To delete the test account, type **DELUSER test**. If you're using the delete command to manage users that are handled by a Primary Domain Controller, be sure to target the Primary Domain Controller when typing this command. You may also need to synchronize the domain after adding users with this command. One final note: Don't use the version of Addusers.exe from the Windows NT 3.51 Resource Kit on an NT 4.0 system; instead, use the Addusers.exe from the Windows NT 4.0 Resource Kit.

I showed you this command because intruders already know about it, and the first thing they do when they gain access to your system is to look for Addusers.exe or a batch file that launches it for them. If they're successful in locating it, you're in more than a bit of danger — you're wide open to any attack. Only user-level permissions are required to dump a user database with this tool, and user names are 50 percent of the puzzle when someone wants to break into your machines using a live account. Don't leave these tools on your systems. You may want to keep them on a floppy disk or on a secure server somewhere on your network that's not accessible from the Internet.

Tip

Never use Addusers.exe to add users over the Internet unless you are *certain* that you're protected by encryption and very strong authentication (using protocols such as PPTP and Kerberos). Otherwise, you're completely vulnerable to packet sniffers and man-in-the-middle attacks anywhere along the route between your networks. Also, don't leave this utility lying around on your NT systems — keep it on a floppy and copy it to a machine when you need to use it; delete it immediately when you're finished.

DumpACL.exe

Somarsoft's DumpACL, a Windows NT program, dumps the permissions (DACLs) and audit settings (SACLs) for the file system, registry, printers, and shares in a listbox so that holes in system security are readily apparent.

DumpACL also dumps user, group, and replication information; it is simply a "must-have" product for Windows NT systems administrators and computer security auditors.

DumpACL solves the problem of having too many files and registry keys to check regularly by producing a concise and readable report of permissions and audit settings. By reviewing this report, you can determine whether users have more access to the file system, registry, and printers than you want them to. You can then use File Manager, the Registry Editor, or Print Manager to set permissions differently.

You can use DumpACL to produce a report of the HKEY_LOCAL_MACHINE registry hive. You may not know that everyone has write and delete access to many registry keys; this much access can become a serious security problem. Any user with local or remote access to the registry can make changes that might disrupt system operations or further compromise security.

Consider the following scenario: An undergraduate student in a university computer lab logs on using another student's account — the password was written in the front cover of the other student's notebook. The student changes the registry of workstations and servers in the lab so that these computers no longer function properly but the malfunction is so intermittent and obscure that only an expert systems administrator could trace the problem to the registry. Because the damage was done using another user's account, there is no way to identify the perpetrator. The only way to correct the damage is to reinstall NT, but the perpetrator can come back and break the system again. Undergraduate students are notorious for finding such mischief a great source of amusement and for having the time on their hands to engage in it.

It is possible to disable remote connection to the registry by removing read access for the Everyone group to the root key HKEY_LOCAL_MACHINE. Do *not* propagate the resulting permissions to registry sub-keys. Removing read access for the Everyone group may cause problems for services running on the local machine. However, it is easy to reverse this change if you experience problems.

The long-term solution is to disable remote connections to the registry explicitly. The default for a newly installed NT server is to disable remote connections, just as the Guest account is disabled by default. Because ordinary users cannot normally log on to an NT server locally, the registry is protected by disabling remote connections. However, keep in mind that someone might later re-enable this feature, so you need to examine it often. DumpACL is a great way to monitor the situation.

When you install a copy of this software, included on the CD-ROM with this book, read the Help File section called "Known bugs, limitations and planned enhancements." It contains information you need to use the utility properly.

DumpEL.exe

In a stand-alone configuration, the Windows NT operating system is certified by the NCSC at the C2 level, as defined in the Orange Book (discussed in Chapter 2). Two requirements of the C2-compliant configuration involve event logging. First, C2-level security requires that a security audit log is maintained such that events in the log are not automatically overwritten. (To set this option, use the Event Viewer's Log Settings menu.) Second, C2 security requires that a system shut down after the event log is full (\CurrentControlSet\Control\Lsa\CrashOnAuditFail must be set to 1 — see MS Knowledge Base article Q140058 at http://www.microsoft.com/kb for more details). The idea is that if someone hacks your system, you can find out what happened, how it happened, and quite possibly who did it.

An intruder who gains administrative-level access to your system can clean up all traces of his or her presence, including the event logs. In this case, the system generates security event # 517, "The audit log was cleared." Usually, it takes significant time for an intruder to gain administrative-level access. Therefore, if you back up your event logs regularly, you are much more likely to have at least the beginning of the attack logged and stored on your tapes, which you can use to trace the break-in to its origin.

The DumpEL.exe utility from the NT Resource Kit helps you dump your event logs. You can run this command-line utility from any batch file and schedule it to execute regularly. Quick help is available by typing **DUMPEL /?**.

Full syntax of the command is

```
dumpel -f file [-s \\server] [-l log [-m source] [-e n1
    n2 ... n10] [-r] [-t]
```

where

- -f file is the file name for the output file. The default is the screen (stdout).
- -s server is the server for which you want to dump the event log.
- -l log is the system, application, or security log to dump.
- -m source is the source to dump records. Only one source can be supplied. If this switch is not used, all events are dumped.
- -e *n1 n2 ... n10* defines up to 10 filters for event ID *nn*.
- -r defines records to be dumped. If the -r switch is not used, only records of these types are dumped; if -r is used, all records except records of these types are dumped. You cannot use this switch without the -m switch.

- -t sets the output format to tab delimited. If -t is not used, the format is space delimited.

For example, to dump all security events on the local server to a file called Security.log, type

dumpel -f security.log -l SECURITY

Keep in mind that you must have administrative privileges to dump the security event log. To dump all failed logon events (event ID 529) to the Logon.log file, type **dumpel -f logon.log -l SECURITY -m SECURITY -e 529 -t**. A normal dump of this log shows only a few failed logon attempts. If you have a lot of failed logon attempts, you may be under a password attack (see the section below about password crackers).

If you use Windows NT Server or Workstation connected to an untrusted network (e.g., the Internet), I do *not* recommend configuring your server to halt after the event log is full. Granted, this specification *is* a requirement for meeting C2 security, but it's still not a great idea. Such a configuration potentially lets an intruder from an untrusted network like the Internet generate lots of events, all logged, which eventually shut down your system. If your systems must meet C2 requirements, I highly recommend that you increase the size of your security event log and schedule regular dumps and backups of the event log.

As I mentioned, you usually need administrative rights to dump the security event log. No additional privileges are required to view application and system logs. However, Windows NT 3.51 Server or Workstation (with service pack 2 or higher installed) and Windows NT 4.0 Server or Workstation have a new feature that lets you disable everyone's access to the event logs. Follow this procedure:

1. Open the Registry Editor (Regedit.exe).
2. Select HKEY_LOCAL_MACHINE\SYSTEM\CurrentControlSet\Services\ EventLog.
3. Select Permissions from the Security menu.
4. Remove everyone from the list of users allowed to access the key.
5. Insert the users you want to have Read Event Log Permission and give them Read-Only privileges.
6. Set the permissions with the Replace Permission on Existing Subtree option checked.

You shouldn't leave this tool on any accessible machines either, because an intruder may use it to determine the level of auditing you use. This information gives intruders a sense of the appropriate comfort level they have. In other words, if intruders see that your auditing is weak, they may actually do much more harm than they would have otherwise.

Password Crackers and Grabbers

According to recent industry surveys, approximately 20 percent of all computer break-ins occur through compromised passwords, probably the oldest known method of breaking into a system. In spite of this fact, Digital Equipment Corp. studies show an alarmingly high percentage of insecure passwords on typical systems, ranging from 30 percent to 70 percent of all passwords used. Therefore, password policy should be one of the important parts of your security policy. Password policies on NT systems should always include at least these items:

- Minimum password length of at least seven characters, if not more
- Periodic password expiration, with a recommended maximum password age of approximately 30 days
- Password histories of old passwords (at least the past three passwords)
- Account lockout after several bad logon attempts, no more than five at most; preferably two or three
- Audits of invalid logon attempts and regular checking of the security event logs
- Periodic check for easily guessed passwords
- Firm policy about password selection

The key point is that password-cracking programs can compromise passwords. Therefore, it's important to audit invalid logon attempts frequently and regularly. If you've established a good password lockout policy of five or fewer attempts, the user accounts being cracked lock out after the specified maximum number of bad passwords. Intruders almost always attempt to crack the Administrator account, because it won't lock out from bad password attempts; hence, you need to rename this account to something obscure.

The best practice is to try to break your users' passwords before an intruder does. ScanNT (http://206.222.24.74/products/scanNT/index.html), a cracker created for this purpose, is a very useful tool, especially for administrators of medium and large networks.

ScanNT uses a plain-text dictionary file as its database of passwords and checks the password strength for selected local accounts. The current version

Tip

Set your password lockout policy to two bad attempts. This way, you can quickly discover cracking attempts against your regular user accounts by monitoring your logs or by user complaints. Also, leave your Administrator account in place, take away *all* its rights and permissions, and create a new "administrator" account with a different name and a maximum-length, super-hard-to-guess password. Then cracking attempts against the built-in Administrator account can go on indefinitely without much risk but without alerting the intruder, which gives you an opportunity to catch him or her.

of the software can attempt up to 10,000 logons per minute on Windows NT Workstation with a 100 Mhz Pentium CPU and 24 MB of RAM. The professional version of this software produces a log file in the following format:

```
User1, message1
User2, message2
User3, message3
Etc.....
```

User$X$ is the account name of the Xth user and Message$X$ is the message for the Xth user. Possible messages are defined as follows:

- OK (*N* attempts) — the password was not cracked after *N* attempts.
- Cracked! <password> (account temporarily disabled) — the password was cracked, but this account is temporarily disabled by the administrator.
- Cracked! <password> (unauthorized time of day for this account) — the password was cracked, but this time of day is unauthorized for this account.
- Cracked! <password> (the account is not authorized to log on from this station) — the password was cracked, but this account is not authorized to log on from this station.
- Cracked! <password> (logon time restriction violation) — the password was cracked, but this log on time is unauthorized for this account.
- Cracked! <password> (password has expired) — the password was cracked, but the password has expired.
- Account Locked — the account is currently locked out and cannot be tested.
- Account Cracked! <password> — the password was cracked. As an administrator, you must prompt this user to change the password as soon as possible.

To run ScanNT, you must temporarily block your password policy by changing the Account Lockout option to "No account lockout." Also, for better performance you should temporarily disable security auditing for user logons on the NT system you're checking. This software is included on the CD-ROM that comes with this book and is available at www.ntsecurity.com/Products/ScanNT/index.html.

Crack 5.0 for NT, which was ported from Unix, and L0phtcrack are other password-cracking programs. Both are easily available at numerous sites on the Internet.

Although password *crackers* are one thing, password *grabbers* are an entirely different story. With the release of Windows NT 4.0, Microsoft has added hooks to its Software Developer's Kits (SDKs) that let you use more than one security notification package during password changes. All you have to do is create a .dll and put the name of that .dll in a certain registry key. After the file and registry key are in place, this .dll is called on every single password change, which of course opens the doors up for password Trojan horses. For complete details about this particular exploit, look at http://www.ntsecurity.net, which includes a sample .dll and complete source code written in Visual C++.

Tip

Check your registry routinely for new entries to the key HKEY_LOCAL_MACHINE\
SYSTEM\CurrentControlSet\Lsa\Notification Packages. Don't overlook the possibility that someone has put Trojan horses on your systems. It's a good idea to check this key after you've installed new software while logged on with an administrator account.

It is of paramount importance to try cracking your own passwords — I learned this from firsthand experience. I used to be naïve enough to think my passwords could not be cracked. But one day, I decided I "didn't have anything better to do" so I got one of the password crackers, a dictionary file, to see how my network fared. I ran the program overnight, and while I slept I cracked well over 200 user passwords on my network with no trouble at all, and the program hadn't checked 25 percent of the user database yet. To make matters worse, two of these passwords were used by my system administrators and had incredibly high levels of access. Since then I've become religious about cracking my own passwords, and you should too.

NTFSDOS

Mark Russinovich and Bryce Cogswell did a great job of showing the importance of physical security for NT-based systems and networks when they created

NTFSDOS. Physical security is a complete concern unto its own, but I want to cover this software in detail here, because it's used to attack your systems.

NTFS is widely used today, and not only on NT. The NT model presumes that NTFS is an entirely secure file system. However, the security of this file system is based on the Access Control List (ACL) and Audit Control (AC) mechanisms, which are available inside the NT operating system itself. Data is stored unencrypted in the NTFS volume. Remember that NT in a C2-compliant configuration must have its floppy drive disabled or removed; otherwise, it is possible for someone to boot another operating system from a floppy and gain access to the NTFS volume.

You can handle inaccessible NTFS partitions (e.g., a partition with lost administrator passwords) in many ways. One way, and the most obvious, is to connect the hard drive to another computer with NT installed on it. The administrator of the new NT machine has a full access to this newly installed hard drive. Other ways of gaining access to an NTFS partition and bypassing its permissions are listed below.

- Boot from floppy or CD and install NT to a new directory, thereby gaining access to the new Administrator account and password.
- Access the hard drive with any kind of "physical sector access" software that can read NTFS data.
- Install the NTFS driver on a Linux (a Unix version) machine, and mount it from there.
- Boot to DOS using a floppy and use the NTFSDOS program to gain access.

NTFSDOS is an NTFS file system driver for DOS and Windows that recognizes and mounts NTFS drives for transparent access — currently in read-only mode. This program makes NTFS drives appear indistinguishable from standard FAT drives, which lets you navigate, view, and execute programs on them from DOS or Windows, including Windows 3.1 File Manager and Windows 95 Explorer. The current version of NTFSDOS (version 1.21) can be loaded from a DOS command line and used for read-only access to the NTFS drive.

To those who are optimistic about the read-only access, I make two brief points:

- A write-access version of NTFSDOS 1.5 is expected to be available sometime in 1997. NTFSDOS 1.5 allows some write capability, aimed at helping recover dead systems. This version will cost just $35 and provide file renaming and over-write capability.
- Because NTFSDOS 1.5 is not available as I write this book, I give details for the read-only version here. Read-only access to the NTFS *system partition*

is all that is required to recover the Administrator password. At least one company is currently offering this service. In other words, a stolen NTFS drive is in fact, accessible.

This great administrative tool is also a key piece of any hacker's toolkit. If your NT Server is publicly or physically accessible (and has a floppy disk installed or an easily opened cabinet), be acutely aware that a malicious user can boot from the floppy, run NTFSDOS, and read all files on that partition. The current edition of the software supports

- NT 4.0 NTFS formatted drives
- Large drives (more than 2 GB) if extended INT13 services are present in the BIOS
- Many hard drive types, including SCSI, without any extra DOS drivers
- Compressed files and directories

The utility is extremely easy to use. Simply typing **NTFSDOS** and pressing Enter brings up a display like the one below.

```
D:\WINNT40\TOOLS>NTFSDOS

NTFS File System Redirector for DOS/Windows Vx.x ...
Copyright (C) 1996 Mark Russinovich and Bryce Cogswell

Initialized 500KB of XMS cache.
Mounting NTFS partition (0x80:3) as drive: H

D:\WINNT40\TOOLS>
```

It appears that the program has found and mounted a new drive for you. Look at the last line in the previous example. You can easily use the H: drive as a local drive for read-only access, including program execution — that is, until they release the version that supports read and write access. Your best recourse is to assume that everyone in your company and everyone on the Internet has this tool, and protect your systems accordingly. Specifically, follow these precautions:

- Install no floppy drives at all until you need them, then remove them after you're done.
- Lock the system's cabinet.
- Lock the server in a secure room.
- Use BIOS boot passwords.
- Disable floppy booting in the BIOS.

In other words, control physical access to the machine.

Routers and Routing

Probably the most popular way to connect different network segments (e.g., LAN to LAN or LAN to the Internet) is with a router. A router uses a complex addressing procedure to determine the destination for all network packets and whether to retransmit (re-route) the data to the right destination.

An Internet router is a TCP/IP-based router that connects trusted networks to the un-trusted Internet. The native Microsoft Windows protocol NetBEUI is not routable without specialized hardware, so it cannot be used effectively on large networks. However, Microsoft encapsulates NetBIOS packets so they can be transmitted by TCP/IP, which is called "NetBIOS over TCP/IP" (NBT). NBT is a built-in feature of NT that uses the existing NetBIOS and TCP/IP protocols. Remote WAN access and administration of Microsoft systems is now possible using the Internet.

From the security standpoint, it is extremely important to protect routers because they handle most of your network traffic. A compromised router can sniff traffic, change the routes and gateways, and potentially compromise your entire corporate network security system.

An administrator should understand all their routers' abilities. Most routers allow direct Telnet access in the configuration, so be sure the password on your router is complicated and very hard to guess. Many routers support Simple Network Management Protocol (SNMP), so make sure this feature is either disabled or highly secured (more on SNMP later in this chapter). If your router supports the Router Internet Protocol (RIP), you need to control this feature as well — RIP can be used to re-route packets, modify routes, break routes, and more.

Windows NT itself can be configured to serve as a simple router. NT uses a static routing table and supports RIP if you load it into your network configuration. The NT-based Route command manually configures network routing tables in much the same way that the Unix version of this command does. You should never leave this command on any systems exposed to the Internet — delete it or copy it to a floppy. The syntax of the Route command is similar to the Unix version, as shown in the example below:

```
route [-fs] [command [destination] [gateway] ]
```

The Route command uses these switches:

- -f: clears routing tables
- -s: packets for which no destinations are found are routed to the smart gateway

You use Route with these additional commands:

- add: adds a route
- delete: deletes a path
- print: prints a route
- change: changes an existing route

The Route command is a powerful tool to handle Internet traffic. Suppose your network is under attack from a SYN flood effort (SYN attacks are covered in depth later in this chapter), which you either suspect because your system is performing very poorly or discover using the Netstat command covered in the next section. You can change your routing tables to disable connections from the attacking IP address. The idea is to set up a fake (bad) route for all connections to a specific IP address on your network. Let's use MALICIOUS_IP as the address of the attacker and FAKE_GATEWAY_IP as the address where you send the attacker's traffic. First, issue the following command from a DOS command shell:

```
route PRINT
```

This command prints a list to your screen of all routes known to this machine. You're looking for your current (valid) gateway address. You could find your gateway address by looking in the Network Control Panel applet, but that doesn't mean that the gateway is currently set as you configured it — someone could have tampered with the gateway address in a number of different ways, so use the Route command to see what it is. As shown below, you find your gateway address as the first item on the display, under the heading Gateway Address; also on that line is a Network Address of 0.0.0.0 and an Interface Address of your machine IP address.

```
Active Routes:
Network              Gateway
Address    Netmask   Address       Interface       Metric
0.0.0.0    0.0.0.0   209.11.144.1  209.11.144.17   1
```

Record your gateway address; you'll use it later to repair the route. To force the intruder's traffic into la-la land and away from your machine, simply pick an unused address from your IP address pool. We call this address FAKE_GATE-WAY_IP in this example. Now issue the following command:

```
route    add    MALICIOUS_IP    FAKE_GATEWAY_IP
```

To make sure that all traffic between your computer and a malicious computer is disabled after the routing is changed, ping the attacking address. If the ping gets through, the traffic is not disabled. If the ping doesn't get through, it's either working as planned or the attacker's machine doesn't respond to ping requests. You can also use the Netstat command, described in the next section, to determine whether the attacking machine is still establishing sessions with your machine.

Netstat Commands

If your NT system is connected to the Internet, you're probably wondering what part of your system is accessible from the outside world. Because the Internet uses TCP/IP as a transport protocol, you need to find out which TCP and UDP ports are in listening state. Windows NT's Netstat command was designed to answer this question. It is supposed to list all listening ports on an NT box, but in fact, it didn't until the release of Service Pack 3 for NT 4.0. The following command now lists listening ports if you have the Service Pack installed:

```
netstat -a -n
```

Many articles in the MS Knowledge Base (such as article Q131482) relate to this problem with Netstat. All of the articles I've found describe the bug as "Netstat does not display TCP ports that are in the listening state" and confirm the old problem. With Service Pack 3 installed, Netstat is very useful because it enumerates all TCP incoming and outgoing connections to that particular machine, which is handy when it comes to determining TCP/IP-related problems. To get a list of every open connection to a particular NT machine, open a DOS command shell and type the following command:

```
netstat -n -p tcp
```

The results show open connections and their connection state. If, for example, your system is under SYN flood attack, you may see lots and lots of connections in the SYN_RECEIVED state. You can also use the Netstat command to display your current routing tables. If you issue the following command, you see output similar to the output from the Route Print command described earlier in this chapter:

```
netstat -rn
```

None of Netstat's uses relate to actually attacking a machine; instead, they determine various aspects of the TCP/IP protocols running on your machine, which could help you find and eliminate attacks. To get extensive help with this command, simply type **Netstat ?** to display all possible command switches and options.

NBTStat Command

You recall that earlier I mentioned NETBIOS over TCP/IP, commonly known as NBT; that's the origin of the name for this command. The NBTStat command can be both handy and dangerous at the same time, in that you can discover a lot about your network simply by issuing one of the following commands:

```
nbtstat -A IP_ADDRESS
nbtstat -a HOST_NAME
```

In the above examples, IP_ADDRESS is the NT machine address, and HOST_NAME is the TCP/IP fully qualified domain name (e.g., host.domain.com). With these commands, you can discover several key pieces of information about a particular NT machine, most notably the actual NETBIOS machine name, an essential piece of information required for attacking an NT machine at the share level. Before you get too concerned, simply blocking UDP port 137 on your firewall, router, or packet filter (there's one built into NT 4.0) stops this tool from being used against you.

The output of the NBSTAT command looks something like this:

```
C:\WIN95\Desktop>nbtstat -A 11.210.30.42
NetBIOS Remote Machine Name Table
Name                      Type            Status
-------------------------------------------------------
MPG                       <00> UNIQUE     Registered
MPG                       <20> UNIQUE     Registered
MYNET                     <00> GROUP      Registered
MYNET                     <1C> GROUP      Registered
MYNET                     <1B> UNIQUE     Registered
MYNET                     <1E> GROUP      Registered
MPG                       <03> UNIQUE     Registered
ADMINISTRATOR             <03> UNIQUE     Registered
MYNET                     <1D> UNIQUE     Registered
POSTLADY                  <03> UNIQUE     Registered
..__MSBROWSE__.           <01> GROUP      Registered
MPG                       <01> UNIQUE     Registered
INet Services             <1C> GROUP      Registered
IS MPG                    <00> UNIQUE     Registered
MAC Address = 00-C0-F0-0C-75-EF
```

Even without knowing all the codes, you can easily learn several items of information about this system and its network. The word GROUP appears in the middle column of several rows; moving to the left on several of them, you see the word MYNET, which is probably the NT domain name. The first entry in the middle column is the word UNIQUE, and moving to the left, you see MPG, which is probably the actual NETBIOS machine name (server name). Further down the list, you see several other entries listed as UNIQUE. Any one of these *could* be user names, so let's examine them further. Wow. Right there in plain sight is ADMINSTRATOR. Uh-oh. We know this account is real because it's logged in. We've just hit a bit of pay dirt.

Remember where I state emphatically that you should always rename or cripple your Administrator account? Even renaming your account doesn't help unless you block UDP port 137 from incoming traffic on your network.

So what else can we learn? In the last 5 lines, we find still other great information, if you're an intruder. POSTLADY is obviously a user account name, probably the one that runs the mail server; Inet~Services reveals that this machine runs IIS; IS~MPG is the IIS Web server anonymous user account IUSR_MPG.

These displays look different each time you use this command against an NT machine, depending on what's happening on that particular NT system at the time. You may see different user names and different entries. If you use this command against a machine running Windows 3.x, WfW, or Windows 95, you can get the machine name, the workgroup or domain name, and the user's name — all bad news in the hands of an intruder. The first thing intruders do with this information is add it to their LMHOSTS files and start hacking away at your shared resources and accounts, so beware!

With all this juicy information at hand, retrieved using only one simple command and without even knowing how to read it correctly, I've learned way too much about this network without really trying. Therefore, if someone were to ask me, "What is the single most important thing I can do to secure my NT network?" I'd say, *"The single best starting point is to block all incoming traffic to ports 137, 138, and 139 at the routers that serve your Internet connections."* They're a gold mine for intruders. It's very similar to building a house and not putting up the doors — anyone can walk right in.

Net Command

The Net command (used in a DOS command window) is very handy and uses many aspects of the SMB protocol. The command is useful for monitoring NT domains or workgroups, starting and stopping services, and mounting network resources. The syntax of the command is

```
net [ ACCOUNTS | COMPUTER | CONFIG | CONTINUE | FILE |
    GROUP | HELP |HELPMSG | LOCALGROUP | NAME | PAUSE |
    PRINT | SEND | SESSION |SHARE | START | STATISTICS |
    STOP | TIME | USE | USER | VIEW ]
```

More help on every command is available by typing **net COMMAND /?**
Here are a couple of examples using the Net command:

- To enumerate all available servers and workstations on the DOM_NAME domain: **net view /domain:DOM_NAME**
- To enumerate shares on a Windows machine (any version) named COMP_ NAME: **net view \\COMP_NAME**
- To find out whether you have the necessary permissions to connect to the remote share SHARE_NAME on the computer COMP_NAME:

    net use x: \\COMP_NAME\SHARE_NAME

When securing your network, remember to disable your Guest account and never grant the Everyone group access to a shared resource. If you set up the accounts correctly, the Net Use command in the last example works only if the user has the correct permissions. If not, the user is prompted to enter a password. You can see that the Net Use command is a great way to hack away at passwords, although it's rather slow because of the amount of time it takes between password attempts.

- To enumerate users on a local computer: **net user**
- To enumerate users on the domain: **net user /DOMAIN**

The Net Use command does not require any privileges beyond simple guest privileges. In the previous section I mentioned intruders placing information in their LMHOSTS file — after intruders know your NetBIOS machine name and your IP address, they simply add them to the LMHOSTS file and then use a barrage of Net commands to test your system's defenses. Believe it or not, lots of administrators create shares with incredibly lax security permissions, and this situation is what intruders love to find. The Net commands make it all possible.

Reminder

Block all incoming access to ports 137, 138, and 139 right at the routers that serve your Internet connections. This way, any SMB traffic, like that generated by Net commands, does not enter your network.

TCP/IP Port Scanners

A port scanner is a nifty little software tool that lets you probe a machine for all listening TPC/IP ports. You can easily find unwanted services, secret Web sites running on your employees' workstations (there's nothing like a little free bandwidth!), unwanted FTP sites, and many other oddities you don't want. On the other hand, as with most of the tools in this chapter, port scanners are a vital part of the hacker's toolkit — yet another reason why they must be a vital part of *your* toolkit as well.

Several port scanners are available for the NT platform. Blue Globe Software's product, Port Scanner, uses an intuitive interface that lets you specify the starting and ending addresses to scan, along with the ports you want to look for. Port Scanner comes preset to scan for the most common TCP/IP services and provides a way to add new ports to any scan.

In addition to port scanning, WhatsUp from IpSwitch Software offers

- Graphical display of monitored components and their status
- Ongoing confirmation of network connections
- Monitoring of a wide range of network elements, including hosts, servers, workstations, bridges, routers, hubs, LAN concentrators, and printers
- Initiation of visual and audible alarms when any network element does not respond to polling
- Remote notification by digital beeper, alphanumeric pager, or e-mail
- Automatic Telnet to monitored hosts
- Monitoring of unmanageable as well as manageable network devices

Both utilities are available on the Internet and are listed in Appendix C of this book.

When you use a port scanner against your network, make sure you scan for the sensitive NT service ports: UDP ports 137 and 138 and TCP port 139. You must disable these ports with your packet filter if at all possible. If you use them to span your network to another network across the Internet, you should take a different approach; these ports are necessary to access NT resources — which intruders know all too well. Most port scanners do not include TCP port 139 in the list of predefined ports, so you will probably need to add it manually. Also, port scanners do not help you with UDP ports in a listening state; instead, check for these ports using the NBTStat command as described in the previous section.

Network Monitors and Packet Sniffers

The most widely used networking architecture today is Ethernet. Therefore, you should be aware that it is usually possible to capture all network traffic from an Ethernet-based computer and that a packet sniffer is the tool for the job. An administrator usually uses a packet sniffer to perform LAN and WAN diagnostics, monitoring, traffic generation, and troubleshooting. Sniffers are also popular among the hacker community, where they're used as an easy way to compromise network security from a single workstation.

For example, during an SMB session (used by NT for file and print sharing), user data is transmitted in clear text. Therefore, if you do not use any special hubs, network cards, or software packages to encrypt a session, a malicious user could use the sniffer to capture your user data during an SMB session. The risk of password-capturing is supposed to be eliminated by the NT authentication challenge–response mechanism; however, a password can still be captured in many applications used on your LAN. For example, Telnet clients transmit information in clear text, as do FTP clients.

Packet sniffers come in two varieties: hardware-based and software-based. The software-based sniffers are most commonly used, because they are typically easy to get and less expensive. Plenty of network sniffers are available for almost any platform, including Unix, DOS, and Windows, and several packet sniffers are available for NT. The Microsoft Network Monitor, part of the Microsoft SMS package, offers much more than simple frame-capturing — it sports a robust capture/display filter language, powerful protocol parsers, and a very snazzy user interface. Windows NT 4.0 Server also has a version of the Network Monitor that captures local packets only. One downfall of the Network Monitor shipped with SMS is that it uses weak password encryption. Two different passwords are used by the sniffer: one to view previously captured sessions and one to activate the sniffer on a remote machine. Be aware that at least two password crackers are available on the Internet that are designed specifically to crack these passwords.

NetXRay, by Cinco Networks, Inc., is another powerful packet sniffer designed especially for Windows NT and Windows 95. It can capture every packet on a network and decode several layers of the network protocols. A copy of NetXRay is on the CD-ROM that accompanies this book.

After you have loaded one of these tools, you should run it for a while to see what information you can collect. Put it on a machine that isn't being used for any other mission-critical tasks and simply let it run for several hours, perhaps even several days. Once you've grabbed lots of packets, peruse them, looking for information that may be of value to an intruder. Beware: *You're monitoring user activity, which may violate your firm's policies and perhaps even your local laws. Be sure to get permission from someone in authority at your firm and have that person oversee your adventure and accept the accountability.*

Software-based packet sniffers require a network card that can be set up in promiscuous mode to capture *all* network traffic. Cards without this feature can be used to capture only those packets arriving at the *local* machine. Therefore, your procurement department should have a policy stipulating that they *must* purchase network cards *without* this capability. This step greatly minimizes the chances of packet-sniffing on your network. Also, your ISP can quite easily sniff all packets coming out of your network that are destined for the Internet, and you cannot easily detect or guard against this sniffing. If you're using the Internet to span your network to a remote network for sensitive company information exchange, use heavy encryption and don't trust your ISP blindly.

Tip

SNMP Monitors

Simple Network Management Protocol (SNMP) was designed to manage large heterogeneous networks and to solve communications problems between different types of networks. Computers on a network can exchange network information through simple messages. SNMP messages can read terminal data, write data, and monitor network events such as startup or shutdown. SNMP can be a big security hole because it gives network intruders access to the information carried along the network and stored in the network systems. For example, NT publishes information about the computer name, OS version, system up time, network cards, and network configuration parameters.

Attacking a network with an SNMP monitor is very easy. You only need to know three things: the IP address, the Read Community name, and the Write Community name — unless these parameters have been set correctly or protected in some fashion. Many administrators simply install SNMP and leave it configured with all its default settings, which is a huge mistake. Every intruder knows that the default community names are "public" and/or "read" and "write" and don't have any password protection.

SNMP monitors can perform huge amounts of discovery work in much the same way that TPC/IP port scanners do. Intruders give them blocks of network addresses and instructions to scan every address, testing for SNMP capabilities. Some of the better SNMP monitors can even discern what type of machine it is, what version of the OS is running, which SNMP drivers are loaded, and which capabilities those drivers have. Lots of SNMP services can even change parameters on key system services. In fact, on Windows NT, it's incredibly easy to grab information such as all machine names in the domain, all user names in a domain, routing tables, services running on the server, IP address, and share names. Don't take SNMP lightly — it's dangerous.

Testing your network for SNMP vulnerabilities is quite simple: Just get a good SNMP monitor, such as NTManage (http://www.lanware.net), and set it up to probe every address on your network. Probe your addresses routinely and often. You may be amazed at what you find, and it is certainly well worth your effort.

A case in point: Recently, I inspected the network of an acquaintance, at his request. I probed his entire network with NTManage from the comfort of my home office, far away from his location (in other words, it can be done from anywhere on the Internet). What I found floored me. After the discovery process was complete, the software quickly built a graphical map of his entire network, then listed every machine that was SNMP enabled, including several of his NT servers.

The owner of the network dives off the deep end with everything but rarely checks the water depth first. When he installed NT and Internet Information Server, he loaded (in accordance with his normal habits) every single SNMP service and driver that came with them, which is fine — except that he didn't configure them at all; he simply left them in the default configuration. The really stupid thing is that he didn't use SNMP on his network for any practical purpose; he was simply in the habit of loading everything and checking it out later.

Once I had identified which of his systems were SNMP enabled, I used my SNMP monitor to examine them in detail. I learned his domain names, his machines' names, his user names, his share names, his IP addresses and subnet masks, his routing tables, the services that were loaded, the services that were running and those that were not. I could also manipulate most of these items at will, with some minor exceptions, like not being able to add users.

From this adventure, I learned most of the information I needed to infiltrate his network. In fact, the only thing I *couldn't* get were his passwords, which I could have found with a simple brute-force password cracker. The moral of the story is this: *Never run services you don't need*. If you can't resist temptation, load them if you like, but disable them until you really need them. Even then, consider the security impact.

Tip

First, block UDP ports 161 and 162 at the routers that serve your Internet connections to prevent any SNMP snooping into your networks. Next, *never* leave SNMP installed and running in its default configuration. Always change the community names to something obscure, and use passwords for SNMP communications whenever possible.

SYN ATTACKS

SYN attacks (SYN is short for synchronize) are common on the Internet because they are easy to instigate. SYN is a packet sent on TCP/IP that asks a remote system for permission to establish a connection. When a system is under SYN attack (sometimes referred as *SYN flooding*), some or all network services are rendered unavailable, at which point error messages appear on network client screens. One such message is "The connection has been reset by the remote host." Most operating systems, including Windows NT, are vulnerable to this type of attack.

Hackers can target an entire machine or just a specific TCP service (such as Web services). SYN attacks are not operating system attacks per se, but instead attack TCP/IP services without regard to the operating system. For explicit details about SYN attacks, see the CERT Advisory CA-96.21 located at ftp://ftp.cert.org/ pub/cert_advisories.

SYN packets establish a form of handshaking, where a system requests a connection to another system. Upon a successful handshake, the host system allocates some of its resources to handle the connection. Keep in mind here that on any system, resources are limited. SYN attacks deplete system resources until the system can longer accept requests — thus, SYN attacks are a kind of denial-of-service attack. Here's how SYN attacks work:

1. A TCP connection request (SYN packet) is sent to the target computer. The source IP address in the packet is spoofed, or replaced with an erroneous address that won't lead back to the attacker. An attacker sends a large number of these TCP SYN packets to tie up as many resources as possible on the target computer.

2. Upon receiving the connection request, the target computer allocates resources to handle and track the new connection, then responds with a SYN-ACK packet. In this case, the response is sent to the spoofed (and nonexistent) IP address.

3. Because the IP address is fake, no response is received to the SYN-ACK. In its default configuration, a Windows NT 3.5x or 4.0 computer retransmits the SYN-ACK packet five times, doubling the time-out value after each retransmission. The initial time-out value is three seconds, so retries are attempted after 3, 6, 12, 24, and 48 seconds. After the last retransmission, 96 seconds pass before the computer gives up on receiving a response and de-allocates the resources that were set aside earlier for the connection. The total elapsed time that resources are in use is 189 seconds (more than 3 minutes) — way too long.

If you suspect that your computer is the target of a SYN attack, you can type the following command in a DOS command shell to reveal connections that are in the SYN_RECEIVED state:

```
netstat -n -p tcp
```

This command may cause the following text to appear on your screen:

```
Active Connections:

Proto   Local Address        Foreign Address      State
TCP     127.0.0.1:1030       127.0.0.1:1032       ESTABLISHED
TCP     127.0.0.1:1032       127.0.0.1:1030       ESTABLISHED
TCP     10.57.8.190:21       10.57.14.154:1256    SYN_RECEIVED
TCP     10.57.8.190:21       10.57.14.154:1257    SYN_RECEIVED
TCP     10.57.8.190:21       10.57.14.154:1258    SYN_RECEIVED
TCP     10.57.8.190:21       10.57.14.154:1259    SYN_RECEIVED
TCP     10.57.8.190:21       10.57.14.154:1260    SYN_RECEIVED
TCP     10.57.8.190:21       10.57.14.154:1261    SYN_RECEIVED
TCP     10.57.8.190:21       10.57.14.154:1262    SYN_RECEIVED
TCP     10.57.8.190:21       10.57.14.154:1263    SYN_RECEIVED
TCP     10.57.8.190:21       10.57.14.154:1264    SYN_RECEIVED
TCP     10.57.8.190:21       10.57.14.154:1265    SYN_RECEIVED
TCP     10.57.8.190:21       10.57.14.154:1266    SYN_RECEIVED
TCP     10.57.8.190:4801     10.57.14.221:139     TIME_WAIT
```

If a lot of connections are in the SYN_RECEIVED state, it is possible that the system is under attack. You can use a network analyzer or packet sniffer to track the problem further. You might consider contacting your ISP for assistance in tracing the source of these packets. The attack's impact will vary from machine to machine, depending upon the TCP/IP stack you use and the applications that are listening on the TCP ports. For most stacks, the number of connections that can be in the half-open (SYN_RECEIVED) state is limited. After the limit is reached for a given TCP port, the target computer responds with a reset to all further connection requests until enough resources are freed up.

Microsoft has confirmed that the TCP/IP protocol in Windows NT versions 3.51 and 4.0 are vulnerable to these attacks, as seen in Microsoft Knowledge Base article Q142641. They released a supported update for Windows NT 3.51 and 4.0. If you haven't loaded the latest service packs on your NT systems, you should do so quickly. SYN attacks are nasty and hard to trace. This attack makes it easy for almost anyone to keep your NT systems at bay around the clock, including any services they run, such as Web and mail access. You really don't need to test your machines' vulnerability to these attacks — *they are vulnerable unless you've loaded the correct service packs.*

SOURCE ROUTING

In source routing, an intruder inserts into TCP/IP packet headers a source IP address that's an address inside the network under attack. In other words, source routing makes the packet *appear* as if it originates from inside your own network, when it actually comes from someplace outside your network. The idea is that your network obviously trusts itself and acts on the packets as if they are from a trusted source. In this way, intruders easily send packets into the network that are normally denied access.

It is difficult to test your network for vulnerability to source routing. The simplest way is to learn every detail about the capabilities of your perimeter security network — whether your routers and firewall software are configured to deny access to these types of packets. Your firewall system, whatever it may consist of, should understand that packets arriving at its network interface attached to an external untrusted network should not come from that direction at all. If your firewall has this feature, which all good ones do, it simply ignores these packets, thus protecting you from this type of attack.

Make sure your router or firewall system can stop source routing packets in their tracks, and configure it to do so. *If it can't, get one that can and install it quickly.*

Tip

ICMP REDIRECTS

An ICMP redirect tells the recipient system to override something in its routing table. Routers legitimately use it to tell hosts that the host is using a nonoptimal or defunct route to a particular destination; in other words, the host is sending it to the wrong router. The wrong router sends the host an ICMP redirect packet that tells the host what the correct route is. If you can forge ICMP redirect packets, and if your target host pays attention to them, you can alter the host's routing tables and possibly subvert the host's security by causing traffic to flow in a path the network manager didn't intend.

ICMP redirects also may be used in denial-of-service attacks — a host is sent a route that loses connectivity or an ICMP Network Unreachable packet saying it can no longer access a particular network. Many firewall builders screen ICMP traffic from their network, thereby limiting the ability of outsiders to ping hosts or modify their routing tables.

IP SPOOFING

IP spoofing plays on the weaknesses of authentication systems. Far too many systems on the Internet rely on IP addresses for their authentication. Of course, this procedure is bad news because IP addresses provide *identification*, not *authentication*.

In addition, far too many routers and gateways route packets with "bad" source IP addresses; in other words, they accept and deliver a packet in which the source IP address and the destination IP address should be on the same side of the router. Routing these packets could be described as incorrect behavior; and in the past, I think most people setting up routers have viewed this error as somebody else's fault.

Here's how the exploit works.

1. The intruder's machine sends a legitimate packet to a target machine, with the packet destined for a legitimate service running on a certain port.

2. The target machine responds with a legitimate acknowledgment, including a packet sequence number.

3. The intruder's machine uses the incoming sequence number to guess the next sequence number and sends a packet destined for some type of service (rsh, for example) to the target machine, using a forged source IP address belonging to a machine that the target trusts. The intruder sends this packet blindly — the intruders don't need to see the responses. That's why they use spoofed (forged) addresses.

4. In the packet in the previous step, the intruder includes some type of command, such as Echo '++' >> .rhosts. The victim's machine acts on the packets, because they're supposedly from a trusted host.

5. In the meantime, the intruder distracts the machine whose address was used for the attack by sending it garbage — TCP packets with intentionally bad sequence numbers. This diversion keeps this machine from becoming involved in the packet exchange between the target and the intruder.

The only quick solution is to configure your routers and firewalls to stop forwarding packets with bad source addresses — something all good security systems should do. The long-term solution is to get programmers to understand the difference between identification and authentication.

Although this type of attack is normally targeted at Unix systems, it is not unique to them, and NT systems are just as vulnerable as any other — especially if they're running any type of "r" services (explained in Chapters 1 and 2). Any system that authenticates hosts or users based on IP addresses alone is vulnerable. This attack was officially announced by CERT in its advisory number CA-95:01, available via FTP from ftp://info.cert.org. Of course, if you use a good authentication system, in theory you can make this whole problem go away.

Make sure you configure your routers and firewalls to stop packets with bad source addresses in their tracks. If your systems can't, *get some that can and install them quickly.*

Tip

PROGRAMMERS AND THE GIFT OF SOFTWARE

You gain many advantages by being a competent programmer. Mark Russinovich and Bryce Cogswell (authors of NTFSDOS) and Jeremy Allison (author of the password-grabber .dll) are three perfect examples. These gentleman have used their programming skills to their advantage and have discovered serious ways to exploit NT along the way. Granted, these gentleman are legitimate programmers who harbor no bad intent, but many code slingers do, and many of them are top-notch intruders (if there is such a thing).

A simple look at NTFSDOS and a quick peek at the NT password-grabbing technique both show why having good programming skills gives intruders the edge. Let's consider another case in point: the ability to develop useful software. Sounds legitimate, right? Well, it is, but it isn't if you consider that many break-ins are socially engineered. You may say, "Social engineering? Isn't that government work?" Not at all. Today, it's the work of the advanced intruder.

Let's say I'm a programmer who wants access to your network. First, I survey your Web site to learn the functions your shop uses. Why? To give me an idea of the kind of software you're likely to load and try. With that in mind, I write a quick little utility or some other program I'm fairly certain you won't be able to resist. As I write this software, I add a feature to give me access to your systems, such as

- Inserting a back door in the form of a service listening on a port that isn't blocked by a firewall or router.

- Including a password-grabbing Trojan horse that e-mails me passwords as they change.
- Granting myself high-level access by forcing you to establish a user account for my software to run under. I get by e-mail the user name and password for this account and I set object permissions so I can access them at will.
- Simply grabbing the files I want and e-mailing them to myself.

I might also take many other actions, but the point is that if I can get you to install my software using an administrator account, I've basically got you where I want you. Because administrators can do almost anything on an NT system, if you use these accounts to install my software, I can have my software do almost anything I want.

Not only can a programmer write programs that open doors and insert Trojan horses into the system, but they can also delve into the lower levels of the operating system, looking for weaknesses. By the way, *many* of the known exploits for NT and other systems are discovered by programmers.

Let's look at a real-world example. By default, most NT services run under a local System account. It is important to recognize that the System account, like the built-in Administrator account, is all-powerful. Microsoft apparently tried to ensure that its Web server (IIS) is a bit more secure because it runs under the authority of a regular user account called IUSR_COMPUTERNAME. However, this account is not as secure as you may think. It's quite simple to make a programming call to a Windows NT API function called RevertToSelf(), using a standard ISAPI script. After this function is called, the IIS server reverts its user account to the local System account, and therein lies the danger. With access to the System account's authority at a program level, you can issue malicious commands. Look at the two lines of code that make it possible:

```
...
RevertToSelf();
system( "malicious commands go here" );
...
```

The second line of code is where the danger lies. Anyone familiar with developing Windows-based applications knows that the system() function passes commands to the operating system, and these commands can be just about anything you can think of. Using this method of attack, a programmer may develop a seemingly harmless ISAPI program with this hidden trap that triggers whenever the intruder runs the script with certain parameters.

It is incredibly important to make sure you trust the people giving you ISAPI scripts to run on your servers. If you don't trust the developers, examine the source code for strange code segments like the one I described. Once you've examined the scripts carefully, compile them yourself and use *your* compiled version, not the developer's.

Never install new software on a production machine, especially if the machine is exposed to the Internet. Never use an administrator account to install software unless it's absolutely forced upon you by the software installation program. Never assume any software is safe from Trojan horses, especially shareware and freeware (remember Microsoft's software auditing and e-mail reporting in the early releases of Windows 95, and beware). Always examine the registry for changes after installing new software (using a utility like DumpReg from Somarsoft).

Tip

GRABBING A LIST OF USERS

Before Service Pack 3 for NT 4.0, a user could easily grab a list of users from a neighboring NT domain. This snooping attack is very easy; it exploits an NT bug in establishing interdomain trusts. Following the steps below, you can test this exploit to see how it affects your network security.

1. Log on to an NT server on the same network as the NT server you want a list of users from.
2. From the User Manager, create a trust relationship with the target. When prompted for a password, enter whatever you want — it doesn't matter. You get a response stating that NT couldn't validate the trust because of a bad password. However, the target is now on your trusting list.
3. Launch Explorer, right-click on any folder, and select Sharing.
4. From the Sharing dialog box, select Add.
5. From the Add menu, select the target NT server.
6. Voila! You can now see the entire group listing of the target. If you select the Show Users command, you'll see the entire user listing, along with full names and descriptions.

At this point, you have half the necessary information you need to launch a brute-force attack against the target NT domain, which makes this problem incredibly dangerous. I mentioned previously that this procedure works on NT 4.0 with (up to) Service Pack 2 installed. Microsoft fixed this anomaly in Service Pack 3, which is another great argument for always checking the changes in new service packs. Don't skip loading them because your systems work fine right now — you never know when the Service Packs will contain subtle, yet important changes.

ABUSING THE ANONYMOUS ACCOUNT

Many people don't realize this, but NT contains an anonymous user account, appropriately named Anonymous. This account doesn't appear in User Manager because it's a built-in account used for certain system-level operations. However, if you examine your Security Log using Event Viewer, you will probably see numerous entries attributed to this account, which can give you an idea of what it's used for.

Would-be intruders can use the Anonymous account to exploit an NT system, as demonstrated by the RedButton program released in April 1997 by Midwestern Commerce in New York. RedButton connected to an NT system remotely, extracted sensitive information from the registry, and displayed a list of all available shares — hidden or not. You can download a copy of Red-Button from Midwestern's Web site (http://206.222.24.74/redbutton), or you can try some tests manually.

To begin, decide upon an NT system to test and open a DOS command shell. Once it's open, type the following command:

```
NET USE \\NTSERVER_NAME\IPC$ "" /USER:""
```

Be sure to replace NTSERVER_NAME with the correct NT NetBIOS machine name. With the command above, you're connecting to the Inter-Process Connection share, used by NT systems to communicate with each other. The additional parameters after the UNC tell your NT to make the connection to the remote NT system using the Anonymous account, indicated by blank parameters enclosed in quotes. Once connected, you have an open channel that can be used in conjunction with Registry Editor and other tools.

Open the Registry Editor and choose Select Computer from the menu. After the list appears, select the machine you're testing against. It opens the remote system's registry, and what you do from there is up to you.

Stopping this attack is a simple as adding Service Pack 3 for NT 4.0. If you can't or don't want to install Service Pack 3 for some reason, you can try one of the two suggestions below for fixing this hole.

- Stop the Server service or unbind the Server service using the Network control panel applet. Although this step prevents the NT system from sharing resources on the network in the typical Microsoft fashion, it's highly recommended if your system is exposed to the entire Internet.

- On NT Servers, modify or add the Registry key HKLM\SYSTEM\CCS\Services\LanManServer\Parameters\AutoShareServer, setting its value to 3D0. On NT Workstations, the last part of the key is AutoShareWks instead of AutoShareServer. This modification disables the default administrative shares (shares with names ending in $).

Tip

SERVICE ATTACKS

The inherent problem with running TCP/IP services under Windows NT is that we are making these services available for Internet use, but we are not 100 percent certain that they are safe from attack. Worse, we can't always test them to look for problems. Therefore, as someone once said, "the best defense is a good offense."

In the computer world, a good offense means watching the Internet for new information about potential exploits and vulnerabilities. You must watch the mailing lists, newsgroups, Web sites, and other informational stores for new items of interest daily. If you do, you'll be almost as wise as most of the hacker community, if not in exact step with them. I say *almost* because not all exploits come to the surface as fast as we'd like. Fortunately, most potential intruders are less knowledgeable than the few leaders, so in most cases, they wait for someone to tell them about a particular problem instead of finding them themselves. However, exploits spread among hacker groups like wildfire in a dry forest. Appendix B lists many well-known hot spots for gathering information; use them to your advantage.

One example that came to the surface as I was writing this book has a huge effect on machines running IIS. A bug in IIS versions 1.x and 2.x allows a certain URL to be issued that completely crashes the IIS process and all its dependent services, such as your MS Proxy Server. It was first reported to an Internet mailing list, where I saw it. Simply use Telnet to connect to port 80 on an IIS system. Once connected, type **"GET ../.."** and press Enter. In just a few seconds, that IIS will crash completely, taking down the dependent services with it. It sounds too simple, doesn't it? But it's true. Even though I and at least one other person told Microsoft about this problem directly, they *never* announced it publicly that I am aware of. However, they immediately released Service Pack 1a, and soon thereafter, they released SP2.

Herein lies the problem: service packs fix problems with software, but it's never in a vendor's best interest to tell the world what problems they have. Vendors leave it up to you to obtain the service packs and install them. You can see how important it is to install service packs in any network environment.

Not all NT services are TCP/IP-based, but most of us run multiprotocol networks and we don't always know whether a particular service is listening on a TCP/IP port. Therefore, it may be wise to scan your systems regularly to look for listening TCP/IP ports, especially after installing new software. For example, you may discover that your network administrator configured MS SQL Server to use TCP/IP instead of some other specified protocol. Several security risks are associated with the MS SQL Server service, as listed below:

- After a user has accessed the SQL server as SA (system administrator) using SQL Enterprise Manager, the SA's password is stored *unencrypted* in the registry.

- The probe account (complete with a clear password) is always created by SQL Server by default. This account can enumerate all SQL users and databases.

- If a user can execute the xp_cmdshell stored procedure, the user can execute every command-line command in the context of the all-powerful NT local System account.

- Some system administrators, especially those from an Oracle background, enable TCP access to SQL via the default port of 1433, which is normally not protected by firewalls.

Another problem service is the NT FTP server. Apparently, security checks are not consistent with the actual file permission settings. In particular, several releases of the FTP service under NT had a problem with what has become known as the "cd.." bug. Try connecting to your FTP server as a restricted user (a user restricted to certain directories), and after you're connected, see how far you can go using the "cd.." command. You may be surprised, but if you've kept up with the service packs, you may not.

I can't tell you how to test every possible NT service, but I can give you some advice that prevents many of attacks from being successful: Run only services you definitely need and run them with regular user accounts.

For example, the Scheduler service, installed automatically with NT, runs automatic commands at set time intervals. Using a DOS command shell (or a program), an intruder can use the AT command to add items to the Scheduler's command queue. These items can be anything allowed to run on that NT machine, such as adding users or e-mailing files. The problem with Scheduler is that many administrators allow this service to run under the System account, which is a bad idea. When Scheduler runs under the System account, you can set up an AT command that launches the Registry Editor. When it's running, the Registry Editor has the authority to examine and modify any key in the Registry, even the NT security database (known as the SAM). If the Scheduler is using a normal user account, such as the Administrator account, it can't get to the Registry Editor. If you must use the Scheduler service, establish a normal user account for it to run under.

Tip

- **Do not run services under the System account unless you absolutely have to.**
- **Always monitor the information sources on the Internet for new problems and possible exploits.**
- **Block all unnecessary ports on your firewalls.**
- **Install the new NT services packs quickly.**

Let's look at some common services that are loaded on almost every NT system during a TCP/IP configuration: Chargen, Echo, Daytime, and Quote of the Day. These services are known in Microsoft lingo as "Simple TCP/IP Services" and are seen in the Control Panel | Services listing as such. Each of these harmless services has a purpose, although the services typically go unused on NT networks. However, left running, they can be an open invitation to a denial-of-service attack.

For instance, the Echo port simply returns any character sent to it. It's there for testing purposes. The Chargen port generates a complete set of ASCII characters over and over as fast as it can and is also used for testing. Putting two and two together, we can see that if we spoof a connection from the Chargen port to the Echo port, we get a never-ending stream of data flowing back and forth. This attack can effectively eat lots of horsepower from the NT system, and detecting this attack is incredibly difficult because you don't readily notice this activity without looking for it explicitly. On the other hand, preventing this type of attack is a walk in the park with one of the following techniques.

- Block access to these ports at your router if possible.
- Do not install Simple TCP/IP Services. If they're already installed, disable them completely.
- Use the built-in TCP/IP filtering to block access to these ports.
- Disable the individual Simple TCP/IP Services by changing registry values under the HKEY_LOCAL_MACHINE/SYSTEM/CurrentControlSet/Services/SimpTCP/Parameters key. Look for parameters associated with each individual

service and change them from 1 to 0, which turns them off. For example, the Chargen entry looks like this: EnableTCPChargen, with a value of 1.

SHARE ATTACKS

As you may have gathered from the previous sections on the Netstat, NBTStat, and Net commands, Windows shares can be vulnerable to attack. The information in those sections should give you an idea of how to test the strength of protection on your shares. However, let me point out a few additional tidbits that may help you strengthen the security of your shared objects.

First, remember that NT creates several default file shares upon installation; two of the most prevalant are C$ and D$, which give the Administrator group access to C:\ and D:\. Although other default shares are established during NT installation, these two are attacked most often. Remember to rename these shares to something obscure.

As a general rule, NT requires a user name and password to access shares, but there are several important exceptions. NT does not require a password if the Everyone group has access, and the Guest account is enabled with blank password. Therefore, it is always wise to disable the Guest account unless using it is absolutely necessary. In that case, pick an incredibly hard-to-guess password.

Writing programs that attack shares is pretty easy. In fact, all that's needed is the machine name, IP address, and the share name, which are easy to obtain with the NBTStat command. With a little luck, NBTStat might provide an actual user name as well. Such a program includes a small loop that reads a text-based dictionary file one line at a time and pipes the words into a command such as

```
net use x: \\MACHINE_NAME\SHARE_NAME dictionary_word
    /USER:username
```

It's not hard, but it *is* rather slow.

Other dangerous shares under Windows NT include the registry share. The registry is not exactly a share in the true sense of the word because it can't be unshared, but it does allow access from machines across a network. NT uses the native Remote Procedure Calls (RPC) mechanism to access the registry on the remote computer. Until recently, this registry share was, by default, made available with *read* permission to *Everyone* after a fresh installation of Windows NT. Because most programs store sensitive information in the registry (including NT's own user security database, SAM), the presence of this share creates a great security threat.

Microsoft finally realized that blindly sharing the registry is not a good idea and released SP2 for NT 3.51 to make it possible to disable network access to the registry. Simply create the following key; only the users listed in the ACL for this key can access the registry remotely. The key on NT 4.0 is

```
HKEY_LOCAL_MACHINE\System\CurrentControlSet\Control\
     SecurePipeServers\winreg
```

When information about the registry share vulnerabilities spread in the NT community, some sources started recommending removing the Everyone group's access from the HKEY_LOCAL_MACHINE key without propagating permissions through the entire tree. On the surface, this method works well, but remember, a malicious programmer could still use the Windows NT API to grab any subkey within the HKEY_LOCAL_MACHINE key.

Never let anyone remotely administer your registry — completely disable remote registry access. Never use the Guest account — disable it. Never blindly grant access to shares to the Everyone group.

Tip

PHYSICAL ACCESS TO THE NETWORK

Most people take for granted the physical aspect of protecting a network. They see the camera downstairs at the front door, the card key reader right below it, and all those keylock doors and assume they're protected from this possibility, but they're wrong. Here's a perfect example.

As I mentioned elsewhere in this book, I used to own and operate a large ISP in Houston. That ISP was located in a building with these protections: we had a camera at the entrance to the building, a key card reader for after-hours access, a required telephone to call security if you didn't have a card, and locks on every single door. One night after being absent from the office for more than four months, I visited the offices just to see what shape things were in, and boy was I surprised.

I didn't have a key card with me, and I needed to get into the building. I simply picked up the security phone, waited for the guard (at a remote site) to answer, gave him a name, and asked him to open the door. Because I didn't have a valid key card, I didn't really tell him who I was — I gave him the name of someone else, an employee who had a valid key card. The guard didn't even think twice; he looked up the name I gave him in a database to verify that a working card key was assigned to this person and opened the door for me. I was in the building.

Once inside, I went upstairs to my suites and found the cleaning crew doing their normal nightly routine. This cleaning crew was new and didn't know who I was. The doors were unlocked because they were taking out trash, so I walked right in like I knew what I was doing, and they never stopped me or asked me a single question. I walked around to the executive offices and found a young man cleaning them. The door to one office was open, so I waltzed right in without a single confrontation. I found sensitive file cabinets unlocked and secret business negotiation documents and memos on the desk.

Then I went to our supposedly secured network room, only to find that someone had left the door unlocked. How convenient! I went in the network room, and guess what I found? Our system administrators had left one Unix box and two NT servers logged in with Administrator privileges. Apparently, they thought it was okay to leave them this way because the door was going to be locked and no one had the keys except them. Boy, were they wrong. First, I created a few new accounts for myself to leave a trail that I was there; second, I logged those machines off, but not before I changed the administrative passwords, thereby locking out the administrators.

The ease with which I gained access to my suite and our network room scared the daylights out of me, but the story doesn't stop there. I know that all commercial office buildings have telephone equipment rooms somewhere, so I found the one on our floor. And guess what? The door was unlocked. I went in and found our phone lines and dedicated circuits that tie us to the Internet. I could have cut the wires, cut the fiber circuits, tapped the phones, tapped the data link — anything. Needless to say, I was a bit upset.

My recourse was to contact the president of the building management company to let him know that his cleaning crew was lax about people in the offices after hours and that the entire building was a security nightmare for any business. I also had a long talk with the man charged with running my ISP business who wasn't attending to the daily security needs of our facilities.

The moral here is never assume that people are doing what they are supposed to. We all have good intentions but frequently fall short of our goals for one reason or another. You should try testing your facilities the way I did. Don't assume that the security systems in place are doing their job — and that goes for employees as well. You may be a bit surprised at the *real* state of affairs.

NAÏVE EMPLOYEES

Naïve employees are perhaps one of the biggest personnel-related security risks. I'd much rather hire a person that questions everything than a person who isn't suspicious enough. In many work environments, suspicion creates problems, but when it comes to security, you could say that an ounce of suspicion is worth a pound of cure.

One of the most common ways an intruder socially engineers your company is manipulating the help desk. The bigger the company, the easier the target because in large firms, it's rare that any staff member knows every other staff member. Let's suppose I want to gain access to your network. First, I'd see if I could get my hands on your company directory, which really isn't that hard to do. I may find an old one in the trash, or I may simply walk in and ask the receptionist if I could borrow one for a moment. Then I'd look for the names of the people in the departments whose information I want access to. Or I might surf your voice mail system to the correct department and hope that someone has left a name somewhere. Once I have the name of some key employees, I would pick an appropriate time to call your help desk — maybe the middle of lunch or just before closing on a Friday. After calling your help desk, I'd pose as this employee, asking the help desk to reset my password because "I just drew a blank and can't remember it to save my life, and I've just got to get this work done before the boss gets mad and I lose my job."

With any luck, they'll accommodate me, and I have what I need to access your network. Although this procedure isn't the only way to get things done, it does work. I know because I've done it myself twice, working on behalf of one of my customers. In one case, I obtained direct access to a network from the Internet, and in another case, I locked a Senior System Engineer out of the system all weekend by simply calling and telling the help desk to change the password.

Other problem areas are your visitors and outside contractors. In one case, two detectives practiced a little trash-digging until they discovered that a particular firm was contracting with a large insurance concern. These detectives wanted some secret information from this company, and using that newfound knowledge from the trash, they posed as two representatives for the insurance firm one Friday afternoon. They walked into offices, claimed to be from the insurance company, presented their newly made and bogus business cards, and requested that certain reports be generated and printed immediately so that they could work on them over the weekend. Guess what? The company was more than accommodating. Within an hour they had the reports. Never take people at face value, no matter what credentials they present. Be suspicious of people you haven't met before, even if they *are* from a partner or

client's business. Check on them before granting their wishes, and you'll probably be appreciated for your security consciousness.

Tip

**Never assume a person's credentials are real — check them out thoroughly. Adopt
policies that require all users to authenticate themselves with your help desk and
system administrators with some additional information — perhaps a Social Security number, driver's license number, mother's maiden name, or better yet, a simple
proprietary code similar to your user passwords.**

SUMMARY

In this chapter, you've learned several ways of attacking your own networks
looking for possible security problems. You learned about some of the tools at
your disposal and how to test your shared objects with these tools. You've
learned about the risk that naïve employees pose, as well as the risk of
assuming a person's credentials are legitimate. Later in this book, we take a
close look at Microsoft Proxy Server and show you how to integrate this security software into your network. First, let's go over some background information about firewalls.

CHAPTER 10

FIREWALL BASICS

Connecting to the Internet spawns a new set of responsibilities for IS departments: They must deliver reliable Internet services to corporate users while ensuring that systems and information stay secure from the outside threats, such as hackers, that an Internet connection brings. The most important tool for protecting a corporate network from Internet intrusions is a firewall — an intelligent device that controls traffic between two or more networks for security purposes.

In this chapter, Philip Carden examines firewall architectures. After looking at the difference between firewalls and a perimeter network, we explore the difference between three common firewall architectures — packet filters, proxy systems, and stateful inspection systems. Next, we look in detail at some of the more advanced firewall features an organization may need. As we get to the end of this chapter, you should begin considering your own organization's needs and how they may best be met — a topic we discuss in detail in Chapter 11.

FIREWALLS AND THE PERIMETER NETWORK

Before we get into our discussion of firewall technologies, I want to define two terms: firewall and perimeter network. Just as a firewall blocks the spread of a real fire, a *network firewall* is a hardware and/or software barrier between two or more networks. The firewall controls who can access the information behind the barrier and how they can access it. MPS is one example of a firewall; however, many other firewall products are available. Mostly, these other firewalls are software systems based on Windows NT or Unix, though hardware platforms (such as routers) may also run firewall software systems. Today, firewalls are usually associated with Internet connections, but you can also use firewalls to control traffic between parts of an intranet or between parts of networks belonging to different companies.

Often, companies use more than one type of firewall to provide a greater level of security. A key part of security planning is ensuring that your protection does not depend on any one particular system. It is common, for example, to use routers to augment the security already provided by more advanced firewall solutions. See Chapter 5, "Multiprotocol Environments," for helpful diagrams about combining security measures.

A *perimeter network* is any combination of firewall systems and connecting hardware that is placed between your trusted network and an untrusted network, such as the Internet (or even a business partner's network).

DEVICE CLASSIFICATIONS IN A PERIMETER NETWORK

Perimeter networks contain three main classes of devices: simple packet filters, proxy systems, and stateful inspection systems. Proxy systems and stateful inspection systems, which are similar to proxy servers, both provide a high level of protection against attack. Simple packet filters do not protect so well — but because companies often use packet filters to enhance the security provided by more advanced firewall architectures, it is important to understand their operation.

PACKET FILTERS

The simplest and most popular form of firewall is the packet filter, also known as a *screening router*, which has some kind of built-in capability that restricts traffic between destinations. A simple packet filter operates only at the network level and makes decisions about which packets to pass through and which to prevent based on the contents of the TCP/IP packet headers. Packet filters are very fast, very flexible, and inexpensive, but they lack the ability to provide detailed audit information about the traffic they transmit. They are vulnerable to attack because they assume that the software on the hosts behind them is configured correctly. For this reason, many experts prefer to avoid packet filters as a sole defense.

These three capabilities of packet filters can enhance your overall security:

- You can establish a traffic filter on a router that allows IP traffic only from a specific source or destination IP address that corresponds to the Dynamic Host Configuration Protocol (DHCP) scope used for your client workstations.

- You can add another filter that specifically disallows TCP port 139 — the port NetBIOS uses for connections over TCP/IP when Windows clients running TCP/IP attempt to access resources on an NT machine.

- You can filter User Datagram Protocol (UDP) traffic on ports 137 and 138, which NT uses to advertise computer names and related information.

With these steps, your simple packet filter helps prevent outsiders from directly connecting to an internal server while it allows internal users to access Internet services.

The packet filter is far from perfect. For example, suppose your network uses DHCP and an intruder tries to connect to each machine on your network, looking for a machine using FTP (normally found running on TCP port 21). Scanning your DHCP scope, the intruder might find a machine running FTP server software. The intruder could then upload a file with a similar filename to a file the user has recently downloaded, except that this new file does unexpected things when a user runs it, like installing a password grabber or keystroke grabber. The best security approach to prevent intrusions such as this one is to disallow all traffic to and from all TCP and UDP ports except those your users really need.

Figure 10.1 shows how to set up a packet filter to allow FTP packets from the Internet to pass into the internal network. As packets move from the Internet to the internal network, the packet filter examines each packet when the packet attempts to pass through the firewall. If the packet meets the criteria for acceptance as defined in the rule base illustrated in Table 10.1, the filter permits it to continue to the internal network.

The rules in Table 10.1 let a single client workstation (198.21.132.5) download files from any FTP server on the Internet. The rules could easily be modified to allow such access from an entire DHCP range. However, you should

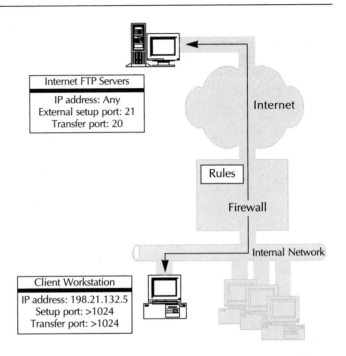

Figure 10.1
*Packet Filter
for FTP*

TABLE 10.1 RULE BASE							
Rule	Direction	Source IP Address	Destination IP Address	Protocol	Source Port	Destination Port	Action
1	Out	198.21.132.5	External	TCP	> 1024	21	Accept
2	In	External	198.21.132.5	TCP	21	> 1024	Accept
3	In	External	198.21.132.5	TCP	20	> 1024	Accept
4	Out	198.21.132.5	External	TCP	>1024	20	Accept
5	Either	Any	Any	Any	Any	Any	Reject

use such an approach only to augment the security provided by a more sophisticated firewall architecture, such as a proxy system.

Even when you create a filter that permits only essential traffic, packet-filtering devices alone don't provide adequate security for two reasons. First, packet filters can't determine whether an IP source address is valid — a hacker can use a forged address; second, they can't ensure that a TCP source port is used only for the service commonly associated with that port. In other words, a connection from port 21 of a client computer doesn't mean that a user is actually using FTP, which normally runs on port 21. A hacker can run any client or server program on a source port running through your packet filter. Because certain protocols, such as FTP, use a wide range of different port numbers, you must allow a wide range of port numbers through the packet filter device. For example, rules 3 and 4 in Table 10.1 allow any system on the Internet to connect to any port above 1024 on the internal machine at IP address 198.21.132.5. For these reasons, packet filters should not be used as your only line of defense against Internet attacks.

However, packet filters are well-suited to supplementing the protection that a more advanced firewall provides. For example, you can place routers with packet filters on one or both sides of a separate firewall to increase overall security and limit your organization's dependence on a single machine (see Figure 10.2).

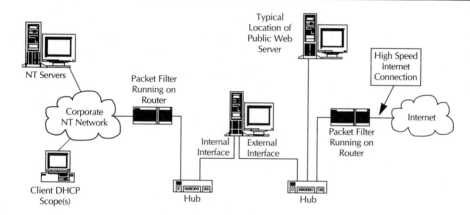

Figure 10.2
Perimeter Network Using Two Packet Filters

In the setup in Figure 10.2, the packet filters running on the routers on either side of the advanced firewall provide backup security if the firewall is compromised. In that case, the router on the left monitors the corporate network to search for passwords. You might also implement a filter that allows communications only to and from client DHCP scopes so that an intruder cannot reach a server. The advanced firewall in the middle has primary responsibility for the security of the Internet connection. The packet filter on the right, an external router, is configured to allow communications only to or from the IP address of the NT firewall's external interface (208.142.13.1). If the NT firewall is compromised, a hacker still cannot reach internal clients and servers because none of them use that address. To help assure that outsiders cannot log on to the NT firewall, you might also disallow traffic on those ports used by the router (TCP on 138 and UDP on 137, 138).

This type of perimeter network is very common and is particularly effective if you implement *address translation* — mapping internal addresses to unique internal network addresses — on an advanced firewall.

PROXY SYSTEMS

A second form of firewall is the proxy system, also known as an *application gateway* or *application firewall,* which consists of a host running both a proxy server program and a proxy client program. The firewall host usually has two network adapter cards: one that communicates between the firewall system and an internal network and another that communicates between the firewall and an external network, such as the Internet. Internet communications might use a modem that acts like a network card on NT. This setup is called a *dual-homed gateway.*

For example, a dual-homed gateway with a proxy for Web traffic has some agent that manages the requests to the remote networks on behalf of the user. Proxy systems are attractive to many sites because the proxies can perform detailed audits of the data passing through them. Many experts also believe proxy systems to be more secure than other firewall types because you can customize them to deflect attacks that the host software is known to be vulnerable to. The main disadvantage of proxy systems is that they are sometimes not completely transparent and they do not support protocols for which a proxy has not been developed. I point out more disadvantages of proxy systems in a moment.

Before you can understand the differences in the architectures of sophisticated firewall products, let's look at an operating proxy server in detail. A user connecting to the Internet first connects to the proxy server running on the firewall using proxy-enabled software. On behalf of the real client, the proxy client (also running on the firewall) establishes a session with the destination host. For example, to establish a Web connection, a Web browser connects to a proxy Web server running on the firewall machine. After verifying that this connection is allowed, the proxy Web server starts a proxy Web client, which in turn connects to the destination Web server, retrieving the requested information and returning it to the client workstation. A proxy system for FTP access is illustrated in Figure 10.3.

In this example, the Internet FTP server communicates with the proxy client at address 208.142.13.1. The internal client workstation (198.21.132.5) establishes an FTP session with the firewall (proxy) FTP server. The proxy server checks the rules to see whether client 198.21.132.5 is permitted to establish an FTP connection with the Internet FTP server in question; if so, it instructs the proxy FTP client to start a session on behalf of 198.21.132.5. From the perspective of

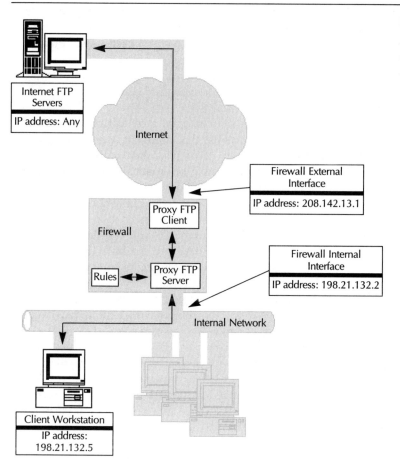

Figure 10.3
*Proxy
System for
FTP Access*

Internet FTP
Servers
IP address: Any

Internet

Firewall External
Interface
IP address: 208.142.13.1

Proxy FTP
Client

Firewall

Firewall Internal
Interface
IP address: 198.21.132.2

Rules ↔ Proxy FTP
Server

Internal Network

Client Workstation
IP address:
198.21.132.5

the FTP server on the Internet, it is transferring a file to a regular FTP client at
an address of 208.142.13.1.

Most proxy systems support transparent connections, which means the
firewall is not apparent or obvious to an authorized user. It appears to the
client workstation that it is connecting directly to its chosen Internet site.

A proxy system is a secure solution because it protects an internal corporate network from the hazards of a direct IP connection. To Internet hackers, a
site with a proxy system appears as a single computer with a single IP address
that establishes Internet connections — the proxy system firewall completely
hides the rest of an internal site's Internet-connected systems and IP addresses.

Besides providing security, a proxy system conserves IP address space.
Because the number of Internet-connected systems worldwide is huge and still

growing, the number of IP addresses is limited. Each Internet-connected system must have a unique IP address. With a proxy system, you need only one unique and valid IP address, the one that the proxy itself uses. You're free to use any addressing scheme you want for your internal systems. If you want to use false internal IP addresses, you must ensure that your firewall software can map internal addresses to unique IP addresses and that your internal system has no direct link to the Internet.

Because proxy systems provide a simple, secure way to implement basic Internet services, many firewall products use this approach or combine proxy systems with other protection methods to accomplish their goals.

Recently, vendors have released a number of products based on *dynamic packet filtering*. This kind of firewall is a cross between a proxy system and a packet filter. To the end user, it looks like it's operating only at the network level, but in fact the firewall examines all traffic that passes, as a proxy system does. When a user connects outward through the firewall, the dynamic packet filtering firewall records that fact and allows data to come back in to the user for the duration of that session. Dynamic packet filtering is an attractive technology that is still evolving and shows a lot of promise.

A disadvantage of the proxy system is that you must use a separate proxy service for each Internet service you want to support. In addition, many vendors support proxies for the most common Internet services (HTTP, FTP, Gopher, SMTP, Telnet) but not for less-common services such as Real Audio, Internet Relay Chat (IRC), and protocols for newsgroups. Sometimes the proxy vendor has not developed the proxy service far enough, and sometimes the particular Internet service is not well suited to a proxy solution. Services based on the connection-oriented TCP are better suited to a proxy solution than are connectionless UDP-based services because the proxy approach is connection-oriented: A proxy client establishes a connection with the real destination based on an already established connection between the real client and the proxy server.

STATEFUL INSPECTION DEVICES

Vendors have come up with several ways to overcome the disadvantages of the proxy system. Because of proxy limitations, many firewall products provide additional ways to connect through an Internet gateway. For example, Raptor Systems' Eagle NT firewall software not only provides predefined proxies for FTP, Gopher, HTTP, SMTP, and Telnet but also lets an administrator custom-define unidirectional or bidirectional service-passing proxies for less common services, such as Real Audio.

However, many firewall vendors are developing an entirely different approach called *stateful inspection*, which monitors connections after they're made to give a greater degree of security. Check Point, maker of the widely used FireWall-1, claims to be the inventor of both the approach and this term, though several other firms now produce products with a similar approach, including the NT-based Guardian from NetGuard and Firewall/Plus from Network-1. Stateful inspection works just like packet filtering but provides better security because it examines application-level information within IP packets and keeps track of a connection's context.

To explain the difference between packet filtering and stateful inspection, let's consider the TCP-based FTP as an example. An FTP client opens a TCP connection to port 21, the FTP command port, on the FTP server. The FTP client automatically picks a random TCP port, usually greater than 1024, for the data channel and tells the FTP server via the command port that the client will listen for data on that port. The FTP server then opens a TCP connection to that high TCP port on the client and transfers the data. Because you don't know which port the FTP client will pick, to let this service pass with a simple packet filter, you need to allow a destination TCP port of 21 for connections originating from the client to the server and allow all destination TCP ports greater than 1024 for connections from the server to the client.

You can tighten this design a little because FTP definitions tell us that the client source port for the command phase is greater than 1024 and that the server sends data from port 20. However, if you want to let users download files from anywhere on the Internet, you still need to let a host on the Internet establish a session from its port 20 to any port greater than 1024 on your internal clients. The problem is that you have no way of telling whether that connection is really being used for FTP data transfer or for some other malicious purpose. This flaw exists because such types of packet filters provide no way of tracking the context of the connection.

In contrast, Check Point's FireWall-1 does track the context or state of the connection. When FireWall-1 sees an attempt to connect to port 21 (assuming that a rule in the FireWall-1 rule base permits FTP), the program examines the application information in the packet to confirm that the packet is FTP. The program then allows packets from the destination FTP server (with a source port of 20) to destination ports greater than 1024 on the client that originated the connection. In short, the program keeps track of which FTP data connections are associated with which FTP command connections and allows only those high TCP destination port connections that have a valid reason to be there.

TRADEOFFS INHERENT IN FIREWALLS

Firewalls, like many other security systems, are not perfect. The tradeoffs they present are related to ease of use and security. The more rigorously the firewall checks the user's identity and activity, the more likely the user is to feel interrupted, pestered, and resentful. When you choose a firewall, don't discount user resentment as a factor in your decision. Users who dislike your system will find a way around it: Many sites with firewalls have internal networks festooned with uncontrolled dial-in/dial-out modems, installed by users to bypass the firewall. If the security system you choose is not easy to use, your users will bypass it unless you have sufficient authority to prevent them.

Proxies provide better auditing and finer control over access than packet filters, but many do not have sufficient capacity to support network connections faster than Ethernet speed. If you're planning to use ATM networks or T3 lines, you may not have a choice other than a screening router firewall.

CATEGORIES OF FIREWALL REQUIREMENTS

You should now understand the differences between the protection offered by different firewall architectures. Your perimeter network should probably consist of a proxy system or a stateful inspection system, preferably augmented by one or two routers running simple packet filters.

But how do you choose which proxy system or stateful inspection firewall is right for you? After all, different organizations have different firewall needs, and a wide range of different firewall features are available. To help you get a grip on them, I've grouped them into five main categories:

- Basic requirements
- Greater flexibility
- Advanced security and control
- Remote users and virtual private networking (VPN)
- Enterprise-level functionality

In addition, you may want to consider NT-specific features separately. Let's explore the type of features that are important in each of these categories.

BASIC REQUIREMENTS

When evaluating your organization's perimeter network requirements, start with the basic functions and add more complex ones as you need them. A basic perimeter network that supports common Internet services and that consists of a proxy or stateful inspection system and a packet-filtering device can be enough for a small organization. Large organizations and those with sophisticated needs can require multiple firewalls that support more Internet services.

A basic firewall lets corporate network users access common Internet services while preventing unauthorized outside users from accessing internal systems. A security administrator sets up rules for the types of connections allowed and disallowed. In addition, a basic firewall ensures that internal IP addresses remain invisible to the Internet. It must also allow the IP address range you use inside your firewall to be different from, and larger than, your company's registered Class A, B, or C address range.

Firewalls can also log network activity in detail, filter the log to produce meaningful reports, and alert a network administrator when the network has reached a predefined threshold. Make sure your firewall software supports at least these Internet services:

- HTTP
- FTP
- Gopher
- SMTP
- Telnet
- DNS name resolution, preferably by letting you run DNS on the firewall and on an internal system

Like any software, a basic firewall system needs to be easy to use. In particular, you should find it easy to add rules to firewall software and to analyze previously entered rules.

A good firewall should have a graphical user interface (GUI), especially if the firewall is administered by a staff member who is accustomed to Windows NT. Finally, a firewall needs high-quality documentation that clearly explains how to configure each type of Internet service and explains address-related issues, such as setting up DNS and configuring Web browsers.

GREATER FLEXIBILITY

Products that let you configure custom services in addition to predefined proxies and products that use stateful inspection provide greater flexibility than products that provide only a limited number of predefined proxy services. You should seriously consider more flexible products if your users must access less common or more sophisticated Internet protocols or if you have so many users that you must allow for unforeseen requirements. Also, look for firewall products that provide many predefined services because they can minimize your configuration efforts.

ADVANCED SECURITY AND CONTROL

Many firewalls provide security beyond source, destination, and service rules. For example, some firewalls allow rules based on time of day, day of week, and even date ranges. Other firewalls provide features such as configuration verification and virus scanning. Some other firewall products also monitor the processes running on the firewall system and halt unknown processes.

One measure of a good firewall is certification by an independent agency such as the National Computer Security Association (NCSA). NCSA tests firewall products against a standardized suite of attacks performed while the firewall still lets authorized users accomplish significant business functions. NCSA certification provides an objective, practical way for you to evaluate the level of security a firewall provides.

At press time, four of the Windows NT firewall vendors — CheckPoint Software Technologies, Raptor Systems, Network-1, and Digital Equipment — had NCSA-Certified firewall products (they've passed the NCSA Version 1.0 set of tests). However, according to Jeff Lolley of NCSA, only Digital's and Raptor's NT firewall products had been tested separately from the non-NT versions. NCSA posts information about firewall-testing procedures and maintains a current list of certified products on its Web site at http://www.ncsa.com. The NCSA is constantly updating information about certification, so check its web site often and be sure to determine whether the NCSA has tested the NT version of the firewall separately from non-NT version.

User Authentication and Authorization

An important advanced firewall security feature is user-oriented authentication, which is the ability to allow or deny certain connections based on a user name and password combination or some other, more advanced identification scheme. NT-based firewall products that support user-oriented authentication include Eagle NT, FireWall-1, Global Internet's Centri Firewall for Windows NT, and Microsoft Proxy Server (MPS).

Various authentication technologies are available. The simplest forms require typing a user name and a reusable password. This method is suitable for controlling only outbound Internet access, because password guessing and eavesdropping attacks are likely on inbound access attempts.

For inbound access, one-time passwords using a scheme such as Bellcore's S/KEY provide a higher level of security. The S/KEY scheme calculates a six-word (96-bit), one-time password based on a sequence number, a firewall-supplied seed word, and a user's secret password. Users type a different password each time they connect.

Better still, some firewalls can integrate one or more credit card-sized handheld token generators that automatically generate and display the next password the user types. Examples include Security Dynamics' SecurID, AssureNet Pathways' (formerly Digital Pathways') SecureNet Keys (SNKs), CRYPTOCard's CRYPTOCard RB-1, and Digipass S.A.'s Digipass.

Integrating Different Security Subsystems — TACACS+ and RADIUS

In larger organizations, you can quickly build a complex security environment that's difficult to maintain if you implement different types of authentication control for different purposes. Implementing a centralized authentication server can greatly simplify your enterprise-wide authentication. This centralized authentication server maintains all the authorizations for users regardless of where the user is located and how the user is connected to the network.

For example, this approach lets you maintain a single user name/password database for both telecommuters connecting directly via ISDN and mobile users connecting via the firewalled Internet connection. Although proprietary authentication servers (such as AssureNet's Defender) are available and supported by certain firewalls (including Check Point's FireWall-1 release 3.0), you should probably consider using an authentication server that is based on one of the two standards for authentication servers — RADIUS and TACACS+. Check Point supports RADIUS in FireWall-1 release 3.0, and Raptor supports both RADIUS and TACACS+ in Eagle release 3.0. Note that RADIUS still transmits authentication packets unencrypted across the network, which means they are vulnerable to attacks from packet sniffers.

As security environments become more complex, it is more important to integrate the different security systems you use. The features of TACACS+ and RADIUS are compared in Table 10.2.

As you can see, TACACS+ clearly offers a stronger set of features. However, because the firewall and the authentication server usually communicate on a trusted network, the encryption features offered by TACACS+ aren't necessarily as important as they might appear. If you are certain that encrypted information will never travel across an untrusted network, RADIUS can provide an equally viable solution. Moreover, RADIUS has somewhat wider vendor support; the one notable exception is Cisco, who initially threw its considerable weight behind TACACS+.

TABLE 10.2 TACACS+ VS. RADIUS	
TACACS+	**RADIUS**
Uses TCP	Uses UDP
Full packet encryption between client and server	Encrypts only the passwords
Independent authentication, authorization, and accounting	Combined authentication and authorization
Passwords in the database may be encrypted	Passwords in the database are in clear text

What Are Your Employees Doing?

Besides securing the network, many organizations want to control employees' access to Internet sites. Limiting this kind of outbound access is called *content-filtering*. First generation NT-based firewall products, including MPS, let you filter content by manually maintaining lists of allowed and prohibited URLs or IP addresses — a tedious process, to say the least. But advanced content-filtering capabilities have appeared in the second round of releases of major NT firewall products, including both Check Point's FireWall-1 and Raptor's Eagle.

Implementing content-filtering without using the firewall is also a possibility. Because content-filtering is a productivity and legality issue instead of a security issue, you can choose to keep the firewall simple and filter content elsewhere. One alternative is to use specialized content-filtering servers that sit between the users and the firewall (or between the firewall and the Internet) and use a database of URLs supplied by a third-party vendor that classifies sites for you. You can then allow or disallow classes of sites, such as adult, gambling, sports, and leisure, based on criteria such as time of day or day of the week. Another alternative is to rely on content providers to begin using RSACi (the Recreational Software Advisory Council's Internet content rating system) to rate their sites. If you use an RSACi-enabled browser (currently only Internet Explorer 3.0 or greater), you can set up the browser to allow access only to rated sites that meet your criteria.

Remember that lots of Internet sites have malicious ActiveX and Java code on them, designed to damage the client machine. Usually this damage is limited to changing certain settings on the browser or spawning copies of the browser until the system crashes. Limiting access to certain Internet sites can remove a lot of these problems and reduce your administrative headaches when your system gets trashed by a malicious Web site.

REMOTE USERS AND VIRTUAL PRIVATE NETWORKING

If your company's mobile users (or telecommuters) must connect to your corporate systems via the Internet, or if you want to establish Internet links with business partners, suppliers, or customers, you should definitely use encryption between the remote locations and your firewall. Using encryption to enable private communications across the Internet is called a *virtual private network* (VPN). Unfortunately, few NT firewall products currently support the emerging VPN encryption standards; instead, vendors still use proprietary encryption techniques, which means that all members of your VPN must use products from the same vendor for compatibility.

Encryption standards are especially important for Internet connections among trusted business partners (e.g., to support EDI applications); with such standards in place, partners need not have the same firewall to exchange information. The IETF has already defined the main set of VPN encryption standards — the IP Security (ipsec) standards. They include

- Encapsulation Security Payload (ESP), detailed in RFC 1827, a protocol for encryption
- Authentication Header (AH), detailed in RFC 1826, a protocol for authenticating TCP/IP packets

RSA Data Security, a leading encryption vendor, has introduced S/WAN, which uses the proprietary RC5 encryption protocol, as an alternative to ipsec. The IETF continues to evaluate standards for a key-management protocol, which is the way encryption keys are automatically passed between computers. For more information about encryption and key management resources, see the Bibliography.

If you plan to connect to other organizations across the Internet in the next two years, you should find out whether the firewall vendors you're considering have participated in testing VPN standards. You may also want to find out whether they plan to introduce ipsec support, including Internet Security Association and Key Management Protocol (ISAKMP)/OAKLEY key management. ISAKMP has strong support from vendors and is likely to be chosen by the IETF as the key management standard. Both FireWall-1 and Raptor claim that the next release of their NT firewall products will support ipsec.

If you want to establish a VPN that includes only your company's sites, you can use proprietary VPN technologies to implement a secure working solution right now. Similarly, if you want to let remote users connect via dial-in Point-to-Point Protocol (PPP), many vendors can provide a solution that uses software on a remote PC to provide an encrypted path back to the firewall.

Another common approach is to provide encryption between a remote system and a server inside the firewall. However, this approach requires establishing a path through the firewall, which can open a security hole.

ENTERPRISE-LEVEL FUNCTIONALITY

Large organizations usually require an enterprise-capable firewall system that is made up of at least two firewalls, each of which has many network interfaces. An *enterprise-capable firewall* is a firewall that lets a network administrator centrally manage remote firewalls over an encrypted path, as one entity, with a central point for logging network information. Many firewall products achieve this configuration by separating the management interface program from the rule-processing engine.

Some firewall vendors, including Check Point and Raptor, also let you download packet filters to routers such as those from Bay Networks and Cisco Systems. An enterprise-capable firewall also needs to provide real-time notification of suspicious activity via e-mail and pager and generate SNMP traps that you can integrate with the enterprise network management system. (SNMP is a standard protocol that network management systems use to collect information from network devices.) Another issue that becomes much more important at the enterprise level is centralized authentication using TACACS+ or RADIUS, as discussed earlier in this chapter.

NT-SPECIFIC FEATURES

If you plan to run your firewall on an NT system, answering a few additional questions can help determine your needs. For example:

- When you install the product, does it automatically configure NT to maximize security? For example, does the firewall disable IP forwarding, nonessential services such as the server service, and the guest account?
- Is the product tightly coupled with native NT features such as User Manager for Domains, Event Viewer, and the Performance Monitor?
- Does the product run on the DEC Alpha version of NT?
- Does it run on your version of NT (3.51 or 4.0)?
- Is the product integrated with Microsoft's DNS Server or does it require a different DNS server? This question is more important if you intend to use NT 4.0, which includes Microsoft's DNS Server.

THE GOTCHAS — USER CONTROL CHALLENGES AND SPECIAL DHCP CONSIDERATIONS

Now you have a good idea of some of the features that may be important when selecting a firewall for your organization. Let's look at some of the hidden surprises to watch for if you evaluate firewalls on your own.

Security is about preventing intruders from breaking into your network, right? Well, partly. Security is also about controlling what internal users can do on the network and what they can access outside of the network. Unfortunately, many firewall products are still much better at keeping intruders out than they are at controlling outbound access from within the corporation.

BROWSER-INITIATED FTP

Employee use of the Internet creates real risks, including reduced productivity; legal exposure; operational risks, such as the threat of downloading virus-infected files; and other security risks, such as disgruntled employees who could transfer valuable data to other locations. Most Internet usage policies therefore include restrictions on such activities. For such policies to be meaningful, it's necessary for employees to agree, in writing, to the terms of Internet use before they have access to the Internet.

It is not unusual for an Internet usage policy to state that users are permitted to download files using FTP only if they are specifically approved to download files and if the download site itself is approved. Ideally, all access rights are tied to NT domain user identities, and rights to use WWW, FTP, and other services are assigned separately so that users are aware of the firewall only when they attempt to do something that isn't permitted. You can use MPS to set up your network this way; however, if you want to go beyond HTTP, Gopher and FTP Read are useful only in a pure Windows environment where you can use MPS's Remote Windows Sockets component. A less ideal but acceptable solution is to prompt users for a user name/password combination when they start their browsers and prompt them again if they click on an FTP link, at which point the authentication rules determine whether they are allowed access.

Most products fall short of enforcing comprehensive Internet usage policies because they focus on controlling FTP access into the corporate network instead of controlling employees' access to the outside world. These products work well if FTP downloads are initiated from the command line (or a dedicated

FTP tool) and if you follow the somewhat convoluted instructions for typing gateway and destination user names and passwords. The high-end products require users to enter remote_username@remote_hostname firewall_username on one line, followed by the remote password and the gateway password.

Few products handle FTP initiated from within a Web Browser, as opposed to command-line FTP or a special FTP client. Of the many products I have tested, only Centri provides separate control over browser-initiated FTP. For example, to make limiting browser-initiated FTP work with FireWall-1 v2.1, I had to add acceptance of higher TCP port numbers to the FTP rule. Version 3.02 of Raptor doesn't allow the separate definition of rules governing HTTP and browser-initiated FTP — if you allow HTTP, you also allow browser-initiated FTP. Even MPS's Proxy Server component (not incorporating the RWS server) supports only FTP Read, not FTP Get and Put, which means that files go to the screen instead of being downloaded to the local file system — a useful setup for reading text files, but little else. However, firewall products are evolving rapidly and several new products will be released soon. I suggest checking these FTP details explicitly with each vendor on your short list.

You should also be aware that users can download files using HTTP instead of FTP if your browser supports this feature, which both Internet Explorer and Netscape Navigator do. The URL for this kind of link begins with http:// instead of ftp://. For an example, check Microsoft's page for downloading Internet Explorer 3.0 (http://www.microsoft.com/ie). Unfortunately, I have not seen any firewall that controls downloading with HTTP. If you are testing how a firewall controls browser-initiated FTP, make sure you are testing it against an FTP link.

CONTROLLING FTP IN A DHCP ENVIRONMENT — THE NEED FOR AUTHENTICATION

If you use DHCP in your NT environment, you have another challenge in controlling users. Unless you want to grant the same privileges to all members of a DHCP scope, your rules governing FTP cannot rely on IP information because IP addresses are dynamically allocated by the DHCP server. Therefore, you need user-based rules, which in turn means you need some form of user authentication on the firewall.

If a firewall you're interested in supports NT domain authentication (as both Raptor Eagle NT and Microsoft's products do), you can build rules based on groups set up using NT's User Manager for domains. Be sure to check whether the firewall machine needs to be a domain controller to support this type of authentication.

If the firewall doesn't provide NT domain integration, users of restricted services must enter a user name/password combination to identify themselves. Obviously, it is not desirable to use one-time password schemes even though it provides a form of stronger authentication, because using a one-time password in this situation means users needs new passwords each time they need to access the firewall. In other words, every time your session expires, you'll need a new password, which could happen dozens of times a day. Therefore, find out whether your candidate firewall supports reusable passwords.

The user authentication schemes in many products validate only "pure" FTP connections; that is, those initiated from the command line or from generic FTP client software, rather than browser-initiated FTP connections. As an alternative to user authentication, Check Point's FireWall-1 offers client authentication, which you can use to restrict access to any service. Although it is not very user friendly — users must log on in a Telnet session — it is a good solution if you permit only a few users to use a specific service, and you can use it with browser-initiated FTP.

CONTROLLING WEB ACCESS IN A DHCP ENVIRONMENT

To control who has access to the Web, you need to ensure that your firewall does not require users to retype passwords every time they click a new link. For example, FireWall-1 lets you define a period of time that a user, once successfully authenticated, is permitted to surf the Internet. If you operate a predominantly NT environment, you need to use NT domain-based authentication so you don't have to create a whole new user database. You may even wish to use a combination of two firewall products to meet the requirements that a single product alone cannot. For example, you might use MPS in series with one of the advanced firewall products.

SUMMARY

In closing this chapter, let me remind you that the possible solutions to your security concerns are numerous. This chapter has defined the major products on the market and pointed out their pros and cons, which should make your job easier at shopping time. This chapter also gives you the information you need to weigh competitors in the firewall arena. Be sure you understand your requirements, both now and in the future, before choosing a solution for your network. Making the right decisions now offers you the flexibility and functionality that you desire in the end — without any regrets down the road.

CHAPTER 11

HOW TO CHOOSE AN INTERNET FIREWALL

In this chapter, we discuss how to choose an Internet firewall. We look at some generalized categories your company might fit into. I also list questions you should ask a firewall vendor. We then consider issues involved in testing a firewall and ways to test firewalls for yourself. Finally, we provide an overview of some of the currently available NT-based firewall products, exploring how these different firewall products address particular types of Internet connectivity needs.

This chapter incorporates the opinions and wisdom of Marcus J. Ranum, a longtime firewall designer and Chief Scientist for V-ONE, as well as the opinions and wisdom of Philip Carden, Managing Consultant for The Registry's network systems consulting practice in New York. Mr. Ranum provides a baseline for choosing a firewall in general, while Mr. Carden provides an overview comparing important features of various Windows NT-based firewall implementations.

GENERAL CASE STUDIES

In this section, we look at a few case studies, not looking at specific companies but instead generalizing about types of organizations. This approach clarifies the different problems and situations that you may face with your own networks.

AN ACADEMIC ORGANIZATION

Academic organizations, such as universities, typically have the most trouble setting up firewalls for two reasons: first, academic organizations have a tradition of academic freedom and easy access to information; second, an academic user community is usually curious, interested in experimenting with a variety of network features, and resistant to restrictions. In fact, academic users tend to actively resist or circumvent a firewall. Additionally, academic departments often have independent budgets and semiautonomous use of the campus network, which makes it difficult to enforce a common security approach. If one department in the university installs a security system that interferes with another, the second department can simply purchase new network links to bypass it.

One approach that seems to work for many academic environments is to isolate critical computing systems behind internal firewalls. You should isolate systems where student records, loan information, and paychecks are processed from the main campus networks by placing them behind screening routers or commercial firewalls.

A RESEARCH LAB

Research labs are often another difficult case. Scientists expect to use the network for collaboration and require access to late-breaking information, which implies that they need a fairly open system. In many cases, however, their research may be economically significant and should be protected. Research labs suffer many of the same problems as academic organizations because their users want to be on the cutting edge and do not tolerate interference.

The most important aspect of security in such an environment is the protection of intellectual property. You should isolate and protect systems containing patent applications and designs for proprietary products; you can also consider adding a second network that connects to the Internet but that is physically separate from the internal research network. Many research labs are connected to the Internet behind commercial proxy-based firewalls, which are fairly conservative but also permit access to the Web and other sources of information. Other research labs rely on separated networks or isolated systems for storing proprietary information.

AN ELECTRONIC COMMERCE APPLICATION

As electronic commerce becomes more important and prevalent, the need to pass commercial traffic through firewalls will become more crucial. Analyzing service requirements is a useful tool for designing and implementing such systems. Suppose an organization wants to put a Web server on an external network and to provide access from that server to a database on a system behind a firewall. In this case, the service requirement is to get data back and forth from SQL only. You might configure a screening router firewall that allows only SQL data between the outside Web server and the inside, or you might choose a commercial firewall that permits a generic proxy or that supports an SQL service. Protocol isolation techniques may also be appropriate here.

MANAGING FIREWALLS

This section should help you think about some issues surrounding firewalls from a manager's perspective — from who will maintain it, what a firewall vendor generally provides, and questions to ask a vendor to issues to consider if you want to build a firewall yourself.

FIREWALL MAINTENANCE

Typical firewalls require about an hour a week to maintain, not counting other tasks a firewall administrator might perform, such as checking for patches and upgrades. Internet connectivity often brings with it a need for personnel to serve as postmaster, Webmaster, FTP manager, and Usenet news manager. These tasks are all time-consuming and can be full-time jobs for a single person. Often the firewall administrator is responsible for many tasks besides the firewall and is the first person called when a user detects a problem.

TYPICAL FIREWALL INSTALLATION

In the past, most firewalls came with consulting packages, including on-site assistance with installation and support. In the "bad old days," many sites that were connecting to the Internet had no local TCP/IP expertise, so the installer's job also encompassed tasks such as configuring routing and setting up internal

DNS and e-mail. Some vendors still provide this level of service, while others simply ship a power-on-and-configure turnkey solution.

Typically, when you install a firewall, the Internet connection must be ready but not connected to the protected network. The firewall installer arrives, tests the machine's basic function, and then may lead a meeting in which you work out the details of how the firewall will be configured. You should discuss issues such as access control policies you want to put in place, where e-mail will be routed, and where logging information should be forwarded. After the installer has a good idea of how to configure the firewall, the installer connects the firewall to the Internet and tests it for correct operation with the network. The firewall is connected to the protected network only after you install and check its access control rules. Typically, the installer performs some basic interoperation tests, such as accessing the Web and sending and receiving e-mail. When everything checks out, you're on the Internet and free to surf.

WHAT VENDORS TYPICALLY PROVIDE WITH A FIREWALL

Besides the installation service just described, most vendors provide support for some time period when you can ask basic questions about the firewall. Often, a difficult part of setting up a firewall is getting various packages behind the firewall to communicate correctly with the firewall itself. Some vendors provide direct support for tasks such as hooking PC LAN mail systems into the firewall's mailer or configuring DNS. If you do not have technical skills in these areas, having a vendor to support your configuration is a big time and energy saver.

Some ISPs offer a supported firewall as part of their connectivity service. For organizations new to TCP/IP or in a hurry, ISPs are an attractive option because the same vendor provides support for the network, the leased lines, and the firewall. However, you're also putting a huge amount of trust in your ISP, which isn't always a smart move — some of them unknowingly hire hackers.

The single most important service a vendor can provide with its firewall is an understanding of how to make a sensible security policy. Unless you're sure that you understand what you're allowing in and out of your network, you may not be safe if you install a firewall that lets you point and click to decide what to allow through. Because some firewall designers assume that administrators are experts and know what they're doing, inexperienced administrators can actually configure a firewall to permit unsecure connections. Support from the vendor in getting set up with a reasonable baseline helps keep you from accidentally configuring a firewall so that you leave holes that may allow an attack.

WHAT VENDORS TYPICALLY DON'T PROVIDE WITH A FIREWALL

Vendors typically do not configure internal legacy systems to work with the firewall. For example, most firewalls assume that they are talking to the Internet on one side and a TCP/IP network on the other. Usually, it's the customer's responsibility to have TCP/IP-capable systems on the inside network.

For e-mail, firewalls primarily support only SMTP, and it's the customer's responsibility to have an SMTP-compatible system someplace on the inside. Often it's the customer's responsibility to know any system-specific configuration changes necessary to get the internal SMTP system to forward all outbound Internet mail to the firewall. Unless you're buying your firewall from an ISP, it's usually your responsibility to have IP network addresses and a domain name.

Few, if any, firewall vendors or consultants on the planet — in their right minds — guarantee a firewall as 100 percent secure. If you need a 100 percent guarantee, you will probably be responsible for it yourself through diligence and perseverance.

QUESTIONS TO ASK FIREWALL VENDORS

You should ask a firewall vendor several questions. The typical set of questions below cover security, credentials, support, engineering, documentation, and operation.

Security

- What are the security design principles of your firewall?
- Why do you think it's secure?
- What third-party experts have reviewed it?

Corporate Credentials

- How long have you been selling this firewall?
- What is the size of your installed base?
- Do you have reference accounts that we can contact?

Support and Engineering

- How many full-time support engineers do you have?
- What hours does your support operate?
- How much does technical support and maintenance cost?

- What is your patch, fix, and upgrade policy?
- Does the product include any warranty for the hardware or software?

Documentation

- Can we review a copy of the documentation?
- What kind of audit reports does the firewall generate?
- Can we review a real audit report before making a buying decision?

Operation

- Does the firewall include hardware or is it completely software-based?
- What kind of network interfaces does the firewall support? For example, will we need Token-Ring-to-Ethernet routers?
- What is the management interface of the firewall like?
- Can we manage the firewall remotely? If so, how is remote management secured?
- Can we test-drive the firewall before making a buying decision? If so, will your staff perform the initial configuration?

Choosing a firewall is a lot like choosing a car. By the time most of us can afford a car, we have most of the information we need to be able to assess the performance and convenience tradeoffs that different cars present. Similarly, the best way to make sure you get a firewall that suits your needs is to make an educated buying decision. See "For More Information" at the end of this book for suggested reading.

BUILDING IT YOURSELF

A number of tools are available for building your own firewall. Trusted Information Systems, Inc.'s Internet firewall toolkit (FWTK) for Unix is a freely available reference implementation of a set of firewall application proxies. It's available via anonymous FTP at ftp://ftp.tis.com/pub/firewalls/toolkit and may have been ported to NT by the time this book is published. If you're building your own firewall using a router and this toolkit, you can take advantage of the router's built-in screening.

It's important to weigh the cost of staff time when deciding whether to build or buy. Unless your time is free, you may find that having an employee spend a week building a firewall is not cost-effective. You may also be forced to provide your own support, which further increases costs. Before a variety of commercial firewalls were available, many companies hired consultants to build their firewalls. Now, custom firewalls are not cost-effective because consultants cost more than a commercial firewall and may not be able to support or enhance the firewall over time.

TESTING FIREWALLS

Internet firewalls are a hot commodity, and an increasing number of products are coming to market. In the past, about five vendors produced firewalls. In 1997, about 35 vendors sold firewalls, and more vendors appear every day. Vendors and their sales teams are constantly asked to differentiate their products from those of their competition, and the pressure is intense. The result is that similar products are touted as being very different, and some types of technologies are cast as inadequate, while others are positioned as superior. It's difficult to sort out the hype from the substance.

As you know, firewalls have very different design goals and objectives. Some, such as router-based firewalls, are designed for cost, speed, and flexibility. Properly configured commercial routers, which provide excellent security in some applications, may not be adequate for other customer needs, such as advanced audit trails, traffic screening, or restrictive access policies. Indeed, for some applications, a correctly configured Windows-based SMTP gateway (for example, a cc:Mail SMTP server) might provide all the firewall functions a site needs, thus providing adequate security.

Predictably, firewall customers have responded with confusion. How do you know if a firewall is secure? It's very difficult because firewalls are so flexible. A safe rule of thumb is that the more the firewall lets in and out, the less resistant it is to attack. The only firewall that is absolutely secure is one that is turned off! Customers who want a firewall but aren't familiar with all the ins and outs of the technology are justifiably worried that they may buy a product that is not quite right for them. Testing firewalls to see whether they provide adequate security is a logical step for bewildered consumers. Let's look at some issues related to firewall testing.

FIREWALL TESTING ISSUES

When it comes to testing a firewall, two good approaches are programmed checklist testing and design-oriented testing. These approaches are not necessarily mutually exclusive or incompatible, but each approach has pros and cons.

Checklist testing could be as simple as running SATAN++ (an enhanced version of the SATAN toolkit) against the firewall and deciding the firewall fails if SATAN++ finds a hole. The problem with this approach is that it's very limited: a bug that SATAN++ doesn't test for could slice right through the firewall tomorrow. The advantage of the checklist approach is that it's cheap, quick, and easy, and it lets a vendor put a certification seal of approval on its product.

In design-oriented testing, you walk into a room with the engineers who created the firewall and ask them, "Why do you think this firewall protects both networks and itself effectively?" Depending on the answers they give, you formulate a set of tests that verify the properties they claim the firewall has. In other words, the test matches the design of the system as you understand it from the designers. The problem with design-oriented testing is that it's hard and it's hard to find people who are good at developing appropriate tests. The process is expensive, slow, and hard to explain to a non-expert — design review requires a pretty high level of expertise.

HOW TO TEST A FIREWALL

The top-down, design-oriented approach to testing starts looking at the firewall from a very high level to see whether it makes sense. Then you look at it at increasingly lower levels until you're looking at the components or you've pushed your tests as far as it's sensible to go.

Determining how far is sensible is a difficult judgment, and it depends a lot on the arena in which the firewall is used. If the firewall is protecting the launch console for an H-bomb, it is entirely appropriate to review not only the high-level design but all the source code as well, including the source code for system library routines, the compiler they were compiled with, the operating system kernel itself, and the processor it runs on. We normal folks must develop some happy medium, and it depends on what you have at stake. You must keep your network in perspective.

Many sites have firewalls, and the firewall is the only aspect of their network that is remotely close to being secure. For example, they have an Internet link on the other side of the firewall and five T1 lines to their business partners, with little or no protection on those links, and the business partners in turn have links to their competitors and the Internet. In such an environment, the firewall is the last thing that is likely to be broken into. It's worth checking that the firewall works, that it's nailed down tightly, that it appears to have security properties that meet the requirements, and that the properties are implemented correctly. It's probably not worth worrying about a Trojan horse in the firewall's compiler.

Postulating and Testing for Problems

To test the design of a firewall, you first must know what you're testing, how it works, and why it works the way it does. You need to interview the designers or have access to very high-quality design documentation. After all, if the high-level design makes no sense, you may not need to test any further. Understanding the high-level design lets you guess which parts of the implementation are particularly critical to the firewall's proper functioning. If the designers and design documentation do not demonstrate that they recognized and countered these potential areas of weakness, you may have found a fruitful area for penetration testing.

If the high-level design is comprehensive and comprehensible, it should be easy to determine what the basic assumptions of the firewall are. From these basic assumptions, derive some simple tests. Some of the tests may be those that are incorporated in tools like SATAN, which are effective tools. For example, if you're testing a firewall that blocks all traffic between two networks, you should be able to run a complete maximum SATAN network scan on a network behind the firewall and it should come up 100 percent dry.

You should continue to postulate problems based on the properties of the firewall as identified by the designers. For example, if a firewall has no IP address, it should not respond to Address Resolution Protocol (ARP), and it should not respond if I ping the network broadcast address — in other words, it should act as if it has no IP address.

Last, determine the protective relationships that the firewall creates. If the firewall passes some of the responsibility for security to hosts behind it, determine what those responsibilities are and how they are documented. For example, if a screening router permits Telneting from the outside to specific hosts on the inside, those hosts may be vulnerable to holes in the vendor-supplied Telnet daemon, and the documentation should reflect this vulnerability.

Design-oriented firewall testing is, perforce, a rambling process. Essentially, you must play the role of a detective, re-creating the design path the engineers followed and turning up any clues they missed.

DOES MORE EXPENSIVE EQUAL MORE SECURE?

Two common misconceptions about firewalls are that you get what you pay for and that the more expensive a firewall is, the more secure it is. Nothing could be further from the truth. Unlike the PC hardware market, which is a commodity market, the firewall market has not yet settled down enough for consistent and competitive pricing to evolve. In 1996, most commercially available firewalls cost from $10,000 to $20,000, but more expensive products can cost $80,000 and up. You should show some healthy skepticism about cost versus value. If one firewall costs twice as much as another, the seller should be able to clearly explain why the more expensive product warrants doubling the cost.

WHAT ABOUT LIABILITY?

Vendors or testers likely will not assume liability for security problems with firewalls. Firewalls are, by their nature, easy to configure and reconfigure. They are also easy to bypass. Anyone assuming liability for a firewall's installation would need a guarantee that the customer — or anyone in the customer's organization — would not somehow alter, weaken, or bypass it.

However, if you're worried about the quality of a firewall from particular vendor, use common sense and ask the same kinds of questions you ask about any other mission-critical product. Vendors should be able to clearly articulate how the design of their firewall improves its security. Don't just accept hand-waving or insinuations that their competitors' products are insecure.

Another problem with assigning liability is determining the origin of the attack. In many break-ins, it's almost impossible to tell how the attacker got into the network — no firewall vendor or testing authority will be happy to defend their firewall when a customer's network is broken into via a modem pool.

OVERVIEW OF WINDOWS NT-BASED FIREWALLS

This section is an overview, compiled by Philip Carden, of the firewall products that run on the NT platform. To ensure that I isolated specific Windows NT issues and real-world network considerations, I evaluated the products against the actual requirements of a medium-sized, NT-based software distribution firm. The firm's environment consisted of multiple sites, multiple NT and Unix servers, multiple NT domains (with the single master domain model), Windows 3.1 and NT workstation clients, and enterprise-wide use of WINS and DHCP. Our test setup included the screening and choke routers (chokes are a packet-filtering gateway and an application gateway combined and are located on the internal side of the router) that formed part of the final perimeter network and used an AT&T frame relay-based Internet connection.

I group the firewalls so that your organization can more easily select the product or combination of products that meet its requirements, based on different sample Internet security policies. Again, I stress that products in this arena are developing rapidly; therefore, by the time you read this, new versions of some products may address the weaknesses I mention. This section is not intended as a thorough review but instead as an overview. Although some products are clearly better-suited to advanced needs than others, no single "best firewall solution" exists. The best solution for your organization depends on your requirements.

Full-featured firewalls first emerged from the primordial Unix swamp in January 1996 when Raptor dragged its Motif interface onto an NT screen that was, in many cases, not quite big enough (Raptor forces you to use an 800 by 600 display to see the entire interface). Cosmetics aside, Raptor's Eagle for NT represented a strong solution to a significant market need and held center stage for more than six months. But times change — now more than eight NT-based firewalls are competing to survive. Other Unix or DOS-descended products include Check Point's FireWall-1, Digital's AltaVista Firewall for NT, and Network-1's Firewall/Plus. Some of the NT-only products are Cisco's Centri (formerly Global Internet's product, sold to Cisco in late 1997), NetGuard's Guardian, Batetech's iWay-One, and Devon Software's Kyber Pass.

OPEN OR PROPRIETARY?

In this section I explain how Microsoft Proxy Server (MPS) compares to other products. MPS is composed of two distinct components — Proxy Server and RWS server. Although the two components complement each other, for the rest of this chapter I treat them separately because it simplifies the understanding of where they fit with other firewall products. To keep matters simple, I use the name MPS as the combined name and refer to the components as Proxy Server and RWS.

The Proxy Server supports WWW, FTP Read, and Gopher initiated from any client machine (Windows, Mac, Unix, etc.) with a standard TCP/IP stack. In contrast, although RWS supports a wide range of Internet services, it works only with Windows clients running the RWS client component.

This proprietary client-side approach was shared by BateTech's iWay-One, which also mandated using Windows-based clients. I use the past tense because in October 1996, BateTech became the first company to move out of the NT firewall wars. Here is the text that appeared on their Web site, which explained their exit from the market. Keep in mind here that Catapult (a beta codename) refers to MPS.

> Due to Microsoft's drive to dominate the Internet tools market with tools like Catapult (witness their battle with Netscape), Workgroup Systems, and its subsidiary BateTech Software is discontinuing the development and shrink-wrap sales of iWay-One and will instead focus on its help desk product, Customer-One (soon to be Customer Ixchange). As promised, iWay-One version 2 will be completed and released as an upgrade for owners of version 1.

Even though the split client/server approach is not appropriate for large corporate environments with a mix of client systems, it is still unfortunate that RWS server is the only product left in the split client/server class. In most cases, an open approach using a standard TCP/IP stack on the client is more desirable, particularly in larger organizations that consider openness strategically important or in any organization with a mix of different client machine types.

Another product that requires a proprietary client-side component is Devon Software's Kyber Pass. Again, the clients must run Windows; however, the reason in this case is security. The product is promoted as an authentication server, and it supports strong authentication and VPN using public-key encryption. If all the machines you need to connect to the Internet are Windows-based (including your mail gateway), if you are prepared to run the proprietary client software, and if you need authentication features, this product also serves as a proxy firewall. However, in medium-sized or large organizations, this product is more likely to augment authentication provided by another firewall, not as the primary firewall itself, because of the Windows-client limitation.

GROUPING THE OPEN FIREWALLS

Because of their more general applicability, *open* firewall products — that is, products that support communications initiated from any client running a standard TCP/IP stack — are the subject of the remainder of this chapter. Two distinct criteria emerge. First, either the products provide advanced enterprise-level functions (FireWall-1, Eagle, Firewall/Plus) or they don't (Centri, Guardian, Proxy Server, and AltaVista). Second, the architecture is either a proxy (Eagle, AltaVista, Centri, Proxy Server) or a stateful inspection system (FireWall-1, Guardian, Firewall/Plus). Based on these criteria, the products fall neatly into one of four quadrants, as shown in Figure 11.1.

Both FireWall-1 and Eagle have matured in their Unix incarnations — and it shows. Guardian is a FireWall-1 look-alike without VPN capabilities, though it has added authentication in release 2.0; Centri looks and feels like a baby brother to Eagle. Proxy Server offers tight integration with NT, including permissions based on NT domain user definitions, but it supports only WWW, FTP, and Gopher. The strengths of Digital's AltaVista are similar to Eagle's — automatic modification of NT, ease of installation and configuration, and good logging and reporting. However, it lacks enterprise functions, such as centralized management and logging, and offers only one form of authentication — SNK, which is not appropriate for controlling outbound access.

One of the more interesting products is Network-1's Firewall/Plus, which can control not only IP but also a number of other protocols including IPX, NetBEUI, VINES, Digital Pathworks (LAST), and SNA. The original incarnation ran on DOS; the NT version first appeared at the 1996 Fall INTEROP and is now in full release. If you need to control a multiprotocol intranet, you should investigate this product. Of all the current NT-based contenders, it is the only

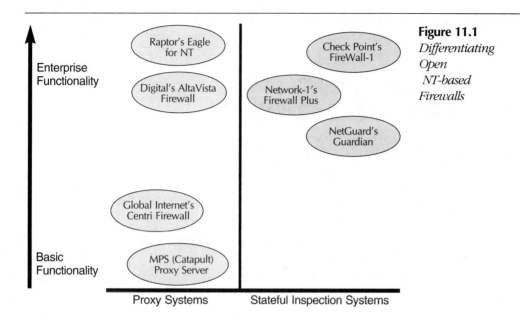

Figure 11.1
Differentiating
Open
NT-based
Firewalls

product that promises the breadth of functions necessary to compete with Fire-Wall-1 and Eagle as an enterprise solution.

It is surprising that many of the basic firewalls have significant features that FireWall-1 and Eagle lack. Centri is the only product I have tested that differentiates between FTP accessed from within a Web browser and FTP initiated from a client software package. Guardian is the only product that lets you define a range of network entities — you can implement a rule applying to a range of addresses, such as 121.131.163.10 to 121.131.163.170. This feature is particularly important in NT environments where it is necessary to differentiate between DHCP scopes (used for clients) and server or router addresses that may be on the same subnet. Both Centri and Guardian also provide much clearer step-by-step installation instructions than either Eagle or FireWall-1. AltaVista offers some unique features, including automatic conversion to NTFS, as well as an installation wizard that takes you through the setup of both the firewall and DNS.

No product currently available can enforce all my Internet requirements; consequently, I can't recommend one product over the others. Indeed, the lack of a complete solution led me to use two products in a recent implementation, combining FireWall-1 and Proxy Server. Each product is appropriate to a different set of needs. Our list of primary needs for that implementation could also have been met by Firewall/Plus, Eagle, or AltaVista (if used in conjunction with its sister product AltaVista Tunnel to provide VPN capabilities).

For those organizations that need a secure firewall to connect to the Internet and do not need VPN capabilities, both Centri and Guardian offer credible solutions that are less difficult to set up than FireWall-1 and Eagle.

MATCHING A PRODUCT TO YOUR INTERNET ACCESS REQUIREMENTS

Matching an existing set of security tools to your needs is not always an easy task. However, it's likely that your Internet access requirements are similar to one of the following scenarios:

- Single point of access to support users who need Web access for research purposes
- Single point of access to support more sophisticated Internet services (such as RealAudio)
- Advanced requirements — multiple firewalls or sites, user authentication, or VPN

Let's examine each of these user requirement classes and discuss which firewall products are appropriate for each class.

The Web from a Single Access Point

Firewall security is most likely to be breached not through product failure but through a configuration error. Therefore, given a limited number of support staff, the simpler the firewall implementation, the more secure it is. If you need to provide only Web browsing and e-mail capabilities, and you *do not* consider the risk associated with a security breach to be large, I recommend either the Centri firewall or MPS. Figure 11.2 shows the Centri Interface.

Centri is a proxy-based solution. Proxy systems are inherently secure if the operating system is not compromised and provide address translation by default. Unless you introduce a generic proxy to support Usenet news, you have little room to introduce a security hole. The product is well documented, and the manual takes you step-by-step through each item to change in the NT configuration, DNS setup, and browser setup on client workstations. It is the only firewall product I have ever installed that worked immediately after I followed the instructions in the installation manual.

MPS is also a good solution for simple Web browsing. MPS is easy to install and configure, as we demonstrate in Chapter 15. It offers strong logging capabilities and lets you define permissions based on existing NT domain user definitions. A large part of this book is dedicated to MPS because it is a very

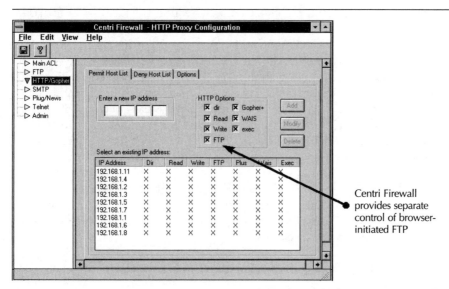

Figure 11.2
*Centri Firewall
— A Strong
Alternative
to MPS*

Centri Firewall
provides separate
control of browser-
initiated FTP

attractive solution for pure Windows shops. However, you might choose Centri because it provides broader support in mixed-client environments, and it doesn't force you to use Windows NT 4.0 (Centri runs on NT 3.51).

If your risk of exposure is great, you should select a product that is more mature, and you might also look for NCSA certification. At press time, Eagle NT or AltaVista were your choices — both FireWall-1 and Firewall/Plus also have NCSA certification, but not for the NT versions of their products. Eagle is less difficult to configure than FireWall-1 and is a better choice if you want a proven firewall and want to minimize the time you spend learning and managing it. It also supports NT domain-based user authentication. Though I haven't tested AltaVista, it appears to be similar to Eagle NT in ease of use, but it won't be suitable if you want to authenticate outbound connections because it supports only strong authentication, which is too inconvenient for outbound users.

Sophisticated Services from a Single Access Point

Let's say that your users need access to RealAudio and next week will want access to something you've never heard of. If you don't need user authentication or VPN and you're providing access from only one or two sites, Guardian is a good solution. The product's GUI is practically identical to FireWall-1's, except that it adds the ability to include the time in its rule definition. In contrast, FireWall-1 supports time-of-day verification only for rules where authentication is used. Guardian also provides GUI access to the network address translation service, whereas FireWall-1 requires you to use a character-based interface in console-mode, which significantly reduces the utility of its network entity definitions.

If you want NSCA certification and a track record, by all means spend the extra money and buy FireWall-1 — it will serve you better than Eagle NT if you need flexibility. It comes with a much larger number of predefined services, and its frame-filtering architecture means that you can quickly add new services as required. Its interface is also much better suited to complex rule bases than Eagle NT, because you can view and comprehend many rules at the same time. It's easy to see how the rules relate to one another and spot gaps in the firewall rules.

Authentication, VPN, and Centralized Management

Currently, only two products provide a full suite of advanced features: FireWall-1 and Eagle NT. AltaVista doesn't quite make the grade for large enterprise deployment for these reasons:

- it lacks the ability to centrally manage multiple firewalls
- it offers only one form of authentication
- it supports VPN only through the use of a sister product (the AltaVista Tunnel), which requires establishing a hole through the firewall

Firewall/Plus comes a little closer, and it is the only NT-based firewall product that controls protocols other than IP between different parts of a corporate network, but it doesn't have the breadth of features FireWall-1 and Eagle NT offer.

Eagle NT provides better management capabilities than FireWall-1. It also provides a great deal of detail in its log and lets you see and kill current connections. The only weakness I found is that the log information is not organized into fields, so sorting and searching the log is not possible. Eagle NT is easier to set up than FireWall-1. Figure 11.3 shows the odd-sized Eagle Interface.

Because FireWall-1 operates at the packet level, it relies on the NT operating system to route packets to their destination correctly. On NT 3.51, you must set up a number of static routes so that traffic coming back from the Internet knows how to find its way to any subnet not directly attached to the firewall. If you need address translation, this setup not only further complicates routing but also requires you to create an address translation table using a command-line interface. Although none of this configuration is particularly difficult, it means that you must make three different changes to support a new internal subnet, and it makes problems more difficult to isolate. You may consider using NT 4.0 instead of NT 3.51, which supports Routing Information Protocol and therefore reduces the complexity of your static route setup.

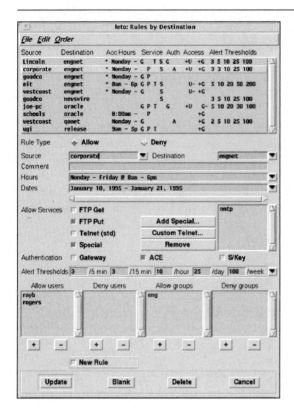

Figure 11.3
*Raptor's Eagle NT
Motif Interface*

However, once set up correctly, FireWall-1's interface (shown in Figure 11.4) is easy to use and makes it easy to add new services. It supports many predefined services, and it is easy to add rules to support new services. It's also very easy to see how the rules relate to one another.

Figure 11.4
*FireWall-1's
Easy-to-Understand
Interface*

Both FireWall-1 and Eagle NT offer many features, and each can probably meet your needs. In many respects, the decision comes down to flexibility versus manageability: FireWall-1 is more flexible, Eagle NT is more manageable. FireWall-1 comes with a large number of predefined services, so it's easy to add less-common services securely. FireWall-1 offers more user authentication options, including a client authentication option that you can use for any service, and is incredibly flexible.

Raptor's Eagle NT, on the other hand, offers much more detailed log information and the ability to view current connections. Versions after 3.05 also offer NT domain integration, which should significantly reduce operational overhead if you authenticate internal users in an NT environment. Eagle NT is more easily configured and provides better management. My guess is that the development side of your company will favor FireWall-1, while the operations team will go for Raptor's Eagle NT.

MY VERY SHORT WISH LIST — TIME FOR A PARADIGM SHIFT?

Firewall vendors need to understand that network managers are trying to address two very different issues when providing browser-based Internet access to Web, FTP, and Usenet services. One of these issues is security; that is, protection from hackers — rule bases, anti-spoofing, address translation, VPNs, and inbound authentication. The other issue is operational control — logging, reporting, traffic analysis and control, adding/deleting internal users, and viewing current connections.

What I'd like to see is a product that not only addresses both issues but also lets an organization split control of those issues between different sets of IT staff. When a user calls to complain that Internet access is slow, I want the operations staff to be able to check the current connections and stop a connection, especially when the connection was initiated in error. And when a manager requests that a new employee be given Web and FTP access, I want the operations staff to be able to handle that request. I also want the operations staff to be able to block sites that are being used heavily and inappropriately.

However, I do not want to give that same operations staff access to my rule base. When I have finished setting up and auditing the firewall, I want to know that only one or two people can make changes to the firewall setup. I don't want to give operators the ability to change rules to meet user requirements. None of the products I have tested, including FireWall-1 and Eagle NT, differentiate among classes of firewall administrator. This lack of differentiation is a big security problem, and it needs to change quickly.

WHAT IF YOU WANT IT ALL?

Well, you can't have it all. But you might come close by using two or more products. I was recently involved in an implementation that required a great deal of flexibility because a significant part of the firm's business is developing Internet-related software. It also required better-than-normal control for similar reasons — for example, they e-mail 700 MB files to clients in the middle of the day.

Because the firm has only Windows-based clients, I used MPS on the inside of the choke router (the router on the inside of the firewall) and Fire-Wall-1 between the choke and screening routers. I set up the choke router filters so that only the MPS server and mail servers could communicate with the FireWall-1 machine. If I hadn't used MPS, I would have set those same filters to the client DHCP scopes. In this way, I achieved not only the dual objectives of flexibility and manageability but also managed to separate the control of security and administration. The operations staff can do everything it needs to do on the MPS system, including setting Web permissions based on existing NT domain user definitions. However, the operations staff doesn't have access to the rule base running on FireWall-1, which means that responsibility for security remains very well defined and isolated.

You might achieve an even better result using Eagle NT (instead of MPS) in series with FireWall-1, if you have sufficient money in the budget to do so (our real-world client didn't). Those organizations with a very high risk of exposure might want to use two firewalls anyway. But for most organizations, using two different products to achieve a reasonable level of functionality is not acceptable.

Many security products are available today, and only the fittest will survive. Firewall vendors now have one more opinion (mine!) of what it takes to become "the fittest" in the brave new world of NT-based firewalls.

SUMMARY

As you can see from this chapter, it is impossible to give exact advice. This material has shown you that you need to base your decisions on your own present and future requirements. Common sense is the best approach, and the more knowledge you can gain about firewalls, the better buyer you'll be. This material has offered you a starting point in this education process.

CHAPTER 12

INTERNET INFORMATION SERVER

In this chapter, we discuss installing and configuring Microsoft's Internet Information Server (IIS) and its associated components. I also suggest some security issues to consider when implementing IIS. IIS is a prerequisite for running Microsoft Proxy Server (MPS). The information in this chapter gives you the understanding and insight you need to administer IIS properly, which in turn will help you administer MPS.

IIS COMPONENTS

IIS consists of several components:

- Internet Service Manager — the administrative program that lets you easily manage each Internet service, including MPS and the complete Microsoft Commercial Internet System platform (MCIS, formerly codenamed Normandy)
- WWW Service — the core Web server software that lets you create and publish information content to be used with a Web browser
- Gopher Service — software that lets you publish documents that can be searched using keywords
- FTP Service — software that lets users upload and download files from your server
- Internet Explorer — a Web browser for Windows 95 and Windows NT that can browse almost any Web site
- ODBC Drivers — drivers and administrative programs that let you connect databases to your Web pages
- Help and Example Files — the usual help material and some great sample Web pages to use as a starting point for building a Web site

IIS comes as a standard part of the Windows NT 4.0 distribution CD-ROM. You can also get it directly from Microsoft's Web site: http://www.microsoft.com/ntserver/default.asp. Be sure to monitor that site occasionally to get the latest updates and information, which is always a good security practice.

HARDWARE CONSIDERATIONS

Although this book focuses on security, we also take a quick peek at the requirements you should have in place before installing and running IIS. A few things can make a big difference in the overall performance of your server, so we cover them quickly in this section.

CPU

A computer's CPU is much like a car's engine. In most cases, the bigger the engine, the faster the car. The same holds true for computers. If you use an Intel-based system, be sure to use a Pentium processor if you can. They offer great performance increases over the older 486 processors.

A great choice for a non-Intel system is the DEC Alpha series, which is always among the fastest in the world. Today, DEC is offering Alpha chips that run as fast as 500 Mhz, and even faster processors are in the testing labs. You may opt to use a PowerPC or MIPS processor, both of which are also great choices. However, you should be aware that most software vendors produce software for Intel and Alpha systems first, with PowerPC and MIPS versions following, which could delay your plans to implement a given piece of software.

TAPE DRIVES

A tape backup system is one of the best investments you can make in securing your data. Every network should have at least one of these invaluable tools. Without a current backup, you could find yourself dead in the water in the event of failure or burglary.

Several great choices are at your disposal, ranging from 4 mm Digital Audio Tape (DAT) to higher-capacity QIC tapes, depending on your needs. The most important thing to remember about backups is that you must do them regularly and not store them on site. A tape backup of all your data is useless if a building fire destroys your tapes! Store the data off-site someplace. You can contract cold storage facilities or even a safe deposit box at a bank if you like.

HARD DISK DRIVES

SCSI storage systems are among the fastest available, and NT provides great support for SCSI tape subsystems. RAID (Redundant Array of Inexpensive Disks) storage systems provide excellent data recovery features that help secure your data. Although RAID systems can recover lost data without a tape backup, you should still use a tape backup to make it easy to get your data off-site.

Another issue to consider when selecting a disk drive is performance. NT relies on paging files to swap data to disk, using disk space as a RAM equivalent. Therefore, the faster the drive, the faster the overall system performance.

UPS SYSTEMS

Uninterruptable power supply (UPS) systems, another invaluable resource, are battery backups that take over when your normal power fails. They can keep the system up and running for a short time during intermittent power outages and can automatically perform a clean system shutdown if the power is not restored in a given amount of time. I highly recommend using UPS on all your systems.

During installation, Windows NT attempts to detect all hardware attached to the system, including the serial ports, which could confuse UPS software or

Windows NT. You should disconnect the UPS devices before you begin installing NT, then reconnect them after installation.

INSTALLING AND TESTING IIS

IIS installation is quite simple. You should have already installed TCP/IP on your network if you're making your Web site available over the Internet. We'll go over the basic steps in this section to get your IIS server up and running quickly.

INSTALLATION REQUIREMENTS

Installing IIS for use on the Internet requires

- Windows NT Server installed and configured.
- TCP/IP installed on the server for Internet connectivity. You install TCP/IP using the Network icon in the Control Panel.
- NTFS installed for maximum security configuration.
- A link to the Internet.
- An IP address for your Web server.
- A registered domain name for your network. The domain name is not mandatory but makes getting to your Web site much easier.

PREINSTALLATION CHECKLIST

Before you start installing IIS, go over the following items in addition to the installation requirements to make sure you have not overlooked anything.

- Close all programs and applications that use ODBC to avoid error messages during installation.
- Configure DNS settings properly for TCP/IP.
- Check that you have at least one IP address assigned to your network interface. If you are multihoming your Web server, you'll need additional IP addresses assigned to the interfaces.
- Check the rights and permissions of your users and groups to make sure you have not assigned any excessive privileges.
- Make sure you don't have any unwanted members in your Administrators group.

- Define and propagate your policies and procedures about the use of the Web server.
- Check for unnecessary network protocols and bindings to ensure proper security.
- Enable some level of auditing on your file system.
- Check for correct permission settings on your network shares.

INSTALLATION AND TESTING PROCEDURE

To install IIS, you must be logged on as a member of the Administrators group. If you're installing from the CD-ROM, insert the CD in the drive and follow the steps below. If you're downloading IIS from Microsoft over the Internet, run the downloaded file to start the installation and skip the first three steps below.

1. Click Start, Programs, and choose the Windows NT Explorer.
2. Navigate through the Explorer to your CD-ROM, and locate Setup.exe in the IIS directory.
3. Double-click this file to begin the setup process. The IIS opening dialog box appears; click OK (Figure 12.1).

Figure 12.1
*IIS Installation
Dialog Box*

4. If asked, type the path to your IIS installation files and click OK. All options are set to be installed by default. Simply uncheck any of the ones you don't want installed — remember, *don't run any services you don't need*. To change the directory where IIS is installed, click Change Directory, type a new path, then click OK.

5. The Publishing Directories dialog box appears, as shown in Figure 12.2.

Figure 12.2
Publishing Directories
Dialog Box

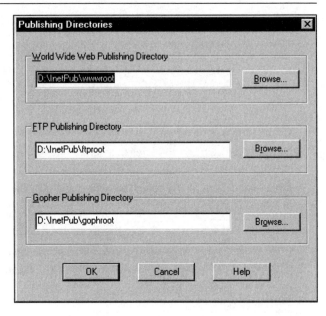

You may either accept the default directory names or type new ones. When you're finished, click OK. If you are asked whether you want the directories created, click Yes.

6. The Create Internet Account dialog box appears. Type and confirm a password. IIS uses this account for security issues during all anonymous access sessions. Setup.exe then installs the appropriate IIS files.

7. If you opted to install ODBC Drivers, the Install Drivers dialog box in Figure 12.3 appears. Select the SQL drivers to install from the list and click OK.

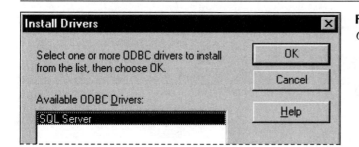

Figure 12.3
ODBC Dialog

That's all there is to the initial installation. Now, you want to test it. To get started, open your Web browser, then follow these steps:

1. Make sure that your DNS and/or WINS servers are running. If you're using DNS and have configured it with an Internet domain name and a host name of www, simply type **http://www.*yoursite.com***, where *yoursite.com* is your Internet domain name. If you're using only WINS, type **http://*machine-name***, where *machinename* is the NetBIOS name of your Web server. You can also test your Web server by typing its IP address prefixed with http://. For example, type **http://207.91.166.2**, where 207.91.166.2 is your Web server's IP address.

2. After you've typed a test address, your Web browser should present the default IIS home page installed during the setup and configuration. If it's working correctly, at this point you can copy over any Web pages you've already developed.

The installation software includes the Internet Explorer (IE) Web browser clients for various platforms (in the \clients directory) and the Internet Service Manager (ISM) (in the \admin directory), which you can run from a remote NT system to administer IIS. Be sure to read the information in the next section, because it contains additional information on configuring and securing IIS.

USING INTERNET SERVICE MANAGER

Now that you've installed and configured IIS, you need to open ISM and review the additional settings at your disposal. These options and settings let you tailor many aspects of the IIS server. The ISM has three basic views: Report, Server, and Service. We cover each of these in this section.

However, before we look at the individual views, let's review the groups of icons that are common in each view, using the Report View in Figure 12.4 as an example.

Figure 12.4
The Report View

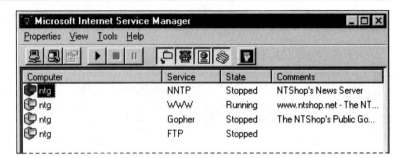

The first three icons, from left to right, let you

- Connect to a specific IIS server
- Locate all the IIS servers on a network
- Display a property sheet for a service

The middle group of icons, from left to right, let you

- Start the selected service
- Stop the selected service
- Pause the selected service

The last group of three icons

- Display FTP service information
- Display Gopher service information
- Display Web service information

If you installed parts of the Normandy platform from Microsoft when it was in beta testing, you'll see additional icons in the last group of icons mentioned above. Normandy was the code name for a set of Internet services, including SMTP/POP3, NNTP News, Chat, Content Replicator, and Personalization.

The icon on the right opens the Key Manager.

THE REPORT VIEW

To bring up the report view shown in Figure 12.4, first open the ISM by clicking Start and choosing Programs. Then click Microsoft Internet Server and choose

Internet Service Manager. You'll be presented with the default Report View. To switch to other views, select a different view from the View menu.

The main window lists computers, services, states of the service, and any comments that have been defined for each service. Clicking on the headings in the columns sorts the lists, and double-clicking any particular computer opens the property pages for the associated service. The status bar at the bottom shows the number of servers and the number of services currently running.

THE SERVERS VIEW

The Servers View, shown in Figure 12.5, is useful for sites with several IIS services running on the same NT Server. This view displays each IIS server on the network in a tree. You can click the plus sign next to a given server to reveal the services it provides. Double clicking on a given service opens that service's properties page.

Figure 12.5
The Servers View

THE SERVICES VIEW

The Services View lists IIS services by type, as shown in Figure 12.6. Clicking the plus sign next to a service reveals which servers are running that service. This view is useful for networks in which IIS services are distributed among several different NT Servers.

Figure 12.6

The Services View

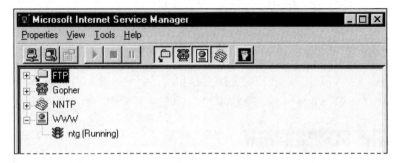

SERVICE PROPERTIES

Each service in the ISM has the same basic set of properties available for configuration. To examine any of the properties, simply double-click one of the services listed in the ISM window. A dialog box with four basic tabs will appear. The Service tab, shown in Figure 12.7, controls which users may use your server and lets you specify the account used for anonymous connections.

Figure 12.7

The Service Tab

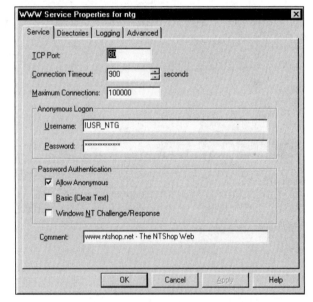

At the Service tab, you can determine the following settings:

- TCP Port — sets the port that the Web server listens on. The default for Web servers is port 80, but you may use other port numbers if you need to.

- Connection Timeout — sets the maximum time for each connection before the server automatically disconnects an inactive user.

- Maximum Connections — specifies the maximum number of simultaneous connections your server accepts at any one time.

- Anonymous Logon — sets the account name and password used by the service to control access. The rights assigned to this user account become the rights for all anonymous connections to the service. By default, this account is the IUSR_computername account established by the installation program.

- Password Authentication — defines the level of security authentication for the service to use. These levels are

  - Allow Anonymous — enables anonymous logons, meaning the someone can connect with the Anonymous user name in combination with any password.

  - Basic (Clear Text) — this level of authentication sends unencrypted user names and passwords over the network and can be a risk to security.

  - Windows NT Challenge/Response — this setting tells the service to authenticate users with the Windows NT Challenge/Response mechanism, currently available only to Internet Explorer users.

- Comment — defines an informational comment that is displayed in the ISM window next to the service in the Report view.

One note about the Password Authentication: If you leave the Basic and Windows NT Challenge/Response boxes unchecked and check the Allow Anonymous box, all client requests are processed as anonymous requests. Users who provide a username and password are ignored and the anonymous account is used instead, with all the security restrictions that may apply to the anonymous user account.

If you're setting up FTP service and the Allow Anonymous Connections box is checked, users may connect to the FTP server as Anonymous in combination with any password they choose. With anonymous FTP connections, the password serves no purpose; normally, users enter their e-mail address for the password so the administrators know who is connecting to the service. If you leave the Allow Anonymous Connections box unchecked, all users must enter a valid Windows NT user name and password to gain access to the service.

DIRECTORY PROPERTIES

The Directories tab, shown in Figure 12.8, lists the directories used by the service.

Figure 12.8

The Directories Tab

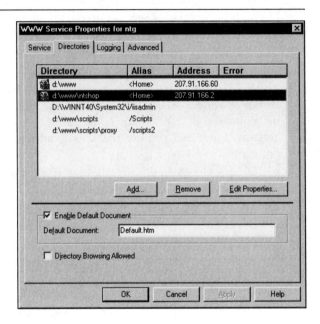

You can configure two boxes on this page:

- Enable Default Document — checking this box allows a default document to be used if a user does not specify a particular document when entering a URL. In most cases, this file is named default.htm, although you may use any file name you choose.

- Directory Browsing Allowed — directory browsing lets users browse the contents of a directory, showing them every file in that directory. This option is generally considered a security risk unless you know that the file permissions do not let a user navigate the directory tree. Use this option with great care.

If you check both the Enable Default Directory box and the Directory Browsing box and the user's desired directory doesn't contain a default document, the Web server displays the directory contents instead, similar to the way you see it in the Windows Explorer.

Adding directories to this property page gives users access to those directories. You may also define virtual directories, which are aliases for real directory names, that you can use to simplify a directory name or to hide the real location of a directory. To add a directory, follow these steps:

1. Double-click the appropriate service in the ISM.
2. Click the Directories tab and click Add.
3. Check the Home Directory or the Virtual Directory checkbox and type the name of the directory in the appropriate box.
4. Set the Access Permissions by choosing the appropriate checkboxes.
5. Click OK.

Some FTP client software requires that FTP information be presented in Unix format instead of NT format. If you are running a public FTP server, you should set the Directory Listing Style to Unix rather than MS-DOS for maximum compatibility; otherwise you can use the NT listing style.

Also, keep in mind that if you're going to enable Secure Sockets Layer (SSL) for secure communication to a particular directory, you'll need to obtain and install your certificate first. See the section below entitled Using the Key Manager for complete details on obtaining and installing the certificate.

LOGGING PROPERTIES

At the Logging tab, shown in Figure 12.9, you specify how IIS logs information about its services. You should always enable some level of logging for your services to ensure you have the information you need for security analysis. Remember, most break-ins occur on systems that are not monitored closely.

After you select the Enable Logging checkbox, which turns on IIS logging, you can set other parameters.

- Log to File — this selection tells IIS to log its data to a standard text file. If you choose this logging method, be sure to choose an interval for creating new log files. If you don't, your log information will be written to the same file continuously, and the log file will grow until the system runs out of disk space.

- Log to SQL/ODBC Database — this choice tells IIS to log its data to an SQL/ODBC-style database. Using this style of logging requires that you specify the Data Source Name (DSN), table, and a user name and password that the server uses to access the database.

Figure 12.9
Logging Tab

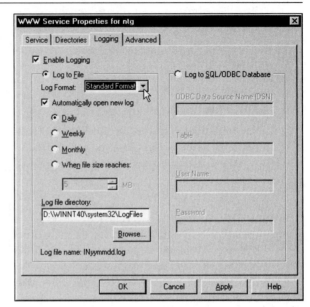

When you log data to a file, the maximum length of a log line is 1,200 bytes, and each field in a log entry is limited to 150 bytes. When you log to an SQL/ODBC database, each field is limited to 200 bytes of data.

ADVANCED PROPERTIES

The Advanced tab, shown in Figure 12.10, lets you control access to your server in a few different ways. Figure 12.10 shows sites that have been denied access to The NTShop Web site for a variety of security reasons specific to our site.

Two checkboxes control the way access works:

- Granted Access — this checkbox lets all computers access your server except the ones you specify by IP address.
- Denied Access— this checkbox denies all computers access to your server except the ones you specify by IP address.

You can also limit the total bandwidth all the services on your IIS system use. This feature can be incredibly handy if your network links are already burdened with traffic loads. It can also help when intruders try denial-of-service attacks on your network, because it limits the amount of artificial traffic they can generate.

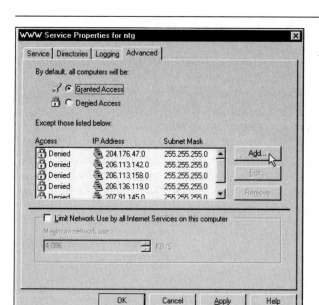

Figure 12.10
Advanced Tab

On the other hand, any time you introduce a configuration, you are creating a dependency, so be aware that when you limit bandwidth usage, users may perceive the server as being slow at times.

MESSAGES PROPERTIES

The FTP service has another property page that lets you configure certain messages presented to the users of the service. These messages are defined as follows:

- Welcome Message — FTP clients see this message when they connect to your FTP server (before they are asked to log on). For example, you may set this message to something such as "Welcome to the XYZ FTP Server."

- Exit Message — clients see this message when they disconnect from your FTP server. For example, you may want this message to say "Thanks for visiting our FTP Server."

- Maximum Connections Message — clients see this message when they try to connect to your FTP service but the service has reached the maximum number of connections allowed. For example, your message may say "Sorry, this server is at maximum capacity at the moment; please try later."

WEB TRAFFIC SECURITY

You can establish several security selections in IIS. In this section, I point out what to look out for. If your security selections in IIS differ from those set in NT itself, the stricter settings are always used.

FLOW OF SECURITY CHECKS

IIS uses the underlying security systems of NT and those built into NTFS and adds its own security with IP address filtering, directory access controls, and authentication. When IIS receives a request from a user, it performs the following series of checks before processing the request.

1. IIS receives a request from a user.
2. IIS checks to see whether the IP address is permitted.
3. If the IP address is permitted, IIS checks to see whether the user is permitted.
4. If the user is permitted, IIS checks whether the permissions allow access to the requested resource.
5. If the IIS permissions allow the access to the resource, IIS checks to see whether the NTFS permissions also allow access.
6. If the NTFS permissions allow the access, then access is allowed.

If any single test fails, access is denied.

PRE-USE CHECKLIST

Now let's look at a checklist you may want to use before you put your Web server on the Internet. Some of these items may seem like common sense, and some of them I've said before, but it never hurts to be careful.

- Never run services you don't need.
- Never allow directory browsing from the Web server unless it is absolutely necessary.
- Never use your Web server as a file server — allow only data on that server that directly pertains to the Web site.
- Never enable anonymous FTP unless you absolutely have to.
- Never make sensitive information available for internal use through the same Web server shared by public users from the Internet.

- Always enable some level of auditing on your file system and review the log files at least daily so that you can detect possible intrusion attempts as early as possible.

- Always unbind any unnecessary network protocols from NICs connected to your Internet link or network segments shared with the Internet link.

- Always triple-check permissions on all your shared resources to be sure you have set them up correctly.

- Always triple-check your file permissions on all your files and directories.

- Always review the IUSR_COMPUTERNAME account to make sure it has the fewest privileges necessary to operate correctly.

- Always review your FTP settings, and test FTP user accounts yourself before allowing their use.

SECURE SOCKETS LAYER

Secure Sockets Layer (SSL) is a communications scheme that lets Web servers communicate securely with SSL-compatible Web browsers across a network. SSL performs server authentication, encryption, decryption, and data integrity checks. Let's take a look at each of these checks now:

- Authentication — assures that data is being sent to the right server and that the server is secured with SSL.

- Encryption/Decryption — transforms the data so that only the correct Web client/Web server pair can reveal the content of the data. SSL uses a public key encryption system to encrypt Web traffic.

- Data Integrity — ensures that the data stream has not been altered during transmission and reception.

SSL creates an intermediate layer between the upper-level HTTP and the lower-level TCP/IP. Web browsers and Web servers make calls and requests directly to the SSL, which manages the task of setting up a secure communications channel and passing or receiving information from TCP/IP. You can find more information about SSL at http://home.netscape.com/newsref/std.

To enable SSL on IIS you must

1. Generate a security key pair file and a request file.
2. Request a digital certificate from a Certification Authority.
3. Install the certificate on your IIS server.
4. Activate SSL security on your IIS server.

We cover the details of generating the files you need and applying for a certificate in the next section; they're also outlined in the IIS online documentation. You may acquire an SSL digital certificate by contacting a certifying organization such as VeriSign (http://www.verisign.com).

After you have a certificate and SSL security has been enabled on your server, you need to remember that only SSL-enabled Web browsers can access your SSL-protected directories. URLs that point to SSL-protected directories must be accessed with the https:// format of URL encoding instead of the normal http:// format.

USING THE KEY MANAGER

The Key Manager lets you build the information files you need to apply for a digital certificate. First, you need to create a key pair file following these steps:

1. Click Start and select Programs. Choose Microsoft Internet Server and then select Key Manager.

2. In the Key menu, select Create New Key.

3. Click on the WWW service in the left window, then choose Create New Key from the Key menu to open the Create New Key and Certificate Request dialog, as shown in Figure 12.11.

Figure 12.11

Request to Create a New Key and Certificate

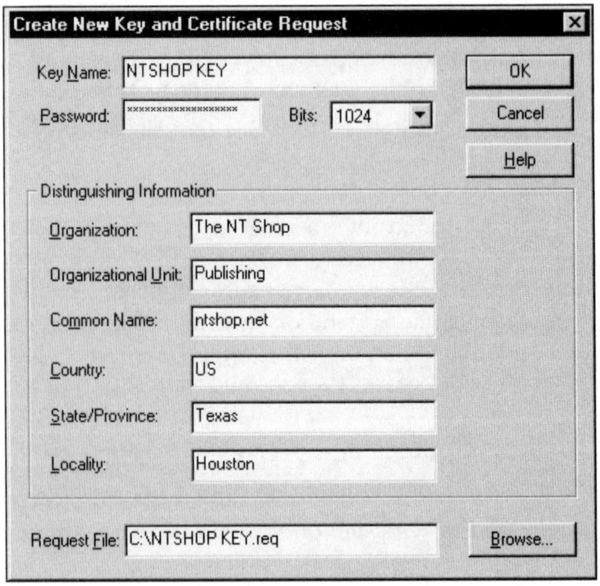

4. Fill in the information for all the fields. Table 12.1 describes the fields. Do not type commas into any field because commas are interpreted as field separators and generate invalid requests. When you are finished, click OK.

TABLE 12.1 FIELDS IN THE DIALOG BOX	
Key Name	Name of the key pair you are creating.
Password	Password used to encrypt the private key (use long passwords).
Bits	Number of bits for the key pair. The default is 1,024 bits; I highly recommend using this setting.
Organization	Your company name or your own name.
Organizational Unit	Name of the division of your company.
Common Name	Internet domain name of your server.
Country	Two-letter abbreviation, such as US, UK, AU, or JP.
State/Province	Your state or province, such as Texas or Alberta.
Locality	Complete name of your city, such as Houston.
Request File	Name of the file you are creating.

5. Type the password once more when you are prompted for it and click OK. Your key will appear in the Key Manager window under the appropriate computer name.

6. Send the certificate request file to an authority according to their procedures. You should receive a digitally signed certificate. Use the Key Manager to install the signed certificate by choosing the Install Key Certificate option on the Key menu. After installing the certificate, activate SSL on IIS by configuring the Directories properties using the Internet Service Manager.

SCRIPTS: ACTIVEX, JAVA, AND CGI

While we're on the subject of secure Web site traffic, let's touch briefly on programs and software that run on your Web server and can be launched by your Web pages. These types of software pose serious threats to your network security.

In Chapter 2 we covered scripts, and I want to remind you again of the dangers. Although these types of tools for Web design and functionality can be extremely alluring, be cautious when you use them. Some tools contain malicious code designed to insert back doors, copy files, create or delete accounts, format drives, change information, or manipulate networked devices like PBXs and fax servers.

As a rule, you should *never* assume that code, components, and controls you download from any source on the Internet are safe for your network, especially your Web server. Screen them carefully by analyzing the code or running the software on isolated test systems before using them in a production environment. Monitor the software to see whether it generates any unusual Event Log entries.

DANGERS OF MIME MAPPING

Multipurpose Internet Mail Extensions (MIME) is widely used on the Internet to encode data that moves between systems. Although the name implies that it's used with e-mail, Web servers and browsers also use MIME attachments.

Windows maps MIME files to associated programs that open or run the MIME file after you receive it. MIME can be convenient, but it can also be a security risk. When you run the IIS Web server, you should always disable the MIME types for .bat and .cmd file extensions so they cannot be executed by the Web server. Past Web servers, including IIS, had a bug that let users execute DOS commands from remote locations without any special permissions. A typical URL entry looked something like this: http://www.yoursite.com/scripts/ something.bat?DIR. The Web server told NT to open a command shell and pass the shell two parameters: something.bat and DIR. When NT realized it could not locate something.bat, it acted on the second parameter instead, causing NT to do a directory list. Imagine what could happen if that DIR command were a FORMAT or DELETE command. This hole in IIS security was fixed in version 2.0 of IIS.

Similarly, a user could also use a simple batch file as a script to pass commands to the operating system. I won't go into the details here, but a typical batch file contained just one line that looked something like this: %1 %2 %3 %4 %5 %6 %7 %8 %9. If you understand DOS batch file processing, you understand how this worked. Trust me, you don't want this mess on your Web server.

To disable the .bat and .cmd extensions, select View from the Windows Explorer, and then choose Options. When the dialog box appears, click the File Types tab. Scroll through the list of MIME file types until you find .bat and .cmd, then simply highlight them and click Remove. Click OK to close the dialog box, and reboot the machine to make changes take effect immediately.

FTP SERVER ISSUES

FTP is a TCP/IP application that lets users upload and download files across a network. FTP supports a wide range of file types and formats, including ASCII, binary files, and Extended Binary Coded Decimal Interchange Code (EBCDIC), an 8-bit character code used by IBM on their mainframe and midrange systems.

Before establishing an FTP server, make sure that you really need one. You can easily link Web pages to files for downloading, which eliminates the need to run FTP and reduces the security burden on your systems.

Determining the need for an FTP server can be confusing at times. An FTP server can be used to offload the process of downloading files from your Web server, or perhaps to provide a means to upload files, because uploading files with a Web client to a Web server can be a tricky business and require special software. There are other possible scenarios, but these are the two that you're most likely to encounter.

FTP CLIENTS

Intruders may use FTP commands after they gain access to the FTP server. You should learn them so you can test your FTP user accounts before allowing them to be used on the network.

Windows NT ships with a terminal-based FTP client that you run by opening a DOS Console and typing **FTP**. The FTP client presents this prompt: FTP>. To get a list of valid commands, type **?** and press Enter. FTP clients provide a whole range of commands, some of which are listed below:

- open — establishes a connection to a remote computer
- ascii — sets the file transfer type to ASCII
- bin — sets the file transfer mode to binary
- get — transfers a specified file from the server to the client system
- put — transfers a specified file from the client to the server system
- quit — closes the connection to the remote computer and terminates the FTP session
- cd/directory — changes directories on the FTP server
- pwd — displays the current directory on the FTP server
- lcd/directory — changes directories on the local client machine

You can also use most Web browsers to access FTP sites by prefacing the URL with ftp instead of http. For example, ftp://ftp.company.com/ connects you to the FTP server of company.com. Remember, you cannot upload files from a Web browser; you may only download them.

If you allow uploads to your FTP server, you may run into some strange file names that seem suspicious to you. Let's go over a brief list of these less-common extensions:

- GIF — graphics file in GIF format
- gz — Unix file compressed by the GNU gzip utility
- HQX — compressed Macintosh file
- JPG — graphics file in JPEG format
- MPG — video file in MPEG format
- ps — PostScript file that may be printed on a PostScript printer
- shar — Usenet newsgroup archive file created by the shar program
- shar.Z — compressed shar file
- SIT — Macintosh file compressed by the StuffIt program
- tar — tape archive file created by the Unix tar utility
- tar.Z — compressed tape archive file
- TIF — graphics file in TIFF format
- TXT — standard text file
- uue — uuencoded file
- uue.z — compressed uuencoded file
- z — compressed file created using pack
- Z — file created by the Unix compress utility
- ZIP — compressed file created using PKZIP

You can uncompress and view most of the compressed file types mentioned above with WinZip software for Windows 95 and Windows NT. You can get a copy of WinZip at http://www.winzip.com.

FTP SITE CONTENT

If you're going to run an FTP server, be sure to organize your files logically, using directories where necessary. For example, if your firm wants to offer driver updates from its Internet site or if you're offering slide shows and demo products, good organization helps you later when you're trying to survey your systems for inappropriate material. The list below is a quick reminder for managing FTP files:

- Each directory can contain a file that is displayed automatically when a visitor navigates to that directory. This file can contain a legal notice and disclaimer about your files and your site. It won't keep intruders out, but it will give you more legal ammunition against them when you catch them. Create a hidden file with the name ~FTPSVC~.CKM.

- Use a file called Index.txt in each directory to tell people exactly what the directory contains. You can use the contents of this file to list file names and descriptions for the directory.

- You can also restrict users to their own directories if you want to. Simply create a subdirectory in your FTP root directory with the same name as the user name. When users log in to the FTP server, they land in their own directory. You can also eliminate their ability to navigate to any other directories using Windows Explorer by removing the Execute permission from the Special Directory Access permissions for their home directory — and for the Anonymous user logon.

ALLOWING ANONYMOUS FTP AND UPLOADS

Anonymous FTP is very popular on the Internet. In a nutshell, it's easy to administer, because each user uses the same Anonymous user account to log on, and those users are not transmitting a password in the clear over the Internet while logging on. However, I don't recommend using it because it gives no control over who logs on to the FTP server, which is particularly troublesome if you allow uploads to your server.

The real jeopardy in allowing the combination of anonymous FTPs and uploads is that an anonymous user can launch a denial-of-service attack on your systems by uploading files until your disk fills up. You have almost no way of finding out who did it — I say "almost" because the FTP server records the IP address of each user that logs on, but an IP address alone doesn't always let you positively identify someone. In most cases, you need the cooperation of the network operator that controls that address. Many ISPs don't track who uses which IP address at specific times, in which case you're out of luck.

The best practice is not using anonymous FTP. Use your Web site to deliver files instead, because the Web site doesn't allow uploads. If you must allow anonymous FTP uploads, consider installing a disk quota management system. Disk quota managers limit the amount of data a user can store in a directory so that users can't bombard your system with data. New Technology Partners (NTP) sells a disk quota manager for NT. For information about contacting NTP, see "For More Information" at the end of this book.

The other problem in allowing uploads to your FTP server, especially anonymously, is that software pirates and pornography peddlers sometimes use your site as a drop zone for their wares. This situation can create all kinds of legal headaches, especially if someone in your company knows about this activity and doesn't take action to stop it. Don't risk it — don't allow uploads to your FTP server, and don't allow anonymous access.

GOING ONLINE WITH FTP

Be certain that you test your FTP site thoroughly before you let others use it. Log on with FTP user accounts as you create them and make sure the restrictions you've applied work as planned. Try navigating directories and changing drives. It never hurts to be careful.

Also remember to monitor, monitor, monitor. You should also establish some degree of auditing on your FTP directories and files.

GOPHER SERVER ISSUES

Gopher lets users locate files by keywords. The Gopher interface is a series of menus that are easy to navigate, typically containing a hierarchy that lets users point and click without learning complicated commands. The Gopher server automatically navigates to the specified file or connects to other Gopher servers, if necessary, in a way that is transparent to the user. Gopher performs many different functions, including logging on to remote computers automatically, performing file transfers, and conducting searches.

CONFIGURING YOUR GOPHER SERVER

Setting up a Gopher server is straightforward. Here's a brief rundown of how to set it up with the Internet Service Manager:

1. Establish a directory to contain your Gopher searchable files.
2. Create tag files.
3. Specify the maximum number of connections you allow to your Gopher server at any one time, and establish a maximum duration for each connection.
4. Configure activity logging.

CREATING GOPHER TAG FILES

Gopher clients use two different kinds of files in their efforts to process a request. *Tag files* build the Gopher menu display, and the other files contain the content.

All management information for the Gopher client is contained in a tag file that Gopher users never see; it contains information such as the display name, host name, port number, creation dates, administrator's name, and administrator's e-mail address. Gopher clients work by loading these tag files when necessary and presenting them as a menu. If the menu item happens to be another tag file, then that new menu is displayed to the client, and if the menu item happens to be a document, then the document is displayed instead.

To create your Gopher tag files, type the following command into the DOS Command console:

```
gdset -c -gn -f "description" -a "name" -e email
     filename
```

The following list defines each part of the command.

- -c — creates or modifies a tag file
- -g*n* — specifies the Gopher ID number that defines the style of the document
- -f "*description*" — adds the specified text description to the tag file
- -a "*name*" — adds the specified administrator name to the tag file
- -e *email* — adds the specified e-mail address to the tag file
- *filename* — the name of the tag file you are creating or modifying

GOING ONLINE WITH GOPHER

Be sure to complete these two tasks before putting your Gopher server into use. They can save you some headaches down the road.

- Check your file permissions carefully to avoid giving intruders a way in.
- Create an outline of your Gopher system. It makes it much easier to make changes later.

IIS LOGS EXPLAINED

Each IIS service can generate log entries. This section explains what you can expect to find in those entries and how you might use them to track down problems and potential security violations.

You should always make it part of your routine checks to review the IIS logs thoroughly. You can even develop small programs to routinely look for certain entries and e-mail them to you, which helps automate your log analysis. If you do create robotic helpers, you should still review the logs because you never know what you might find. The log entries that use a standard text file are comma delimited. The following list details the contents of a log record:

- Client IP address
- Client user name
- Date and time of request
- Service type
- Server name
- Server IP address
- Request processing time
- Bytes received
- Bytes sent
- Service status code
- NT status code
- Operation name
- Target of operation
- Parameters

Many log analysis tools can present statistical information in a variety of layouts and format. IIS can log information in NCSA format, and you may also convert your logs to EMWAC format. Most of the popular log analysis tools available support one or more of these logging formats.

DETECTING PROBLEMS

All sorts of problems can pop up in relation to your Internet services. The wide array of possible problems sometimes makes it difficult to determine the real cause. Many factors can influence server behavior patterns. Let's look at some of the obvious items to keep in mind when tracking down trouble:

- Server's link speed
- Server's traffic and request loads
- User's communications link speed
- Speed between client and server
- Route between client and server
- User's computer type and capabilities

- User's client software type and version
- Current connections to the server
- Miscellaneous processes running on the client and server
- Server processor performance and RAM capacities
- Disk access time on the server
- Network interfaces — 16-bit or 32-bit?
- Malfunctioning Web pages or corrupt FTP files
- Damaged cabling
- Cabling too close to large electrical fields from lights, air conditioners, etc.
- Firewall limitations

Many users' problems are directly related to their individual setup and perceptions, so gather all the facts before trying to find solutions. Use the NT Performance Monitor to your advantage, because IIS services post statistics for this utility that can show you information such as service loading and network traffic loads. The IIS documentation clearly points out the performance counters that are particularly helpful to monitor.

SUMMARY

This chapter gives you much to consider when you use IIS components. You've learned how to install and configure IIS, establish security access controls, and establish secure communications channels between the clients and servers using SSL.

Finally, let me remind you again: don't take logging for granted. Use it heavily and review your logs carefully and routinely. Don't run anonymous FTP or allow uploads to your FTP server unless absolutely necessary. Review the permissions of the IUSR_COMPUTERNAME user account carefully; IIS uses this account when giving users access to the services.

CHAPTER 13

MICROSOFT PROXY SERVER DETAILS

Most people have heard of proxy servers, but not everyone understands what they are and how they work. This chapter offers some insight into the inner workings of proxy servers in general, as well as detailed information about the Microsoft Proxy Server (MPS) application. You learn what a proxy server's job is, how it gets that job done, and what features MPS has to offer. A small portion of the information in this chapter might be better understood by a programmer, but you don't necessarily need to know any of it to run the MPS correctly. The information is provided for those of you want a really technical look at the software.

MPS ARCHITECTURE

Proxy architecture is both simple and complex. Although the overall philosophy is quite simple, the actual inner workings of such a product can get rather complex. In this section, I provide an in-depth look at the overall MPS design and architecture and then look at the two basic parts of MPS: the Proxy Server and the Remote Windows Sockets service.

OVERVIEW OF A PROXY SERVER

In a general sense, a *proxy* is "the authority or power to act on behalf of another." In a networking environment, a proxy server does exactly that — it acts on behalf of other client machines on the network.

The MPS provides access to TCP/IP networks such as the Internet while keeping the workstation address anonymous. When the workstation is anonymous, a potential intruder has no way of knowing what client address to attack. Proxy servers hide the inner details and specifics of your network's layout and architecture. This type of workstation anonymity makes intruder attacks on your machine almost impossible; however, a Trojan horse or virus can still infiltrate your workstation through a file you download from the Internet, so to be completely safe at the workstation level, you need more than a proxy server.

Proxy servers are also known as application gateways, because they are essentially designed for use with very specific applications. The proxy server was developed as the security system for the Web's HyperText Transfer Protocol (HTTP). HTTP and the first programming libraries to support Web clients and Web server applications were developed as Unix-based services at Switzerland's Conseil Europeen pour la Recherche Nucleair (European Laboratory for Particle Physics, a.k.a. CERN). As the developers at CERN continually added support for application-aware proxies to their programming libraries, the Web community steadily built on these additions. Systematically, the CERN proxy protocol became an accepted industry standard, which Microsoft used as the basis for its own Proxy Server software, thus making it CERN-compatible.

Although CERN-compatible proxy services — such as MPS — all support HTTP, FTP, and Gopher requests, a client and the proxy server communicate using only HTTP. Proxies automatically translate other protocols into HTTP. HTTP itself defines a set of commands, commonly called methods, that a client sends to a server. The two most common methods are GET and POST. GET passes a Universal Resource Locator (URL) to a server for processing. The URL serves as a request for a resource, which the URL identifies. POST sends requests for action to a server, as in the GET method, except that POST URLs are accompanied by additional data. In most cases, this additional data is the input from some type of Web-based form, such as a search engine query, that the server will act on in some way.

Proxies service TCP/IP requests for the client. First, the client workstation makes a TCP/IP-based request, such as pulling up a Web page with a particular URL. The client sends the request to the proxy server and waits for the reply. The proxy server receives the request, substitutes its own server address for the client address, and sends it to the destination address, thus keeping the client address anonymous. The destination processes the request and sends the results to the proxy server, which returns the results to the client.

Here's a step-by-step flow of the actual end-to-end process with MPS as the proxy server, assuming that a Web browser asks MPS to return a Web document:

1. The Web browser sends a proxy-formatted request to MPS.
2. MPS receives the request and parses the URL.
3. If the URL is in the MPS cache, MPS sends the request to the Web browser from the cache and is finished. If the URL isn't in the MPS cache, MPS follows the rest of these steps.
4. MPS confirms that the request is in HTTP format.
5. MPS resolves the domain name in the URL to an IP address.
6. MPS sends a request for the document to the Web server (identified by the IP address) using the appropriate protocol. In this example, it uses HTTP.
7. The Web server receives the request and responds by sending the requested document to MPS, also using HTTP.
8. MPS receives the document and forwards it to the Web browser in HTTP.
9. The Web browser receives the document and displays it on-screen.

Simple enough, right? One of the secrets of establishing a proxy server is making sure it serves as the only route to your workstations and other servers. However, the proxy server does need at least one valid, routable IP address. If a real route doesn't exist to the rest of your network, traffic can't reach your machines.

You can eliminate alternative routes in two ways. The first way is to choose an arbitrary Class C network pool to use internally. For example, you can pick something such as 204.176.47.0 for one of your Class Cs. This choice gives you 204.176.47.1 through 204.176.47.254 as internal addresses. This Class C network pool is probably assigned to someone already, and the routes on the Internet point to that network, not yours, so you're safe using arbitrary addresses in this way. However, when you choose an arbitrary address, you need to make *absolutely certain* that your network does not accidentally announce routes for these arbitrary addresses to the Internet. If you do, you can cause strange problems on your network, not to mention on the network that owns the addresses you've used.

The second way to eliminate alternative routes is to use what I call test address pools. Several non-routable test address pools are assigned by the InterNIC — the U.S. organization that manages domains and IP addresses for the Internet. Many people all over the Internet use these test addresses. None of the backbone ISPs include routes to these addresses, so they are useless for routable traffic — and thus perfect for internal use behind a proxy server.

You're safe using Class C addresses out of the Class A network test address pool of 10.0.0.0, which provides more than enough IP addresses for an average intranet. If you need fewer than 254 addresses, use a Class C network from this pool. For example, you can have a Class C network ranging from 10.0.0.1 through 10.0.0.254, which uses a subnet mask of 255.255.255.0. If you need more than one Class C for internal use, simply subnet the 10.0.0.0 again (break the pool into more manageable pieces for routing in different directions), creating additional address pools. Subnetting can get rather complex, so seek administrative help if necessary, or consult a book dedicated to TCP/IP. Chapter 1 touches on routing and subnetting issues; for more detailed information, check a guide to TCP/IP networking.

THE PROXY SERVER COMPONENT

MPS's Proxy Server component is the heart of the software. It serves all Web, FTP, and Gopher application requests on behalf of the clients using it. Application-level proxy services are designed and built to have knowledge of the protocol used by the applications they support. With this knowledge built in, a proxy server can offer additional features, such as user authentication, protocol conversions, and caching of retrieved content. These features allow an administrator to control security, improve response time, and decrease network traffic.

A Web proxy actually acts as both a client and a server. In the server role, it receives Web requests from network clients, and in the client role, it requests content from Web servers on the Internet. The Proxy Server component runs as an Internet Server Application Programming Interface (ISAPI) extension dynamic-link library (DLL) to the IIS. All ISAPI DLLs run in the same physical process as IIS, which means that the code runs faster than normal CGI programs because CGI programs always spawn separate processes each time they are called. ISAPI server extensions are loaded only once and are simply recalled each time they are needed, which increases performance.

MPS's Proxy Server component consists of two basic parts: the Proxy ISAPI Filter and the Proxy ISAPI Application (for more information about Microsoft's ISAPI filter interface, see the ActiveX Development Kit, available on the Web at http://www.microsoft.com/workshop/prog/default.asp). Both the Proxy ISAPI Filter and the Proxy ISAPI Application are contained within a single DLL, appropriately named W3Proxy.dll. Because both parts are in W3Proxy.dll, the complete proxy server is initialized at one time during the initial Web server startup. Let's look at each of these components.

Proxy ISAPI Filter

The ISAPI Filter is a software-based interface that IIS calls each time it receives an HTTP request from a network client. Because the filter is called for every client request, it can monitor, log, modify, redirect, or authenticate each request sent to the server. The filter examines each request to determine whether the request is a proxy request or a standard HTTP request.

In effect, the Proxy ISAPI Filter intercepts every request sent to the server and takes some type of action on the request, depending on the exact nature of the actual request. If the request consists of a URL that contains a protocol and domain name (such as http://www.company.com), the filter adds the name of the Proxy ISAPI Application (W3Proxy.dll) to the URL, which causes IIS to forward the request to the Proxy ISAPI Application.

If the request does not contain a protocol and a domain name, the request is assumed to be for a Web resource located on the proxy server itself. In this case, the Proxy ISAPI Filter does not modify the request; instead, it simply passes it along to IIS to service directly.

Proxy ISAPI Application

The Proxy ISAPI Application receives and processes requests from the Proxy ISAPI Filter. The Proxy ISAPI Application is loaded at the same time as the Proxy ISAPI Filter — during IIS startup. The application performs the following specific sequence of tasks to accomplish its work:

1. Authenticates the client using the configured authentication schemes.
2. Applies the domain filter to the URL.
3. Looks for the requested objects in its cache and returns them from the cache if they are there.
4. If the requested objects do not exist in the cache, the server retrieves the objects from the specified server on the Internet and returns them to the client. It also adds the newly requested objects to the cache if the proxy has been configured to do so.
5. Terminates and waits for another request.

You can see that on the surface the application appears rather simple but in reality performs a complex function. The Proxy Server, with its two ISAPI components, acts quite adequately as the liaison between network clients and servers on remote networks. In the course of its tasks, it can also cache the objects it retrieves for later use. The following section discusses the caching capabilities of MPS, which are important tools in reducing network loads and increasing response time.

PROXY SERVER CACHING

The term *cache* means "to store," and the MPS can store most of the Web objects it retrieves on behalf of its clients. However, not all objects can or should be cached — some objects are updated frequently or change every time they are accessed, and others require user authentication before they can be retrieved. Retrieving objects for the client takes some time. As the number of object requests increases, so does retrieval time under a server or network load. When the objects are cached by the proxy server, they may then be retrieved and delivered much more quickly, which in turn improves response time and reduces network traffic.

MPS performs three basic types of caching: passive, active, and negative. Let's review each of these caching types.

Passive Caching

Each time the MPS retrieves an object, it stores the object and an associated time to live (TTL) in its cache. From that point on, each time that same object is requested, the proxy server retrieves the object from the cache (through a call to URLcache.dll) and delivers it to the client.

Before it delivers the object, the proxy server checks the TTL to ensure that it has not already expired. If the TTL has expired, the proxy server retrieves a fresh copy of the object and updates its cache before delivering the object to the client. If not enough disk space is left on the server to cache the new object, older objects are removed from the cache to make room.

Active Caching

Active caching is actually a superset of passive caching. When the proxy server is actively caching, it automatically generates new requests for objects currently stored in its cache — without necessarily being requested to do so by a client. This type of caching lets the proxy server decide which objects should be updated automatically.

When actively caching, the proxy server evaluates and optimizes its choices for cache updates based on several criteria:

- Object popularity — requests likely to be made by a network client are made by MPS as well.

- Object TTL — objects with longer TTLs are less likely to be updated frequently; likewise, objects close to expiration are more likely to be refreshed.

- Server loading — the lower the MPS load, the more aggressive the caching activity.

Active caching offers much better overall performance because objects are more likely to be in the cache. This type of caching can also perform often-requested object updates when the server is not busy. Additionally, during times of low server loading, MPS checks and updates unexpired objects, increasing the chance of returning more accurate data to the client.

Negative Caching

Negative caching is the process of remembering bad URLs. The MPS creates an object in its cache each time a requested URL results in an error return-code, such as 404 — URL NOT FOUND or 403 — FORBIDDEN REQUEST. The cached response is returned for each subsequent request for the same URL. This type of caching is not so different from active or passive caching, but you must explicitly configure MPS to cache bad requests.

THE RWS COMPONENT

The RWS service lets a Winsock-compliant application act as if it is connecting directly to an Internet service, when it is actually connected indirectly through a gateway computer. In the case of RWS, the gateway is the MPS. A client application calls the Winsock API (more on Winsock in a moment). *Calls* occur when one program communicates with a set of external program code — not necessarily part of the main program — and asks it to perform some task. Most Windows-based Internet (TCP/IP) applications use an external library, the Winsock.dll, to offload some of their Internet communications needs, and this is where RWS comes in.

As it communicates with a remote host somewhere on the Internet, RWS acts as a mediator for Winsock calls. This mediation is called *remoting*, which we discuss further in a moment. Just as the proxy service accepts standard object requests from a client, RWS accepts standard remote calls from a client. Remoting fills non-HTTP, non-FTP, and non-Gopher types of Internet application object requests by letting these types of applications appear as if they were directly connected to a remote computer.

The RWS service is capable of working with most Winsock 1.1-compliant applications. You should note that MPS version 1.0 is not yet compatible with

Winsock 2.0; however, you can expect Microsoft to add this compatibility as Winsock 2.0 gains popularity. Now let's take a look at Winsock itself.

Winsock

Winsock, a.k.a. Windows Sockets, is an API that makes possible TCP/IP-specific communications among Microsoft Windows applications. Winsock lets a developer create software using a common standard, without writing low-level network protocol code into the program itself, which makes applications smaller and easier to develop. The Winsock.dll file stores the Winsock API routines.

These applications that communicate with Winsock can be running on the same computer or on networked computers. Besides supporting all Windows-based TCP/IP stacks, Winsock even supports some non-TCP/IP network protocols, such as Novell's Internetwork Packet Exchange/Sequenced Packet Exchange (IPX/SPX) and Microsoft's NetBEUI.

Windows Sockets supports two basic types of connections: point-to-point connections, usually called stream-oriented communications, and multipoint-to-point connectionless communications, or datagram-oriented communications. Stream-oriented connections communicate using TCP, and datagram-oriented communications use UDP. Both protocols are explained in Chapter 1.

The important distinguishing characteristic between these two connection methods is that TCP maintains an open connection and UDP does not. Most Internet-enabled applications use the point-to-point, connection-based TCP. As mentioned in Chapter 1, UDP does not offer data reliability guarantees, whereas TCP does. However, UDP is more performance-oriented than TCP because it has less overhead.

The important things to understand about Winsock-compatible applications are

- They require the presence and use of a Winsock.dll file.
- DLLs are storage files for executable, program-independent application code.
- DLLs store procedures and functions that can be called by external applications.

Applications use Winsock to communicate directly with remote computers across a network. To protect a client machine, the network setup must incorporate a liaison that hides the client's identity, like the proxy service for Web, FTP, and Gopher clients. This function is not built into Winsock, so Microsoft resolved the issue with the Remote Windows Sockets (RWS) service. In the next section, you learn how this new service achieves the desired results.

RWS Components

RWS is a standalone NT service made up of a server-based application and a client-side DLL. Applications use the DLL to communicate with RWS. When the client files are installed, the setup program renames Winsock.dll so that it is not called by a client application. It then installs RWS.dll and renames it either Winsock.dll or Wsock32.dll, depending on whether it's a 16-bit or 32-bit version.

From this point, all applications that call Winsock.dll are actually calling the new RWS file, which determines how to handle the call. The RWS file processes some calls completely on its own and passes others to the old Winsock DLL for processing. Programs communicating completely within your local internal network are forwarded to the old Winsock DLL, while programs communicating with remote external networks (remoting, as mentioned above) use the RWS version of Winsock.dll.

The client software makes this internal/external decision based on the contents of the Local Address Table (LAT) configured during MPS installation. The LAT contains a list of all IP address ranges used on your local network, which is transmitted to the client when an application connects to RWS.

RWS Remoting

As mentioned above, RWS uses two types of remoting: TCP and UDP. RWS performs TCP remoting by creating two connections, one between the client and RWS, and one between RWS and the remote server the client wants to connect to. Data passed from either connection is forwarded to the other connection, thus creating the appearance that the client and server are directly connected to each other, when RWS is really a mediator.

UDP remoting is different from TCP remoting because UDP is a connectionless protocol that can have multiple packets from different source addresses bound for a single destination address. In UDP remoting, RWS creates a mapping table for each host that is sending UDP packets to an RWS client. You should recall that each TCP/IP packet (including UDP) has a header that contains at least a source address, a source port, a destination address, and a destination port. RWS uses this header information to manage UDP remoting.

Each time a new client connects to RWS, a control channel is established between the two. When a remote host sends its first data packet to an RWS client, RWS creates a separate UDP socket for that host and adds the host information to its mapping table. The mapping table is sent to the client each time the table is updated.

Let's look at this in another light: in TCP remoting, the address and port mappings remain constant, so the connection is easy to manage. In UDP remoting, the address and port mappings can change, so a table keeps track of the changes. The mapping table tells the client which address and port the data is coming from, which in turn lets the client use the table to map the data to an Internet application's address and port.

Internal Network Protocols

Because Winsock includes functionality for TCP/IP, IPX/SPX, and NetBEUI, it is possible to provide a level of Internet access without using TCP/IP on your internal networks. Using Winsock can therefore add a level of security — if a client runs IPX/SPX, not TCP/IP, it cannot communicate directly with a remote host running TCP/IP; instead, it must go through RWS, thus preventing an outside machine from directly attacking a client.

When you use TCP/IP on an internal network with valid Internet IP addresses, you increase your chances of an attack. Using valid IP addresses that *are not routed to your network* but that are instead routed to someone else's network, as we discussed earlier, reduces your chances of being attacked.

Using TCP/IP on your internal network certainly has its merits, and TCP/IP is often a great choice for a networking protocol. When your internal network runs IPX/SPX or NetBEUI, the principles of remoting are identical to those of TCP/IP. RWS translates non-TCP/IP packet data to TCP/IP packet format before it transmits client data to a remote host, and it translates the data back to the native format before sending the data to the client. All Winsock application communication attempts in non-TCP/IP environments are remoted to the Internet host, and no LAT information is transferred to the clients.

MPS SECURITY

MPS as a whole relies on the built-in security functions of IIS, which in turn relies on the built-in security features of NT.

In most cases, inbound Internet traffic destined for one of your Internet services (Web, FTP, Gopher) is handled using the anonymous logon account established for your IIS server. Remember, it is wise to change the user name and password of the anonymous account (by default, IUSR_MACHINENAME) to something hard to guess. If you create a new account instead of modifying the default account, be sure to grant the new account the Log on Locally permission, or your services will not function correctly.

You may also wish to use SSL, which supports data encryption and server authentication schemes. SSL can greatly enhance the security of your data transmission and user authentication. MPS and IIS also let you create your own security schemes for encryption and authentication. Check out the ISAPI Software Development Kit. ISAPI supports user-developed filter DLLs that let you develop your own systems for handling specialized security needs.

MPS FEATURES

MPS is a secure barrier you can install between networks that offers isolation and secure communications. MPS is actually composed of two parts: the Proxy Server service and the Remote Windows Sockets (RWS) service. Let's look at the features and their functions in a nutshell.

The Proxy Server service

- Is a CERN-compatible proxy service, which offers maximum client compatibility
- Supports most of the popular Web, Gopher, and FTP client software packages
- Offers Internet object caching for increased performance and lower network use
- Uses TCP/IP on your internal networks
- Provides user-level security for each protocol
- Provides secure, encrypted logons for clients that support NT Challenge/Response authentication
- Supports Secure Sockets Layer (SSL) specification

The Remote Windows Sockets (RWS) service

- Supports TCP/IP and IPX/SPX on the private network
- Is compatible with most applications that are compatible with Windows Sockets (Winsock) version 1.1
- Offers complete control over inbound and outbound access using port numbers, protocols, users, user groups, domain names, IP addresses, and subnet masks

Both the Proxy Server service and the Remote Windows Sockets service

- Block external (Internet) users from accessing your private internal network and computers
- Hide your internal IP addresses from Internet users
- Offer extensive logging information about usage patterns
- Integrate seamlessly into Microsoft's Internet Service Manager

SUMMARY

From this chapter, we can see that the MPS is complex at the deeper level yet relatively simple on the surface for the administrator — not to mention its near-transparency to the user. MPS offers a robust way to secure a private network that needs to be connected to remote hosts over an unsecured communications medium such as the Internet, while offering a platform that can interoperate with a wide assortment of network clients. Careful MPS planning, installation, and configuration, along with a good set of policies and procedures for usage, monitoring, and maintenance, can really benefit your effort to secure your networking environment.

CHAPTER 14

ESTABLISHING YOUR PROXY DESIGN

The way you install and integrate Microsoft Proxy Server (MPS) makes or breaks your security system. Before you begin, you need to decide how MPS will interoperate with TCP/IP-based services on the Internet, even if your network does not use TCP/IP.

This chapter discusses integration and topology considerations, usage policies and procedures, and the legal groundwork you need. When you complete this chapter, you should have a good idea of what lies ahead and how you can get the job done effectively.

INTEGRATION CONSIDERATIONS

At this point, you should understand what a proxy server is and how it accomplishes its tasks. Now we consider finding a place for the proxy server on your network. Connection and integration are key factors in securing a network with this type of software. We start by looking at where a proxy server may fit into your topology and how you may need to change your environment to accommodate the security system. Several factors influence your decisions, including network size, network protocols, and your network connection type.

TOPOLOGY MAPPING

I can't tell you how many times I've walked into a network shop to do some work, only to find myself mapping the network just to get a clear view of where things stand. Every network, no matter how large or small, should be completely and accurately mapped on paper or on computer. You gain many benefits from mapping your network, and I can't think of a single drawback beyond the time it takes — and imagine the time you'll spend a year from now trying to remember how you built your network if you don't map it.

Mapping your network

- Expedites future modifications
- Gives you a clear view of how the network connects everything
- Reduces time spent in future planning
- Helps you analyze traffic issues and concerns
- Shows you places you may be able to improve the network itself
- Gives you an idea of vulnerabilities
- Gives outside vendors a quick, clear view of your network topology
- Saves you money by saving you time

If you don't already have a map of your network, draw one before you install the MPS server. You need a clear view of where it will be installed physically and what effect it will have on the overall network design. Be sure to include your network protocols on your map as well as your workstation and server types. The more information you record, the less you'll have to gather later.

Think carefully about storing your map — it's now a proprietary and sensitive corporate asset. Don't hang it on the wall where visitors and employees who don't need access can easily see it. Intruders need to know certain information about your network to attack it successfully, and the less information you give away, the harder it is for them. Thieves have a harder time stealing something when they can't find out where it is!

WHERE DOES IT FIT?

Before you can decide where MPS fits in your network, you must understand what you already have in place. Everyone's network is different, so I can't offer a one-size-fits-all solution. Instead, let's focus on general questions and issues you should analyze before you proceed, including network size, protocols, and connection type.

You need to consider the size of your network because network size affects the form of name resolution you use. Smaller networks running NetBIOS-based protocols such as IPX/SPX use broadcasts to resolve computer names to network addresses. This setup may be entirely acceptable for your environment, but if your network has more than fifty hosts connected to it, you may want to consider using a Domain Name System (DNS) server or a Windows Internet Naming Service (WINS) server to assist in resolution. I cover name resolution in more detail in the next section.

Network protocols are a definite consideration. If your network runs the NetBEUI protocol, you need to enable either IPX/SPX or TCP/IP because MPS uses only those two protocols to communicate with clients. If you don't have one of these protocols running on your network yet, you should consider using TCP/IP because it offers better performance than IPX/SPX.

Your network connection type is another consideration in implementing MPS. You may be using a standard modem, ISDN, or even a dedicated circuit to connect to the Internet. Each of these connection methods requires a slightly different configuration of the NT software and the server hardware.

The basic reason to add a proxy server to your network is to control the flow of traffic in and out of your network. No traffic should be able to travel into your network unless you specifically want it to; likewise, no workstation clients should have a route out to the Internet unless you want them to. You accomplish this control by physically wiring MPS between your network and the Internet.

Your MPS server needs two network adapters to correctly isolate your network. Typically, one adapter is plugged into a network hub, along with all your workstations; the hub thus gives them a common point of communication. The other network adapter in your MPS server is usually connected to the hub where the device supporting your Internet connection is — which is typically some type of router.

When clients have traffic destined for the Internet, MPS client software forwards that traffic to your MPS Internet gateway, which passes it to its destination on the Internet. In theory, it's that simple. Depending on the structure of your network, however, the process could realistically be much more complex. Just remember, the idea is to isolate the Internet connection on one side of your MPS server and force all client traffic to use the MPS for Internet access. Figure 14.1 shows a simple proxy integration design.

Figure 14.1
*Simple Proxy
Integration Design*

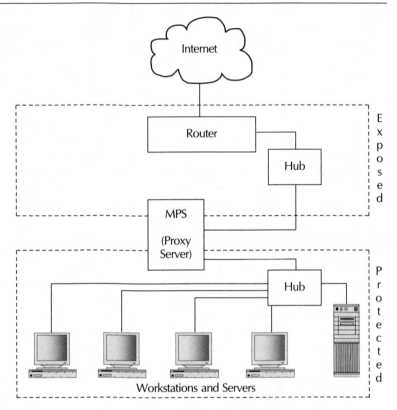

On networks with lots of clients that need Internet access, you may need to install more than one proxy server to balance the client load. Chapter 15 discusses how to configure the software for load balancing. Figure 14.2 shows how you might integrate several proxy servers in a load-balanced environment using one Internet connection.

If you use equipment such as an Ascend ISDN router for your Internet connection, the router has a TCP/IP address that is typically used as the gateway address on your client workstations. You need to be sure that none of the client TCP/IP stacks has a gateway configured. Instead, the MPS client

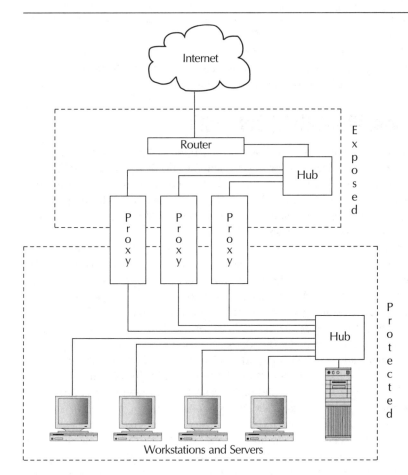

Figure 14.2
Multiple Proxy Servers for Load Balancing

software, once installed, will handle gateway routing by forwarding traffic to the MPS server.

If your router has packet-filtering capabilities, you may want to exclude traffic from all your network addresses except those that need *direct* Internet access, such as your SMTP mail server or your Web server. This filtering prevents mischievous users from reconfiguring your TCP/IP stacks to include a gateway address, which could quite easily bypass the MPS server. For example, on my network I stop inbound traffic destined for all ports except port 25 (mail), port 80 (Web), and port 53 (DNS). For outbound access, my filters open only those ports necessary for access to outside systems, such as port 25 for my ISP's mail server — on the rare occasion I need to use its server. Other custom tools, such as IISA (an IIS Web server monitor), require a filter to open outbound access to port 60 so that IISA can look up the origins of users visiting my site.

Also, keep in mind that if your client workstations run Windows 95, you may want to implement user policies restricting access to the Network Control Panel Applet; this restriction prevents reconfiguration.

HOST NAME RESOLUTION CONCERNS

You recall from Chapter 1 that all hosts on the Internet have host names and domain names, which together form fully qualified domain names. If you want your client workstations and MPS server to communicate with other computers on the Internet, they need to be able to resolve those names to IP addresses. Several network services, including broadcasts, DNS, WINS, and a combination of services, can perform resolution.

I highly recommend using DNS, whether you run your own server or use someone else's DNS service. You can easily use your ISP's DNS servers — you need only the IP addresses for those machines, which your ISP should provide at no cost. Then configure the addresses into your TCP/IP, and they should work immediately, assuming your Internet connection is working properly.

You can also use broadcasts or WINS to resolve host names. Bear in mind two primary drawbacks of using broadcasts to resolve host names — they create additional traffic on your network and do not work across routers. Also, be aware that both broadcasts and WINS have no way to resolve Internet host names and addresses. If you're building a secured private network connection that communicates only with another Windows-based network (even if it uses the Internet as a wide area network), you're safe to use WINS or broadcasts because you never need to access an Internet host. However, the moment you try to connect to an Internet site, your clients and the MPS server won't be able to resolve the names to usable addresses. Although WINS helps map NetBIOS computer names to their associated IP addresses, it doesn't understand Internet computer names (hosts) and addresses. You need to get WINS some help or replace WINS. Both Microsoft and Metainfo offer DNS servers designed specifi- cally for Windows NT that can either interoperate with WINS or be used alone to resolve Internet host names. Microsoft's DNS server ships with Windows NT 4.0, and Metainfo's DNS server software is available at http://www.metainfo.com.

CONSIDER THE ROLLOUT

You should carefully plan and manage the process of installing the MPS client software, which is commonly called *client roll-out*. Don't just install the client on every machine — consider which clients need Internet access. You never want to use services you don't need, not even for the sake of convenience.

MPS installation establishes a share on the MPS server; your network client machines connect to this share and from there install the MPS client software. See Chapter 15 for details about the network share. You can handle this share in several ways: your shop may use SMS to push software to client machines, you may have an administrator who installs new software for your users, or you may even let users install new software themselves.

In any event, *control the rollout.* If you simply install the software on everyone's machines, eventually they will use it. That's what it's for, of course, but you may not want them to use it yet. Don't just assume your users won't use it if you tell them not to. Remember, part of securing a network is controlling how the network is used. The first step in your client rollout should be educating your users about installing and using the MPS Internet gateway. To adequately prepare your users, you first need policies and procedures that govern the way they use the network.

POLICIES AND PROCEDURES

Chapter 7 is devoted entirely to establishing and enforcing policies and procedures. However, you also need a few policies specific to MPS that lay down rules for your network's users. Once the users are informed and educated, they have no excuse for deviating from the status quo. Policies and procedures also arm you to take action against violators, whether the violations are intentional or unintentional.

I recall one instance at an isolated, secure federal government network installation in which a user innocently logged on to an IRC server. The user didn't realize that IRC clients often give away a user's IP address, e-mail address, domain name, and other clues that help an intruder find a way into the network. Had this user been educated in these areas, that network's security may not have been compromised.

UNDERSTANDING THE POTENTIAL USE

The great thing about the Internet is that it is full of fun and useful information. The bad thing about the Internet is that it is full of fun and useful information. It is human nature to explore new things, including the Internet. I don't know a single person who has been introduced to the Internet and not become incredibly busy surfing its vast expanses.

The Web's popularity is spreading like wildfire. The comparable phenomenon in the past 20 years was the personal computer explosion in the early 1980s. Besides the Web, IRC chat systems, e-mail, and news groups are the primary features people use on the Internet.

If you give a man a gun, sooner or later he will shoot it. The same holds true for the Internet and client access software. That's why I stress that you should not install client software that you don't want clients to use. If you control software access and installation, you go a long way toward strengthening your network security.

ESTABLISHING THE GROUND RULES

You are not investing in an Internet connection for the sheer fun of it. You probably have a valid justification for this decision to plug in. If you don't, back up and find one or rethink your decision to connect to the Internet. You can't control something if you don't know why you want to use it.

Perhaps your goal, like so many other businesses today, is to gain e-mail access and establish a Web site to promote your firm. Or you may want to use the Internet as a WAN to connect remote networks economically. Whatever your reasons, be certain they are clear to you. Your ground rules governing employee use of your Internet connection are based on your company's intended use.

Businesses complain of users surfing the Internet on company time. Work productivity falls off, attentiveness falls off, quality falls off, and of course, revenues suffer. Several firms have developed software systems that monitor and control your Internet connection. You may consider adopting one of these products. On the other hand, if your company has a disciplined staff, this type of software may not be necessary.

Several issues surrounding network use and data accumulation have far-reaching ramifications for your business. The Internet is full of data — software, multimedia, and other types — all easily downloaded to a user's workstation. If your users download pirated software, your firm could get in trouble; likewise, users may download pornography. This material can cause your firm significant problems. Because you provide the Internet link and the client tools necessary to use that link, in the eyes of the law, you are accountable for its use. The situation is similar to owning a firearm and being negligent about where it's kept. If your child grabs the gun and shoots a neighbor's kid, you're essentially responsible for not controlling access to and use of the weapon. Internet access software and Internet connections are both productivity tools and weapons. You are accountable for your network and its use.

In your policies and procedures, don't forget to include ways to report security incidents at the appropriate levels. You need to know when someone does not follow the rules, because that person is jeopardizing your business.

Management should know of every incident that occurs, no matter how insignificant it seems. These incidents should be reviewed routinely and often, so each team member is aware of the incidents. What one person sees, another person may overlook.

ASSIGNING AUTHORITY AND RESPONSIBILITY

One of the best ways to begin controlling any situation, including network security, is to assign authority and responsibility, which leads to accountability. Someone must see that the rules are followed. You may opt to bestow this responsibility on your network administrator, or you may give these tasks to someone else. How you handle it is up to you; however, you should not let your network administrator both govern your security and enforce procedures. Keep the responsibilities separate whenever possible.

Separating the tasks between two people (at least) decreases the likelihood of any sanctioned illegal activity because consent from more than one person is required. Ideally, you should have one person enforce policies and procedures, another person handle user accounts and user security issues, and yet another person handle network administration concerns. Spreading the load reduces the possibility of any wrongdoing.

LEGAL ISSUES

Don't overlook the legal avenues for remedying a situation. Some employees may do something so unethical that you are morally obligated to turn them in to the authorities. Doing so lessens the chance that they'll do the same thing again. Anyone who gets away with something is likely to try it again or try something worse. Involving the authorities may be your best option to resolve a problem and the best way to set an example for others. At least it sends a message to all employees that your firm does not tolerate unauthorized or illegal use of the Internet.

IIS CONSIDERATIONS

Part of establishing a good proxy server design for your network is understanding that MPS runs on top of Internet Information Server. Therefore, IIS must be installed first for MPS to operate correctly. When MPS is installed on top of IIS, it reconfigures IIS so that it *does not* listen for Internet requests on the network interface connected to the Internet, thus disabling inbound requests from the Internet. However, in this default configuration, it does listen for any request that comes from your internal network, presenting no threat to security.

MPS was designed to facilitate outbound Internet connections for private internal network clients. However, using the same server to offer other Internet Web services is not a good idea; in fact, doing so decreases security and increases the chances of an intrusion. I recommend that you use separate servers for MPS Internet access and IIS Internet publishing.

If cost is a big factor in adding a server, you can lease Web server space on your ISP's Web server or a server belonging to a Web-hosting company. Leasing space offloads bandwidth use to the ISP and lets you keep your network security at its maximum when using MPS.

If you must enable Internet Web publishing services on the same server that runs MPS, do so with the following steps:

1. Open the Internet Service Manager and double-click on the server name running MPS.

2. When the Service Properties window appears, select the Service tab.

3. Check the Enable Internet Publishing option box, which is not checked by default. Checking this box tells IIS to listen on port 80 (the Web port) of the server's external network interface, which is connected to the Internet. This switch lets incoming traffic reach your Web service. Choosing this option does not affect FTP and Gopher, which you control using the permissions settings for those services. If you don't want to allow access to them at all, simply disable them.

4. Click OK to complete the task.

If you opt to use one server for both Web and MPS services, consider following these recommendations to further strengthen the security of your configuration:

- Install Microsoft Proxy Server and IIS separately on different servers and in different Windows NT domains. Establish a one-way trust between the MPS server's domain and your private internal domain. For example, if you have a private internal NT domain called Internal that you use with your internal computers, you can add a domain called Proxy that includes your MPS and your IIS servers that publish Internet content. Then set the Proxy domain to trust the Internal domain. This way, users in the Internal domain can be granted access to services and resource in the Proxy domain, but users on the Internet can't get through to your Internal domain because no trust is established that allows access.

- Never add external Internet IP addresses to the Local Address Table (LAT) the MPS uses; if you have some external addresses in your LAT, remove them using the configuration dialog box. Having external IP addresses on your LAT exposes your entire network to the Internet, defeating the purpose of the MPS altogether.

- Wherever possible, ensure that your network shares have read-only access.

- Set the default access rights on your MPS cache directories and the Internet publishing directories on the MPS server to allow read-only access for all users. You can assign this right to the Everyone group or its replacement.

- Don't use mapped network drives for storing Internet publishing content. If your server can access other shared network resources, so can a potential intruder. This one safeguard can be a critical point in securing your network.

- Avoid using CGI, ActiveX, Java, JavaScript, VB Script, and other types of Web programming tools. Bugs in these applications can open your systems to intrusion. Furthermore, assume scripts acquired from untrusted sources are dangerous unless you examine all the source code before using them. Use the NTFS file and directory permissions to secure your scripts directory, ensuring that scripts cannot run from other areas of the hard disk.

- Always enable auditing and logging for all your network services and shared resources.

SUMMARY

In this chapter, you've learned the importance of mapping your network and keeping that information protected. You've also learned basic placement ideas for your proxy server. And you should understand now that policies, procedures, and accountability are equally important parts of proxy server design. Additionally, you've learned that because MPS runs on top of IIS, IIS presents additional design considerations for your proxy implementation. Refer to this chapter any time you plan to add a new proxy server to your network.

CHAPTER 15

IMPLEMENTING MICROSOFT PROXY SERVER

In this chapter, I give step-by-step instructions for installing Microsoft Proxy Server (MPS). By the time you complete this chapter, you will have a configured, working security server. Before you get started, be sure you read Chapter 1, "Understanding TCP/IP," and Chapter 2, "Network Security Overview." The material in those two chapters gives you insight into what you're working with when you install and configure the software.

INSTALLING MPS

This section covers the basic installation of the Microsoft Proxy Server, which is straightforward. The initial setup process is very simple — you don't need to allocate more than about 30 minutes to install the entire product set. However, configuring settings after initial installation could take considerably longer, depending on the number of users who need access.

PREINSTALLATION CHECKLIST

Before we get too far, let's review a list of items you should check before installation. The last thing you want is for something to go wrong when your halfway through. Review this list carefully before proceeding.

- You must install and correctly configure both Internet Information Server (IIS) and Windows NT 4.0 or greater. Chapter 12 covers IIS installation and configuration.

- Inform all your users of the downtime you expect. If your server already runs other Internet services, such as IIS, be sure to notify your users that the services will be unavailable while you are installing MPS.

- Make sure you have one of these two setups — two network cards installed in your machine, one preconfigured with a nonroutable address, or a modem connected to a COM port to connect to the Internet.

- Do not run any applications on the server other than those that are absolutely necessary. The setup program overwrites particular files on the server, and if they are being used by other programs, the setup program cannot continue. If you don't stop all Microsoft Internet services, the MPS setup program stops them for you.

- Log on as Administrator or as a member of the Administrators group before starting the installation. You need administrative privileges to complete the installation correctly.

- Gather all the IP address ranges in use on your network. You need them during the installation process. If you are not sure of all the addresses, consult the network administrator that manages your IP addresses before you proceed.

- Find out which client operating systems the workstations on your network use so you can install the appropriate client packages during the setup routine. The setup program automatically creates a network share that client workstations use to install the MPS client software.

- Be sure that the disk drive where you plan to install MPS has 3.2 MB of free space for the server software itself. You need additional disk space if you plan to have MPS cache Web pages for better performance.

STEP-BY-STEP INSTALLATION

Before we begin the installation itself, let's look at some assumptions:

- You have performed the tasks specified in the preinstallation checklist
- You want to install MPS on your D partition or disk drive
- Your internal TCP/IP network uses addresses from the 10.0.0.0 Class C network, with addresses ranging from 10.0.0.1 through 10.0.0.254 (refer to Chapter 1 for details about TCP/IP network addressing)
- Finally, this installation of MPS is the only proxy server installed on your network and that it uses the NetBIOS machine name of IAS1.

With these assumptions understood, let's begin installation.

1. Find Setup.exe on your CD-ROM and double-click it to start installation. The opening dialog box is typical of Microsoft software installations. It shows a brief warning message telling you that you should close all applications before proceeding and contains information about copyrights and End User License Agreements (EULA). Review the complete license agreement when you get a moment. License violations can get you into a lot of hot water, and you don't need that problem. Click Continue to proceed.

2. The setup program searches for any installed Microsoft Internet components. If you have already installed IIS, the setup program automatically integrates MPS into this configuration. After the search is complete, you see a dialog box. Select the folder where you want the software installed. The setup program checks that the folder exists; if it does not, the setup program prompts you for confirmation before creating it. After you have the correct folder, click the large Installation Options button to continue.

3. The dialog box shown in Figure 15.1 appears, giving you installation options appropriate for your configuration. The two primary options are Install Server and Client Installation Share and Install MPS HTML Documentation.

    The Install Server and Client Installation Share option lets you install the MPS client software packages on your server. The setup program automatically creates a network share so that workstations can connect and

Figure 15.1

Installation Options

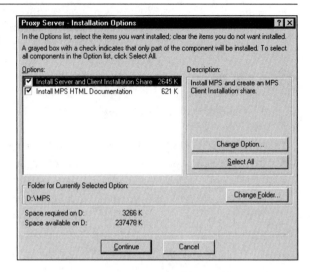

install the clients across the network. The available client packages include Windows NT versions for Intel, PowerPC, MIPS, and the Alpha, as well as Intel-based Windows 95 and Windows 3.x clients. Figure 15.2 shows the client selection options.

Figure 15.2

Install Server and Client Installation Share

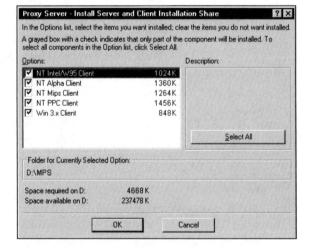

The Install HTML Documentation option in Figure 15.1 lets you install the documentation into a directory on your server. With the documentation in HTML format, you can easily use any standard web browser to read it.

4. After selecting your installation options, click Continue shown in Figure 15.1. The setup program detects and stops any other Microsoft Internet services that may be running. After the installation is complete, the setup program automatically restarts the services for you.

5. After the setup program stops all the Internet services, you see a dialog box like that shown in Figure 15.3. Choose the drives where MPS stores Web pages so it can reload them more quickly if they are requested again within a certain time period. The setup program recommends that you choose drives with at least 50 MB of free space. Using drives with less space limits how much you can store in the cache. Highlight the drives in the left pane you want to use and click Select to include them. When you are finished, click OK.

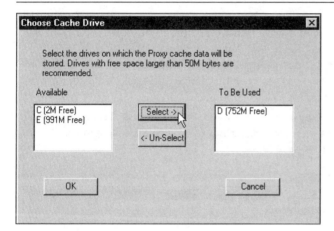

Figure 15.3
Choosing Cache Drives

6. The Network Configuration dialog box is shown in Figure 15.4. This dialog box lets you define the IP address ranges used on your internal networks.

You can type your IP address range or click the big button labeled "Load from internal NT routing table." If you click the button, the setup program analyzes the *current* routing table and includes the address ranges it contains. If you use other IP address ranges on your network that aren't currently in the routing table, you cannot add them by simply clicking here. You must insert them manually. Be sure you know the full scope of IP address ranges in use on your network before completing this dialog box. See Chapter 1, "Understanding TCP/IP," for a more complete understanding of IP addresses and routing.

Figure 15.4

Network Configuration

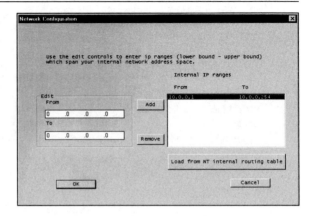

To see what the routing table contains, click "Load from NT internal routing table." You can always remove anything you don't want from the table before you click OK at this dialog box.

Remember that in this example, we are using addresses ranging from 10.0.0.1 through 10.0.0.254, so type that range and click Add. After you've added all the range, click OK to continue.

7. The next part of the installation configures client access. You see a dialog box like that shown in Figure 15.5; it has two parts: Remote Windows Sockets Access and Proxy Access.

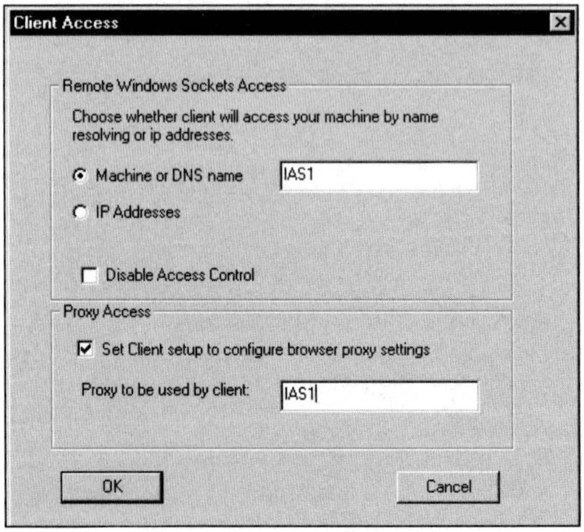

Figure 15.5

Client Access

You need to configure two settings in the Remote Windows Sockets Access box. The two buttons tell the client software package how it contacts MPS. Your options are "Machine or DNS name" and "IP Address." Choosing "Machine or DNS name" means that client packages contact MPS by name, not by address. Because names are far easier to remember than long numeric addresses, this option may be the best choice for your network. The "IP Address" box tells the client packages to contact MPS by address.

Type the proper name or address of the option you choose — for "Machine Name or DNS name," type the NetBIOS name of the server; for "IP Address," type the IP address of this server.

When you select the Disable Access Control check box, any client package that has the correct name or address for the server can use it as its proxy server. If you want to control who can and cannot use this access server, do not check this box. If you do not want to regulate the use of this access server, check this box.

The Proxy Access box contains a check box labeled "Set Client setup to configure browser proxy settings." Selecting this check box tells the setup program to configure the client packages so that they automatically configure themselves for use with a given proxy access server. The "Proxy to be used by client" box lets you determine the IP address or machine name of the proxy access server that the client packages stored on this computer will use.

For this installation, we assume that you are installing the only proxy server in use, so check the box and type this server's NetBIOS name (IAS1 in our example) in the data entry window as shown in Figure 15.5. When you are finished, click OK.

8. The setup program checks that you have the necessary disk space to install the software. After confirmation, the setup program copies all the necessary files to your hard drive. You see a status window during the copy process. After it's finished copying, the setup program establishes the network share for the client software and restarts any stopped Internet services.

9. When the files are copied successfully, the installation is complete. You see a standard final dialog box.

THE NUTS AND BOLTS OF MPS

In this section, I go through MPS configuration in detail. We quickly review the Internet Service Manager (ISM) — the tool you'll use to configure and manage the MPS — and also go over each setting you find in the MPS property pages.

USING ISM

Now that MPS is installed, you need to review the additional settings at your disposal. You manage MPS in the same way you manage all Microsoft Internet services — with the ISM. We looked at the ISM in detail in Chapter 12 during the IIS installation and configuration, so I won't go over all that material again. However, let's quickly review some of the features of the ISM for your convenience.

First, open the ISM by clicking Start and selecting Programs, Microsoft Internet Server, and Internet Service Manager from the subsequent menus. The main dialog box, shown in Figure 15.6, appears.

Figure 15.6

Internet Service Manager

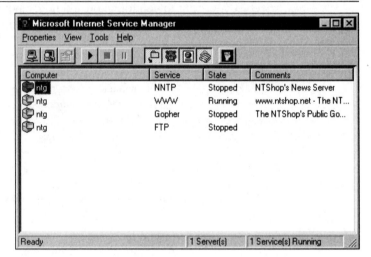

No matter which view of the ISM you use, you'll always see the same groups of icons across the top of the interface. Let's review them briefly:

The first group of icons

- Connects to a specific IIS server
- Locates all the IIS servers on a network
- Displays the properties of a service

The second group of icons

- Starts the selected service
- Stops the selected service

- Pauses the selected service

  The third group of icons

- Displays FTP service information
- Displays Gopher service information
- Displays Web service information
- Displays Proxy service information
- Displays Remote Windows Sockets information

  The last icon opens the Key Manager.

  You may see other icons in the third group if you have installed other Microsoft Internet services, such as parts of the Microsoft Commercial Internet Systems (MCIS) platform. You may recall from Chapter 12 that Normandy is a set of Internet services that includes SMTP/POP3, NNTP News, Chat, Content Replicator, and Personalization servers.

  Now let's quickly review the different views of the ISM:

- The Report View shows a list computers, services, states of the service, and any comments that have been defined for each service. You may click on the headings in the columns to sort the lists. The status bar at the bottom shows the number of servers found and the number of services currently running.
- The Servers View is useful for sites with several IIS services running on the same NT Server. This view displays each Microsoft Internet service installed on the network. You can click the plus sign next to a given server to reveal the services it provides.
- The Services View shows Internet services by type. You may click on the plus sign next to a service to reveal which servers are running that service. The Service View is useful for networks where IIS services are distributed among several different NT Servers.

  Each service controlled with the ISM has the same basic set of properties available for configuration. To examine any of the properties of a particular service, simply double-click on that service in the list. Doing so presents four basic tabs — Service, Directories, Logging, and Advanced — with particular sets of properties; remember, though, that these tabs can vary from service to service. Later in this chapter, we look at the properties of MPS you can configure, but for now, let's quickly review the four basic tabs.

- The Service tab contains the TCP port for the service, the Connection Timeout setting for each connection to the service, the setting for the Maximum Connections allowed to the service, the parameters for the Anonymous Logon account, the Password Authentication type to be used with the service, and a brief descriptive comment.

- The Directory tab lists the directories used by the service. Each service presents a different specific dialog box that corresponds to the way the service uses the directory settings.

- The Logging tab lets you specify how service logging is performed for each service individually. You should always enable some level of logging for your services to ensure you have the information you need to analyze security aspects of these services. *Remember, most break-ins occur on systems that are not monitored closely enough.* You have two basic means of logging at your disposal: Log to File and Log to SQL/ODBC Database. Each has its own merits. Logging to a file writes all log information to a standard text file using a standard layout for each record. Logging to a database writes log information to the database of your choice, which gives you a greater degree of control over how you can analyze the data.

- The Advanced tab gives you control over access to your services by granting or denying access based on the client IP address. This page also lets you set the maximum amount of bandwidth used by your installed Internet services.

ADVANCED MPS CONFIGURATION

Now that we've taken a close look at the basic installation of MPS and quickly reviewed the ISM, let's take an in-depth look at some of the details of configuring MPS once it has been installed. Go over this section thoroughly before putting MPS into service on your network.

Configuring the Proxy Server Component

You recall from Chapter 13 that MPS's proxy server component is the heart of MPS; it controls access to Web, FTP, and gopher sites. You manage the MPS through the ISM, so start up the ISM. If you have other Internet services installed on your NT machine, you'll see them in the ISM display. The configuration settings are on a set of tabs for each individual service. To display the tabs for a particular service, you can either double-click the service name in the ISM or right-click the service name and select Service Properties. The tabs for the proxy server component (Figure 15.7) are Service, Permissions, Caching, Logging, and Filters. Let's look at the individual settings on these pages.

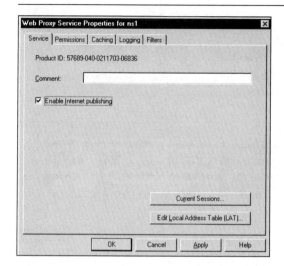

Figure 15.7
Proxy Service Tab

The Service tab in Figure 15.7 is for information only. It contains nothing to configure beyond a comment field; the text in the comment field appears in the ISM. Clicking Current Sessions displays a list of the users connected to the Proxy service at any given moment.

The Permissions tab, shown in Figure 15.8, lets you grant or deny the right to use the proxy server component for Internet access to various users and groups. You can manage three types of access here — FTP, WWW, and Gopher.

Figure 15.8
Permissions Tab

To allow access to a particular service, first select that service in the Rights list, then click Add. You will see the familiar Add Users and Groups dialog box, where you can make selections. After you have added the users and groups you wish to grant access, click OK to close the dialog box. To revoke access rights to a user or group, select the user or group in the window and click Remove.

Tip

You can use the User Manager for Domains to create a group containing the user accounts of all users who need access to WWW, FTP, or Gopher. Then you set permission for each service only once for the entire group, rather than for each individual member. This feature can be a real time saver!

The Caching tab, shown in Figure 15.9, presents the cache property settings. You can configure the service to store Internet objects on your local hard drive for a period of time, which can greatly reduce response times and bandwidth utilization. The cache has two modes of operation: passive and active. In passive mode, MPS copies each object requested from the Internet to the hard disk of the computer running the MPS Server. In active mode, MPS updates objects in the cache periodically, whether a user requests them or not.

Figure 15.9

Caching Tab

[Screenshot: Web Proxy Service Properties for ns1 dialog box, Caching tab selected (Service, Permissions, Caching, Logging, Filters tabs). Enable Caching checked. Cache Expiration Policy slider from "Always request updates" to "Fewest Internet requests". Enable Active Caching checked, with slider from "Most client cache hits" to "Fewest Internet requests". Cache Size section showing Total Cache: 50 MB and Change Cache Size button. Reset Defaults and Advanced buttons. OK, Cancel, Apply, Help buttons.]

You can configure five settings for the Proxy cache:

• The Enable Caching check box enables and disables the cache.

- The Cache Expiration Policy setting lets you adjust the freshness of objects stored in the cache. Freshness is a measure of how long a copy of an object in the cache is stored and used before it is updated from the original Web site. Use the slider bar to adjust this setting. Moving the slider bar toward "Always request updates" keeps objects fresher but increases the amount of traffic the MPS server generates. Moving the slider bar toward "Fewest Internet requests" lengthens the amount of time objects are stored before they are refreshed but decreases the amount of traffic the MPS server generates.

- The Enable Active Caching setting ensures the freshness of Internet objects stored on the hard disk by letting the cache manager generate its own request for an Internet object without a prompt from a client. Move the slider bar toward "Most client cache hits" to update the cache more frequently. Move the slider bar toward "Fewest Internet requests" to reduce the frequency of update requests to Internet sites.

- The Cache Size setting lets you add and remove disk drives from caching and set the amount of disk space used for caching Internet objects.

- The Advanced button displays Advanced Cache Options, which let you specify which objects are to be cached, specify the maximum object size to cache, enable server protection, and enable cache filtering. Cache filtering lets you select, by file name, directory name, and domain name, the objects that are always or never cached.

The Logging tab (Figure 15.10) lets you turn logging on or off, select regular logging or verbose logging, and determine whether your data is logged to a text file or a database. Each log record contains the user name, client type, client protocol, time and date stamp, and size of the requested object.

Figure 15.10
Logging Tab

The Filters tab, shown in Figure 15.11, presents the filtering properties that give you control over access to Internet sites through the server.

Figure 15.11
Filters Tab

The filtering mechanism works by granting or denying access based on the IP address or domain name of particular Internet sites. For example, to block access to particular web sites, select Denied, click Add, select Domain, and then type the web address to which you want to prevent access. That's all there is to it.

Remote Windows Sockets Service

Now let's take a look at the Remote Windows Sockets (RWS) service. The RWS is a mechanism that makes a Windows Sockets-compatible application running on an private network perform as if it were directly connected to the Internet, when a gateway computer actually connects the two networks. In this case, the gateway is the MPS.

To get to the set of configurable properties for the RWS, follow the same steps as for the Web proxy server: open ISM and double-click on the RWS service. You can choose from five tabs: Service, Protocols, Permissions, Logging, and Filters. Let's look at each tab.

The Service tab, shown in Figure 15.12, has only a comment field where you define a description of this service that is visible in ISM.

The Protocols tab, as seen in Figure 15.13, allows you to add, delete, and modify custom protocol settings. Quite a few popular protocols are already configured, and you will likely add more as more interesting Internet tools become available. You control the list with the Add, Edit, and Delete buttons.

Figure 15.12
Service Tab

Figure 15.13
Protocols Tab

The Permissions tab, shown in Figure 15.14, has many configuration possibilities. You can add, change, and remove protocols and control who has access to each protocol. This tab has the following elements:

• The Service element lists the Internet protocols available to RWS users on this server. To add a protocol to this list, click Protocols and complete the dialog box that appears. To grant a user access to a protocol, select that

Figure 15.14

Permissions Tab

protocol from the Service box, click Add, and complete the dialog box that appears. In that dialog box, the box on the right lists the users and groups that are permitted to use the protocol on this server.

- The Add button lets you grant a user or group the right to use a protocol. First select the protocol from the Services box, choose Add, and then complete the Add Users and Groups dialog box that appears.
- The Remove button removes a user or group granted the right to use a protocol on this server.
- The Protocols button displays a dialog box that lets you add a protocol, modify an existing protocol configuration, or remove a protocol altogether.

The Logging tab (Figure 15.15) gives you the same options as the Logging tab for the proxy server component. It lets you turn logging on or off, select regular logging or verbose logging, and select whether your data is logged to a text file or a database.

The Filters tab, shown in Figure 15.16, lets you grant and deny access to Internet sites that are accessible through the RWS. You can use filters to prevent access to specified sites or to allow access to only the sites specified. The filtering applies to all users who access the Internet through the RWS service on this server.

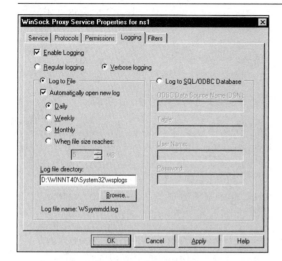

Figure 15.15
Logging Tab

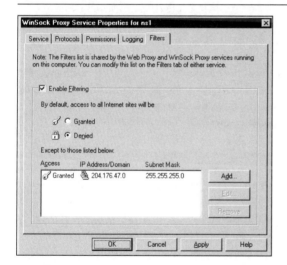

Figure 15.16
Filters Tab

Configuring the Proxy and RWS to Work Together

You can configure the proxy server component and RWS to work together, which lets you use IPX/SPX on your internal network. This feature eases integration for Novell shops because they don't have to migrate to TCP/IP. Having the Proxy and RWS work together also lets you use streaming and datagram Internet protocols as well as the Windows NT Challenge/Response authentication between the client and MPS Server.

To configure the proxy server component to work with RWS, follow these simple steps:

1. Configure the client's Internet browser to use the MPS proxy server component.

2. Configure the client computer to use any RWS server on the internal network.

3. If the private network is running TCP/IP, use MPS setup to configure the Local Address Table (LAT) to remove the Proxy server's internal IP address from the LAT, which forces the use of RWS between the client and MPS server. The LAT must be modified on all MPS servers on the private network. If your internal network runs on IPX/SPX, you can skip this step because you won't have TCP/IP routing tables to manage.

Balancing Loads on Proxy Gateways in a DNS Environment

Using several proxy server gateways is becoming more common in large network environments. As the number of users that need Internet access grows, balancing loads on multiple proxy servers is increasingly important.

You balance your network traffic with MPS by creating a group name in your LMHOSTS file and assigning all client computer applications to this group. The group contains a list of all the machine names and IP addresses for each proxy server on your network. The LMHOSTS file includes sample entries that demonstrate how to create entries in to this file correctly. The following steps show how to create the balancing group in the LMHOSTS file.

1. Open LMHOSTS, located in SystemRoot\System32\Drivers\Etc. If you have not already configured an LMHOSTS file for use on your network, open the LMHOSTS.SAM sample file and save it in the same directory to a new file called LMHOSTS.

2. Create a new group name for the proxy servers that you want to participate in load-balancing. In this example, I'll use the name proxygate. Be sure the group name does not conflict with existing group names or NT domain names. Type the group name to make new proxy server entries, one per line, in the LMHOSTS file. The proxy denotes groups by looking at the #DOM tag at the end of each proxy server entry. Be sure that each proxy server's entry includes the IP address, the NetBIOS machine name, and the #DOM tag with the group name. See Figure 15.17 for an example of these entries in the LMHOSTS file.

   As the example shows, you can use the #PRE tag, which tells NT to preload these entries when the operating system boots up. Using #PRE

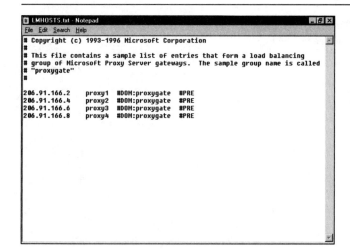

Figure 15.17
Sample LMHOSTS File

increases performance slightly because NT won't have to read and parse the file from disk each time it needs to access the information.

3. Save the file and exit the editor.

4. Configure your client software to use the new proxy group name.

That's all there is to it. When you use a group in the LMHOSTS file, client computers requesting an Internet object through the group name tell your DNS to cycle through the list of gateways in the group, one at a time. The first request uses the first entry in the list, the second request uses the second entry in the list, and so on. This cycle balances the load on the servers, easing the burden on any particular proxy server.

Balancing Proxy Loads in a WINS Environment

If your network relies on WINS instead of DNS for name resolution, you can use WINS to configure a multihomed environment to facilitate Internet object requests. This feature is similar to the DNS environment in that you create one entry that contains the list of IP addresses for all the proxy server gateways.

To establish a load-balanced environment using WINS,

1. Open the WINS Manager by clicking Start and selecting Programs, Administrative Tools, and WINS Manager from the subsequent menus.

2. Select Mappings and click Static Mappings. You see a dialog box similar to the one shown in Figure 15.18.

Figure 15.18
Static Mappings Dialog Box

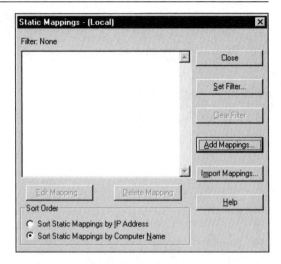

3. Click Add Mappings to call up the dialog box in Figure 15.19. Here, select Internet Group, which tells WINS you are creating a list of computers and their associated IP addresses.

Figure 15.19
Add Static Mappings
Dialog Box

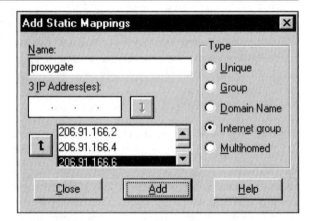

4. Type a name for the Internet Group. In this example we use "proxygate."
5. Type the IP addresses for each of the proxy servers that will participate in load balancing.
6. Click Add and then click Close. Your load balancing proxy group is now added, as shown in Figure 15.20.

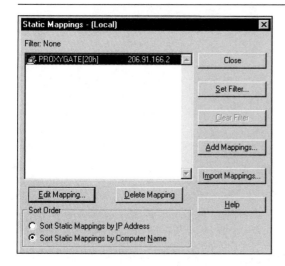

Figure 15.20
The "proxygate" Group

Now configure your client software to use this new group. You also need to make sure that those client workstations point to your WINS server in their TCP/IP protocol configurations. Without the WINS entry in the TCP/IP configuration, the clients won't be able to locate the load-balancing proxy server group.

In this configuration, WINS provides three levels of name resolution. First, the WINS server attempts to match a client's request with the client's IP address. Next, WINS seeks a proxy server on the same subnetwork as the client. Then WINS seeks a Proxy server on the same network as the client. If WINS cannot match a client to a gateway, it randomly picks a gateway from the WINS list of gateways to facilitate the Internet object request.

Load Balancing RWS with Multiple Gateways

By default, clients on the internal network use the RWS gateway that they were configured to use. You can balance the load by installing RWS on the clients from *each* of the gateways you want the client to use. For example, if you expect a particular group of users to produce heavier-than-normal traffic to the RWS service — as in the case of video conferencing — then distribute the users across all your gateways to lighten the load on any particular server.

SUMMARY

We have walked through the initial installation and preliminary configuration options and settings. From this exercise, you can see that setting up this security measure is easy and goes quickly. The complete Proxy Server package is not large and not complex to configure. The only tricks to installing MPS are listed in the pre-installation checklist at the beginning of this chapter. Be sure to review the list carefully each time you need to install MPS.

CHAPTER 16

PLANNING MPS CLIENT ROLLOUT AND SUPPORT

In this chapter, I address the client rollout and the support you need to give your users when they start using Microsoft Proxy Server (MPS). Besides explaining ways to handle the client rollout, I detail how to configure client software and the underlying network settings. I also discuss the importance of training your users, which makes using MPS easier for them and lightens the load on your help desk.

AUTOMATING THE CLIENT INSTALLATION

Most organizations implement many MPS clients; therefore, automating the installation process may be challenging but necessary. Although MPS clients are fairly simple to install, having different client platforms can make establishing different configurations more complex.

For example, with Unix clients, you need to configure only a proxy-compatible Web browser, but on Windows 95 clients, you may also need to install Winsock Proxy Service (WPS), depending on the functions you want the client to perform. If you are running IPX/SPX instead of TCP/IP, you need the Winsock client instead; it redirects Winsock calls that are not destined for your network to the proxy server, which in turn processes the request on behalf of the client.

In any event, several products can help on medium to large multiclient rollouts. One of the best tools is Microsoft's Systems Management Server (SMS). Let's look at it more closely now.

SYSTEMS MANAGEMENT SERVER

SMS can perform many useful tasks, one of which is the remote installation of software on multiple client computers, or *pushing out* software. To use SMS to push out client software, install a copy of the client software on an SMS server and create an SMS package to run the setup program on selected computers. An *SMS package* describes a set of files that install a program. SMS packages are placed in jobs, which are scheduled to run at certain times.

When it is installed, SMS inventories your network, so it already knows about potential client machines you have installed. You can choose the clients you want to install software on, and SMS keeps track those clients for you. SMS also includes a run-time version of Microsoft Test to help administrators implement packages using installation scripts. *Installation scripts* automate the execution of the install program. Keep in mind that to create install scripts, you must purchase a full retail version of Microsoft Test or use another scripting program such as Winbatch to perform the task for you.

WINBATCH

Winbatch, created by Wilson WindowWare, is a scripting language that can be used on all Windows operating systems. Besides simple file and program manipulation, Winbatch gives you the power to pause in the middle of a sequence of actions and display a status message or prompt a user to answer a question. Winbatch files can base decisions on items such as current system values or a user's response.

Winbatch lets you manipulate window size and location, make network connections, and perform math computations and string manipulation. Additionally, you can read and modify registry values and even see whether a mouse button or Shift key is being pressed.

In short, Winbatch gives you more than 500 features that let you control what scripts actually do, including push out MPS client software. For more information about Winbatch, see their Web site at http://www.windowware.com.

END-USER INSTALLATION

Your end users can install MPS clients if you wish. When you install MPS, it creates a shared directory on the server per your specification. It places the client software setup programs in this shared directory automatically, including only the selections you've chosen.

Once MPS installation is complete, users with access to the shared directory are free to install the software. The software can be installed in three ways.

- You may notify users that the new directory share is available and give them instructions for connecting to the share and installing the client package, explaining how to run Setup.exe.

- You may send users a default URL (created during the installation process) that helps guide them through the setup process. This default URL http://www.domain.com/msproxy, where www.domain.com is your MPS server's fully qualified domain name.

- You may use an automation package such as SMS to push the software out to the client workstations.

If users already have Web browsers installed, using the Web page as a guide is probably the better way to approach end-user installation because it offers the user a small amount of assistance that may curb calls to your help desk. If your users don't use Internet Explorer or Netscape Navigator, their Web browsers must support CERN-compatible proxy servers and need to be configured manually, specifying the MPS server name and port numbers.

MANUAL INSTALLATION

In some instances, you may need to install client software manually on each machine by simply running Setup.exe, located in the MPS client software directory. You can use several command-line switches when you're installing client software manually. Let's look at them now.

Keep in mind that all command-line switches are optional. The basic form of the command is as follows: setup [/r] [/u] [/q[1,t]].

- /r — Reinstalls the client. Note that you can't use the /r switch with 16-bit clients, such as computers running Microsoft Windows 3.1 or Windows for Workgroups (WfW).

- /u — Removes the client application but leaves shared components. Note that you can't use the /u switch with 16-bit clients, such as computers running Microsoft Windows 3.1 or WfW.

- /q — Runs the client setup program in quiet mode. The screen displays progress windows and a setup completion dialog box, but it doesn't prompt the user to approve or modify installation settings. Quiet setup always installs the client software into the default directory (Mspclnt), and you can use quiet mode only for an initial setup. If a client is already installed, you cannot reinstall or remove it using the /q option.

- /q1 — Same as /q, but it also hides the setup completion dialog box.

- /qt — Same as /q, but it also hides the progress windows and completion dialog box. After the installation is complete, the client computer is restarted if necessary.

To install the client software manually from a shared directory on a server, connect to the server's Mspclnt share and run the setup program with any of these command line switches.

CONFIGURING CLIENT SOFTWARE

Let's look at configuring some of the more popular client software packages that you might use with MPS. You'll see that configuring any proxy-enabled client software for MPS is straightforward, once you know and understand the fundamental parameters.

Before we get too far, you should know that if you've created a load-balanced environment as described in Chapter 15, you need to use the group name as the client's proxy server name. If you don't want a particular client software package to use the load-balancing group, simply configure that client software with the proxy server name that you want it to use instead.

In some cases, you may need to bypass the proxy server altogether to reach a certain Internet site if that site is behind a firewall. A proxy running on a host server *outside* a firewall cannot connect to a server *inside* the firewall.

To work around this firewall restriction, you must bypass the proxy to access the system.

If your network uses nonroutable IP addresses, you won't be able to bypass the proxy to reach sites on the Internet, because your network has no valid routes in and out. However, you can still reach sites on your local network if your administrator establishes the proper routes. When configuring your proxy server and clients, it's probably a good idea to use routable IP addresses instead of nonroutable ones to help you avoid unnecessary headaches down the road.

The Web browser is probably the most common type of client software used on the Internet today. Let's walk through configuring two of the more popular Web browsers on the market — Internet Explorer and Netscape Navigator. We also look at RealAudio, a popular live audio software tool.

INTERNET EXPLORER 3.0X

Configuring Internet Explorer 3.0x for Windows 95 and Windows NT is straightforward. Follow these simple steps to get to the MPS Settings:

1. Click Start.
2. Select Settings.
3. Select Control Panel.
4. Double-click the Internet icon.
5. Select the Connection tab.
6. Choose "Connect Through a Proxy Server."
7. Click Settings.

The MPS Settings dialog box is shown in Figure 16.1. Figure 16.1 has two boxes: Servers and Exceptions. In the Servers options group, you can type addresses for each of the following protocol types: HTTP, Secure, FTP, Gopher, and Socks. You can define a different proxy server for each of these Internet protocols. Just type the appropriate proxy server information in the associated fields.

If you prefer to use a single proxy or group of proxies for all protocol types, check "Use the same proxy server for all protocols." When you check this box, you can type an address in only the HTTP fields. Type the proxy server or proxy group's URL and port number in the appropriate HTTP fields.

You can configure two settings in the Exceptions box. If you want certain protocols to bypass your proxy server — providing a direct connection instead — type them in the "Do not use proxy server for addresses beginning with"

Figure 16.1
*Proxy Server Settings
Dialog Box*

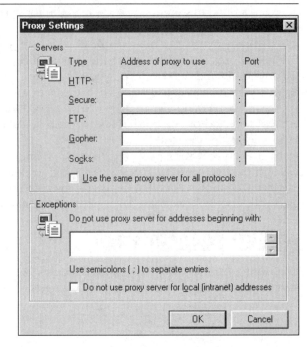

Special Note

Even though you type the information into the HTTP fields, the proxy server uses these settings to process all other protocol requests.

field. For example, if you want all FTP connections to bypass the proxy server, type **ftp** in the box provided. Separate all entries in this box by semicolons.

Check the second option in the Exceptions box, "Do not use proxy server for local (intranet) addresses," to tell the client software to connect directly to servers on your intranet, bypassing the proxy. Checking this box can improve the performance of client software packages because it removes the added overhead of communicating with the Internet Access Server. MPS uses IP addresses and subnet masks to determine whether the destination is local.

NETSCAPE COMMUNICATOR 4.0

Configuring the Netscape Communicator proxy is also straightforward. Follow the steps below to begin configuration:

1. Open Netscape Navigator.

2. From the Edit menu, select Preferences.

3. In the left pane, click the plus sign next to the Advanced label to expand the menu.

4. In the left pane, select Proxies, which changes the dialog box in the right pane.

5. Select Manual Proxy Configuration and click View to display the dialog box in Figure 16.2.

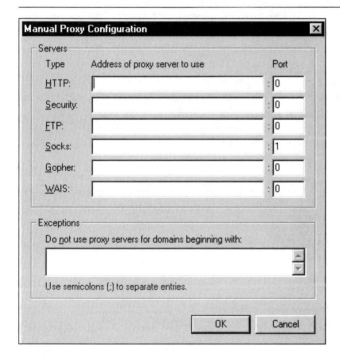

Figure 16.2
Netscape Manual Proxy Configuration Dialog Box

Now that you're in the proper dialog box, you simply type the host name or IP address of the computer running the proxy server and its port number in each proxy field (HTTP, Security, FTP, Socks, Gopher, and WAIS). In the "Do not use proxy servers for domains beginning with" field at the bottom of the dialog box, type addresses for hosts that you want to access directly, bypassing the proxy server. For example, if you want Navigator 4.0 to connect directly to Netscape's public Web server, type **http://www/netscape.com:80**. As always, be sure to insert a colon before the port number.

REALAUDIO

RealAudio is a popular software tool that is widely used to deliver all sorts of creative audio content across the Internet, ranging from live radio broadcasts to recorded speeches or mission statements from corporate executives.

MPS supports RealAudio through the Winsock Proxy Server (WPS) service, but it's more complicated to configure than a simple Web browser. To configure the RealAudio Player software, you must understand how data moves across the Internet.

RealAudio supports two basic types of transmissions: TCP and UDP. I won't go into all the details of these two protocols, but briefly, UDP is less reliable than TCP. UDP provides no error correction and no guarantee that UDP packets arrive at their intended destination. When UDP packets do arrive at their destination, they do not necessarily arrive in the order you send them. However, UDP requires less overhead than TCP and is therefore faster.

Some networks incorporate a separate packet-filtering firewall system, in addition to a proxy server, that may not let UDP traffic enter your intranet. In these cases, you must either reconfigure your packet-filtering firewall to allow UDP packets for RealAudio or reconfigure RealAudio to use TCP. The choice is simply a network administration decision.

Here, I focus on configuring RealAudio to be used with WPS and UDP. Because WPS handles all Winsock applications transparently, you do not need to configure RealAudio to use the proxy server. Be sure the proxy server is disabled in the RealAudio preference settings.

To configure the RealAudio Player to receive audio with UDP protocol (the default), follow these steps:

1. Start RealAudio Player.
2. From the View menu, choose Preferences.
3. Select the Network tab, which displays the dialog box in Figure 16.3.
4. Select UDP.
5. Next, select the Proxy tab, which displays the Proxy properties page.
6. Clear the Use Proxy field.

The "Use Specified UDP Port" setting on the Network tab defines a port number that the WPS service uses to receive RealAudio data. If you use this setting, it must match the setting on the WPS service, which you configure using ISM; the setting is on the WPS Permissions tab.

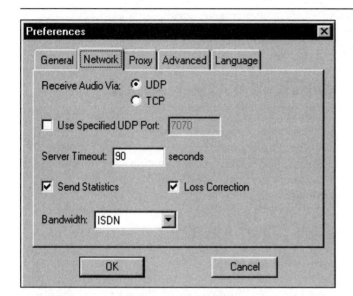

Figure 16.3
RealAudio Preferences
Dialog Box

MACINTOSH, UNIX, AND OTHER CLIENTS

You can configure other types of operating system clients to use MPS as easily as in the examples above. You can configure any software that can use a proxy server (or software that is Winsock compatible) to use MPS. All you need are a few simple parameters, including the name of the computer running MPS and the port number for the particular protocol you want to support.

WINDOWS CLIENTS

If the client installation goes well, you should not need to configure anything else — MPS setup creates a file, Mspc1nt.ini, and the options you specify in the Client Configuration dialog box in the server setup are placed in this file. When the setup program is run from a client, this file is copied to the client.

CLIENTS ON THE PROXY SERVER

Using a proxy-enabled client such as a Web browser on the MPS server itself requires a slightly different configuration when defining the MPS server name. Instead of using the computer name to point to the proxy gateway, you must use the IP address of the actual network card in the MPS server that has the direct connection to the Internet. This change is necessary because the Local

Access Table MPS uses shouldn't have an entry for this IP address. If you do use the machine name instead of the IP address, you'll get an "Access is Denied" error message.

PROXY CONFIGURATION ON IPX-ONLY CLIENTS

Problems can arise when you try to run a proxy client on systems using only IPX/SPX if that system is configured to use the MPS server name instead of the MPS server's IP address. To avoid this situation, be sure to use the server's IP address. Also, if you're using a load-balancing configuration, you must manually balance your IPX/SPX clients by assigning each to a server based on your judgment of each server's load.

LOGONS WITH 16-BIT CLIENT SOFTWARE

When you use 16-bit proxy client software on systems running Windows 95 and WfW, a Domain Credentials dialog box may appear. This dialog box requests the domain name, user name, and password. Typing this information allows the connection to be completed.

TRAINING, DOCUMENTATION, AND SUPPORT

Besides showing your users what to do when it comes to using a proxy server, it is important that you also explain why the proxy is used that way. Many situations requiring slight adjustments may arise. For example, if your users use laptops at home with a dial-up account through an ISP, they must reconfigure their browser to not use a proxy server, or it simply won't work correctly for them. These specialized situations can lead to a higher volume of technical support calls to your help desk if you don't address them up front.

Documentation is very important in all aspects of a networking environment, including MPS client software. After you decide how to roll out the clients on your particular network, document the procedure — don't wait until later to do it, because invariably you'll forget something that you didn't annotate completely or thoroughly.

In addition to documentation, you should give your users some level of training before sending them off on their own. Again, a little training helps relieve the burden on the help desk by reducing the number of user calls. For your users who travel with laptops, document the subtle yet important changes they need to make to the system configuration and let them make those changes themselves. Consider walking users through the reconfiguration process the first time so they know the ropes.

Having policies in place that govern what types of software may be used, and by whom, also eases the burden on the help desk. Many software packages come out each month, and it is hard to resist trying some of them. Users may not understand that your network has certain blocks in place to regulate traffic in and out of the Internet, and thus they may not comprehend why a particular software package isn't working. Invariably these users call the help desk asking for assistance. Documenting this information beforehand and making sure users know and understand it curbs these calls.

Most situations that cause users to call for help using MPS can be avoided by simply training the users on usage, policies, and procedures.

SUMMARY

In this chapter, we covered a lot of client software configuration, which is a large part of the support process. You learned how to pre-configure the client software and several ways to install the client software. You've also learned how to configure some of the more popular software packages that you're likely to use with MPS, including some of the needs of specialized proxy clients. You also learned how to curb the number of help desk calls you're likely to face when installing any new software package, including MPS. In Chapter 17 we look at troubleshooting, monitoring, and maintaining the MPS server itself.

CHAPTER 17

MPS TROUBLESHOOTING, MONITORING, AND MAINTENANCE

In this chapter we discuss troubleshooting, monitoring, and maintaining your Microsoft Proxy Server (MPS) servers. For the most part, proxy servers are simple to install, operate, and maintain, but this chapter alerts you to a few problems and gives you tips to make your tasks simpler. We look at some of the more common problems you may run into and the methods and tools available for monitoring these servers. We also explore important items to remember during your maintenance routines.

TROUBLESHOOTING MPS

If you carefully plan and execute the installation of your MPS, you shouldn't see many problems. In this section, I talk about some of the more common items that may cause you trouble, but keep in mind that Microsoft's documentation (included with MPS) on troubleshooting is extensive and very inclusive. Therefore, instead of repeating the documentation, I focus on some of the more common problems you're likely to experience in everyday use.

PROXY SERVER ACCESS PERMISSIONS

Traffic running in and out of the Proxy Server is regulated by the permissions settings that grant and deny access to specific users. By default, MPS installs itself, allowing only the Administrator access to the particular supported protocols. When you're ready to let other users start using the MPS server, be sure to add each user to each service you want to grant access to.

Remember that users are expected to authenticate with MPS unless you have selected Allow Anonymous users, which I don't recommend. When this setting is enabled, all client applications use it and no user is forced to authenticate with MPS. In other words, enabling Anonymous logins circumvents all access permissions.

WEB SERVER DOCUMENT ROOT

If you are running MPS on top of a live IIS Web site and you move your root document directory to another network drive while MPS is running, you may experience a server error. The error is generated because MPS is running and doesn't obtain the dynamic changes to the Web document root directory.

You can avoid this problem by one of the following methods:

- Map the network drive to a drive letter, and use that drive letter to specify a root document location.
- Create a virtual directory to the new document root and use that name instead.

In either case, after making the change, you may need to stop and restart MPS for the changes to be seen by the proxy server.

WINSOCK PROXY

A common problem I see occurs when an internal subnet is not reachable through a Winsock Proxy client application. This problem is usually caused by problems in the Local Address Table (LAT). Some companies put their LAT on a separate network system instead of on their actual MPS servers for better performance or easier management. Although this layout works well, it creates a dependency that it is easy to forget about.

LATs are automatically updated by MPS *if they reside on the MPS server itself.* If the LATs do not reside on an MPS server, they must be managed and updated manually. Remember that MPS clients refresh their LATs periodically and automatically. Adding new addresses to your network can immediately generate a problem when clients can't perform some action through the MPS server. Invariably, the problem is caused by the fact that these new addresses are not properly indicated in the LAT.

If you want to locate your LAT on some other server, plan for and schedule adjustments to the LAT when necessary.

WINSOCK PROXY DIAGNOSTIC UTILITY

When you install an MPS client, a Winsock Proxy Diagnostic Utility is automatically installed into the Mspclnt directory on the client. This program contains configuration information that can be helpful in isolating certain problems. On systems using 32-bit operating systems, such as Windows 95 and Windows NT, this program is called Chkwsp32.exe, and on 16-bit operating systems, such as WfW, this program is called Chkwsp16.exe.

To use the Winsock Proxy Diagnostic Utility most effectively, run it from a DOS command prompt with the -f switch, which tells the program to print all diagnostic information on the screen. The ensuing output resembles the following:

```
*** Winsock Proxy Diagnostic Information **** CONFIGURATION:
Winsock Proxy Service - Configuration Location: C:\mspclnt\
Proxy Name (IP Addr): 207.91.166.199
SERVERNAME: LIASON
IP: Installed
IPX: Not Installed

16-bit RWS CLIENT:
Winsock Name: C:\WINDOWS\winsock.dll
Version: 1.0.193.4
Description: Microsoft Remote Windows Socket 16-Bit DLL
```

```
32-bit WSP CLIENT:
Winsock Name: C:\WINDOWS\SYSTEM\wsock32.dll
Version: 1.0.193.4
Description: Microsoft Remote Windows Socket 32-Bit DLL
Version Type: FREE
Client version of control protocol: 9

WSP SERVER:
Testing against server: 1.1.1.1 (SERVERNAME)
Version: 1.0.193.4
Version Type: FREE
Server version of control protocol: 9
Windows version: 4.0
Windows build number: 1381
Client control protocol version MATCHES the server
    control protocol
```

Notice that in the last group of parameters displayed, the WSP server performs a basic test and displays whether control protocol versions match. In some cases, new software installations may inadvertently overwrite Winsock DLLs, which can lead to problems when using MPS because control protocols will no longer match. To correct the problem, you need to copy the correct version to the client.

MOBILE USERS

As I've said before, mobile users encounter problems when trying to use their proxy-enabled systems through a non-proxied network, such as those found at ISPs. When users connect their portable computers to a proxied network, everything works fine. But when they take the machine home or on the road and use it to connect to an ISP, they find that almost nothing works correctly. The reason is that the machine is configured to use a proxy server.

The simple way to correct the situation is to disable the proxy server setting using the Internet Control Panel applet. Simply open the applet, click the Connections tab, and clear the "Connect through proxy server" box.

When users return to the office network (or proxied network) they need to go back to the Internet Control Panel applet and re-check that same box. Simply training users to adjust the setting greatly reduces the strain on your help desk and ensures that your users are equipped with the information they need to work with MPS efficiently.

USING APPLICATIONS

Another source of confusion for MPS users is attempting to run a Winsock application for the first time using the proxy server. Each time a new Winsock application is launched without some other previously used Winsock application running, it prompts the user for credentials.

Tell your users to type their username, password, etc., and click OK to continue. I know this advice seems obvious, but believe me, I have taken too many support calls about this question. Sending a simple memo to the users (and incorporating this procedure into the training class) reduces the volume of calls right away.

PERFORMANCE PROBLEMS

From time to time, you may experience what appear to be performance problems. Many variables contribute to overall performance, but in my experience, one problem in particular arises more often than others.

The LAT stores the IP address of all internal systems so that proxy clients can connect to those systems directly on your internal network. If a machine is not in the LAT, proxy clients attempt to use the MPS server to make the connection, which slows performance by introducing another step in the connection process.

If performance is slow for requests from Winsock Proxy clients to any particular servers on your private network, check that the IP addresses of those servers are included in the LAT. Again, remember that the information in the LAT identifies the range of IP addresses of your private network. If an internal server is not listed in the LAT, Winsock Proxy clients redirect their connections to it through MPS, slowing down the overall process.

MONITORING YOUR MPS SYSTEMS

Monitoring your network and its services is one of the most important tasks you can perform to improve your network security. You can monitor your MPS systems in several ways. This section outlines some of the tools you can use and what they reveal.

NT SERVER MANAGER

The NT Server Manager or Server Manager for Domains gives you a 10,000-foot view of the NT system running MPS. It also gives you a fairly good look at who's currently using the MPS server. Server Manager is available for Windows 95 and Windows NT and is installed by default on NT systems. You start the Server Manager on NT by clicking Start, selecting Programs, and choosing Administrative Tools. Then click Server Manager.

After the server manager starts, you see a list of NT systems in your domain and can view various aspects of those systems. To see installed services on an MPS system, click an MPS server, then choose Services from the Computer menu. You see the standard NT-style Services dialog box, where you can adjust properties and start and stop the services.

To see who is currently using a particular MPS server, double-click on that server. You see the properties dialog box, as shown in Figure 17.1.

Figure 17.1
Properties Dialog Box

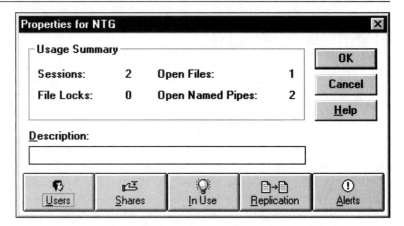

To see which users are connected to the server, click Users, which displays the User Sessions dialog box (Figure 17.2).

Figure 17.2
User Sessions Dialog Box

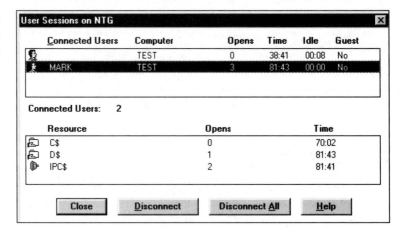

You may disconnect a user by clicking on a user and clicking Disconnect. To disconnect all users, simply click Disconnect All.

You may also send a message to all users connected to an MPS machine with this Server Manager interface, but keep in mind that you must have set up and be running the Alerter and Messenger services to send the message successfully. This feature can be handy when you need to perform some type of emergency change or announce upcoming maintenance. To send users a message, select the computer and choose Send Message from the Computer menu. The dialog box shown in Figure 17.3 appears; simply type a message and click OK to send it.

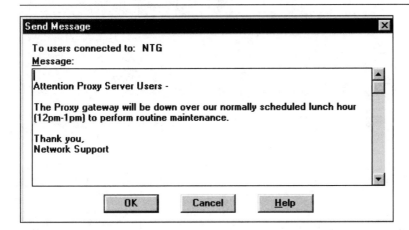

Figure 17.3
Send Message Dialog Box

NT NETWORK MONITOR

The Microsoft NT Network Monitor is a network packet analyzer that captures, filters, and analyzes network traffic. The Network Monitor lets you capture packets from the network; display, filter, and edit them; and transmit them back to the network.

The Network Monitor, shown in Figure 17.4, is a basic part of SMS and Windows NT Server, but the NT version is limited compared to the SMS version. The version that ships with NT captures only those packets that are destined for or generated by the computer it runs on. Therefore, if you want to use the NT version of Network Monitor to troubleshoot MPS, you need to run it on that particular MPS system. On the other hand, if your shop has SMS installed, you may use the SMS version of Network Monitor to inspect MPS traffic from any network location you choose.

Packet sniffers are handy tools capable of copying packets from the network for closer examination. You may need to capture packets to help find

Figure 17.4

NT Network Monitor

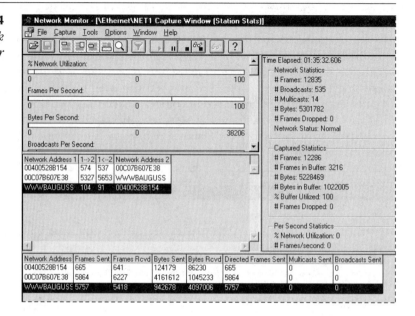

the root of a problem, especially on a larger network, where traveling to a user's workspace is time-consuming. For example, if the user has an IP address not listed in the LAT, you may discover this problem after capturing packets destined for the MPS server, at which point you can see the source IP address and compare it to the LAT. Figure 17.5 shows a list of packets grabbed with the Network Monitor.

PERFORMANCE MONITOR

NT comes with a nice tool, Performance Monitor, that gives you a look at system performance characteristics. MPS offers three sets of performance counters that you can use with Performance Monitor to trace particular characteristics.

- Web Proxy Server Cache — counters specific to URL caching performed by the Web Proxy service
- Web Proxy Server Service — counters specific to the Web Proxy Server service
- Winsock Proxy Server — counters specific to the Winsock Proxy Server service

Performance may be an issue on larger networks in particular, and using this tool may help isolate the problem. Determining whether your network is large or small in relation to MPS is really a matter of comparison between your

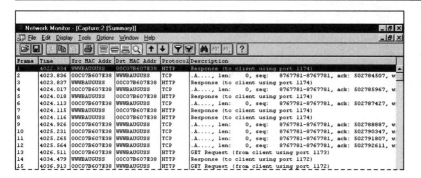

Figure 17.5
*Network
Monitor
Capture
Summary*

MPS server's performance capabilities and the amount of traffic it is serving. As such, making this determination is truly a matter of feel. In any case, if you think the MPS system is not performing as best it could, using Performance Monitor in conjunction with those MPS objects you can monitor can help reveal any existing problems.

Figure 17.6 shows the Performance Monitor tracking performance statistics for an MPS system.

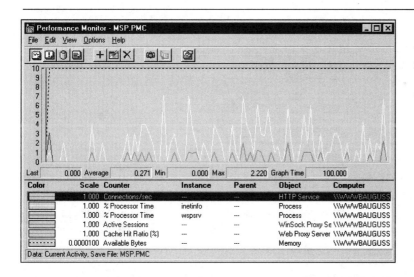

Figure 17.6
*Performance
Monitor
Watching an
MPS System*

This particular chart shows several characteristics of the MPS, including connections per second, processor time, active sessions, cache hit ratio, and available bytes of memory. It's easy to see through the statistics that this particular MPS server is using all its available memory, which could be dragging down performance.

SNMP MONITORING

If your shop uses Simple Network Management Protocol (SNMP) monitoring, you can use the SNMP Management Information Base (MIB) files provided with MPS to enable SNMP monitoring for the Web and Winsock Proxy services.

The MIB for the Web Proxy service is called W3p.mib; the MIB file for Winsock Proxy service monitoring is called Wsp.mib. Remember, the setup program does not install these files on the MPS server; however, you can find them on the MPS CD-ROM in the Perfctrs directory under the proper processor type (e.g., DEC Alpha MIBs are under Alpha\Perfctrs).

As with any SNMP-enabled device, using these MIB files with an SNMP monitor requires that you first compile them with the MIB compiler that comes with your SNMP software. The SNMP service uses Object Identifiers (OIDs) for MIB processing. The OID for W3p.mib is 11, and the OID for Wsp.mib is 12.

Besides compiling the MIB files, you must also start the Web Proxy service and the Winsock Proxy service before configuring and starting the Windows NT SNMP service on the computer running MPS. After you start the SNMP service on both the remote SNMP monitoring computer and the local MPS computer, you can use any SNMP monitoring software (such as NTManage) to monitor MPS services.

Keep in mind that SNMP can represent a security risk to your network if you don't configure it correctly. Be sure to understand Microsoft's SNMP service. Probably the most important action you can take is changing the default community names to something obscure, because the default community names are well known and intruders can use them easily to find critical system information, such as your routing tables.

EVENT LOGS AND OTHER LOGS

The standard Windows NT Event Log receives various messages from MPS servers. These messages can be any of the three allowable types of messages: Application, Security, and System. Typically these messages pertain to MPS services themselves, not to the overall operation of the system. One exception is when a user is being incorrectly authenticated, which is revealed in the Security Event Log.

Both Winsock Proxy Service and the Web Proxy Service can log to separate log files — separate from each other and separate from the standard NT Event Logs. I covered how to configure logs during installation and configuration in Chapter 15. At this point, let's take a look at what those logs contain.

In either log (Winsock Proxy or Web Proxy), each record contains the user name, client type, client protocol, time and date stamp, and size of the requested object. Let's look at a Winsock Proxy Server log entry:

```
200.200.200.128, MJE, -, N, 3/19/97, 6:17:30, 2, -, -,
    news.ntsecurity.net, -, -, -, -, -, -, -, -, -, -,
    Unknown, 0
```

This entry shows that a client, whose user name is MJE, accessed the server from an IP address of 200.200.200.128 on March 19, 1997 at 6:17 a.m. The user MJE accessed a system called news.ntsecurity.net. Next, you see several dashes in lieu of data. Not all object requests generate information for all possible log fields.

Now, let's look at a sample entry from the Web Proxy Server:

```
200.200.200.10, anonymous, Mozilla/2.0 (compatible; MSIE
    3.0B; Win32), N, 3/24/97, 12:15:25, W3Proxy, WWWBAU-
    GUSS, -, www.microsoft.com, -, 80, 941, 445, 453,
    http, tcp, GET, http://www.ntsecurity.net/ntis.gif,
    image/gif, Inet, 200
```

This entry includes more information than the Winsock Proxy Server entry. It reveals that an anonymous user using Internet Explorer 3.0b sent a Web request for an image called ntis.gif located at http://www.ntsecurity.net and that the request was successful. It also reveals that the transport used was HTTP over TCP and that the transaction took approximately 941 milliseconds, sending 445 bytes and receiving 453 bytes.

For a complete explanation of each possible log entry field, see the documentation accompanying MPS.

MAINTAINING MPS SYSTEMS

A proper maintenance routine for MPS does not have to be complex. However, the larger the network, the more strenuous your maintenance plans may be. In any event, MPS is a simple network service to maintain.

I've outlined some of the more important maintenance tasks below. Consider each one carefully to see whether it applies to your environment.

- Check the permission settings for all users and limit the membership of groups used to provide proxy access.
- Check any shared directory permissions on MPS systems for proper configuration.

- Archive log files either during your routine backups or through a special process you establish for this task. Keep your logs for some standard time period in case you need to refer to them. I recommend keeping at least a full month of logs.

- Check the network adapter bindings on MPS systems to ensure they remain as you've set them.

- Make sure IP forwarding remains disabled on MPS systems. Remember that if you install the Remote Access Service (RAS), IP forwarding is enabled and you must disable it after completing the RAS installation.

- Use data collected from Performance Monitor to see what upgrades or adjustments you want to make to a particular MPS server.

- Adjust bandwidth settings on your MPS servers as necessary, depending on user loads.

- Check the usefulness of your cache settings by examining Performance Monitor statistics and adjust the settings as necessary. In some cases, you may be able to reclaim unnecessarily allocated disk space. Remember that caching increases performance and reduces bandwidth use significantly. Performance Monitor can provide numerous useful statistics on cache operation, including the total number of bytes retrieved from the cache and the most frequently used URL in the cache.

- Check Microsoft's Proxy Server Web site (http://www.microsoft.com/proxy) for new patches, fixes, updates, and other useful information. New developments are likely to be revealed here first.

SUMMARY

In this chapter, we discuss some of the more common problems you're likely to encounter while using MPS and ways to correct those problems. You also learned several ways of monitoring various aspects and characteristics of MPS systems and several key items about proper Proxy Server maintenance.

APPENDIX A

OUT-OF-THE-BOX NT SECURITY CHECKLIST

This appendix helps you strengthen your out-of-the-box security with Windows NT systems. Although it doesn't contain everything you could possibly consider, it does serve as a great way to get started. Performing the recommended actions in this appendix will definitely leave you with a much safer NT system.

This checklist was compiled by Rob Davis with the help and advice of several other people, as well as information found on Microsoft's Web site. Thanks to everyone who contributed towards this effort.

INTRODUCTION

As you know, Microsoft's Windows NT operating system provides several security features. However, the default out-of-the-box configuration is highly relaxed, especially on the Workstation product, and you really should tighten it further upon installation.

As you have learned in this book, one particular installation's security requirements can differ significantly from another. Therefore, you should evaluate your particular environment and requirements before implementing a security configuration. Remember here that implementing security settings can affect system configuration. Certain applications installed on Windows NT may require more relaxed settings to function properly because of the nature of the product. You are therefore advised to carefully evaluate any recommendations in the context of your system configurations and usage.

If you install a Windows NT machine as a Web server or a firewall, you should definitely tighten up the security on that box. A system exposed to an untrusted network, such as the Internet, is more likely to be attacked than those that are not.

Although this checklist cannot be implemented in its entirety on all systems, it does offer some sound advice in a consolidated resource for many system configurations. Let's begin by going over some physical security items to check, and then proceed to harden the operating system itself.

Reminder

After you've finished securing your system, be sure to update your Emergency Repair Disk(s) in case you need them.

PHYSICAL SECURITY CONSIDERATIONS

Let's start with physical security, because it's equally important in the grand scheme of things. With physical security issues, use common sense and take the same precautions you take with any other piece of valuable equipment.

USE LOCKS AND OTHER FORMS OF PROTECTION

Protect your network and its components against casual theft. This step can include locking the computer room when it's not in use or attaching a lockable cable to the unit and securing it to a wall. You might also establish procedures for moving or repairing the computer so that the computer or its components cannot be taken under false pretenses.

Next, consider using a surge protector or power conditioner to protect the computer and its peripherals from power spikes. Perform regular disk scans and defragmentation to isolate bad sectors and to maintain the highest possible disk performance.

You may want to keep unauthorized users away from the power and reset switches on the computer, particularly if your computer's rights policy denies them the right to shut down the computer. The most secure computers (other than those in locked and guarded rooms) expose only the computer's keyboard, monitor, mouse, and (when appropriate) printer to users. The CPU and removable media drives can be locked away where only specifically authorized personnel can access them. Use long extension cables so the video, keyboard, and mouse cables can be passed into a less-secure area for proper system access.

MAKE BACKUPS

Regular backups protect your data from hardware failures and honest mistakes as well as providing virus recovery abilities.

Obviously, files must be read to be backed up, and they must be written to be restored. Therefore, backup privileges should be limited to administrators and backup operators — people whom you trust with Read and Write access on all system files.

CONTAIN NETWORKS

Containing the network completely in a secure building minimizes the risk of unauthorized taps. If the cabling must pass through unsecured areas, use optical fiber links rather than twisted-pair wiring. This step helps foil attempts at tapping the network cables to collect data.

RESTRICT THE BOOT PROCESS

Most personal computers today can start a number of different operating systems. For example, even if you normally start Windows NT from the C drive, someone could start another version of Windows from another drive, including a floppy or CD-ROM drive. If so, security precautions you have taken with your normal version of Windows NT could be circumvented.

In general, you should install only those operating systems that you know you need. For example, don't load Windows 95 on the same system as

Windows NT, because you don't need both, and loading both compromises security. The same logic holds true for multiple copies of NT on the same system.

For a highly secure system, consider removing the floppy drives and CD-ROM. In some computers, you can disable booting from the floppy drive by setting switches or jumpers on the system motherboard.

If the CPU is in a locked area, away from the keyboard and monitor, nobody can add drives or change or hardware settings to make it possible to boot from another operating system. Another great way to limit access is to edit the boot.ini file so that the boot timeout is 0 seconds — it is then a little more difficult to boot to another system, but not impossible.

On many hardware platforms, the system can be protected using a *power-on password*. A power-on password prevents unauthorized personnel from booting any operating system without the correct password. Power-on passwords are a function of the computer hardware, not the operating system software itself. Therefore, the procedure for setting up the power-on password depends on the type of computer, but you can usually find it in the system BIOS settings.

HARDENING YOUR NT OPERATING SYSTEM

This section explains how to further secure the operating system itself after installation. Be sure to use caution when performing changes to the registry, because mistakes can lead to an unbootable system.

A checklist for each of these tasks is at the end of this Appendix. Where a task includes several subtasks, a shorter checklist incorporating each subtask is included in the text.

INSTALL LATEST SERVICE PACKS AND HOT-FIXES

Install the latest recommended Microsoft Service Pack for the NT operating system if at all possible. Once you have done this, install the necessary hot-fixes as well. In some cases, not all hot-fixes are necessary, but if you are not sure, load them all. Remember that the order in which hot-fixes are installed is very important — later hot-fixes sometimes supersede earlier hot-fixes. Be sure to pay attention to the date and time stamps on the files listed on Microsoft's FTP site (ftp://ftp.microsoft.com/bussys/winnt/winnt-public/fixes) and install them in chronological order.

If you add any services, you must reinstall the latest Service Pack and hot-fixes.

PROTECT FILES AND DIRECTORIES

NTFS provides more security features than the FAT system; therefore, you should use NTFS whenever security is a concern. The only reason to use FAT is for the boot partition of an ARC-compliant RISC system such as a DEC Alpha. *A little-known fact is that a system partition using FAT can be secured in its entirety using the Secure System Partition command on the Partition menu of the Disk Administrator utility.*

Among the files and directories you need to protect on any partition are those that make up the operating system software itself. The standard set of permissions on system files and directories provides a reasonable degree of security without interfering with the computer's usability. For high-level security installations, however, you might also set directory permissions to all subdirectories and existing files as shown in the following list *immediately after Windows NT is installed.* Be sure to apply permissions to parent directories before applying permissions to subdirectories.

First, apply these permissions using the ACL editor.

Directory	Permissions	Complete
\WINNT and *all* *subdirectories*	Administrators: Full Control CREATOR OWNER: Full Control Everyone: Read SYSTEM: Full Control	

Now, in the \WINNT tree apply the following exceptions to the general security permission settings:

Directory	Permissions	Complete
\WINNT\Repair	Administrators: Full Control	
\WINNT\System32\ Config	Administrators: Full Control CREATOR OWNER: Full Control Everyone: List SYSTEM: Full Control	
\WINNT\System32\ Spool	Administrators: Full Control CREATOR OWNER: Full Control Everyone: Read Power Users: Change SYSTEM: Full Control	

\WINNT\Cookies
\WINNT\Forms
\WINNT\History
\WINNT\OCCache
\WINNT\Profiles
\WINNT\Sendto
\WINNT\Temporary
  Internet Files
	Administrators: Full Control
	CREATOR OWNER: Full Control
	Everyone: Special Directory Access
	  — Read, Write, and Execute
	  Special File Access — None
	SYSTEM: Full Control	

Several critical operating system files exist in the root directory of the system partition on Intel 80486- and Pentium-based systems. In high-security installations, you should seriously consider assigning permissions as follows:

File	C2-Level Compliant Permissions	Complete
\Boot.ini \Ntdetect.com \Ntldr	Administrators: Full Control SYSTEM: Full Control	
\Autoexec.bat \Config.sys	Everybody: Read Administrators: Full Control SYSTEM: Full Control	

\Temp directory	Administrators: Full Control
	CREATOR OWNER: Full Control
	Everyone: Special Directory Access
	  — Read, Write, and Execute
	  Special File Access — None
	SYSTEM: Full Control	

To view these files in File Manager, choose the By File Type command from the View menu, then select the Show Hidden/System Files check box in the By File Type dialog box.

Reviewing the permissions on various partitions to ensure that they have been properly secured, per your changes, is extremely important. To check the permissions, use Explorer or a specialized tool such as Somarsoft's DumpACL.

LIMIT ACCESS TO SERVICES AND NETBIOS FROM THE INTERNET

For a standalone Web server or firewall system, consider the guidelines in this section for NT services.

You should *not* start the services in the table below.

Service	Installed	Not Installed	Disabled
Alerter			
ClipBook Server			
Computer Browser			
DHCP Client			
Directory Replicator			
Messenger			
NetLogon			
Network DDE			
Network DDE DSDM			
Plug and Play			
Remote Procedure Call (RPC) Locator			
Server			
SNMP Trap Service			
Spooler (unless you need to spool printing)			
TCP/IP NetBIOS Helper			
Telephony Service			
Workstation (Required for Raptor Firewall)			

After you stop Workstation and Server services, you cannot perform most administrative functions. Install these two services and start them up when you need them, but be certain to stop and disable them before the system is used openly on the network. Also note that some applications (such as Raptor's EagleNT Firewall) may require that the Workstation and/or Server service be running. In this case you may also need a network protocol associated with the service, so be certain not to choose TCP/IP — use NetBIOS instead.

Special Note

You *must* start these services.

Service	Installed	Not Installed	Disabled
EventLog			
NT LM Security Support Provider			
Remote Procedure Call (RPC) Service			
Any other necessary application services, such as WWW or FTP			

You may use these services if you need them for system operation.

Service	Installed	Not Installed	Disabled
Schedule			
UPS			

Reminder

Remember: if you use the Schedule service, be sure to change the account that it runs under. By default, this account is the SYSTEM account, which is a very dangerous way to leave it running. Consider using a normal user account instead.

RECONSIDER USING ALERTER AND MESSENGER SERVICES

The Alerter and Messenger services let a user (or a service, such as a printer service) send messages to administrators or other users to alert them to problems; these messages appear in a window on the user's desktop. These services may be an unnecessary risk because they have been used in social engineering attacks, such as requesting a user's password. Don't laugh, it happens! Some users actually respond to a request to change their password, create a share, or otherwise open holes in the network. A side effect of running this service is that it causes the name of the current user to be broadcast in the NetBIOS name table, which gives an attacker a valid user name to use in brute-force intrusion attempts.

UNBIND UNNECESSARY SERVICES

Disable the NetBIOS Interface, Server, and Workstation network bindings from the "WINS Client (TCP/IP)" unless the service is required for a specific application. Whenever possible, use the Bindings feature in the Network application in Control Panel to unbind any unnecessary services from any network adapter cards connected to the Internet. For example, you might use the Server service to copy new images and documents from computers in your internal network, but you might not want remote users to have direct access to the Server service from the Internet. In this case, you may require the Server service to work correctly on your *private* network, but not on the public network side. Therefore, you should disable the Server service binding to any network adapter cards connected to the Internet or other public (or untrusted) networks.

By removing the NetBIOS binding to the TCP/IP protocol, the native file-sharing services (using the Server and Workstation services) will not be accessible via TCP/IP network and the Internet. Other NetBIOS-related services are accessible via other protocols if any are installed and already bound to NetBIOS.

OBSCURE THE ADMINISTRATIVE ACCOUNTS

It's a great idea to disable the built-in Administrator account, because this account is incredibly dangerous to leave available for use. The best practice is to assign Administrative-level permissions and rights to an account that is a member of the Administrators group, and then remove all rights and permissions from the built-in Administrator account. Do this using the User Manager and Explorer.

The reason for disabling the Administrator account is that any intruder worth his salt knows that this account exists by default on all NT systems. Therefore, it's a likely target of attack. Intruders may spend days, weeks, or even months trying to gain access to that account, but if you cripple it, even a successful break-in gives them access only to a useless account.

Besides obscuring administrative accounts, consider the following changes:

- Remove the "Log on from the network" right from the Administrator's group as a whole
- Add the "Log on from the network" right for individual accounts that require administrative access
- Adjust user account policies to lock out users after more than three failed logon attempts
- Require passwords be exactly seven characters in length for maximum strength (because of to the algorithm Microsoft uses to encrypt NT passwords, this length is the hardest to crack)

DISPLAY LEGAL NOTICES AT LOGON

Windows NT can display a message dialog box with the text of your choice when a user logs on. Many organizations use this message box to display a warning message that notifies users that they can be held legally liable if they attempt to use the computer without proper authorization. The absence of such a notice could be construed as an invitation, without restriction, to enter and browse the system. Consult with your attorney as to the best wording.

You can use the logon notice in special scenarios, such as when NT serves as an information kiosk. In this case, users might need instructions for supplying a user name and password for the appropriate account. This message dialog box could supply that information in addition to legal notices.

To display a legal notice on your NT system, use the Registry Editor to create or assign the following registry key values:

Hive: HKEY_LOCAL_MACHINE
Key: Software\Microsoft\WindowsNT\Current Version\Winlogon
Name: LegalNoticeCaption
Data Type: REG_SZ
Value: Title shown on the logon notice dialog box

Hive: HKEY_LOCAL_MACHINE
Key: Software\Microsoft\WindowsNT\Current Version\Winlogon
Name: LegalNoticeText
Data Type: REG_SZ
Value: Text shown in the logon notice dialog box

Here's a sample notice:

> You have reached the XYZ Corporation Network
>
> This system is for the use of Authorized Users only.
> Activity on this network may be monitored and recorded.
>
> If you do not agree to be monitored and recorded,
> or if this act is illegal in your place of origin,
> you must log off immediately.

DISABLE THE GUEST ACCOUNT

Make sure your Guest account is disabled or removed. You can provide limited access for casual users through the built-in Guest account, but you need to make certain you've adjusted all resources so that the account is limited to only those resources you wanted used by guests.

SECURE YOUR SCREENSAVERS

Turn on the NT screensaver feature with the Password Protected option, setting the activation time to a low value — somewhere in the range of one to ten minutes. This way, when a user walks away from the system without logging off, the screensaver activates and locks the system from unwanted access. Although it can become incredibly annoying to deactivate screensavers continually, it's well worth the effort.

ALLOW ONLY LOGGED-ON USERS TO SHUT DOWN THE COMPUTER

Normally, you can shut down a computer running Windows NT Workstation without logging on by choosing Shutdown in the Logon dialog box. This setup is okay if the user can access the computer's power or reset switches, but if you've concealed those switches, you also need to remove this Shutdown option from the Logon dialog box.

On NT Server, this option is disabled by default, but on NT Workstation, you need to create or adjust the following registry key:

Hive:	HKEY_LOCAL_MACHINE
Key:	Software\Microsoft\WindowsNT\Current Version\Winlogon
Name:	ShutdownWithoutLogon
Data Type:	REG_SZ
Value:	0

The changes take effect the next time the computer is rebooted.

HIDE THE NAME OF THE LAST USER

By default, Windows NT places the name of the last user to log on in the Username field of the Logon dialog box. This idea is that it makes it more convenient for a frequent user to log on — but it also provides 50 percent of the puzzle needed to break into a system!

To keep the username from appearing in the Logon dialog box, use the Registry Editor to create or assign the following registry key value:

Hive: HKEY_LOCAL_MACHINE
Key: Software\Microsoft\WindowsNT\Current Version\Winlogon
Name: DontDisplayLastUserName
Data Type: REG_SZ
Value: 1

RESTRICT ANONYMOUS NETWORK ACCESS TO THE REGISTRY

Service Pack 3 (SP3) for NT 4.0 includes a security enhancement that restricts anonymous (null session) logons when they connect to specific named pipes, including the one for registry access. SP3 provides for the use of a registry key value that defines the list of named pipes that are exempt from this restriction. The key value is:

Hive: HKEY_LOCAL_MACHINE
Key: System\CurrentControlSet\Services\LanManServer\Parameters
Name: NullSessionPipes
Data Type: REG_MULTI_SZ
Value: Add or remove names from the list as required by the configuration.

Be sure to read Microsoft's Knowledge Base (KB) article Q143138 for complete details before modifying this key. Find the KB on the Web at http://www.microsoft.com/search.

RESTRICT ANONYMOUS LOOKUP

Windows NT has a feature that lets users of the anonymous logon feature list domain usernames and enumerate share names. Customers who want enhanced security have asked Microsoft for help in restricting this feature as they see fit. Service Pack 3 for NT 4.0 (as well as a hot-fix for Windows NT 3.51) gives you this ability. To implement your restrictions, use the following registry key and value.

Hive:	HKEY_LOCAL_MACHINE
Key:	System\CurrentControlSet\Control\LSA
Name:	RestrictAnonymous
Data Type:	REG_DWORD
Value:	1

Microsoft's Knowledge Base article Q143474 contains complete details on this function.

ENFORCE STRONG USER PASSWORDS

Service Pack 2 or NT 4.0 (and later Service Packs) include a password-filtering DLL file called Passfilt.dll that lets you enforce stronger password requirements on users.

Passfilt.dll implements the following password policies:

- Passwords must be at least six characters long. (You can increase the minimum password length by setting a higher value in the Password Policy for the domain.)
- Passwords must contain characters from at least three of the following four classes:
  - English uppercase letters (A, B, C, etc.)
  - English lowercase letters (a, b, c, etc.)
  - Westernized Arabic numerals (0, 1, 2, etc.)
  - Non-alphanumeric (special characters), such as punctuation symbols
- Passwords may not contain your user name or any part of your full name as recorded in your account (as seen in User Manager).

These requirements are pre-programmed in Passfilt.dll and cannot be changed through the user interface or registry. You can however, get a copy of the source code and modify it, if you wish.

To use Passfilt.dll, copy the file into your %SYSTEMROOT%\System32 directory and add the DLL name to the following registry key on all your domain controllers:

Hive:	HKEY_LOCAL_MACHINE
Key:	System\CurrentControlSet\Control\LSA
Name:	Notification Packages
Data Type:	REG_MULTI_SZ
Value:	Add Passfilt to existing strings

DISABLE LANMANAGER PASSWORD HASH SUPPORT

Windows NT supports LanManager (LM) challenge/response and Windows NT challenge/response for authentication issues. When they provide access to servers that support only LM authentication, NT clients by default send user information in both authentication types. If you know your network is not using any LM servers, disabling this feature enhances your security. Simply install the post-SP3 LanManager hot-fix located on Microsoft's FTP site and configure the following registry key:

> **Hive:**   HKEY_LOCAL_MACHINE
> **Key:**   System\CurrentControlSet\Control\LSA
> **Name:**   LMCompatibilityLevel
> **Data Type:**   REG_DWORD
> **Value:**   0,1,2 (Default 0)

Setting the value to 0 sends both Windows NT and LM password forms; setting it to 1 sends Windows NT and LM passwords only if the server requests it; setting it to 2 never sends the LM password.

If you set this key to 2, that system cannot connect to systems that support only LM authentication, such as Windows 95 and Windows for Workgroups. For complete information about this feature, refer to KB article Q147706.

ERASE THE SYSTEM PAGE FILE
DURING A CLEAN SYSTEM SHUTDOWN

The virtual memory feature in Windows NT uses a system page file located on a disk as a way to expand the physical memory installed in the system. On a running system, this page file is opened only by the operating system and is well protected. However, best practice is to erase the page file when the system shuts down cleanly to ensure that sensitive information from memory processes is not available to an intruder. To configure your NT system to erase the page file, adjust the following registry key:

> **Hive:**   HKEY_LOCAL_MACHINE
> **Key:**   System\CurrentControlSet\Control\SessionManager\
>   Memory Management
> **Name:**   ClearPageFileAtShutdown
> **Data Type:**   REG_DWORD
> **Value:**   1

Note that this protection works only during a clean shutdown; therefore, it is important that untrusted users cannot power off or reset the system manually. If they can, they might then be able to gain access to the page file through some other means.

PROTECT THE REGISTRY

By now you know that the initialization and configuration data NT uses is stored in the registry. Some processes modify their own keys, while other keys must be modified using the Registry Editor. It is possible to configure the NT registry remotely, and therefore you should restrict this type of access wherever possible. To do so, create the following registry key:

Hive: HKEY_LOCAL_MACHINE
Key: System\CurrentControlSet\Control\SecurePipeServers
Name: winreg

The security permissions set on this key define which users or groups can connect to the system for remote registry access, so adjust them accordingly. By default, this key is not defined in NT Workstation and does not restrict remote access to the registry. The NT Server default setting permits only Administrators to gain remote access to the registry. Consider disallowing everyone remote registry access, Administrators included.

SECURE THE EVENT LOGS

By default, NT lets guests and anonymous users view System and Application Event Logs. The Security log is protected from guest access by default, but users with the Manage Audit Logs user right can see it. The Event Log service uses the following key to restrict guest access to these logs:

Hive: HKEY_LOCAL_MACHINE
Key: System\CurrentControlSet\Services\EventLog\[LogName]
Name: RestrictGuestAccess
Data Type: REG_DWORD
Value: 1

Set the value for each log to 1 to restrict access and reboot the system. Besides changing this key, you should also change the user access permissions to disallow access for all users other than Administrators and the SYSTEM account — otherwise an intruder might be able to reset the key value and gain access.

CONTROL PRINT DRIVER INSTALLATION

Windows NT uses a registry key to control who can add printer drivers to the system. In some cases, you may not want anyone other than administrators installing drivers on the system. For example, when users can't copy data to a floppy or e-mail it someplace, they may print it instead.

To limit who can install printer drivers, change the value for the following registry key to 1, which causes the NT Spooler service to restrict this operation to Administrators and Print Operators (NT Server) or Administrators and Power Users (NT Workstation).

Hive: HKEY_LOCAL_MACHINE
Key: System\CurrentControlSet\Control\Print\Providers\LanMan
             Print Services\Servers
Name: AddPrintDrivers
Data Type: REG_DWORD
Value: 1

LIMIT THE SCHEDULE SERVICE (AT COMMAND)

The Schedule service (sometimes referred to as the AT command) is used to schedule tasks that run automatically at a predetermined time and date. These tasks run under the context of the defined account used by the Schedule service, which by default is the all-powerful SYSTEM account. Besides running the Schedule service under a normal user account, you can further secure this function by adjusting a registry key.

By default, only Administrators can schedule tasks using AT commands, which may be a security problem if you want a user to schedule tasks but don't want that user to have Administrator access. You can assign permission for scheduling tasks to the System Operator group by creating or assigning the following registry key value:

Hive: HKEY_LOCAL_MACHINE
Key: System\CurrentControlSet\Control\Lsa
Name: Submit Control
Data Type: REG_DWORD
Value: 1

Reboot your computer for the changes to take effect. *At the time of this writing, there is no way of allowing other groups permission to schedule tasks.*

REMOVE DEFAULT ADMINISTRATOR SHARES

It's common knowledge that Windows and DOS do not display shares ending in a dollar sign. Therefore, you can use this method of share-naming to hide any shares that you don't want the users to see. This feature is the reason that administrative shares (C$, D$) are not visible when you browse the network. You can connect to hidden shares only if you know the exact share name.

Default administrative shares cannot be removed by simply un-sharing them. Although deleting the share may remove it, that removal is only temporary. The next time you reboot the system, the shares reappear. To remove administrative shares *permanently*, edit the appropriate registry key below. Change the value to 3D0 and reboot the system.

For NT Server:

Hive:	HKEY_LOCAL_MACHINE
Key:	System\CCS\Services\LanManagerServer\Parameters
Name:	AutoShareServer
Value:	3D0

For NT Workstation:

Hive:	HKEY_LOCAL_MACHINE
Key:	System\CCS\Services\LanManagerServer\Parameters
Name:	AutoShareWks
Value:	3D0

SECURE RESOURCE-SHARING

The native NT way of sharing resources is provided for in the SMB protocols, which let systems transparently access files that reside on remote systems. Any item mapped into the file space (such as a printer) is also transparently shared by these protocols.

Installing Service Pack 3 introduces SMB signing to your NT systems — both Workstation and Server. On NT Servers, it's disabled by default, but on NT Workstations, it's enabled by default.

With this feature enabled, SMB sessions are mutually authenticated between client and server, packet by packet, using a strong authentication mechanism. In other words, both client and server transparently agree up front that they will digitally sign each packet to ensure its authenticity.

Keep in mind that you can configure SMB signing in two ways: *enabled* and *required*. *Enabled* means that if a client system also has SMB signing enabled, SMB signing is used as the preferred communication method.

Required means that all clients must use SMB signing to communicate with the NT system.

To enable or require SMB signing on an NT Server, edit the registry as follows:

1. Open HKEY_LOCAL_MACHINE subtree.
2. Locate this key: System\CurrentControlSet\Services\LanManServer\ Parameters.
3. Click Add Value on the Edit menu.
4. Add the following two values:

   Name: EnableSecuritySignature
   Data Type: REG_DWORD
   Value: 0 (disable), 1 (enable)

   The default value is 0 (disable).

   Name: RequireSecuritySignature
   Data Type: REG_DWORD
   Value: 0 (disable), 1 (enable)

   The default value is 0 (disable).

5. Click OK and quit Registry Editor.
6. Shut down and restart NT.

The registry key for NT Workstation is different from the key for NT Server, but it is also located in the HKEY_LOCAL_MACHINE subtree. First, find the following key and value:

   Key: \System\CurrentControlSet\Services\Rdr
   Name: Parameters

Then follow steps 3 through 6, above.

A few final notes here — be advised that you need the updated service packs for Windows 95 and other MS client systems that will participate in SMB signing with an NT system. The current incarnations of those non-NT operating systems know nothing about this new authentication technique and won't work with your NT systems if you've *required* SMB signing. On the other hand, if you've only *enabled* SMB signing, they should work just fine in conjunction with your NT systems, although they remain more vulnerable to SMB attacks. I recommend you take the time to upgrade them; it will be worth the effort! See KB article Q161372 for further details on SMB message-signing enhancements.

Windows NT version 4.0 Service Pack 3 includes another enhancement to the SMB file-sharing protocol. By default, it keeps you from connecting to SMB Servers (such as Samba, Hewlett-Packard LM/X, or LanManager for Unix) with an unencrypted (plain text) password. This feature prevents clear text forms of passwords from being passed over the wire. Refer to KB article Q166730 if you have any reason to let clients send unencrypted passwords over the wire.

LOCK NT WITH SYSTEM KEYS

SP3 introduces another really cool feature called System Keys. You may recall the release of NTCrack and PWDump software in 1997 that dumps the Security Account Manager (SAM) database and attempts to crack the user passwords — system keys go a long way toward preventing this type of attack. With SP3, you can create a server key for NT. Without the key, you can't boot the NT system at all, period.

System Keys use strong encryption techniques to increase the protection of account password information stored in the registry in the SAM database. These passwords are therefore much more difficult to attack, even if someone manages to obtain an actual copy of the SAM, either directly from your NT system or from your Emergency Repair Disk (ERD).

Protect access to your Emergency Repair Disks fiercely, because they contain incredibly sensitive system information, not to mention a complete copy of your SAM database. You should also check the permissions on your %SYSTEMROOT%\Repair directory, because it also has copies of sensitive system information.

Special Note

Normally, only administrators have access to the SAM database using the Registry Editor, and even then, they can't directly view its contents. But it's all too easy to fool NT into granting complete and unhindered access to the SAM. I won't say how it's done in this book (you never know who's reading!), but I will point out that disabling or changing the service account for the Schedule service helps stop it from ever happening to you.

This new strong encryption capability is an optional feature and protects private account information by encrypting the password data using a 128-bit random cryptographic key, also known as a password encryption key. Only the private password information is strongly encrypted in the database, not the entire account database. Every system using the strong encryption option has a

unique password encryption key. The password encryption key is itself
encrypted with a System Key. Strong password encryption may be used on
both NT Server and Workstation, where account information is stored. Using
strong encryption adds additional protection to the SAM, subsequent backup
copies of the registry information (ERD and Repair directory), and system
backup tapes.

To use this new feature, run the Syskey.exe utility installed by SP3 in the
%SYSTEMROOT%\System32 directory. Only members of the Administrators
group can run the Syskey.exe command. This tool initializes or changes your
System Key — the master key that protects the actual password encryption key.

Before you get started, I want to point out a few things: protecting access
to your System Key is paramount. If it's compromised, you could be in for
some trouble. The System Key feature is rather detailed to implement, so
check KB article Q143475 carefully before you get started.

Instead of giving you step-by-step instructions, I explain some of the features and design characteristics of the newfound System Keys. First, you have
three options for managing the System Key itself, all designed to meet the
needs of different NT environments. Those options are as follows:

- Use a machine-generated random key as the System Key and store the
  key on the local system using a complex obfuscation algorithm. This
  option strongly encrypts the password information in the registry and
  allows for unattended system restart.

- Use a machine-generated random key and store the key on a floppy disk.
  This floppy disk is required for the system to boot and must be inserted
  when prompted in the startup sequence for the system to be available for
  users to log on. Using this method of key storage, the System Key is not
  stored anywhere on the local system — only on the floppy disk.

- Use a password chosen by the Administrator to derive the System Key. NT
  prompts for the System Key password during the initial startup sequence.
  The system is not available for users to log on until after the key is
  entered. The System Key password is not stored anywhere on the system.
  An MD5 (encryption algorithm) digest of the password is used as the
  master key to protect the password encryption key.

Of the previous options, the last two introduce a new prompt during the
initialization of the NT operating system, where you manually provide your
key for initialization to continue. These two options also probably provide the
strongest protection, because the Master Key information is not stored anyplace
on the NT system itself, and you can control access to the external password
key or floppy base key.

If your environment requires unattended booting, opt for storing the System Key on the NT system's hard drive. Don't worry too much; the System Key is reportedly stored using a complex obfuscation algorithm and is accessible only to the core operating system security components. In the future, Microsoft says they'll provide a way to obtain the System Key from a tamper-proof hardware device attached to the system, thus creating a fourth and even-more powerful way to handle your System Keys. When will this happen? Your guess is as good as mine.

Let me offer a small warning to all you would-be System Key users: If your System Key is forgotten or the floppy disk lost, it may not be possible to start your NT system at all. Therefore, you should protect System Key information diligently by creating backup copies of the floppy or giving more than one person the password. The only way to recover the system is to restore to a previous version (a backup made before you enabled strong encryption) with a repair disk and start enabling strong encryption from scratch.

To use the password version of the System Key feature, consider using a long password and giving an equal part of the password to several different users — with each person receiving a different part. This way, no single person can boot the system, and all "part holders" must enter their parts in the correct order before the system boots. I hear you thinking, "This is a paranoid approach," but some of you may in fact require this level of control. The choice is up to you.

Additionally, this strong encryption feature may be configured independently on the Primary Domain Controller and on each Backup Domain Controller. Each domain controller has a unique password encryption key and a unique System Key. Keys cannot be used across systems — each system must use its own unique key set regardless of domain participation roles. Before enabling the feature on your domain controllers, you should ensure your BDCs are in complete sync with the PDCs and create a fresh ERD before you get started.

Read KB article Q143475 on this topic. It explains everything in detail, and it really is a "must read" before you get started using this new function.

ENABLE GENERAL AUDITING

Auditing can reveal activity that could be posing a security risk to your network, and it can also identify the user accounts performing that activity. When you establish an audit policy, you must weigh the cost (in disk space and CPU cycles) of the various auditing options against the advantages of these options. You should audit at least failed log on attempts, attempts to access sensitive data, and changes to security settings. Here are some common security threats and the type of auditing that can help track them.

Threat	Audit Settings
Random password-guessing	Audit failed log on and log off events.
Use of stolen passwords	Audit successful log on and log off events. You are looking for unusual activity on user accounts, such as logons at odd hours or on days when you do not expect activity.
Misuse of administrative privileges by valid user accounts	Audit successful use of user rights, user and group management, and security policy changes; also audit restart, shutdown, and system events. Windows NT does not normally audit the use of the "Backup Files And Directories" and the "Restore Files And Directories" rights because of the high volume of events it would record.
Virus contamination	Audit successful and failed write access of program files, such as files with .exe and .dll extensions. Track successful and failed processes. Examine suspicious programs cautiously and examine the security log for unexpected attempts to modify program files or create unexpected processes. These settings generate a large number of event records during routine system use.
Improper access to protected files	Audit successful and failed attempts to access files and objects. With Explorer, audit successful and failed attempts by users or groups to access sensitive files (both read and write access).
Improper access to printers	Audit successful and failed attempts to access file and objects; then use Print Manager to audit successful and failed attempts by users or groups to access the printers.

ENABLE SYSTEM AUDITING

Enabling system auditing can tell you about actions that pose security risks and help you detect security breaches. To activate security event logging, follow these steps:

1. Log on with administrative access.

2. Click Start, choose Programs, Administrative Tools, and User Manager.

3. On the Policies menu, choose Audit.

4. Click Audit These Events.

5. Enable the options you want to use. The following options are available:

- Log on/Log off — logs both local and remote resource logons.

- File and Object Access — logs file, directory, and printer access. Files and folders must reside on an NTFS partition for security logging to be enabled. After you enable auditing file and object access, use NT Explorer to select auditing for individual files and folders.

- User and Group Management — logs any user accounts or groups that are created, changed, or deleted; any user accounts that are renamed, disabled, or enabled; and any passwords set or changed.

- Security Policy Changes — logs any changes to user rights or audit policies.

- Restart, Shutdown, and System — logs shutdowns and restarts of the local system.

- Process Tracking — logs program activation, handle duplication, indirect object access, and process exits.

6. Click the Success check box to enable logging for successful operations and the Failure check box to enable logging for unsuccessful operations. Click OK to close the dialog box.

AUDIT BASE OBJECTS

To audit base system objects, add the following key value.

Hive:	HKEY_LOCAL_MACHINE
Key:	System\CurrentControlSet\Control\Lsa
Name:	AuditBaseObjects
Data Type:	REG_DWORD
Value:	1

Simply setting this value does not start generating audits; the administrator must turn on auditing for the Object Access category with User Manager. This setting tells the Local Security Authority (LSA) that base objects should be created with a default system audit control list.

AUDIT PRIVILEGES

Certain privileges in the system are not audited by default, even when you turn on privilege-auditing, in an effort to control the growth of audit logs. The privileges not audited by default are listed below, with default assignments in parantheses:

- Bypass traverse checking (granted to everyone)
- Debug programs (granted only to Administrators)
- Create a token object (granted to no one)
- Replace process level token (granted to no one)
- Generate Security Audits (granted to no one)
- Backup files and directories (granted to Administrators and Backup Operators)
- Restore files and directories (granted to Administrators and Backup Operators)

Auditing the first item is meaningless, because it's a privilege granted to everyone. Debugging programs is a privilege designed to be used by programmers and should not be granted to any user whatsoever; it's dangerous to assign this right to a user. The next three privileges are not granted to any user or group and should not be unless you're sure it's necessary, because they are highly sensitive rights. The last two privileges are used during normal system operations.

To audit these these privileges, add the following registry value:

Hive:	HKEY_LOCAL_MACHINE\SYSTEM
Key:	System\CurrentControlSet\Control\Lsa
Name:	FullPrivilegeAuditing
Type:	REG_BINARY
Value:	1

DISABLE CACHING LOGON CREDENTIALS

By default, Windows NT caches the logon credentials for the last user that logged on interactively to an NT system. This feature is provided so that if, for example, a system is disconnected from the network or none of the domain controllers is available, the user can still log on to the system.

The credential cache is somewhat protected, but you may want to disable this credential caching completely if your environment requires a high level of security. To disable credential caching, change this entry.

Hive: HKEY_LOCAL_MACHINE
Key: Software\Microsoft\Windows NT\CurrentVersion\Winlogon
Name: CachedLogonsCount
Data Type: REG_DWORD
Value: 0

SECURE THE BACKUP COPY OF SAM

By default, a copy of SAM is kept in the %SYSTEMROOT%\repair directory in a file called SAM._. The directory has the following permissions:

Administrators: Full Control
Everyone: Read
SYSTEM: Full Control
Power Users: Change

These settings are not the optimum for a secure system. Consider reassigning the permissions as follows, using Cacls.exe in the Windows NT Resource Kit:

1. From Explorer, highlight the SAM._ file, right-click, choose Properties, Security, and Permissions. Remove all privileges from this file.

2. Open a DOS Command window and issue this command: cacls %systemroot%\repair\sam._ /D Everyone.

This command denies the Everyone group permission to the SAM._ file and ensures that no share permissions provide access to the file. In effect, the command in step 2 removes access from the file so that no user may access it.

Keep in mind that to update your ERD, you must manually reset the permissions on this file temporarily to regain access, then set them back when you're done. To reset the permissions:

1. Open a DOS Command window and issue the following command, which grants Administrators change permission to the SAM._ file: cacls %systemroot%\repair\sam._ /T /G Administrators:C.

2. After updating the ERD, execute the following command to remove the permissions granted in step 1: cacls %systemroot%\repair\sam._ /E /R Administrators.

AUDIT PASSWORD REGISTRY KEYS

Auditing the password-related registry keys helps you detect unauthorized attempts to gain access to them, a favorite ploy of intruders. To audit these keys, follow the steps below (the following information was contributed by Russ Cooper and can also be found at http://www.ntbugtraq.com):

1. Enable Auditing, then start the User Manager, select Policies, Audit, and click Audit These Events.
2. Choose the items to audit for Failure and Success and close the dialog box.
3. Log on with Administrative authority. This step begins the tricky part: fooling NT into giving you access to the SAM keys in the registry.
4. Using Control Panel, Services, set the Schedule service to run under the SYSTEM account and start (or restart) the service.
5. Open a DOS Command window and check the current time.
6. Add one or two minutes to the time (e.g., if it's 14:10, make it 14:12) and issue the following command at the DOS prompt: at 14:12 /interactive "regedt32.exe".
7. Wait until 14:12, at which time the Schedule service launches the Registry Editor (Regedit32.exe) under the security context of the SYSTEM account. You have complete access to the entire registry; this is a dangerous level of access, so be careful when you edit the registry this way.
8. Select HKEY_LOCAL_MACHINE, locate the SAM tree, and select it.
9. Choose Security from the menu and select Auditing.
10. Click Add then Show Users.
11. Add the SYSTEM account, the Domain Admins group, your trusted administrator account(s), and any other account with the following rights:
    - Take ownership of files or other objects
    - Back up files and directories
    - Manage auditing and security log
    - Restore files and directories
    - Add workstations to domain
    - Replace a process level token
12. Select the "Audit Permission on Existing Subkeys" checkbox.
13. Select Success and Failure checkboxes for the following entries:
    - Query Value
    - Set Value

- Write DAC
- Read Control

14. Click OK and then Yes.

15. Repeat steps 7–11 for the SECURITY key as well. This step is not required if you want to audit only password keys. If you want to track other security-relevant changes to the system, perform this step.

16. Exit the Registry Editor.

17. Stop the Schedule service and reset the service account with a normal user account. Do not restart the service unless you're sure you need to have it running for a particular reason.

At this point, you've applied the changes necessary to initiate auditing on the entire SAM in the registry. The Event Log contains information revealing successful and failed access attempts on these keys.

Enabling this particular level of auditing can generate a large number of log entries because the security subsystem accesses these keys during normal operations. Periodically monitor your Event Logs and archive them as necessary.

Keep in mind that programs running under the context of powerful accounts such as Administrator or SYSTEM are capable of manipulating logs and other items, which means that traces of activity could be removed by an intruder. Therefore, it's always wise to ensure programs run only under the context of a normal restricted user account.

QUICK CHECKLIST

Feel free to photocopy the following page for easy reference when performing Windows NT installations.

Task	Complete	Unimplemented
Install latest service packs and hot-fixes		
Protect files and directories		
Limit access to services and NetBios from the Internet		
Reconsider using Alerter and Messenger Services		
Unbind unnecessary services		
Obscure the administrative accounts		
Display legal notices at logon		
Disable the Guest account		
Secure your screensavers		
Allow only logged-on users to shut down the computer		
Hide the name of the last user to log on		
Restrict anonymous network access to the registry		
Restrict anonymous lookup		
Enforce strong user passwords		
Disable LanManager password hash support		
Erase the system page file during a clean system shutdown		
Protect the registry		
Secure the Event Logs		
Control print driver installation		
Limit the Schedule Service (AT command)		
Remove default Administrator shares		
Secure resource sharing		
Lock NT with System Keys		
Enable general auditing		
Enable system auditing		
Audit base objects		
Audit privileges		
Disable caching logon credentials		
Secure the backup copy of SAM		
Audit password registry keys		

APPENDIX B

FINDING SECURITY HELP ONLINE

Finding help in securing all aspects of your network and its information can be a tough job. Be selective about who you trust with this task. Lots of consulting firms will assist you, and the Appendices of this book list many resources to get you started, both on the Internet and not on the Internet.

NEWSGROUPS

Newsgroups can be a great way to gather information and obtain help. Just be careful what you post on any public message forum! For example, if you have a suspected security problem and you want to ask for help, don't give unnecessary details. Intruders watch these online resources for vulnerable systems and networks to attack later.

- alt.security.* — more than a dozen general security-related newsgroups
- microsoft.public.cryptoapi — discussions about Microsoft's Crypto API for developers
- microsoft.public.microsofttransactionserver.administration-security — issues in safely administering Microsoft Transaction Server
- microsoft.public.proxy — discussions related to Microsoft's Proxy Server
- microsoft.public.windowsnt.* — NT discussion groups on various topics, including security
- comp.security.* — almost a dozen general security-related newsgroups
- alt.2600 — more than a dozen newsgroups that serve as a frequent hangout for those new to hacking; a good place to watch and learn

WEB SITES

NT Security News — the author's site on NT security issues, concerns, and related software; http://www.ntshop.net or http://www.ntsecurity.net

James M. Atkinson, Communications Engineer — a great site relating to electronic eavesdropping, detection, and prevention; http:/www.tscm.com

Andy Baron's NT Password Cracker Page — interactive tests to see if your system is properly secured from Internet hackers; http://www.omna.com/yes/AndyBaron/pk.htm

Big Sur Multimedia, Inc. Windows NT Security — white papers and articles related to NT security; http://www.ntresearch.com

C2 Hack Microsoft — a site dedicated to pointing out the perceived inadequacies in Microsoft products; http://www.c2.org/hackmsoft/

Computer Operations, Audit, and Security Technology (COAST) — a super collection of online security resources; if you can't find it here, it may not exist; http://www.cs.purdue.edu/coast/coast.htm

Computer Research and Technology, National Institutes of Health Security Web Sites — pointers to Web sites, neatly organized by topic, that provide information about computer security; http://www.alw.nih.gov/security/security-www.html

Computer Security Information — general information about computer security, with information organized by source and each section organized by topic; http://www.alw.nih.gov/Security/security.html

Computer Security Institute — the oldest international membership organization offering training specifically targeted to information security professionals (established in 1974), whose primary purpose is to disseminate practical, cost-effective ways to protect an organization's information assets; http://www.gocsi.com/

Electronic Frontier Foundation Archive — a large list of security information relating to privacy, cryptography, and surveillance; http://www.eff.org/pub/Privacy/

FIRST security papers — a large collection of papers about various computer security issues; http://www-itg.lbl.gov/ITG/KDTF/docs/www.alw.nih.gov-FIRST. Security.Papers.html

Information Security Institute at George Mason University — links to many security-related documents, publications, and courses; http://www.isse.gmu.edu/~csis

Information Warfare — many forms of security information, including

- Information Systems Auditing — audit programs, organizations, conferences, news, publications, products, services, and related Web sites
- Information Systems Security — standards, policies, guidelines, organizations, conferences, news, publications, products, services, and related Web sites
- Emerging Technologies — general information, issues, trends, concerns, conferences, news, publications, products, services, and related Web sites
- Control Environments — issues, concerns, policies, guidelines, conferences, news, publications, conferences, products, and services

http://www.rain.org/~lonestar/infowar.htm

LSE Computer Security Research Centre — links to other Internet resources of interest to practitioners and researchers in Information and Computer Security; http://csrc.lse.ac.uk/csrc/gtway2.htm

The L0pht — a well-known hacker hangout on the Web containing many security-related resources, papers, and documents; http://www.l0pht.com

Malachi Kenney's Ping o' Death Page — how to crash many different OSes with ping; http://prospect.epresence.com/ping

Mark Russinovich and Bryce Cogswell's NT Internals Page — loaded with freeware and shareware and other information on NT and Windows 95; http://www.ntinternals.com

Microsoft FrontPage Security Issues — interesting comments about security issues in FrontPage extensions and Unix; http://www.mr.net/~fritchie/frontpage.html

MWC, Inc.'s NT Security Site — http://www.ntsecurity.com

NCSA Web Site and Hotlinks Directory — an independent organization offering objective views and opinions on computer security issues whose site is a wealth of information, including antivirus links and firewall product links; http://www.ncsa.com

New Technology News Time — a readable Web-based magazine about Windows NT; http://www.fbsolutions.com/sdwntug/announce.htm

John Neystadt: How to Create an Internet Site with Windows NT only — a personal opinion about securing an NT system connected to the Internet; http://www.neystadt.org/winnt/site.htm

NT Security FAQ — frequently asked questions about NT security; http://www.it.kth.se/~rom/ntsec.html

Raptor Systems' Security Library — a database of known security problems; http://www.raptor.com

Ron Rivest's Cryptography and Security site — pointers to other web pages about cryptography and security; http://theory/lcs/mit.edu/~rivest/crypto-security.html

RSA Data Security Systems — a great Web site from "the most trusted name in cryptography" listing many items of interest about encryption technologies; http://www.rsa.com

Rusten & Ilene's Windows NT Links — many links to Windows NT related sites; http://www.datawide.com/nt

Rutger's WWW Security References — links to Web sites, mailing lists, standards documents, etc., related to Web and/or Internet security; http://www-ns.rutgers.edu/www-security/reference.html

Somar Software — great information on securing NT when connecting to the Internet as well as some great tools that really help secure your NT systems; http://www.somarsoft.com

Telstra's Security Papers and Documents — a huge informative list of security-related papers and documents; http://www.telstra.com.au/pub/docs/security

U.S. Department of Energy Computer Incident Advisory Capability (CIAC) — organization that provides computer security services to employees and contractors of the DOE; http://ciac/llnl/gov

University of Auckland's Security and Encryption-Related Resources and Links — a long list of cryptography- and security-related resources; http://www.cs.auckland.ac.nz/~pgut001/links.html

Unix to NT FAQ — the place to get a Unix-like superuser tool for NT utilities as well as some very interesting source code; http://nentug.org/unix-to-nt

W3C Security Resources — the World Wide Web Consortium's list of online security resources; http://www.w3.org/pub/WWW/Security/Overview.html

Windows NT Security & Administration — NT-related security white papers and security checklists; http://www.ntresearch.com

WWW Security FAQ — a great list of frequently asked questions about Web security; http://www-genome.wi.mit.edu/WWW/faqs/www-security-fac.html

Search Engines — a great way to find other related information about NT security. Use any one of these, typing the keywords **nt security**:

- http://www.excite.com
- http://www.altavista.digital.com
- http://www.yahoo.com
- http://www.hotbot.com

MAILING LISTS

Mailing lists are a great way to stay on top of new developments and concerns, but they usually produce tons of e-mail (100 or more messages per day each). They're worth monitoring if you've got the time and manpower to do it.

NT Security Digest (NTSD) — an informative newsletter published once a month by the author of this book. NTSD encompasses a world of NT security information, consolidating only relevant security material into a monthly news piece, which saves you lots of time scouring for the information yourself. Urgent and dangerous discoveries are sent to you immediately, while the normal digest is published once a month via e-mail in text or Word document format. http://www.ntsecurity.net

NT Internet Security List — an unmoderated NT security mailing list operated by ISS, Inc. To subscribe, send e-mail to majordomo@iss.net with the words "subscribe ntsecurity" in the body of your message.

NTBugTraq — a mailing list run by Russ Cooper of Canada. The list handles only NT security-related issues and is not a general question and answer forum but instead serves as a technical discussion platform for known NT risks. To subscribe, send e-mail to majordomo@rc.on.ca with the words "subscribe NTBUGTRAQ" in the body of the message.

BugTraq — a great mailing list relating to security risks on all platforms. This is an "information only" list, in which no discussions take place; only security risk announcements are posted here. To subscribe, send e-mail to majordomo@netscape.org with the words "subscribe bugtraq" in the body of the message.

Best of Security — a list summarizing the best of the best from other security lists. To subscribe, send e-mail to majordomo@suburbia.net with the words "subscribe best-of-security" in the body of the message.

Firewalls List — a good general firewalls discussion forum where you'll likely get most of your questions answered sooner or later. To subscribe, send e-mail to majordomo@greatcircle.com with the words "subscribe firewalls" in the body of the message.

CERT Advisory List — a mailing list that announces new security problems for all computing platforms. To subscribe, send your e-mail address to cert-advisory-request@cert.org for instructions on subscribing.

MICROSOFT

Microsoft isn't always quick to release information about security problems in any of their software, but they do fix the problems quietly and release these fixes in Service Packs. Be sure to monitor Microsoft's site for new releases and pertinent information. The Web site is located at http://www.microsoft.com and their Knowledge Base can be searched from http://www.microsoft.com/search. Use the word "security" to get a list of all published material related to Microsoft security issues.

Microsoft recently established a new Web site that gives information about security in relation to Microsoft products: http://www.microsoft.com/security. You can report suspected problems to secure@microsoft.com.

COMPUTER EMERGENCY RESPONSE TEAM

The Computer Emergency Response Team (CERT) is an agency dedicated to alerting the masses to new security problems on any and all computing platforms. Watching the CERT site and subscribing to the CERT mailing list are worthy endeavors. When you suspect intrusion upon your network, CERT is a good place to call, because they offer assistance. They'll help you notify the proper authorities and even lend a hand tracking down the nature of the intrusion.

CERT Contact Information:

CERT Coordination Center
Software Engineering Institute
Carnegie Mellon University
Pittsburgh, PA 15213-3890

E-mail: cert@cert.org
Phone (412) 268-7090 (24-hour hotline): CERT personnel answer 8:30–5:00
　　　p.m. EST and are on call for emergencies during other hours
Fax: (412) 268-6989
Web: http://www.cert.org

APPENDIX C

SECURITY RESOURCE VENDORS

HARDWARE-BASED SECURITY SYSTEMS

Ascend Secure Access Firewall
One Ascend Plaza
1701 Harbor Bay Parkway
Alameda, CA 94502
Phone: 510-769-6001
Fax: 510-814-2300
info@ascend.com
http://www.ascend.com/products/firewall/

Ascend's Secure Access Firewall is NCSA-certified and part of a comprehensive Ascend
network security architecture that offers fully integrated firewall security for Ascend's
MAX and Pipeline products. It is cost-effective enough for network-wide deployment to
protect the entire organization — Corporate LAN, Remote Office LAN, and Telecommuter
LAN. This product is one of *Windows NT Magazine*'s Top Picks of 1996.

Cisco Systems
170 West Tasman Drive
San Jose, CA 95134-1706
Phone: 408-526-4000 or 800-553-NETS (6387)
Fax: 408-526-4100
cs-rep@cisco.com
http://www.cisco.com/warp/public/751/pix/

Cisco Systems' Private Internet Exchange (PIX) provides full firewall protection that
completely conceals the architecture of an internal network from the outside world. PIX
allows secure access to the Internet from within existing private networks and gives
you the ability to expand and reconfigure TCP/IP networks without being concerned
about a shortage of IP addresses.

Livingston IRX Router

Livingston Enterprises, Inc.
4464 Willow Road
Pleasanton, CA 94588
Phone: 800-458-9966 (Customer Service), a toll free number that can be
        accessed from U.S., Canada, Caribbean, and Hawaii
Phone: 510-426-0770
Fax: 510-426-8951
info@livingston.com
sales@livingston.com
http://www.livingston.com

Livingston's IRX Router is advanced technology delivering affordable and flex-ible interconnectivity between networks using Novell/IPX and/or TCP/IP. PortMaster IRX Multiprotocol Internetwork Routers provide wide-area intercon-nectivity between Novell/IPX, TCP/IP, and mixed network environments. The robust feature set of these second-generation routers provides functionality and reliability to extend networks over long distances using WAN links such as Digital Leased Lines (64K, T1), ISDN, Switched 56, or Frame Relay. IRX routers set new technical standards for security, ensuring your remote LAN users secure interconnectivity to critical enterprise resources.

SOFTWARE-BASED SECURITY TOOLS

AFS 2000

1287 Anvilwood Avenue
Sunnyvale, CA 94089
Phone: (toll free) 888-237-ABHI or 408-541-1400
Fax: 408-734-4407
sales@abhiweb.com
http://www.abhiweb.com/afs.html

Internet security is a key issue for companies that must protect confidential information while providing Internet access to employees and customers. The AFS 2000's firewall proxy supports secure use of the World Wide Web, FTP, Telnet, e-mail, news, and gopher. The AFS 2000 firewall works with both pri-vate and public IP addresses inside the network. The AFS 2000's easy-to-use administrative tools manage control of network access as well as reporting.

AltaVista Firewall

30 Porter Road
Littleton, MA 01460
Fax: 508-486-2017
altavista-web@altavista.digital.com
http://altavista.software.digital.com/firewall/products/index.htm

AltaVista Firewall on Windows NT combines trusted application gateways, comprehensive logging, reporting, evasive action, and an easy-to-use Windows GUI. This combination adds up to highly secure and reliable Internet access and secure domains within your intranet. At the time of this writing, AltaVista Firewall was the only NCSA-certified firewall for Windows NT.

OmniGuard Family of Products

AXENT Technologies, Inc.
Headquarters
2400 Research Boulevard
Rockville, MD 20850
Phone: 301-258-5043
Fax: 301-330-5756
sundav@axent.com
http://www.axent.com

OmniGuard is AXENT's answer to an organization's requirement for comprehensive client/server security strategy. This integrated suite of software tools secures and protects information assets across multiple types of client/server environments. OmniGuard products, when combined with AXENT's support and professional services, can provide a total security solution that safeguards an enterprise's distributed data from unauthorized access, modification, or destruction.

Black Hole

13231 Champion Forest Drive
Suite 110
Houston, TX 77069-2600
Phone: 281-631-0477
Fax: 281-631-0848
http://www.milkyway.com

Connecting to an external network is fast and simple, thanks to Black Hole's transparent gateway at both the application and circuit level. By using the Black Hole, the user-to-server connection can now be a one-step process.

BorderWare

20 Toronto Street
Suite 400
Toronto, Ontario M5C 2B8
Canada
Phone: 416-368-7157
Fax: 416-368-7789
webmaster@border.com
http://www.border.com/contents.html

The BorderWare Firewall Server is a complete Internet gateway and firewall security system in one. It combines Internet application-level servers — including World Wide Web, mail, news and name services, with proxies for applications such as Mosaic, Telnet, and FTP — with a transparent IP firewall.

Carmel Software Engineering

P.O. Box 25055
Haifa 31250
Israel
Phone: 972-48-416976
Fax: 972-48-416979
http://fbsolutions.com/ntav/demo.htm

NTAV is designed to identify and eliminate viruses and diagnose suspicious files that may be infected with new virus strains.

Centri Firewall

755 Page Mill Road
Suite A-101
Palo Alto, CA 94304
Phone: 800-682-5550
Fax: 402-436-3036
info@globalinternet.com
http://www.gi.net/security/centridownload/index.html

Centri Firewall 3.1.1 provides evolutionary enhancements for security and ease of use, as well as fixes for anomalies reported in Release v3.1. ActiveX applet blocking is the new security feature and joins the Java applet protection already included in Release v3.1. Together, these two functions provide complete protection from rogue applets traveling on the Internet.

APPENDIX C SECURITY RESOURCE VENDORS 457

CyberGuard Firewall

2101 W. Cypress Creek Road
Fort Lauderdale, FL 33309
Phone: 800-666-4273 or 954-973-5478
Fax: 954-973-5160
cyberguard@mail.cyberguardcorp.com
http://www.cyberguardcorp.com

The CyberGuard Firewall is a member of the CyberGuard Series(TM) of network security products. These products provide security from unauthorized access to local-, metropolitan-, and wide-area networks. The CyberGuard Firewall is a low-cost, highly configurable security solution that leverages the advantages of a Multi-Level Secure (MLS) architecture. Customers with internal networks that hold sensitive data can use the CyberGuard Firewall to prevent security breaches.

Eagle NT Firewall

Raptor Systems, Inc.
69 Hickory Drive
Waltham, MA 02154
Phone: 800-9-EAGLE-6 or 617-487-7700
Fax: 617-487-6755
info@raptor.com
http://www.raptor.com

Eagle NT is the first application-level firewall for the Windows NT platform. More comprehensive than firewalls that only implement packet filters or routers, Eagle NT acts as a proxy server for common TCP/IP applications, including Telnet, FTP, Gopher, WAIS, http (WWW), and SMTP. By proxying these services at the application level, the firewall gains valuable information about the network packet and can therefore discern which packets are permitted or denied access to your network. This gives the network administrator the power to enforce a specific security policy.

Elementrix Technologies, Inc.

850 Third Ave.
New York, NY 10022
Phone: 212-888-8879
Fax: 212-935-3882
sales@elementrix.co.il
http://www.elementrix.co.il/elm_prod.html

Elementrix develops encryption technology and products for secure, private, and practical Internet use. The company's POTP technology is a new method that guarantees the secure transfer of large amounts of information over open high-speed international networks. Elementrix develops products and also licenses its technology for applications covering all types of digital communications. Elementrix is a subsidiary of Elron Electronic Industries Ltd., Israel's leading advanced technology holding company.

FireWall-1
Check Point Software Technologies
400 Seaport Court
Suite 105
Redwood City, CA 94063
Phone: 415-562-0400 or 800-429-4391
info@checkpoint.com
http://www.checkpoint.com

FireWall-1 provides integrated Internet/intranet mobile and remote access control, authentication, encryption, and network address translation. The first shrink-wrapped firewall package and the first to employ an easy-to-use graphical user interface, FireWall-1 is an NCSA-certified solution recognized by users and trade publications for its usability, flexibility, extensibility, and high performance. The product is installed at thousands of customer sites worldwide and is the most widely tested network security solution on the market.

FireWall/Plus
Network-1
909 3rd Avenue
9th Floor
New York, NY 10022
Phone: 212-293-3068 or 800-638-9751
sales@network-1.com
http://www.network-1.com

FireWall/Plus is a fifth-generation firewall solution which operates in the native Windows NT Kernel Mode for maximum performance and security and combines all of the popular firewall methodologies in one package for maximum flexibility. Combined with its support for hundreds of transport protocols including IP, IPX, DECNet, and SNA, FireWall/Plus is the only firewall solution available today that will protect the entire organization from both external and internal threats.

Guardian

Netguard, Inc.
2445 Midway Road
Carrollton, TX 75006
Phone: 972-738-6900
Fax: 972-738-6999
info@ntguard.com
http://www.ntguard.com/free2.htm

The Guardian firewall system is a network security and management software package that cost-effectively prevents infiltration to the private network from the Internet and helps you keep track of what's going on in your network. Guardian, appearing at first glance to be a firewall product, takes a refreshing look at the problems of implementing network security.

Gauntlet Firewall

Trusted Information Systems, Inc.
3060 Washington Road (Rt. 97)
Glenwood, MD 21738
Phone: 301-854-6889 / +1-410-442-1673
Fax: 301-854-5363
tis@tis.com
http://www.tis.com

TIS's Gauntlet Family of Firewall products offers managers the most secure firewall system available today. The Gauntlet Firewall system is application proxy-based. By serving as the only connection between outside, untrusted networks or users and your private, trusted network, a Gauntlet Firewall uses specific software application gateways and strong user authentication to tightly control access and block attacks. Gauntlet Firewalls provide a network strongpoint where strict enforcement of your security policy is concentrated.

Intrusion Detection Inc.

217 East 86th
Suite 213
New York, NY 10028
Phone: 212-348-8900
Fax: 212-427-9185
75162.452@compuserve.com.
http://www.intrusion.com/

Intrusion Detection specializes in Novell, Windows NT, and general network security product development and security consulting. Our flagship product, the Kane Security Analyst™ (KSA), is a state-of-the-art network security assessment tool that allows corporate security managers, network administrators and auditors to instantaneously assess the total security soundness of a Novell 3.x, 4.x NDS, or Windows NT network.

Kane Security Analyst for Windows NT
http://www.intrusion.com/ksant.htm

The KSA thoroughly assesses the overall security status of a Novell and Windows NT network and reports security in six areas: password strength, access control, user account restrictions, system monitoring, data integrity, and data confidentiality. The KSA provides the expertise of seasoned security specialists and streamlines the analysis process.

Internet Scanner SafeSuite
Internet Security Systems
41 Perimeter Center East
Suite 660
Atlanta, GA 30346
Phone: 770-395-0150
Fax: 770-395-1972
iss@iss.net
http://www.iss.net/

The Internet Scanner SAFEsuite is a comprehensive set of network security assessment tools that audit, correct, and monitor all aspects of your enterprise network security. The Internet Scanner SAFEsuite can help you measure the effectiveness of your security policy by providing you with a comprehensive assessment of your network security.

iWay-One
BateTech Software
7550 W. Yale Avenue
B-130
Denver, CO 80227
Sales: 800-743-6238
Phone: 303-763-8333
Fax: 303-763-2783
sales@batetech.com
http://www.batetech.com

iWay-One lets you connect networked PCs to the Internet without the inconvenience associated with installing TCP/IP on each workstation. In addition to substantially reducing the costs and technical challenges of a network-wide TCP/IP installation, it also provides integrated security, firewall protection, administrative capabilities, and a variety of customizable statistical management reports.

KyberPASS

190 Bronson Ave.
Ottawa, Ontario K1R 6H4
Canada
Phone: 800-845-1140
Fax: 613-567-3693
devon@devon.com
http://www.devon.com

KyberPASS is a nonintrusive security solution that is completely transparent to client and server systems. Microsoft Windows and Win95 based client applications, and all TCP/IP networks and server platforms, can be served by KyberPASS. Using a stand-alone hardened Microsoft NT 3.5.n Server, Kyber-PASS runs on the most secure and low-cost platforms possible.

McAfee Associates

2710 Walsh Ave
Santa Clara, CA 95051-0963
Phone: 408-988-3832
security@mcafee.com
http://www.mcafee.com

PCFirewall

PCFirewall runs transparently on your Windows system to protect it from network attacks and denies access to unauthorized users. It repels external and internal hacker attempts to probe for weaknesses with your system.
http://www.mcafee.com/prod/security/pcfire.html

ROMShield

RomShield loads into your system as extended BIOS, before your computer starts the boot process, and automatically scans any floppy diskette in your system to see if it contains a boot sector infection. If the diskette is infected, RomShield can remove the virus from the diskette. RomShield also scans any diskettes placed into the drive before they are accessed.
http://www.mcafee.com/prod/av/romshd.html

BootShield

BootShield, a VirusScan Companion Solution, is an unobtrusive countermeasure which masks the computer's boot image and immediately recognizes any subsequent modification that may be characteristic of boot virus activity.
http://www.mcafee.com/prod/av/bootsh.html

Microsoft Proxy Server

Microsoft Corporation
Phone: 206-882-8080
http://www.microsoft.com

By sharing a single, secure gateway, Microsoft Proxy Server eliminates the need to share one dedicated machine for the Internet among multiple users, or to run multiple Internet lines into the organization to provide each desktop with a separate connection. This shared gateway delivers maximum accessibility, while helping keep costs down and simplify administration. Because Microsoft Proxy Server supports popular network protocols, it works easily with your existing network. That means you can use it to connect to the Internet without eliminating and replacing the technology in which you've already invested. And, if your strategy is to move from a local area network-based IPX/SPX platform to a TCP/IP-based standard, you can move at your own pace, because Microsoft Proxy Server works on both.

MidWestern Commerce, Inc.

1601 West Fifth Avenue
Suite 207
Columbus, OH 43212
Phone: 614-263-0662
Fax: 614-263-0663
services@box.omna.com
http://www.omna.com/Yes/MWC/PRS-index.htm

Windows NT Password Recovery Service

MWC, Inc. Network Security team is happy to announce a new service for Windows NT Community. This service is for those who lost the Administrator's Password. If you have a Windows NT 3.5x or 4.0 Server, PDC, BDC or Workstation it is now possible to recover your Administrator's password if you have forgotten or lost it.

ScanNT

ScanNT is a program that makes repeated attempts at breaking your user's passwords. The program runs against the accounts you select and uses a dictionary to guess the passwords. http://www.omna.com/yes/AndyBaron/pk.htm

Network-1 FireWall/Plus for Windows NT
Network-1 Corporation
Phone: 212-293-3068
Fax: 212-293-3090
http://www.omna.com/yes/AndyBaron/pk.htm

FireWall/Plus is unique. Originally developed to protect copyrighted material and confidential consulting records for major corporations and government agencies, Network-1 meets the demands for a formidable firewall that epitomizes versatility. And now FireWall/Plus supports the Windows NT operating system.

NetAlert
C. B. Consulting
2071 Lakeridge Cr.
Suite 104
Chula Vista, CA 91913
clbrown@netcom.com
http://www.fbits.com/clbrown/

NetAlert monitors the status of a TCP/IP network port by checking to see if the port is listening. When the port goes down or up, NetAlert sends an e-mail alert, a page, or both. You can use this application to check your Internet connection by setting it to check a well-known port on your service provider's network.

NetXray
Cinco Networks, Inc.
1340 Center Drive   or   6601 Koll Center Parkway
Suite 103   Suite 140
Atlanta, GA 30338-4140   Pleasanton, CA 94566
Phone: 770-671-9272   Phone: 510-426-1770
                                  sales@cinco.com
                                  http://www.cinco.com

NetXray is a great packet sniffer that can help solve various networking issues, including analyzing intrusion attempts. The software offers IP address auto discovery, NETBIOS name auto-discovery, separate pre-filters for all real time statistical features, and custom and proprietary packet decoding including SNMP.

NTManage
LANWARE, Inc.
6150 Richmond Avenue
Suite 116
Houston, TX 77057-6202
Phone: 713-975-8050
Fax: 713-975-8335
info@lanware.net
http://www.lanology.com/ntmanage

Designed exclusively for Microsoft Windows NT Server, NTManage is the quick
and easy way to monitor and manage your Windows NT environment across
heterogeneous platforms, regardless of the size or complexity of your network.
If there's a problem with any component of your network, NTManage lets you
know about it immediately, whether you're at your console or away from it.
NTManage is the solution to problems associated with multiple hardware platforms (routers, terminals, servers, workstations or any other addressable network hardware) and a select set of networking software (SNMP, SMTP, DNS
Servers, POP-1 Servers, WWW, FTP, and NNTP News) for Windows NT
Servers versions 3.51 and later.

PORTUS
2825 Wilcrest
Suite 160
Houston, TX 77042-3358
Phone: 713-974-3274
FAX: 713-978-6246
portusinfo@lsli.com
http://www.lsli.com/

PORTUS is an application firewall designed to repel the most sophisticated
attacks from skilled and determined crackers. PORTUS logs and controls all
traffic between secured and unsecured networks. PORTUS can be configured
to match the security policies of an organization instead of imposing its own
policy upon an organization. PORTUS is easy to install, configure, maintain,
and use. PORTUS works with shrink-wrapped applications to provide easy and
transparent access from secured to unsecured (Internet) networks.

Somarsoft Security Products

Somarsoft, Inc.
P.O. Box 642278
San Francisco, CA 94164-2278
Phone: 415-776-7315
Fax: 415-776-7328
info@somarsoft.com
http://www.somarsoft.com

Somarsoft DumpAcl

DumpAcl is a Windows NT program that dumps the permissions (ACLs) for
the file system, Registry, shares, and printers in a concise, readable listbox
format, so that "holes" in system security are readily apparent. A must-have
product for Windows NT systems administrators.

Somarsoft DumpEvt

DumpEvt is a Windows NT program that dumps the event log in a format suitable for importing into a database. Used as a basis for your eventlog management system and for long-term tracking of security violations, DumpEvt is
similar to the DUMPEL utility in the NT resource kit, except that it fixes various
defects of that utility that make the output unsuitable for importing into
databases.

Somarsoft DumpReg

DumpReg is a Windows NT and Windows 95 program that dumps the Registry, making it easy to find keys and values matching a string. In Windows
NT, dumped entries can be sorted by reverse order of last modified time,
making it easy to see changes made by recently installed software. A must-
have product for Windows NT systems administrators.

Somarsoft ReDial

ReDial is a Windows NT service that maintains a full-time dial-up PPP Internet
or other RAS connection by redialing whenever the connection is lost. ReDial
can optionally cycle the EMWAC HTTP server and other WINSOCK services
which lock up when the RAS connection is stopped and restarted. This service
has the option to throttle redialing attempts in cases where there is a cost for
redialing. V1.4 adds the option to issue periodic pings to specified IP
addresses, to handle cases where PPP connection drops after an interval (for
example, 30 minutes) if there is no data traffic. ReDial also adds the option of
dropping and reestablishing the PPP connection if pings repeatedly fail to
handle cases where the PPP connection gets "hung" at the Internet provider.

Somarsoft RegEdit

RegEdit is a DLL callable by 32-bit Visual Basic that can be used to view and/or modify the user Registry profile. For example, a 10-line VBA for an Excel program can change the mail server path in the Registry profiles of all users at once. A great tool for Windows NT systems administrators who can program in Basic. V1.4 adds a new API, and the shareware version is fully functional except for registration message boxes.

SeNTry
Phone: +44-(0)1684-577195
Fax: +44-(0)1684-577197
support@sunbelt.fr
http://www.sunbelt.co.uk

With the increasing use of Windows NT as an enterprise NOS where multiple NT servers exist in multiple domains, a major challenge exits for enterprise administrators needing to collect mission-critical event log information. SeNTry provides the Windows NT administrator with the ability to view and manage multiple events logs on multiple servers.

UniKey
Software Security, Inc.
Phone: 800-841-1316 (U.S.) or 203-656-3000 (all locations)
inquiry@softsec.com
http://www.softsec.com/

Software Security, Inc. is a leading provider of patented software protection technologies and products. The products are a combination of a small hardware device and specialized software that are marketed to software developers who are seeking to protect their vital intellectual properties. The hardware keys are small solid state devices designed to attach to a computer port. The presence of a hardware key on the computer port allows a protected application to operate. When the hardware key is removed, the application can be copied but will not run.

DATA ENCRYPTION SYSTEMS

CryptoSystem
RadGuard
24 Raoul-Wallenberg Street
Tel Aviv 69719
Israel
Tel: 972-3-645-5444
Fax: 972-3-648-0859
info@radguard.com
http://www.radguard.com/products.htm

CryptoSystem is a unique, comprehensive, end-to-end enterprise-wide security
solution based on hardware and software designed and produced in-house. It
provides a complete array of security services for protecting user networks
connected to public networks, including the Internet, forming Virtual Private
Networks.

PGP Encryption
Pretty Good Privacy, Inc.
2121 S. El Camino Real
Suite 902
San Mateo, CA 94403
Main: 415-572-0430
Fax: 415-572-1932
http://www.pgp.com

The new PGPmail 4.5 protects the privacy of millions of e-mail users with the
most advanced cryptography available. Designed for both the corporate and
individual user, PGPmail offers an unprecedented privacy solution that seamlessly integrates into your favorite e-mail package for encrypting messages and
attachments providing state-of-the-art protection for all of your valuable data.
PGPmail 4.5 is a powerful encryption application which now has easy-to-use
controls for encryption, decryption, digital signatures, and basic key management to QUALCOMM's Eudora 3.0 (Windows) e-mail client software (Pro or
Light) and Netscape Mail.

RSA Protect
RSA Data Security, Inc.
100 Marine Parkway
Suite 500
Redwood City, CA 94065-1031
Phone: 415-595-8782
Fax: 415-595-1873
http://www.rsa.com

Discover RSA SecurPC, the award-winning disk and file encryption software for your personal computer. RSA SecurPC lets you create encrypted attachments for your e-mail. It is fast and reliable, and has the most trusted name in cryptography behind it. This software encryption tools integrates right into your mail client and Windows File Manger.

Shade Disk Encryption
Soft Winter Corporation
http://softwinter.bitbucket.co.il

Shade is strong encryption software for Windows NT which allows you to create an encrypted disk device inside a file. Such a device can then be formatted using any file system (like NTFS or FAT) and used as a regular disk, at which point the software will encrypt the data on every write operation and decrypt it on every read operation.

VIRUS DETECTION AND PREVENTION

InocuLAN
Cheyenne Software Corporate Sales
3 Expressway Plaza
Roslin Heights, NY 11577
Phone: 800-CHEY-INC or 800-243-9462
Fax: 516-484-2489
sales@cheyenne.com
http://www.cheyenne.com

InocuLAN 4 is the leading antivirus solution for Windows NT networks, offering unmatched enterprise management and virus protection. Exclusive features of InocuLAN 4 include Real-Time Cure, Universal Manager, Virus Wall, Virus Quarantine, Hands-Free Updates, Extensive Alerting options, Support for Windows NT 4.0 and virus protection for Internet downloads and e-mail attachments. InocuLAN is certified by the NCSA to detect 100% of viruses in the wild, carries the "Designed for BackOffice" logo from Microsoft and won the Editor's Choice from *Windows NT Magazine* in both 1995 and 1996. Ideal for Windows NT (Intel, Alpha, PowerPC, MIPS) and NetWare enterprises, InocuLAN is fully integrated with separate Cheyenne AntiVirus clients for Windows NT, Windows 95, Windows 3.x, DOS, and Macintosh workstations.

McAfee Associates
2710 Walsh Ave
Santa Clara, CA 95051-0963
Phone: 408-988-3832
security@mcafee.com
http://www.mcafee.com

VirusScan

VirusScan supports Windows NT with an extensive array of features to keep your system immune to viruses. http://www.mcafee.com/prod/av/vsnt.html

NetShield

NetShield offers superior antivirus solutions for network servers. NetShield combines McAfee's award-winning proprietary virus scanning technologies with server management capabilities to effectively minimize and manage the virus threat within networks. http://www.mcafee.com/prod/av/netshnt.html

WebScan

Since the Internet and Intranets allow immediate exposure to viruses, how can you proactively prevent such viruses from entering your system? McAfee's WebScan, a VirusScan Companion Solution, integrates the world's leading virus protection with popular Web Browsers and e-mail. WebScan automatically repels distributed viruses. http://www.mcafee.com/prod/av/webscan.html

WebShield

To provide increased security, McAfee developed WebShield, a NetShield Companion Solution, which prevents viruses from penetrating your enterprise. A local LAN or WAN turns into a single line, comprised of routers and/or a firewall, as it connects to the Internet. This Internet Gateway is essentially an on-ramp to the virus-filled superhighway. WebShield automatically scans inbound and outbound traffic at all three potential virus transport mechanisms: Simple Mail Transport Protocol (SMTP), File Transfer Protocl (FTP) and Hyper-Text Transfer Protocol (HTTP). http://www.mcafee.com/prod/av/webshld.html

Companion Solution

A VirusScan Companion Solution is an unobtrusive countermeasure that masks the computer's boot image and immediately recognizes any subsequent modification that may be characteristic of boot virus activity. http://www.mcafee.com/prod/av/bootsh.html

Norton AntiVirus Scanner

10201 Torre Avenue
Cupertino, CA 95014-2132
Phone: 408-253-9600
Fax: 408-253-3968
webmaster@symantec.com
http://www.symantec.com

Norton AntiVirus Scanner provides the most effective protection available against Boot Record viruses and File viruses for your Windows NT system. Simple and easy to use, Norton AntiVirus Scanner is based on the industry-leading technology that's successfully conquered viruses on millions of DOS and Windows systems worldwide. Norton AntiVirus Scanner can be scheduled to automatically run periodic scans that detect and destroy virus infections, under both NTFS and FAT file systems.

SWEEP

Sophos, Inc.
18 Commerce Way
Woburn, MA 01801
Phone: 617-932-0222
Fax: 617-9320251
sales@sophos.com
http://www.sophos.com

SWEEP antivirus software for Windows NT is available for both Intel x86 and Alpha platforms. It operates as a background scanner and Intercheck server, or as a command-line scanner for interactive use. It uses the application event log to record virus detections and problems, and reports virus detections via MS Mail.

Trend Micro

Trend Micro Devices, Inc.
20245 Stevens Creek Blvd.
Cupertino, CA 95014
Phone: 408-257-1500
webmaster@trendmicro.com
http://www.trendmicro.com

InterScan VirusWall and E-Mail VirusWall

E-Mail VirusWall for NT Server is the solution to Internet/intranet e-mail viruses, including the new Word.Concept macro virus (found by the NCSA to be the fastest-growing virus ever).

WebProtect

WebProtect scans HTTP files for viruses and allows the system administrator to block Java applets, ActiveX and unsigned software. WebProtect supports Authenticode.

ScanMail for cc:Mail

ScanMail for cc:Mail is the solution to e-mail viruses, including the new Word.Concept macro virus.

PC-cillin 95

PC-cillin 95 scans compressed files and files attached to e-mail. And now that Windows 95 makes it easier than ever to access on-line services, you have an even greater risk of catching and spreading viruses.

DATA BACKUP AND RECOVERY SYSTEMS

Cheyenne Software
Corporate Sales
3 Expressway Plaza
Roslin Heights, NY 11577
Phone: 800-CHEY-INC or 800-243-9462
Fax: 516-484-2489
sales@cheyenne.com
http://www.cheyenne.com

Cheyenne ARCserve 6 for Windows NT is the High Performance and Automated Backup, Restore, and Disaster Recovery Solution for Windows NT Networks. ARCserve is a multi-threaded, multi-tasking data management software solution. Offering advanced capabilities such as centralized administration, remote management, and intelligent alert notification, ARCserve is designed to back up and restore data across single or multi-site Windows NT enterprises. ARCserve comes in three different editions — Enterprise, Single Server, and Workstation — to meet the needs of different types of customers.

Double-Take for Windows NT

Network Specialists Inc.
80 River Street
Suite 5B
Hoboken, NJ 07030
Phone: 201-656-2121
Fax: 201-656-2727
nsisupport@nsisw.com
http://www.nsisw.com

Double-Take offers real-time continuous backup for as many as 50 servers per backup server. The backup process automatically copies only file changes, which reduces the backup time. IS administrators can use Double-Take for fault tolerance in a many-to-one server environment.

Network Custodian LANRecover

Len Gilbert Associates
10097 Cleary Blvd.
#330
Plantation, FL 33324
Phone: 954-476-1127
Fax: 954-476-1127
lga@paradise.net
http://it-universe.com/lga

LANRecover supports LAN Manager, LAN Server, NetBIOS, NetWare 3.x, NetWare 4.x, VINES, and Windows NT. It provides disaster recovery planning for Windows for Workgroups, Windows NT, and Windows 95 networks. It also includes a template for a recovery plan, a policies and procedures manual, a customizable help desk, hardware inventory, configuration file backup, and report functions. Finally, LANRecover provides built-in access controls for different levels of users.

Retrospect

Dantz Development Corp.
4 Orinda Way
Bldg. C
Orinda, CA 94563
Phone: 510-253-3000 or 800-225-4880
Fax: 510-253-9099
info@dantz.com
http://www.dantz.com

Dantz Development Corporation's Retrospect family of backup products recently grew to include Windows 95 and NT platforms. Following in the footsteps of the company's Remote Pack for Macintosh, its Remote Pack for the Windows 95 and NT Operating Systems gives Mac-based IS departments a way to back up mixed-platform networks that may include Windows 95 and Windows NT.

Seagate Backup Exec for Windows NT

Seagate Software, Inc.
920 Disc Drive
Scotts Valley, CA 95067
Phone: 408-439-2149
diana_l_cartwright@notes.seagate.com
http://www.arcada.com

Backup Exec for Windows NT is the *de facto* standard for proven 32-bit backup that protects the entire Windows NT network. With centralized administration and its exclusive monitoring console, Backup Exec provides true client/server functionality for Windows NT data protection. No other product offers more comprehensive features for data protection and reduced administration overhead. Only Backup Exec supports any combination of clients — on any platform — on your Windows NT network. What's more, it is the only data protection solution providing complete, integrated support for Microsoft BackOffice. In fact, Microsoft selected Seagate Software to protect over 1,500 of their Windows NT servers worldwide. *Formerly from Arcada.*

Ultrabac

Barratt Edwards International Corporation
14850 Lake Hills Blvd.
Suite B-4
Bellevue, WA 98007
Phone: 206-644-6000
Fax: 206-644-8222
info@ultrabac.com
http://www.ultrabac.com

UltraBac lets you back up the registry to a hard drive and then back up the drives to tape. UltraBac features a scheduling capability, which lets you automatically define and then invoke this process. UltraBac also lets you select computers in the network and back up remotely. In support of remote backup, UltraBac includes a utility (UltraVue) that lets you monitor remote events, including remote UltraBac logs. All in all, the software is powerful. Ultrabac ships on a single 3.5" diskette and is written in C++ language.

SECURITY CONSULTANTS

Lots of security consultants operate around the world, many of which can be located using the various search engines on the Internet. The three listed below specialize in Windows NT security and are some of the more reputable firms that you may consult with.

The NT Shop

12667 Memorial Drive
Suite107
Houston, TX 77024
Phone: 713-215-9661
security@ntsecurity.net
http://www.ntsecurity.net

The NT Shop is my company, which offers security consulting services related to Windows NT networks. The NT Shop maintains one of the most comprehensive Web sites related to NT security on the Internet. The NT Shop also publishes a monthly NT security newsletter and offers routine security scanning services that ensure your network is viewed as secure when you look from the Internet inward — we show you what the hackers see.

Midwestern Commerce, Inc. (MWC)

1601 West Fifth Avenue
Suite 207
Columbus, OH 43212
Andy Pozo, Director of Sales
Phone: 614-263-0662
Fax: 614-263-0663
AndyPozo@box.omna.com
http://www.omna.com

Midwestern Commerce, Inc. (MWC) offers a wide range of Internet-related services from Personal Web Hosting for individuals to Turn-key Solutions for Businesses; from consultations for novices to Security Evaluation and Implementation for skilled Webmasters and Administrators.

MWC employs certified Windows NT & Internet Security professionals who would be happy to share their experience with you. MWC specialists will help you to make your part of the Net totally secure. If you are already experiencing difficulties, MWC can assist you. MWC can help in even the most sensitive situations, even if an Administrator's password on your NT machine has been lost.

Network-1
909 3rd Avenue
9th Floor
New York, NY 10022
Phone: 800-638-9751
Fax: 212-293-3090
sales@network-1.com
http://www.network-1.com

Network-1 claims to be the industry leader in network and security consulting services. Network-1 has hundreds of high-profile clients who have benefited from the expertise and experience of their highly trained professional consultants. Consultants from Network-1 are skilled in spending as little of your valuable time as necessary to survey and troubleshoot on site. Network-1 provides an executive summary at the beginning of each report which summarizes our evaluation, recommendations, analysis, and results. Your customized report, written by the consultant with input from our research center, includes information on the standards and specifications that apply to the task about which you have requested Network-1's expertise.

The Registry, Inc.
95 River Street
Suite 3A
Hoboken, NJ 07030
Phone: 201-798-7801
nynscp@tri.com
http://www.tri.com

The Registry's Network Systems Consulting Practice (NSCP) provides a unique service portfolio that serves the key needs of mainstream internetworking users as well as networking vendors, carriers, and service providers. The Practice maintains a staff of subject matter experts in enterprise wide security issues (applications, systems, network, procedures) who have particular expertise in firewall technology, authentication (hand-held tokens and authentication servers), centralized authorization ("universal login"), VLAN- and DNS/DHCP-based group security, encryption, and virtual private networks. The NSCP has also developed a ground-breaking model of *Enterprise Wide Security Cost of Ownership* (based on a study of major U.S. corporations) which can be used to quantify the cost benefit of an integrated approach to enterprise-wide network security. In addition, The Registry is a leading national provider of information technology (IT) consultants on a contract basis for a diversified client base which includes communications companies, financial services organizations, systems integrators, manufacturers, and pharmaceutical firms.

APPENDIX D

FREQUENTLY ASKED QUESTIONS ABOUT FIREWALLS

This appendix answers some of the more commonly asked questions about firewalls. This list of Frequently Asked Questions (FAQ), commonly known on the Internet as "The Firewall FAQ," is maintained by Marcus J. Ranum of V-ONE and is available online at http://www.v-one.com.

WHAT IS A NETWORK FIREWALL?

A firewall is a system or group of systems that enforces an access control policy between two or more networks. The means by which this control is accomplished varies widely, but in principle, the firewall is a pair of mechanisms, one that blocks traffic and one that permits traffic. Some firewalls emphasize blocking traffic, while others emphasize permitting traffic. The most important thing to recognize about a firewall is that it implements an access control policy. If you don't know what kind of access you want to permit or deny, or you let someone else or some product configure a firewall based on judgment other than yours, that entity is making policy for your whole organization.

WHY WOULD I WANT A FIREWALL?

The Internet is a fun little playground and at the same time a hostile environment. Like any other society, it's plagued with the kind of people who enjoy the electronic equivalent of writing on other people's walls with spray paint, tearing off their mailboxes, or just sitting in the street blowing their car horns. Some people get real work done over the Internet, and some must protect sensitive or proprietary data. Usually, a firewall's purpose is to keep the intruders out of your network while letting you do your job.

Many traditional corporations and data centers have computing security policies and practices that users must follow. If a company's policies dictate how data must be protected, a firewall is very important because it embodies corporate policy. Frequently, the hardest part of hooking a large company to the Internet is not justifying the expense or effort, but instead convincing management that it's safe to do so. A firewall not only provides real security but also plays an important role as a security blanket for management.

Last, a firewall can act as your corporate ambassador to the Internet. Many corporations use their firewall systems to store public information about corporate products and services, files to download, bug-fixes, and so forth. Several of these systems (such as uunet.uu.net, whitehouse.gov, gatekeeper.dec.com) have become important parts of the Internet service structure and reflect well on their organizational sponsors.

WHAT CAN A FIREWALL PROTECT AGAINST?

Some firewalls permit only e-mail traffic, thereby protecting the network against any attacks other than attacks against the e-mail service itself. Other firewalls provide less strict protections or block services that are known to be problems.

Generally, firewalls are configured to protect against unauthenticated interactive logins from the outside world. This protection, more than anything, helps prevent vandals from logging on to machines on your network. More elaborate firewalls block traffic from the outside to the inside but permit users on the inside to communicate freely with the outside. The firewall can protect you against any type of network-borne attack if you unplug it.

Firewalls are also important because they are a single point where you can impose security and auditing. If someone attacks a computer system by dialing in with a modem, tracing the perpetrator is impossible. In contrast, the firewall can act as an effective phone tap and tracing tool. Firewalls also provide an important logging and auditing function, summarizing topics such as the kinds and amount of traffic that passed through it and how many attempted break-ins occurred recently.

WHAT CAN'T A FIREWALL PROTECT AGAINST?

Firewalls can't protect against attacks that don't go through the firewall. Many corporations that connect to the Internet are very concerned about proprietary data leaking out of the company. Unfortunately, a magnetic tape exports data just as effectively as the Internet. Many organizations whose management is terrified of Internet connections have no coherent policy about protecting dial-in access via modems. It's silly to build a steel door six feet thick when you live in a wooden house, but a lot of organizations out there buy expensive firewalls and neglect their network's other numerous back doors. For a firewall to work, it must be a part of a consistent overall organizational security architecture. Firewall policies must be realistic and reflect the level of security in the entire network. For example, a site with top secret or classified data doesn't need a firewall at all: it shouldn't be hooking up to the Internet in the first place; at least the systems with really secret data should be isolated from the rest of the corporate network.

Firewalls also can't protect you from traitors inside your company. Although industrial spies might export information through your firewall, they're just as likely to export it through a telephone, fax machine, or floppy disk. In fact, floppy disks are a far more likely way to leak information from your organization than a firewall!

Firewalls also cannot protect you from stupidity. Users who reveal sensitive information over the telephone are good targets for social engineering. Attackers may break into your network, completely bypassing your firewall, by finding a helpful employee inside who is fooled into granting access to a modem pool.

WHAT ABOUT VIRUSES?

Firewalls can't protect against viruses very well. Binary files can be encoded for transfer over networks in too many ways, and too many different architectures and viruses exist to try to search for them all. In other words, a firewall cannot replace users' security consciousness. In general, a firewall cannot protect against a data-driven attack — attacks in which code is mailed or copied to an internal host where it is executed. This form of attack has occurred against various versions of sendmail and GhostScript (a freely-available PostScript viewer).

Organizations that are deeply concerned about viruses should implement organization-wide virus control measures. Rather than screening viruses at the firewall, make sure that every vulnerable desktop has virus-scanning software that runs when the machine is booted. Blanketing your network with virus-scanning software protects against viruses that come via floppy disks, modems, and the Internet. Trying to block viruses at the firewall protects against viruses only from the Internet, and most viruses are passed via floppy disks.

WHAT ARE SOME BASIC DESIGN DECISIONS IN A FIREWALL?

The lucky person who is responsible for designing, specifying, and implementing or overseeing the installation of a firewall should consider a number of basic design issues.

The first and most important issue is how your company or organization wants to operate the system. Is the firewall in place to deny all services except those critical to the mission of connecting to the Internet? Or is the firewall in place to provide a nonthreatening but metered and audited method of access? Varying positions between these two carry with them varying degrees of paranoia; the final stance of your firewall may be a political rather than an engineering decision.

The second issue is the level of monitoring, redundancy, and control you want. Having established the acceptable risk level (that is, your level of paranoia), you can form a checklist of what should be monitored, permitted, and denied. In other words, you start by figuring out your overall objectives, then combine a needs analysis with a risk assessment, and sort the (almost always conflicting) requirements into a laundry list that specifies what you plan to implement.

The third issue is financial. We can't address this issue in anything but vague terms, but it's important to try to quantify the cost of both buying and implementing any proposed solutions. For example, a complete firewall product may cost $100,000 at the high end or it may be free at the low end. The free option — doing some fancy configuring on a Cisco or similar router — costs nothing but staff time and cups of coffee. Implementing a high-end firewall from scratch can cost several person-months, which may equate to $30,000 worth of staff salary and benefits. The systems management overhead is also a consideration. Building a home-brew solution is fine, but it's important to build it so that it doesn't require constant and expensive fiddling. It's important, in other words, to evaluate firewalls not only in terms of what they cost now, but also in terms of continuing costs, such as support.

On the technical side, you must make a decision. For practical purposes, we are talking about a static traffic-routing service placed between the network service provider's router and your internal network. The traffic-routing service may be implemented at an IP level via something like screening rules in a router, or at an application level via proxy gateways and services.

You need to decide whether to place an exposed stripped-down machine on the outside network to run proxy services for Telnet, FTP, news, etc., or to set up a screening router as a filter, permitting communication with one or more internal machines. Both approaches have plusses and minuses — the proxy machine provides a greater level of audit and potential security in return for increased cost of configuration and a decreased level of service provided (because you need a proxy configured for each desired service). The old trade-off between ease-of-use and security comes back with a vengeance.

WHAT ARE THE BASIC TYPES OF FIREWALLS?

Conceptually, firewalls come in two flavors: *network level* and *application level.* They are not as different as you might think, and latest technologies are blurring the distinction to the point where it's no longer clear whether one is better or worse. As always, you need to pick the type that meets your needs.

Network-level firewalls generally make their decisions based on the source, destination addresses, and ports in individual IP packets. The traditional network-level firewall is a simple router because it doesn't make particularly sophisticated decisions about what a packet is talking to or where it came from. Modern network-level firewalls are more sophisticated and now maintain internal information about the state of connections passing through them, the contents of some of the data streams, and so on. Many network-level firewalls route traffic directly though them, so to use one you usually need to have a valid IP address block. Network-level firewalls tend to be very fast and transparent to users.

In Figure D.1, you see a *screened host firewall*, in which a router operating at a network level controls access to and from a single host. The single host is a *bastion host* — a highly-defended and secured strong-point that can resist attack.

Figure D.1
*Screened Host
Firewall*

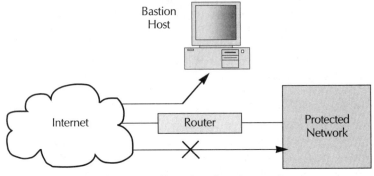

Router permits traffic only to/from bastion host

Figure D.2 shows a *screened subnet firewall.* In a screened subnet firewall, a router at the network level controls access to and from a whole network. It is similar to a screened host, except that it is effectively a network of screened hosts.

Figure D.2
*Screened Subnet
Firewall*

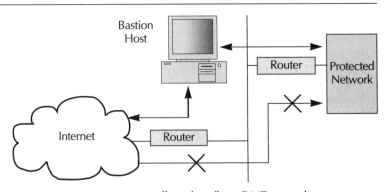

Routers permit traffic only to/from DMZ network

Application-level firewalls are generally hosts running proxy servers, which permit no traffic directly between networks and log and audit traffic passing through them. Because the proxy applications are software components running on the firewall, the proxy is a good place to do lots of logging and access control. Application-level firewalls can be used as network address translators, because traffic goes in one side and out the other after passing through an application that effectively masks the origin of the initiating connection. Having an application in the way may affect performance in some cases and may make the firewall less transparent.

Early application-level firewalls, such as those built using the TIS firewall toolkit (FWTK), are not particularly transparent, and users may require some training. Modern application-level firewalls are often fully transparent. Application-level firewalls tend to provide more detailed audit reports and enforce more conservative security models than network-level firewalls.

Figure D.3 shows a *dual-homed gateway*, a highly secured host that runs proxy software. It has two network interfaces, one on each network, and blocks all traffic passing through it.

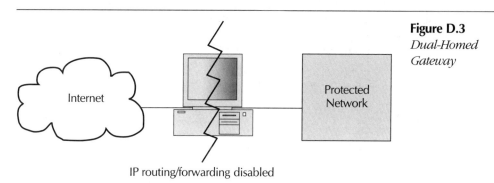

IP routing/forwarding disabled

Figure D.3
Dual-Homed Gateway

The future of firewall technology lies somewhere between network-level firewalls and application-level firewalls. It is likely that network-level firewalls will become increasingly "aware" of the information going through them and that application-level firewalls will become increasingly low-level and transparent. The result will be a fast packet-screening system that logs and audits data as it passes through. Increasingly, both network and application firewalls incorporate encryption so they can protect traffic passing between them over the Internet. Organizations with multiple points of Internet connectivity can use firewalls with end-to-end encryption to make the Internet their "private backbone" without worrying about someone sniffing their data or passwords.

WHAT ARE PROXY SERVERS AND HOW DO THEY WORK?

The definition of a proxy is "the authority to act on behalf of another," and that's exactly what a proxy server does. A proxy server, sometimes called an *application gateway* or *forwarder*, is an application that mediates traffic between a protected network and the Internet. Proxies are often used instead of router-based traffic controls to prevent traffic from passing directly between networks. Many proxies contain extra logging features or support user authentication. Because proxies must understand the application protocol being used, they can also implement protocol-specific security. For example, an FTP proxy might be configurable to permit incoming FTP and block outgoing FTP.

Proxy servers are application specific. A new protocol must be developed for every new application supported. One popular set of proxy servers is the TIS firewall toolkit (FWTK), which includes proxies for Telnet, rlogin, FTP, X-Window, http/Web, and NNTP/Usenet news. SOCKS is a generic proxy system that can be compiled into a client-side application to make it work through a firewall. Its advantage is that it's easy to use, but it doesn't support the addition of authentication hooks or protocol-specific logging. For more information about SOCKS, point your Web browser to ftp://ftp.nec.com/pub/security/socks.cstc. Check the file named Files for a description of the directory's contents.

WHAT ARE SOME CHEAP PACKET-SCREENING TOOLS?

The Texas A&M University (TAMU) security tools include software for implementing screening routers (ftp://net.tamu.edu/pub/security/TAMU). Karlbridge is a PC-based screening router kit (ftp://ftp.net.ohio-state.edu/pub/kbridge). A version of the Digital Equipment Corporation kernel-screening software, screend, is available for BSD/386, NetBSD, and BSDI. A kernel-level packet screen called ipfilter is available for free for BSD-based systems. Many commercial routers support screening of various forms.

WHAT ARE SOME REASONABLE FILTERING RULES FOR A CISCO ROUTER?

The following example, shown in Figure D.4, displays one possible configuration of a Cisco router as filtering router. It shows the implementation of a specific example policy; your policy will undoubtedly vary.

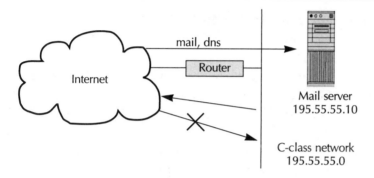

Figure D.4
Sample Cisco Router Configuration

Mail server
195.55.55.10

C-class network
195.55.55.0

In this example, a company has Class C network address of 195.55.55.0. The company network is connected to the Internet via an ISP. The company policy allows everybody access to Internet services, so all outgoing connections are accepted. All incoming connections go through the machine called *mailhost*. Mail and DNS are the only incoming services.

IMPLEMENTATION

Here are the rules this sample implementation uses:

- Allow all outgoing TCP-connections
- Allow incoming SMTP and DNS to mailhost
- Allow incoming FTP data connections to high TCP port (>1024)
- Try to protect services that live on high port numbers

The only packets checked in this configuration are packets from the Internet. The rules are tested in order and stop when the first match is found. An implicit "deny" rule at the end of the access list denies everything else. This IP access list, shown below, assumes that you are running Cisco IOS v.10.3 or later.

```
 1. no ip source-route
 2. !
 3. interface ethernet 0
 4. ip address 195.55.55.1
 5. !
 6. interface serial 0
 7. ip access-group 101 in
 8. !
 9. access-list 101 deny ip 195.55.55.0 0.0.0.255
10. access-list 101 permit tcp any any established
11. !
12. access-list 101 permit tcp any host 195.55.55.10 eq smtp
13. access-list 101 permit tcp any host 195.55.55.10 eq dns
14. access-list 101 permit udp any host 192.55.55.10 eq dns
15. !
16. access-list 101 deny tcp any any range 6000 6003
17. access-list 101 deny tcp any any range 2000 2003
18. access-list 101 deny tcp any any eq 2049
19. access-list 101 deny udp any any eq 204
20. !
21. access-list 101 permit tcp any 20 any gt 1024
22. !
23. access-list 101 permit icmp any any
24. !
25. snmp-server community FOOBAR RO 2
26. line vty 0 4
27. access-class 2 in
28. access-list 2 permit 195.55.55.0 255.255.255.0
```

Configuration Explanation

- Drop all source-routed packets because source routing can be used for address spoofing.
- If an incoming packet claims to be from the local network, drop the packet.
- Pass without further checking all packets that are part of an already-established TCP connection.
- Block all connections to low port numbers except SMTP and DNS.

- Block all services that listen for TCP connections on high port numbers. X-windows (port 6000+) and OpenWindows (port 2000+) are candidates. NFS (port 2049) runs usually over UDP, but it can be run over NFS, so block it, too.

- Check incoming connections from port 20 into high port numbers; they are supposed to be FTP data connections.

- Limit access to the router itself (Telnet & SNMP) with access-list 2.

- Block all UDP traffic to protect RPC services.

SHORTCOMINGS

- You cannot enforce strong access policies with router access lists. Users can easily install back doors to their systems to get past "no incoming Telnet" or "no X" rules. Also, some crackers can install Telnet back doors on systems after they break in.

- You can never be sure what services are listening for connections on high port numbers.

- Checking the source port on incoming FTP data connections is a weak security method because it makes using back doors more difficult, but it doesn't prevent hackers from scanning your systems. Another drawback is that it breaks access to some FTP sites.

Use Cisco code version 9.21 or later (current version is 10.3) so you can filter incoming packets and check for address spoofing. It's always best to use the most current version, because you get extra features (like filtering on source ports) and some improvements on overall filter syntax.

You still have a few ways to make your setup stronger. Block all incoming TCP connections, and tell users to use passive-FTP clients. You can also block outgoing ICMP echo-reply and destination-unreachable messages to hide your network and to prevent the use of network scanners. The Cisco FTP site has an archive of examples for building firewalls using Cisco routers (ftp://ftp.cisco.com/pub/acl-examples.tar.Z). Those examples are a bit out-of-date, but some perl scripts are pretty useful once they've been adjusted for your network.

HOW DO I MAKE WEB/HTTP WORK THROUGH MY FIREWALL?

You have three ways to make Web/HTTP work through your firewall.

- Allow "established" connections an outward path via a router, if you are using screening routers.
- Use a Web client that supports SOCKS and run SOCKS on your firewall.
- Run some kind of proxy-capable Web server on the firewall. The TIS Firewall Toolkit (FWTK) includes a proxy called http-gw, which proxies Web, gopher/gopher+ and FTP. CERN httpd also has a proxy capability, which many sites use in combination with the server's cache of frequently accessed pages. Microsoft has a great Proxy Server that supports most of the functions you might need. Many Web clients, including Netscape, Mosaic, Spry, and Chameleon, have proxy server support built directly into them.

HOW DO I MAKE DNS WORK WITH A FIREWALL?

Some organizations want to hide DNS names from the outside world. Although many experts don't think hiding DNS names is worthwhile, it is one approach that is known to work. If you have a nonstandard addressing scheme on your internal network, you have no choice but to hide those addresses.

Don't fool yourself into thinking that hiding your DNS names slows down attackers. Information about what is on your network is too easily gleaned from the networking layer itself. For an interesting demonstration, ping the subnet broadcast address on your LAN and then issue the "arp -a" command. Also note that hiding names in the DNS doesn't address the problem that host names leak out in mail headers and news articles.

If you want to hide DNS names, you have many options. The following approach is one of many. The success of this approach lies in the fact that DNS clients on a machine don't have to talk to a DNS server on that same machine. In other words, even though a DNS server is on a machine, you can redirect that machine's DNS client activity to a DNS server on another machine.

First, on the bastion host, set up a DNS server that the outside world can talk to so that it claims to be authoritative for your domains. In fact, all this server knows is what you want the outside world to know — the names and addresses of your gateways, your wildcard MX records, and so forth. This server is your public server.

Then set up a DNS server on an internal machine. This server also claims to be authoritative for your domains; unlike the public server, this one is telling the truth. This is your "normal" name server, into which you put all your normal DNS stuff. You also set up this server to forward queries that it can't resolve to the public server (using a forward line in the named.boot table, for example). This approach assumes that a packet-filtering firewall between these two servers lets them talk DNS to each other but otherwise restricts DNS between other hosts.

Finally, set up all your DNS clients (the resolv.conf file, for instance), including the ones on the machine with the public server, to use the internal server. This step is the key.

An internal client asking about an internal host asks the internal server and gets an answer; an internal client asking about an external host asks the internal server, which asks the public server, which asks the Internet, and the answer is relayed back. A client on the public server works just the same way. An external client, however, asking about an internal host gets back the restricted answer from the public server.

Another trick that's useful in this scheme is to use wildcard PTR records in your IN-ADDR.ARPA domains. That way, an address-to-name lookup for any of your non-public hosts returns a response such as "unknown.YOUR.DOMAIN" instead of returning an error. This response satisfies anonymous FTP sites like ftp.uu.net that insist on having a name for the machines they talk to. This strategy may fail when you attempt to connect to sites that do a DNS cross-check in which the host name is matched against its address and vice versa.

HOW DO I MAKE FTP WORK THROUGH MY FIREWALL?

Generally, to make FTP work through the firewall, you either set up a proxy server, such as the TIS firewall toolkit's ftp-gw or Microsoft's Proxy Server, or you permit incoming connections to the network at a restricted port range and otherwise restrict incoming connections using something like "established" screening rules. You then modify the FTP client to bind the data port to a port within that range. Obviously, you must be able to modify the FTP client application on internal hosts.

If FTP downloads are all you wish to support, you might want to consider declaring FTP a "dead protocol" and letting your users download files via the Web instead. The user interface certainly is nicer, and this setup gets around the ugly callback port problem. If you choose the FTP-via-Web approach, your users won't be able to FTP files out, which may be a problem, depending on your setup.

A different approach is to use the FTP PASV option to indicate that the remote FTP server should permit the client to initiate connections. The PASV approach assumes that the FTP server on the remote system supports that operation. (See RFC1579 for more information.) Other sites prefer to build client versions of the FTP program that are linked against a SOCKS library.

HOW DO I MAKE TELNET WORK THROUGH MY FIREWALL?

You can support Telnet either by using an application proxy, such as the TIS firewall toolkit's tn-gw or Microsoft's Proxy Server, or by simply configuring a router to permit outgoing connections using something like the "established" screening rules. An application proxies could be a standalone proxy running on the bastion host or a SOCKS server and a modified client.

HOW DO I MAKE FINGER AND WHOIS WORK THROUGH MY FIREWALL?

Many firewall administrators permit connections to the finger port from only trusted machines, which issues finger requests in the form of *finger user@host.domain@firewall*. This approach works only with the standard Unix version of finger. You can restrict access to services to specific machines by using either tcp_wrappers or netacl from the TIS firewall toolkit. This approach does not work on all systems because some finger servers do not permit user@host@host fingering.

Many sites block inbound finger requests for a variety of reasons, most often because of past security bugs in the finger server (the Morris internet worm made these bugs famous) and because of the risk of revealing proprietary or sensitive information in a user's finger information. In general, if your users are accustomed to putting proprietary or sensitive information in their .plan files, you have a more serious security problem than a firewall can solve.

HOW DO I MAKE GOPHER, ARCHIE, AND OTHER SERVICES WORK THROUGH MY FIREWALL?

The majority of firewall administrators support gopher and Archie through Web proxies. Proxies such as the TIS firewall toolkit's http-gw converts Gopher/Gopher+ queries into HTML and vice versa. For supporting Archie and other queries, many sites rely on Internet-based Web-to-Archie servers, such as ArchiePlex. The Web's tendency to make everything on the Internet look like a Web service is both a blessing and a curse.

Many new services are constantly cropping up. Often they are not designed with security in mind, and their designers cheerfully tell you that if you want to use them, you need to let port xxx through your router. Unfortunately, not everyone can do that, and a number of interesting new toys are difficult to use for people behind firewalls. RealAudio, which requires direct UDP access, is a particularly egregious example; remember that Microsoft's Proxy Server handles RealAudio. If you find yourself faced with one of these problems, remember to find out as much as you can about the security risks that the service may present before you allow it through. It's quite possible the service has no security implications. It's equally possible that it has undiscovered holes you could drive a truck through.

WHAT ARE THE ISSUES ABOUT X-WINDOWS THROUGH A FIREWALL?

X-Windows is a very useful system, but it unfortunately has some major security flaws. Remote systems that can gain or spoof access to a workstation's X display can monitor a user's keystrokes and download copies of the contents of their windows.

Although attempts have been made to overcome problems — for example, MIT "Magic Cookie" — it is still entirely too easy for an attacker to interfere with a user's X display. Most firewalls block all X traffic. Some permit X traffic through application proxies such as the DEC CRL X proxy (FTP crl.dec.com). The TIS FWTK includes a proxy for X, called x-gw, which a user can invoke via the Telnet proxy, to create a virtual X server on the firewall. When a user requests an X connection on the virtual X server, the user is presented with a pop-up menu asking whether it is OK to allow the connection. Although this setup is a little unaesthetic, it's entirely in keeping with the rest of X.

WHAT IS SOURCE-ROUTED TRAFFIC AND WHY IS IT A THREAT?

Normally, the route a packet takes from its source to its destination is determined by the routers between the source and destination. The packet itself says only where it wants to go (the destination address) and nothing about how it expects to get there.

The sender of a packet (the source) has the option to include information in the packet that tells the route the packet should follow to get to its destination; thus the name "source routing." For a firewall, source routing is noteworthy, because an attacker can generate traffic that claims to be from a system "inside" the firewall. In general, such traffic wouldn't route to the firewall properly, but with the source routing option, all the routers between the attacker's machine and the target return traffic along the reverse path of the source route. Implementing such an attack is quite easy; so firewall builders should not discount the possibility.

In practice, source-routing is used very little. In fact, its main legitimate use is in debugging network problems or routing traffic over specific links to control congestion in special situations. When building a firewall, you should block source routing at some point. Most commercial routers incorporate the specific ability to block source routing, and many versions of Unix that you might use to build firewall bastion hosts have the ability to disable or ignore source-routed traffic.

WHAT ARE ICMP REDIRECTS AND REDIRECT BOMBS?

An ICMP redirect tells the recipient system to override something in its routing table. This feature is legitimately used by routers to tell hosts that the host is using a non-optimal or defunct route to a particular destination; that is, the host is sending it to the wrong router. The wrong router sends the host an ICMP Redirect packet that tells the host what the correct route should be. If you can forge ICMP Redirect packets, and if your target host pays attention to them, you can alter the host's routing tables and possibly subvert its security by changing the paths traffic uses. ICMP redirects may also be used in denial-of-service attacks, in which a host is sent a route that loses it connectivity or a host is sent an ICMP Network Unreachable packet telling it that it can no longer access a particular network. Many firewall builders screen ICMP traffic from their network, because screening limits outsiders' ability to ping hosts and modify their routing tables.

WHAT ABOUT DENIAL OF SERVICE?

A denial-of-service attack occurs when someone makes your network or firewall useless by disrupting it, crashing it, jamming it, or flooding it. Denial of service is impossible to prevent because of the distributed nature of the network: every network node is connected via other networks, which in turn connect to other networks. A firewall administrator or ISP has control of only a few of the local elements within reach. An attacker can always disrupt a connection "upstream" from where the victim controls it. In other words, someone who wants to take a network off the air can either take the network off the air directly or take the network it connects to off the air, or the network that connects to *that* network off the air, *ad infinitum*. Hackers can deny service in many ways, ranging from the complex to the brute-force.

If you are considering using the Internet for a service that is absolutely time- or mission-critical, you should consider your fallback position in the event that the network is down or damaged. Microsoft has released hotfixes that address certain types of denial-of-service attacks such as SYN Flooding and giant Ping packets. Be sure to regularly watch for new Service Packs, because they offer new security enhancements that you should put on your systems.

CONTRIBUTORS TO THIS FAQ

Primary Author	Marcus J. Ranum, V-ONE Corporation, mjr@v-one.com
Cisco Config (V2.0)	Keinanen Vesa, vjk@relevantum.fi
Cisco Config (V1.0)	Allen Leibowitz, allen@msen.com
DNS Hints	Brent Chapman, Great Circle Associates, brent@greatcircle.com
Policy Brief	Brian Boyle, Exxon Research, bdboyle@erenj.com

APPENDIX E

HOW TO USE THE CD-ROM

The CD-ROM is set up to run automatically under Windows 95 and Windows NT 4.0. If Autorun is enabled on your machine, you should be able to insert the disk into your CD-ROM drive, and it will start automatically. If Autorun is disabled on your machine, you can choose Run from the Start menu and type z:\security.exe, where "z" is the letter of your CD-ROM drive. In addition, we have provided Microsoft Internet Explorer 3.02 on the CD-ROM for you to install if you don't have a Web browser.

REQUIREMENTS

The Macromedia Director© movie that comprises the shell for this CD-ROM is designed to run under Windows 95 or Windows NT 4.0 with an Intel processor, as is most of the software included on the CD. At minimum, you need a 486 66MHz processor, 8 MB free RAM, a double-speed CD-ROM drive, a 256-color monitor, and a sound card. We recommend using a Pentium 100MHz or better processor, 12 MB free RAM, and an 8x or better CD-ROM, as well as a 256-color monitor and a sound card.

CD-ROM CONTENTS

The disk is organized as a Macromedia Director© movie and is self-running as described above.

SOFTWARE

The CD-ROM contains the following software:

1. Centri — An easy-to-use-and-configure NT firewall.

2. Cinco Networks-NextRay — A cost-effective software-only tool that enables network managers to extract and review vital and detailed information to troubleshoot, manage, and migrate today's complex network environments effectively.

3. Cinco Networks-WebXRay — A tool that can "see" your Internet applications and services and keep you informed in real time, not giving you just bits and pieces of data, but complete information for the overall status of traffic loads and network applications, telling you where the bottlenecks are, which services are available and in use, and how well applications are running, so that you can spot potential problems before they affect your operations.

4. ISS SafeSuite — A security scanning suite that probes your network for vulnerabilities.

5. Kane Security Analyst — A security scanning suite that probes your network for vulnerabilities.

6. Network-1 Firewall Plus (for Alpha and Intel) — An easy-to-use, well-designed firewall for NT Alpha systems.

7. NTManage — A robust TCP/IP network monitoring platform designed specifically for Windows NT that works in heterogeneous networks.

8. ONGuard Firewall — A plug-and-play PC-based firewall system using an industry-standard Intel CPU. The Windows-based ONGuard Manager program provides a graphical environment to establish and maintain security policies and procedures and for receiving logging reports and security alerts. A Windows-based Express Configuration option lets the network administrator easily select the types of traffic and services to accept through the firewall.

9. RadGuard Crypto-Guard — Hardware-based encryption software designed to securely transmit data from point to point.

10. SomarSoft

    • DumpACL — dumps access control list settings so you can easily find errors in security configuration

    • DumpREG — dumps out registry permission settings

    • DumpEVT — exports the event logs so you can import them into other data systems or read them more easily

11. TrendMicro

    • Email VirusWall — works with mail servers to stop viruses from being transmitted in e-mail

    • ScanMail — provides same functions as VirusWall for Lotus cc:Mail

    • PC-cillin — a virus scanner that examines files on a disk for infection

12. Ultrascanner Portscanner — a scanner that checks a range of TCP/IP hosts for listening ports and detects services running on machines scanned.

WEB VENDOR LINKS

The CD-ROM contains the following links to vendor Web sites:

1. Centri — http://www.centri.com

2. Cinco Networks — http://www.cinco.com

3. ISS SafeSuite — http://www.iss.net

4. Kane — http://www.intrusion.com

5. Network-1 — http://www.network-1.com

6. NTManage — http://www.lanware.net

7. ONGuard — http://www.onguard.on.com

8. RadGuard — http://www.radguard.com

9. SomarSoft — http://www.somarsoft.com

10. TrendMicro — http://www.trendmicro.com

11. Ultra Scan Portscanner — http://www.ntshop.net

12. NTSecurity — http://www.ntsecurity.net

DISCLAIMER

All software on the CD is provided on an "as is" basis. Duke Press makes no claims for it nor accepts any responsibility for any damage it may do to an individual user's computer. Support for the CD by Duke Press is limited to the workings of the shell structure only. For support of the software provided on the CD, please contact the individual software vendors.

FOR MORE INFORMATION

GENERAL SECURITY INFORMATION

- http://www.thecodex.com
- http://itd.nrl.navy.mil/ITD/5540/ieee/cipher/readers-guide

SECURITY-RELATED TECHNOLOGIES

Keeping abreast of new and changing technologies can save you money down the road.

HIGHER-BANDWIDTH TECHNOLOGIES

Many industry leaders have Web sites with white papers detailing their efforts to provide higher-bandwidth technologies. For more information on some of these standards, refer to the following documents, which are easily found on the Internet using your favorite search engine:

- IEEE 802.1Q — Draft Standards for Virtual Bridged Local Area Networks
- IEEE 802.1p — Draft Standard for Traffic Class and Dynamic Multicasts Filtering Services in Bridged Local Area Networks
- IETF NHRP (Next Hop Resolution Protocol) — Internet Draft proposal document.

UNINTERRUPTIBLE POWER SUPPLY SYSTEMS

American Power Conversion (APC), in Miami, Florida makes some of the best UPS systems on the market today. Visit their Web site at http://www.americanpower.com.

VIRTUAL PRIVATE NETWORKING, ENCRYPTION, AND KEY MANAGEMENT

See the following articles in *Windows NT Magazine* by Lawrence Hughes:

- "Secure Enterprise Email," May 1996
- "Digital Envelopes and Signatures," September 1996
- "Exchange Email," October 1996

FIREWALLS

The best-known books about firewalls are listed below.

- Chapman, D. Brent and Elizabeth Zwicky. *Building Internet Firewalls*. O'Reilly, 1995. ISBN: 1-56592-124-0.
- Cheswick, Bill and Steve Bellovin. *Firewalls and Internet Security, Repelling the Wily Hacker*. Addison Wesley, 1994. ISBN: 0-201-63357-4.
- Garfinkel, Simson and Gene Spafford. *Practical Unix Security*. O'Reilly, 1991 ISBN: 0-937175-72-2. (Discusses primarily host security.)

Related references include

- Comer, Douglas and David Stevens. *Internetworking with TCP/IP Vols I, II and III*. Prentice-Hall, 1991. ISBN: 0-13-468505-9 (I), 0-13-472242-6 (II), 0-13-474222-2 (III). A detailed discussion about the architecture and implementation of the Internet and its protocols. Vol I (on principles, protocols, and architecture) is readable by everyone; Vol 2 (on design, implementation, and internals) is more technical; and Vol 3 (on client-server computing) is fairly new.
- Curry, David. *Unix System Security — A Guide for Users and System Administrators*. Addision Wesley, 1992. ISBN: 0-201-56327-4.

FTP sites:

- ftp://ftp.greatcircle.com/pub/firewalls — Firewalls mailing list archives, and Firewall Howto, a how-to document for building firewalls.
- ftp://ftp.tis.com/pub/firewalls — Internet firewall toolkit and papers.
- ftp://research.att.com/dist/internet_security — Papers on firewalls and breakins.
- ftp://net.tamu.edu/pub/security/ — Texas A&M University security tools.

Web sites:

- http://www.v-one.com — Internet attacks presentation, firewall standards
- http://www.ntshop.net — NT related security information; risks, exploits, and defenses

Mailing lists:

- Firewalls — A forum for firewall administrators and implementors. To subscribe to the Firewalls mailing list, send "subscribe firewalls" in the body of a message (not on the Subject line) to Majordomo@GreatCircle.COM. Archives of past Firewalls postings are available by anonymous FTP from ftp.greatcircle.com in pub/firewalls/archive.

- NT Security Digest — A consolidation of many security resources, including mailing lists, Web sites, newsletters, and other periodicals. The purpose is to consolidate the relevant information in an effort to save you time in monitoring these resources. Subscribing to NTSD also places you on the distribution list for immediate announcements of new NT security problems. Point your Web browser to: http://www.ntshop.net/security.

- NT Security — An all-NT security discussion mailing list run by Christopher Klaus, founder of Internet Security Systems. To subscribe, send email to request-ntsecurity@iss.net, and use the word "subscribe" in the body of the message.

An independently maintained list of commercial consultants or corporations that sell or service firewalls (no warrantee or recommendations are implied) is on the Web at http://www.access.digex.net/~bdboyle/firewall.vendor.html.

INDEX

New Books in the Duke Press Library

1001 SECRETS FOR WINDOWS NT REGISTRY
By Tim Daniels
Without expert guidance, meddling with the registry can be disastrous. But for the accomplished user, *1001 Secrets for Windows NT Registry* is the definitive reference for system customization and optimization. Organized into sections that cover networking, applications, system management, hardware, and performance, the book also has an exhaustive index to help you quickly find the registry information you need. The accompanying CD is packed with innovative registry monitoring and performance utilities, plus an Internet link to our Registry Secrets home page (www.registrysecrets.com) for registry updates and many interactive services for registry "spelunkers." 350 pages.

THE ADMINISTRATOR'S GUIDE TO MICROSOFT SQL SERVER 6.5
By Kevin Cox and William Jones
This book delivers expert technical advice, practical management guidelines, and an in-depth look at the database administration aspects of the Microsoft SQL Server 6.5 product. 469 pages.

THE MICROSOFT EXCHANGE SERVER INTERNET MAIL CONNECTOR
By Spyros Sakellariadis
This book presents everything you need to know about how to plan, install, and configure the servers in your Exchange environment to achieve the Internet connectivity users demand. 234 pages.

THE MICROSOFT EXCHANGE USER'S HANDBOOK
By Sue Mosher
Here's a must-have, complete guide for users who need to know how to set up and use all the features of the Microsoft Exchange client product. Includes chapters about Microsoft Exchange Server 5.0 and Microsoft Outlook. 692 pages. CD included.

MIGRATING TO WINDOWS NT 4.0
By Sean Daily
This book is a comprehensive yet concise guide to the significant changes users will encounter as they make the move to Windows NT 4.0. Includes a wealth of tips and techniques. 475 pages.

POWERING YOUR WEB SITE WITH WINDOWS NT SERVER
By Nik Simpson
The author explores the tools necessary to establish a presence on the Internet or on an internal corporate intranet using Web technology and Windows NT Server. 661 pages. CD included.

THE TECHNOLOGY GUIDE TO ACCOUNTING SOFTWARE
A Handbook for Evaluating Vendor Applications
By Stewart McKie
If you are involved in recommending or selecting financial software for your department or company, this book is must reading! It is designed to help managers evaluate accounting software, with an emphasis on the issues in a client/server environment. McKie provides a range of useful checklists for shortlisting products to evaluate in more detail. More than 50 vendors are profiled, and a resource guide and a glossary are included. 256 pages.

Developing Your AS/400 Internet Strategy
By Alan Arnold
This book addresses the issues unique to deploying your AS/400 on the Internet. It includes procedures for configuring AS/400 TCP/IP and information about which client and server technologies the AS/400 supports natively. This enterprise-class tutorial evaluates the AS/400 as an Internet server and teaches you how to design, program, and manage your Web home page. 225 pages.

Inside the AS/400, Second Edition
Featuring the AS/400e series
By Frank G. Soltis
Learn from the architect of the AS/400 about the new generation of AS/400e systems and servers, and about the latest system features and capabilities introduced in Version 4 of OS/400. Dr. Frank Soltis demystifies the system, shedding light on how it came to be, how it can do the things it does, and what its future may hold. 448 pages.

Building AS/400 Client/Server Applications
Put ODBC and Client Access APIs to Work
By Mike Otey
Mike Otey, a leading client/server authority with extensive practical client/server application development experience, gives you the why, what, and how-to of AS/400 client/server computing, which matches the strengths of the AS/400 with the PC GUIs that users want. This book's clear and easy-to-understand style guides you through all the important aspects of AS/400 client/server applications. Mike covers APPC and TCP/IP communications, as well as the underlying architectures for each of the major AS/400 client/server APIs. CD with complete source code for several working applications included. 489 pages.

Control Language Programming for the AS/400, Second Edition
By Bryan Meyers and Dan Riehl, NEWS/400 technical editors
This comprehensive CL programming textbook offers students up-to-the-minute knowledge of the skills they will need in today's MIS environment. Chapters progress methodically from CL basics to more complex processes and concepts, guiding students toward a professional grasp of CL programming techniques and style. In this second edition, the authors have updated the text to include discussion of the Integrated Language Environment (ILE) and the fundamental changes ILE introduces to the AS/400's execution model. 512 pages.

Also Published by Duke Press

The A to Z of EDI
By Nahid M. Jilovec
Electronic Data Interchange (EDI) can help reduce administrative costs, accelerate information processing, ensure data accuracy, and streamline business procedures. Here's a comprehensive guide to EDI to help in planning, startup, and implementation. The author reveals all the benefits, challenges, standards, and implementation secrets gained through extensive experience. 263 pages.

C for RPG Programmers
By Jennifer Hamilton, a NEWS/400 author
Written from the perspective of an RPG programmer, this book includes side-by-side coding examples written in both C and RPG, clear identification of unique C constructs, and a comparison of RPG op-codes to equivalent C concepts. Includes many tips and examples covering the use of C/400. 292 pages.